ETHICS AND THE FUTURE OF SPYING

This volume examines the ethical issues generated by recent developments in intelligence collection and offers a comprehensive analysis of the key legal, moral and social questions raised.

Intelligence officers, whether gatherers, analysts or some combination thereof, are operating in a sea of social, political, scientific and technological change. This book examines the new challenges faced by the intelligence community as a result of these changes. It looks not only at how governments employ spies as a tool of state and how the ultimate outcomes are judged by their societies, but also at the mind-set of the spy. In so doing, this volume casts a rare light on an often ignored dimension of spying: the essential role of truth and how it is defined in an intelligence context. This book offers some insights into the workings of the intelligence community and aims to provide the first comprehensive and unifying analysis of the relevant moral, legal and social questions, with a view toward developing policy that may influence real-world decision making. The contributors analyse the ethics of spying across a broad canvas – historical, philosophical, moral and cultural – with chapters covering interrogation and torture, intelligence's relation to war, remote killing, cyber surveillance, responsibility and governance. In the wake of the phenomena of WikiLeaks and the Edward Snowden revelations, the intelligence community has entered an unprecedented period of broad public scrutiny and scepticism, making this volume a timely contribution.

This book will be of much interest to students of ethics, intelligence studies, security studies, foreign policy and international relations in general.

Jai Galliott is Research Fellow at the University of New South Wales, Sydney, Australia. He holds a PhD in military ethics from Macquarie University, Australia, and was formerly a Naval Officer in the Royal Australian Navy. He is the author of *Military Robots: Mapping the moral landscape* (2015).

Warren Reed is a former intelligence officer with the Australian Secret Intelligence Service (ASIS). Trained by MI6 in London, he served for ten years in Asia and the Middle East. He is a regular commentator on intelligence matters, industrial espionage and terrorism.

STUDIES IN INTELLIGENCE

General Editors: Richard J. Aldrich and Christopher Andrew

ETHICS AND THE FUTURE OF SPYING

Technology, national security and intelligence collection

Edited by Jai Galliott and Warren Reed

LONDON AND NEW YORK

First published 2016
by Routledge
2 Park Square, Milton Park, Abingdon, Oxon OX14 4RN

and by Routledge
711 Third Avenue, New York, NY 10017

Routledge is an imprint of the Taylor & Francis Group, an informa business

British Library Cataloguing in Publication Data
A catalogue record for this book is available from the British Library

Library of Congress Cataloging in Publication Data
Ethics and the future of spying : technology, national security and intelligence collection / edited by Jai Galliott and Warren Reed.
pages cm -- (Studies in intelligence)
Includes bibliographical references and index.
1. Intelligence service--Moral and ethical aspects. 2. Espionage--Moral and ethical aspects. 3. Electronic surveillance--Moral and ethical aspects. 4. Electronic data processing--Moral and ethical aspects. 5. Spies--Professional ethics.
6. Political ethics. 7. National security. I. Galliott, Jai. II. Reed, Warren, 1945-
JF1525.I6E89 2016
172'.4--dc23
2015019636

ISBN: 978-1-138-82036-4 (hbk)
ISBN: 978-1-138-82039-5 (pbk)
ISBN: 978-1-315-74391-2 (ebk)

Typeset in Bembo
by Taylor & Francis Books

CONTENTS

CONTRIBUTORS

Matthew BEARD holds a PhD in the area of Just War Theory and Virtue Ethics, a subject on which he has spoken internationally. He is currently Research Associate with the Centre for Faith, Ethics and Society at the University of Notre Dame Australia, as well as the Managing Editor for *Solidarity: The Journal for Catholic Social Thought and Secular Ethics*. Matthew's expertise lies generally in the area of moral philosophy. Alongside several academic articles in international journals, he has published with *The Punch* and *The Conversation*.

Martine BERENPAS is a doctoral candidate at Leiden University, the Netherlands, on the relationship between Heidegger, Derrida and Levinas. She is interested in phenomenology and French existentialism.

Alexander FATIĆ is a philosopher and social scientist based at the Institute for Philosophy and Social Theory, University of Belgrade, Serbia. His interests include applied ethics, political philosophy, and criminal justice theory and policy. He is a prolific author and teacher, with a long history of involvement in high-level training programmes in anti-corruption policy and corruption theory, business ethics and criminology both in university settings and for various governments and inter-governmental organizations. His most recent book is *The UN International War Crimes Tribunals: Transition with justice* (Routledge 2015). He is currently finishing *Virtue as Identity: Emotions and the moral personality* (Rowman & Littlefield). He has also worked in diplomacy and as a consultant on a number of ethics and policy issues, including the development of professional ethics for the intelligence profession and conducting long-term training of justice professionals, policing and intelligence ethics under the auspices of the Swedish and Serbian governments. He teaches applied philosophy internationally and is project leader of a major research project on identity and ethics within the University of Belgrade.

Michael FALGOUST is a Policy Specialist at Google, specialising in technology ethics. He has published in political philosophy, philosophy of law and technology. He has also taught courses on Buddhism and has a deep interest in Asian philosophy and mystical traditions.

Shannon FORD is Lecturer in Intelligence and Security Studies with the Australian Graduate School of Policing and Security (AGSPS), Charles Sturt University (CSU), Australia. He is also a Foundation Director for the Asia Pacific Chapter of the International Society for Military Ethics (APAC-ISME). Mr Ford has taught at the Australian National University (ANU), the Australian Defence Force Academy (University of New South Wales) and the Australian Defence College (Department of Defence). He was also a Research Fellow at the Centre for Applied Philosophy and Public Ethics (CAPPE), CSU, where he was Chief Investigator for a research project on the ethics of cybersecurity (2013–14). Before that, he worked on the Australian Research Council-funded project 'Police Leadership in the Twenty-first Century' (2010–11). Prior to starting his academic career, Shannon spent nearly ten years as a Defence Strategist and Intelligence Analyst (1999–2009).

Jai GALLIOTT is a Research Fellow at the University of New South Wales in Sydney, Australia. His research interests revolve around emerging military technologies, including autonomous systems, soldier enhancements and cyber warfare. His broader interests include military strategy and applied ethics. He holds a PhD in military ethics from Macquarie University, Australia, and was formerly a Naval Officer in the Royal Australian Navy. He now conducts contract research for the Department of Defence. His most recent book was *Military Robots: Mapping the moral landscape* (Ashgate 2015).

John HARDY holds a Master of Letters in Peace and Conflict Studies, a Master of International Security Studies/Master of Policing, Intelligence and Counterterrorism, and a Postgraduate Diploma in Policing, Intelligence and Counter Terrorism. He is currently completing his PhD at the Australian National University's National Security College.

Matthew HARRIS is a prize-winning Oxford graduate who has triangulated his studies between philosophy, theology and history. He is currently researching the philosophical theology of Gianni Vattimo. In addition to writing articles on Vattimo for various philosophy journals, he has published a book on the thirteenth-century papacy. He has also written over 20 book reviews across seven journals. Holding a PGCE, he has considerable teaching experience in one of Britain's foremost independent day schools, Queen Elizabeth's Hospital (QEH).

Jill HERNANDEZ earned her PhD in philosophy from the University of Memphis and her MA from Texas A&M, both USA. She won an 8-month National Endowment for Humanities Faculty Award in 2014 as well as the President's Distinguished Achievement Award in Research and Teaching.

Mark JENSEN is an Associate Professor at the United States Air Force Academy. He holds a PhD in philosophy from the University of Notre Dame, USA, and is author of *Civil Society in Liberal Democracy* (Routledge 2011).

Patrick LIN is the Director of the Ethics + Emerging Sciences Group at California Polytechnic State University, San Luis Obispo, USA, where he is an associate philosophy professor. He is also affiliated with Stanford Law School (Center for Internet and Society), University of Notre Dame (Emerging Technologies of National Security and Intelligence), both USA; and Australia's Centre for Applied Philosophy and Public Ethics. Previously, he held academic appointments at Stanford's School of Engineering, US Naval Academy, and Dartmouth College. Dr Lin has published on the ethics of emerging technologies – including robotics, cybersecurity, AI, human enhancements, nanotechnology, space exploration and more – especially their national security implications. He has provided briefings and counsel to the US Department of Defense, CIA, United Nations, International Committee of the Red Cross, National Research Council, Google and many other organisations. He earned his BA in philosophy from UC Berkeley and his PhD from UC Santa Barbara, both USA.

Kevin MACNISH is a Teaching Fellow and Consultant in Applied Ethics at the University of Leeds, UK. He shares his time between lecturing undergraduates in engineering and computer science, leading online modules for an MA in Applied and Professional Ethics, and undertaking consultancy work with an ethical focus. Kevin's research is in the ethics of surveillance, security and technology. He is the author of numerous articles on surveillance ethics and has organised two international conferences on the subject at the University of Leeds. Kevin has also been interviewed for *The Atlantic* magazine and by the BBC, and has spoken at both the House of Commons and the House of Lords. He conducts ethical analysis for security and ICT projects, and has been involved with a number of European Union FP-7 projects with a focus in these areas.

Seumas MILLER is one of the directors of the Centre for Applied Ethics and Public Ethics (CAPPE) in Australia. Miller is an internationally recognised expert on corruption, terrorism and police ethics. He contributes to projects on complex ethical questions raised by new technologies in the area of war, terrorism and public security, for example neuroenhancement technologies. Miller is also Professor of Philosophy at Charles Sturt University, Australia, and the Australian National University (joint position). He was Head of the School of Humanities and Social Sciences at Charles Sturt University 1994–99.

Warren REED completed two years' national service in the Australian Army and then studied at the University of Tasmania, Australia, graduating in political science and winning the university's prize in international relations. Later, as an Australia–Japan Business Cooperation Committee Scholar, he carried out research on Japan's relations with China and the rest of Asia in the Law Faculty of Tokyo University,

Japan. He then worked for an Australian resources company in Japan, before being recruited into the Australian Secret Intelligence Service (ASIS). After training with MI6 in London, he served as an intelligence officer for ten years in Asia and the Middle East. Later, he worked as a consultant to Australian firms operating in Asia, published a number of books on the region, and also worked for three years as Chief Operating Officer of the Committee for Economic Development of Australia. More recently he has been occupied in writing and commenting in the media on intelligence and security matters.

Brian ROUX obtained a Bachelor of Science and a Master of Science degree in computer science and subsequently completed a PhD in engineering and applied science, all from the University of New Orleans, USA. He obtained his Juris Doctor from Tulane University Law School, USA, where he also received a Certificate in International and Comparative Law. He specialises in e-discovery services and provides expert testimony relating to forensic investigations, data acquisition and preservation, data recovery, query design and data analysis.

Thomas SIMPSON is Associate Professor of Philosophy and Public Policy at the Blavatnik School of Government, University of Oxford, and a Senior Research Fellow at Wadham College, also University of Oxford, UK. He joined the School from University of Cambridge, UK, where he was a Research Fellow (Sidney Sussex College) and also educated (BA, MPhil, PhD). His doctorate was entitled 'Trust on the Internet' and was sponsored by Microsoft Research. Between degrees he was an officer with the Royal Marines Commandos for five years. He served in Northern Ireland as a Troop Commander with 45 Commando; as aide-de-camp to the senior UK General in Baghdad, Iraq; and as an intelligence and operations officer with HQ 3 Commando Brigade RM when it led the UK Task Force in Helmand Province, Afghanistan.

Nicolas TAVAGLIONE holds a PhD in political science from the University of Geneva, Switzerland, and works at that institution. His research interests revolve around bioethics, just war theory and applied ethics more generally.

Patrick WALSH is a Senior Lecturer in Intelligence and Security Studies. He is responsible for the course coordination of the Graduate Certificate/Diploma/MA (Intelligence Analysis) at the Australian Graduate School of Policing and Security, and has academic oversight for all other short intelligence courses offered by the school. Dr Walsh teaches on National Security and Intelligence Issues, and his research interests range across intelligence reform and bio-security. He is also consulted widely by federal and state agencies on intelligence reform/capability and bio-security issues.

Dan WEIJERS is an Assistant Professor of Philosophy at California State University, Sacramento, USA. Previously he was a Postdoctoral Fellow in the Philosophy Department at Victoria University of Wellington, New Zealand. His research interests include normative ethics (especially hedonism, wellbeing and experimental normative ethics, applied ethics (especially prediction markets), and interdisciplinary happiness/wellbeing research.

Jeremy WISNEWSKI is an Assistant Professor of Philosophy at Hartwick College, USA. His latest projects take on torture and the moral questions that surround it. He wants to know what it is, why it's morally problematic, when it might be permissible, whether it can be eliminated, and why human beings engage in it in the first place. Wisnewski has two related projects: two manuscripts, 'The Ethics of Torture' and 'Torture: A Philosophical Analysis'.

INTRODUCTION

Jai Galliott and Warren Reed

The British historian Arnold Toynbee (1995) once likened civilisations to climbers on a cliff-face. Advancing societies climb steadily towards the top, while others plunge to their demise or are trapped on a ledge, unable to ascend any further. At the top of the cliff is a higher state of civilisation with hitherto unimagined levels of security, wellbeing, education and creativity for all citizens. At the bottom are chaos, barbarism and suffering. Toynbee argued that a fall from the cliff-face is not inevitable, but that a civilisation must take measures to ensure its progression, rather than falling into stagnation or decline.

The consequences for societies that fail to recognise the proximity of their fall are evident in the form of majestic ruins and dead languages. Not all declines are so dramatic, however, as the American writer Jared Diamond has pointed out. '[M]uch more likely than a doomsday scenario involving human extinction or an apocalyptic collapse of industrial civilisation would be', he tells us, 'just a future of significantly lower living standards, chronically higher risks, and the undermining of what we now consider some of our key values' (Collins and Reed 2005, p. 4).

Intelligence has always been vital for making progress up Toynbee's cliff. Ascending states use their intelligence wisely, while those slipping down often abuse it. Intelligence provides intellectual and practical means to developing the best technology, choice of route, protection from the ill-intentioned and careless – and even from falling rocks or companions who have lost their grip. It also provides a way of helping other climbers.

The moral strengths of intelligence – a commitment to objective truth and accountability in government – should be valued by society more generally. Its tools – cultural, psychological and technological – should be the best available. Its weaknesses – venality, self-interest and delusion – are also those of society at large. History provides many examples of states misreading their strategic circumstances to their detriment, missing – or worse, ignoring – signs of imminent danger. The tragedy of 9/11 in the United States comes to mind.

Further back in history we find a seminal example: the long-lived Byzantine Empire before its decisive defeat by the nomadic Seljuk Turks, in what is now south-eastern Turkey:

> [The Battle of Manzikert in 1071] was the plunging point from which recovery for the Byzantine Empire proved to be impossible. Byzantium, incomparably the world's greatest power for seven centuries, lost at one blow the richest part of its domain, its heartland, leaving the rest to be plucked at and torn away piecemeal by predatory neighbours until, after the longest death rattle in history, its last remnant, the city of Constantinople, fell to the enemy's sword.
>
> *(Friendly 1981, p. 17)*

Here, a balance of power was shattered – one that had endured since the fall of the Roman Empire. Unlettered pastoralists were a new force confronting Europe. The catastrophe of Manzikert ushered in the Crusades, which still reverberate today throughout the Middle East. Europe, after deserting Byzantium, spent centuries struggling to beat back the Islamic Turks. A British historian, Lord Julius Norwich, identified the major cause of the Empire's collapse: conspirators in Constantinople exploited the disaster at Manzikert to betray, blind and finally kill the emperor – who had defeated the Seljuks on more than one occasion.

As Norwich puts it,

> [b]linkered by their own smug intellectualism and obsessive personal ambition, they made every mistake, threw away every opportunity offered to them. In doing so they martyred a courageous and upright man who, though no genius, was worth more than all of them put together and could, with their loyalty and support, have saved the situation; and they dealt the Byzantine Empire a blow from which it would never recover.
>
> *(Norwich 1995, p. 358)*[1]

Some might think that the world today is fundamentally different and incomparable to earlier historical periods. To be sure, the global community is tighter now than it has ever been, particularly when it comes to the speed of travel and the possibility of virtually instant communication, but the ways in which nation states operate and interact – and the reasons why human beings do what they do – have changed little.

To understand the role of intelligence in the modern world, two misapprehensions must be dispelled: first, that the era in which we live today is vastly different from any that has gone before; and second, that modern technology is a separate field of human endeavour from that of intelligence, except perhaps where intelligence systems use cutting-edge technological devices to aid and abet their clandestine activities. The reality is that the two have been inextricably intertwined from the very beginnings of human society.

An example of the first misapprehension dates from the late 1980s and early 1990s, when the Soviet Union collapsed, the Berlin Wall was torn down and the Cold War – which had largely divided the globe into two camps, the free world and the communist or totalitarian world – came to an end. Because the Cold War had lasted four decades, it had traversed more than one generation, and thus overran the normal career span of the individuals directly involved. Partly due to the resulting discontinuity in intellectual thought, it was asserted that the West could comfortably scale back its military forces and even do away with its intelligence agencies. Nothing could have been further from the truth. Viewed from a wider perspective, the Cold War was a mere aberration in the broad sweep of human – and intelligence – history. Not so many centuries before, Europe itself had endured the Hundred Years War.

The second misapprehension – the common belief that modern technology, because it is more sophisticated and ubiquitous than anything that has gone before, is a separate field of endeavour from that of intelligence – is simply wrong. Even in primitive times, details of how and where a neighbouring tribe's superior cutting tools were made was 'hot intelligence', just as information about development was sought after in the Stone Age, Iron Age and Bronze Age, right through to the Industrial Revolution. Longer and stronger blades, more powerful bows and arrows, the invention of intricate siege machines, gunpowder, guns, cannons and secret navigational charts for the New World all preoccupied spies along the way, including the brilliant mind of Leonardo da Vinci. More recently, the invention of the telegraph ushered in modern eavesdropping, aided by the Italian inventor and electrical engineer Guglielmo Marconi and later Alexander Graham Bell, who invented the telephone.

Intelligence and technology have always been intertwined – if not inseparable twins. The same can be said of both trade and economic intelligence. Yet each of these fields must also confront the vital issue of morality and ethics. Without such considerations, we would quickly lose our grip, and once again experience the kind of loss seen at the Battle of Manzikert and in the fall of the Byzantine Empire. In his masterful work *The History of the Decline and Fall of the Roman Empire*, Edward Gibbon (1776) outlines similar processes.

What is unique to the modern era is the speed at which we can gain access to information and knowledge, and the freedom we have to do so. And concomitant with this development – as those of more senior years are wont to observe – is a widespread confusion of information with wisdom. The attitude of younger generations to intelligence has also changed: with the romantic image of the spy having waned over the past decade, intelligence is less often seen as a 'craft' in and of itself. The modern generation sees the spy less as a covert agent fighting for freedom, and more as a politicised agent possibly fabricating intelligence, who is asked to ignore things that do not fit a particular political narrative.

That suggests that the best and brightest, in the democratic world at least, are looking elsewhere to make their contribution to society. But to what and to whom? And in whose national interest? Take this insight from a historian, citing a young teacher as to how Australia has changed:

the process of stripping away the legitimacy of all major social institutions seems almost complete. Students have been trained to distrust any claim to knowledge or authority. They've been trained to think that being left in ignorance is some form of liberation from oppressive forces. It's not as if it's some sort of conspiracy, it's just the way the system works

(Bendle 2006, p. 13)

Both bemoan the effect of this fallacy, which claims that people are somehow liberated if they have no sense of who they are, where they come from, what they stand for or how they want to develop as a nation.

Intelligence officers, whether gatherers, analysts or some combination thereof, operate in a sea of social, political, scientific and technological change. They are challenged in a variety of ways, some of which seem unimaginable. This book is about those challenges and the ways in which professionals in the intelligence community confront them, usually to the best of their ability and often with great success.

The chapters of Part I examine the moral case for spying. Mark Jensen of the United States Air Force Academy sets the scene in Chapter 1 with a deep philosophical examination of the intelligence trade: 'The virtues of Bond and vices of Bauer: an Aristotelian defence of espionage'. This chapter argues, among other things, that the Aristotelian approach can provide a sophisticated, free-standing account of espionage, together with action-guidance for those interested in establishing ethical practices in the craft of spying. At the same time, this approach proffers a framework for understanding the methods and means associated with espionage, and helps identify excesses and deficiencies. Jensen also discusses objections to his approach, pointing out implications that might be useful to officials interested in cultivating a more ethically sound practice of espionage. His comparisons between a number of ancient and modern philosophers on this issue are enlightening.

In Chapter 2 – 'The limits of intelligence gathering: Gianni Vattimo and the need to monitor "violent" thinkers' – Matthew Harris of the University of Staffordshire examines how twenty-first-century intelligence services have an extraordinarily large amount of data at their disposal as a result of increasingly sophisticated means of surveillance. The very judgment of who should be watched is impossible to make when applied to all of this data. What criteria should be used in order to maximise the likelihood of surveillance providing information of interest to national or even international security? One contemporary Italian philosopher, Gianni Vattimo, makes a distinction between 'strong' and 'weak' thought, which may well provide the answer to dilemmas encountered in monitoring visitors to certain websites. The principal advantage of appropriating Vattimo's philosophical programme for intelligence and surveillance is that it provides a criterion for selecting website and internet groups on which to focus. In his justification of this criterion, Vattimo recognises that we live in an irreducibly plural world, in which surveillance activity must be reconciled not only with the liberal–democratic system of governance common to much of the civilised world, but also with the values of tolerance, diversity and dialogue that inform civil institutions.

In Chapter 3 – 'The epistemology of intelligence ethics' – Alexander Fatić of the University of Belgrade examines the argument that the use of intelligence for the purposes of national security is rarely predicated upon the need to uncover the truth. Rather, it is based upon a 'rights game', where the real objective is the protection of a set of rights arising from sovereignty, citizenship or other forms of belonging to a political or moral community. Most of the current literature rightly insists on drawing conceptual and methodological boundaries between classic intelligence – gathered by states – and criminal intelligence, and highlights many principled differences. Little, however, has been said about what they have in common, especially in the context of intelligence ethics. Fatić's examination of the relationship between knowledge and truth in intelligence is illuminating. 'There is never', he writes, 'an explicit statement of irrelevance of the truth, because such an acknowledgement would instantly delegitimise the intelligence service: people do continue to trust that truth is the ultimate criterion for judging the value of intelligence. Conversely, public opinion would rightly perceive an intelligence service which openly disparages the truth in favour of rights as manipulative and threatening'. The conclusion of this chapter is significant in relation to the professional ethics of intelligence work, as well as for the status of intelligence in ensuring the security of a democratic state.

Part II turns the examination towards interrogation, torture and terrorism. Matthew Beard of the University of Notre Dame Australia is the author of Chapter 4, 'The human costs of torture'. Much of the modern debate about torture, he points out, has understandably centred on the question of whether it can ever be justified. While most find torture unacceptable, it may be morally permissible when the benefits outweigh the moral costs. Thus the question of whether torture is morally acceptable pits the moral requirement for justice against the responsibility of statespeople and intelligence officers to make decisions that protect their citizens. Beard then focuses on the moral challenges that face the torturer, even when that individual's task can be morally justified. The ideal interrogator is a person who is disinclined to resort to torture even in extreme situations; the ideal torturer one who will torture only when it is absolutely necessary. Beard argues that at the very least we ought to ensure that torture is never used when interrogation will do, and that the type of people inflicting torture are never those who would enjoy the process. Rather, we should seek those who are able to avoid the temptations presented by the situation.

Following this, in Chapter 5, Martine Berenpas of Leiden University examines this subject from a different angle in 'The implications of spying and torture on human freedom from a Sartrean point of view'. Sartre argues in *L'Être et le Néant* that humans are ontologically inclined to use strategies such as torture to gain control over the other and to mask freedom as 'for-itself' (*pour-soi*). He claims that 'sadism is the failure of desire'. The sadist does not want to deal with the look of the other and refuses to acknowledge the other as another human, who is also free.

The sadist reduces the other to a mere object by inflicting pain on him. In sadism as well as in torture, an inequality exists between abuser and victim. Berenpas argues that torture is rooted in this existential fear, and as such is always unjust, is a universal crime against human freedom, and can never be justified.

In Chapter 6, Dan Weijers of California State University, Sacramento, introduces us to a new dimension of the ethics of spying in 'Predictive markets as an alternative to one more spy'. He adopts a unique approach, focusing on the continued threat of terror attacks, further showing that this threat makes intelligence gathering essential for modern governments. Yet both budgetary restraints and ethical issues restrict the collection options available. The mixed public response to government-backed phone tapping and torture of suspected terrorists suggests that some forms of intelligence gathering that are *pro tanto* immoral might nevertheless garner public acceptance if they appear to be effective in preventing terrorist attacks. Prior to the 9/11 attacks, scholars had been devising a scheme – Policy Analysis Market (PAM) – that would guide foreign policy, including that related to terrorist attacks. The rationale for PAM was based on the 'wisdom of crowds': the idea that the right kind of aggregation tool could reliably distil useful information from the opinions of large groups of people, even when most of the individuals in a group have very little relevant knowledge. Modern prediction markets are virtual marketplaces in which traders can buy and sell shares in predictions of real-world outcomes, such as political, economic or social events. PAM was to include prediction markets on terrorist attacks, which would allow traders to bet on, and possibly profit from, lethal acts of terrorism. Before its completion, PAM was lambasted for being immoral, ineffective and a waste of money by several politicians and media commentators. As a result, PAM's funding was cut and the programme immediately terminated. In his chapter, Weijers argues that, compared with the torture of suspected terrorists, prediction markets including terrorism are less morally problematic and are likely to be more effective at thwarting attacks. Based on this, he argues that government-backed prediction markets including terrorism should be established and used alongside existing intelligence-collection methods.

Kevin Macnish of the University of Leeds leads us into Part III, which focuses on classificatory problems, with 'Persons, personhood and proportionality: building on a Just War approach to intelligence ethics' (Chapter 7). There are a number of available approaches to intelligence ethics; in recent years, however, theorists have argued that the principles of the Just War tradition can be usefully employed to assess the ethics of intelligence from a deontological perspective. Macnish has argued elsewhere that the Just War principles are helpful for assessing surveillance, which has obvious overlaps with intelligence work. In this chapter, Macnish defends this approach. First, he considers its benefits; he then looks at some important challenges it faces, and answers each in turn. Finally, he accepts that one challenge in particular (that of a lack of real guidance) presents a particular problem, and addresses this challenge through the Just War principle of proportionality as it applies to coercive techniques of intelligence collection. When weighing proportionality, it is tempting to see the assault in coercive intelligence as solely against the individual. Macnish argues that the assault is also against personhood and the wider community, and thus that it goes both deeper and wider than an assault 'merely' against a single person. He concludes that coercive practices in intelligence are not *mala in se*, but are nevertheless justifiable only in rare cases.

In Chapter 8 – 'Just war, cyberwar and cyber-espionage' – Matthew Beard looks at how cyberwar is increasingly common in the landscape of global conflict and intelligence gathering. As such, it represents a dramatic shift away from conventional means of warfare and toward an entirely new security scenario. At the same time, a view has developed among academics that cyberwar represents a 'new' type of war with new ethical requirements, for which the traditional and widely accepted Just War theory is unable to account. On the contrary, Beard argues that Just War theory is adequately equipped to deal with cyberwar, and that while cyberwar does require novel applications of Just War theory, this neither generates a need for a new theory nor demonstrates that cyberwar is a new kind of war. Beard notes that cyberwar and cyber-espionage are not so readily separated, as many suggest. He goes on to argue that spying is not about damage, but about knowledge, which means that the distinction between the physical and non-physical on which his opponents rely is largely spurious. This chapter concludes with remarks on how existing Just War theory might be best applied to the unusual challenges of cyberwar.

Chapter 9 – 'A dilemma for indiscriminate pre-emptive spying' – by Nicolas Tavaglione of the University of Geneva, starts with the observation that spying can take many forms. One may spy on specific individuals or groups on the basis of prior intelligence in order to verify some specific suspicions or to accumulate more evidence: this is discriminate reactive spying. Or one might spy indiscriminately on targets '*en masse*' on the basis of no prior intelligence, in order to identify suspect individuals: this is 'PRISM-style' indiscriminate pre-emptive spying. In this paper, Tavaglione focuses on indiscriminate pre-emptive spying (IPS) and develops the following argument. In order for IPS to be morally acceptable, two conditions (at least) must be met. First, IPS ought to be necessary – as is the case every time one considers violating some well established moral law. For example, if someone wants to violate the prohibition on killing when acting in self-defence, their use of lethal force has to be necessary in order to justify the attack. Second, IPS ought to follow as far as possible the model of 'perfect voyeurism' – 'covert watching or listening that is neither discovered nor publicised', where someone might accumulate massive amounts of information about a person's private life without imposing harm on that person. From this viewpoint, however, it appears that IPS finds itself at a dead end. Either it conforms to the model of 'perfect voyeurism', and as such cannot be necessary as it wouldn't even be useful in the first place, or it gives itself the means of being useful and thus potentially necessary, but then cannot conform to the model of 'perfect voyeurism'. Neither condition renders it morally acceptable. As a consequence, there is no hope of justifying PRISM-style surveillance.

Chapter 10 – 'The morality of unconventional force' – by Thomas Simpson of the Blavatnik School of Government at the University of Oxford, questions moral constraints on the exercise of unconventional force. Force can be unconventional in terms of its target, nature, and social and legal context. Simpson is concerned with unconventional force because it occurs outside of war. US drone strikes in Yemen are one example of unconventional force; espionage is another. The conditions for *jus ad bellum* and *in bello* traditionally given by Just War theorists relate to a parallel enquiry, namely that of moral constraints on the exercise of conventional force. So the Just War tradition is an obvious place to look for principles constraining unconventional force. Others have also taken this step, lightly revising the *in bello* principles to apply them to unconventional force. Simpson, however, argues that this is a mistake and misconstrues the status of the *in bello* principles. Some of the *in bello* principles prohibit certain actions altogether, such as the use of weapons *mala in se*, which relate to how we treat one another – and these likewise apply to spies. But other *in bello* principles attempt to codify rules of behaviour which, if observed, mitigate the more destructive aspects of war. Yet this second type of principle bears no essential tie to the morality of human relationships. One instance of this is the obligation to provide for prisoners of war and not to punish them. As Schelling has noted, the possibility of mutual accommodation between adversaries is as important and dramatic as the element of conflict. Once rules of mutual accommodation are widely followed, it becomes morally obligatory to follow them. In the case of war, such conventions are usually established as regularities of behaviour through positivisation by black-letter law. Espionage is subject to both kinds of moral constraint.

At the beginning of Part IV, we focus explicitly on the often intertwined topics of remote surveillance and killing. In Chapter 11 – 'I, Spy Robot: the ethics of robots in national intelligence activities' – Patrick Lin of the California Polytechnic State University and Shannon Ford of Charles Sturt University examine the ethics of using military robots – which are marching ahead, judging by recent news coverage and academic research. Yet there's little discussion of the use of robots in national intelligence and espionage – both of which are omnipresent, carried out quietly in the background. This lacuna is surprising because most military robots are used for surveillance and reconnaissance, and in the United States they are most controversially used by the Central Intelligence Agency in targeted strikes against suspected terrorists. This chapter proceeds in two parts. First, Lin and Ford survey the diverse range of robots that currently exist or are emerging and explore their value for national security. This includes describing several scenarios in which they have been, or could be, used. Second, they examine interesting aspects of robot use, including the limitations of both humans and robots in the service of national intelligence activities, and relevant laws and treaty obligations. They pay special attention to the ethically and legally problematic trend of shifting from intelligence collection to taking action, which has been both enabled and emboldened by new technology.

In Chapter 12 – 'Emerging technologies, asymmetric force and terrorist blowback' – Jai Galliott of the University of New South Wales looks at how the game of chess has long been seen as a simulacrum of political and military confrontation. He points out that even in early James Bond films such as *From Russia With Love,* the Cold War was represented as a game of chess between two grand masters. While clearly a mega-metaphor, Galliott argues that chess embodies a conception of a very particular type of chivalric military action and, moreover, a conception that has a great deal of significance for our moral assessment of unmanned systems and their use in intelligence collection. When we think of chess, we imagine four-star generals looking at each other across a board, on which there are equally configured forces ready to engage in a perfectly symmetrical contest. Each side has a clear and distinguishable uniform of black and white, presented on a battlefield that is clearly demarcated with similarly coloured squares. The reality, however, is that neither war nor its accompanying intelligence collection embodies the sort of symmetry and equality that characterises the contest that is chess. As modern history confirms, foreign intelligence collection all too often diverges from the chessboard image of war. Here Galliott argues that when the degree of divergence reaches a critical point, we begin to experience serious difficulties in interpreting and applying the Just War criteria as typically applied to justify such actions. More specifically, unmanned systems and their high-powered lenses generate a morally problematic 'radical asymmetry' that puts justice and fairness in conflict or competition with the aims of persistent surveillance.

In Chapter 13 – 'Targeting thresholds: the impact of intelligence capability on ethical requirements for high-value targeting operations' – John Hardy of Macquarie University examines high-value targeting operations, which have become a popular tool in the fight against international terrorism and against insurgents in Pakistan and Afghanistan. High-value targeting operations are intelligence-led operations that culminate in tactical strikes against identified targets. The F3EAD (find, fix, finish, exploit, analyse, disseminate) targeting cycle consists of a large amount of intelligence collection and analysis before strikes, and intelligence exploitation and dissemination after strikes. Although most literature on high-value operations focuses on drone strikes or kill–capture raids, the strikes themselves constitute only a small portion of the targeting cycle. Hardy argues that new collection, exploitation and analysis technologies have enabled coalition forces to create much more comprehensive intelligence pictures of the enemies they target, increasing their understanding of enemy networks and the human terrain of the battlespace, thus improving analyses of high-value targets and enhancing the situational awareness of units on the ground. Hardy argues that this development has had significant implications for ethics of such operations in terms of the threshold for initiating strikes based on the targeting cycle. The capacity to create a more informed intelligence picture carries with it a duty to employ force more selectively in order to minimise harm to non-combatants, coalition force elements and targets themselves, where possible. This is consistent with the *in bello* principle of proportionality, as it serves to limit the application of force to the minimum required to achieve the military objective of capturing or killing a high-value target. It also complements the commanders' duty to avoid exposing force elements to unnecessary risk. Finally, it enhances the operational effectiveness of the targeting cycle by setting quality thresholds, which necessitate the effective use of new intelligence-collection methods and analysis capabilities available to coalition forces.

Part V examines recent intelligence leaks and secrets. In Chapter 14 – 'The NSA, Edward Snowden and the ethics and accountability of intelligence gathering' – Seumas Miller and Patrick Walsh of Charles Sturt University examine the US National Security Agency (NSA) leak perpetrated by Edward Snowden, a former NSA private contractor, which catapulted the ethics and accountability of intelligence gathering to the front pages of major newspapers and media outlets. Miller confronts a range of interconnected ethical issues that are in need of analysis. Perhaps the most obvious is the privacy rights of US and other citizens. He then examines the ethics of whistleblowing: should Snowden have leaked these documents? And should the media have disseminated the material they received? Further, it is evident that, post-9/11, the boundary between domestic law-enforcement intelligence gathering and foreign intelligence gathering has blurred, notably in the legal sphere – for example, under the provisions of the above-mentioned Patriot Act, law enforcement agencies were subject only to the wiretap provisions of the Foreign Intelligence Surveillance Act (FISA) and as such not subject to the normal judicial controls of the criminal justice system. Nor is this blurring restricted to the legal sphere. Whatever the moral principles governing intelligence gathering in domestic law enforcement, they surely differ to some degree from those governing foreign intelligence gathering. However, the phenomenon of international terrorist groups that perpetrate terrorist attacks on domestic soil muddies the waters and, as a result, the specification of appropriate moral principles for the collection of intelligence in relation to such groups is problematic, as it is in other areas of counter-terrorism. This chapter explores these three interconnected ethical issues in the context of the Snowden leaks.

In Chapter 15 – 'WikiLeaks and whistleblowing: privacy and consent in an age of surveillance' – Jeremy Wisnewski of Hartwick College offers a partial defence of Chelsea Manning-type whistleblowing. He does so by considering the test case of privacy, arguing that knowledge of the possibility of an invasion of privacy is required for our ability to consent to such invasions, and hence this knowledge is required for the legitimacy of such invasions. This same line of reasoning applies *mutatis mutandis* to whistleblowing on government activity more generally. Whistleblowing is thus justified, at least to the extent that it preserves the conditions under which a democratic government maintains its legitimacy. Wisnewski also considers the limits of such whistleblowing, showing that there is an important link between privacy and the exercise of autonomy. The ability to maintain a degree of privacy over some areas of one's life facilitates one's engagement in legitimately autonomous action. In democratic societies, at least ideally, there are straightforward mechanisms in place for limiting intrusions into privacy. But the citizens of a nation must be aware of actions carried out by their government. Without this awareness, it is impossible to revoke consent. And if it is impossible to revoke consent, then the 'consent' in question is not worthy of the name. Second, the mechanisms that enable change in existing law must be functional. And if these conditions are not met, the breaches of privacy in question are illegitimate. WikiLeaks, Wisnewski argues, provides a forum that ensures the first condition is met. He does not argue that every page of the thousands released is necessary for meeting this condition. Rather, he argues that exposing government actions more generally – and in particular the surveillance activity of a government – is essential for the legitimacy (or illegitimacy) of such surveillance. Such whistleblowing makes consent (and revoking consent) possible.

Part VI concerns responsibility and governance, and starts with Chapter 16 – 'Ethics for intelligence officers' – by Brian Roux of Tulane University and Michael Falgoust of the University of Twente. They examine instances of intelligence-gathering legislation that have led to serious concerns in the areas of privacy, autonomy and ethics, and examine public information that has been made available in existing mass intelligence-gathering programmes, comparing facets of the programmes to elements of the Just War theory. In so doing, they try to determine whether each programme: (1) has a just cause, wherein the aim of the programme is compliant with international law and societal norms; (2) is conducted by a competent authority established by and accountable to the sovereign government; (3) maintains the right intentions when executing its mandate in connection with the aims established by its cause; (4) is designed to strike a proportional balance between the harm it tries to prevent and collateral damage to privacy interests; and (5) distinguishes between civilian and non-civilian targets, friendly and unfriendly governments, and other dichotomies of proper and improper targets. They then set out an ethical framework for evaluating future operations against the Just War theory.

In Chapter 17, '"Due care" or a "duty to care"? Codes of ethics in intelligence gathering', Jill Hernandez of the University of Texas at San Antonio examines an interesting difference in intelligence-gathering terminology. Michael Walzer's 'due care' criterion asserts that the public has a supervenient right not to be put at risk, so that the government always has better reasons to pursue unhindered intelligence gathering than to ensure individual liberty. Civilians, in short, have a right to due care. Contemporary legal arguments use Walzer's due care doctrine to contend that there are no actual deontic constraints on the state in its use of extraordinary measures to procure intelligence of high national security value. In a post-9/11 shift away from deterrentist ideals towards jurisprudence, favouring proactive, preventative measures, scholars have scrambled to provide a legal or moral standard for governmental powers in the gathering of intelligence. This chapter, however, takes a different tack. Hernandez argues that a jurisprudence of pre-emption and prevention is not inconsistent with certain deontic moral constraints, especially those that are rooted in the values of a duty of ethical care. A due care criterion can be relevant in important national security cases, because the questioning of those in custody can justify detaining enemy combatants during times of war, especially when fighting terrorist networks. She contends, however, that by framing a code of ethics for the intelligence community in an ethics of care, ethical care can function as a deontic check relevant to all means of gathering intelligence. Since ethical care functions as a built-in professional constraint, its values must always be factored in when determining a course of action during intelligence gathering. Finally, a code of ethics can outline conditions under which the deontic base can be overridden: for example when there would be immediate, significant and epistemically determinable consequential benefits.

Warren Reed has the final word. As a former ASIS officer who served in Asia and the Middle East, and now a Sydney-based adviser, author and commentator, he provides a spy's perspective on how the many issues examined in this book impact on the day-to-day professional life of a spy operating in a foreign country. Spying is a decidedly human affair. And the spy is as human as her agents – the providers of secret intelligence – whom she inveigles into committing an act of betrayal. But this is the antithesis of everything for which the spy stands. And yet, despite this perversity and the spy's control over the agent, there must nevertheless be a high degree of mutual trust between the two. The security of their clandestine relationship depends upon this, as do the lives of both, at times. Reed examines the moral challenges and dilemmas that arise in this relationship, and how most spies deal with them.

As co-editors, we trust that the reader will find the issues, ideas and insights in this book useful and informative. Throughout history, intelligence has been an important and unique field of human endeavour. Technology and other innovations affect it in various ways, but at heart it is always a matter of human trust.

Note

1 Reed and Lance Collins (personal communication, 28 February 2005) discussed this and other historical intelligence matters with Lord Norwich in London.

PART I

The moral case for spying

1

THE VIRTUES OF BOND
AND VICES OF BAUER

An Aristotelian defence of espionage

Mark Jensen

Moral assessment of espionage is difficult. In the first place, ordinary citizens are not privy to the day-to-day operations of our intelligence agencies. This is as it should be: if these operations are to be successful, they must be kept secret. While citizens in a modern liberal democracy expect their governments to exercise oversight to ensure the effectiveness and scrupulousness of intelligence agencies, we recognise that we do not need to know what these agencies are doing on a daily basis. But this also means that we are not in a position to make moral judgments on their principles and actions. In addition, our knowledge about past operations undertaken by intelligence agencies is at best sketchy. We know about spectacular successes (Osama bin Laden) and spectacular failures (Edward Snowden). Successes tend to glamorise the practice; failures lead to vilification. There are excellent historical treatments of some episodes, but even these present only a partial picture of the past and tell us little about the present.[1]

Nevertheless, it is possible to evaluate espionage in abstraction: we can work from an operational definition and test it against the main evaluative approaches in normative ethics: deontology, consequentialism and virtue theory. While the philosophical literature includes several 'fourth' approaches, these three, which focus (respectively) on the right, the good and the excellent, lie at the centre of contemporary discussion, are codified across our social and political institutions, and have been at the heart of ethical philosophy for millennia. In this chapter, I will argue that while espionage does not fare well against traditional deontological or consequentialist criteria, a broad defence of espionage is possible under an Aristotelian version of virtue theory. Such a defence will not satisfy everyone (especially those with reservations about virtue theory), but it is robust enough to answer the most worrisome objections and provide guidance for policymakers looking to establish ethical guidelines for intelligence agencies in the modern world. Toward a defence of this perspective, I will first define espionage and distinguish it from related practices. I will then test it against criteria central to the three main approaches. I conclude with a brief consideration of some prominent objections and a vindication of this chapter's title.

What is espionage?

Espionage is a set of practices undertaken by nation-states aimed at discovering the secrets of other nation-states. To clarify these practices, we must describe the actors involved in espionage, differentiate espionage from ordinary intelligence gathering, and distinguish between espionage and acts of war.

First, the form of espionage that concerns us here is that occurring between states. While it is true that individuals and corporations spy on one another, we typically reserve the term 'espionage' for activity in the international arena: sovereign states spying on other sovereign states. At the same time, when we say that espionage is a state activity, we mean this literally: acts of espionage are undertaken by the state, not by individuals. Of course, it is individuals who do the day-to-day work of spying. But these individuals are agents of the state authorised to spy on its behalf. In this way, our ethical assessment of espionage should be analogous to our ethical assessment of war.[2] According to the Just War tradition, soldiers are permitted to do many things in combat that we forbid in civilian life. By analogy, intelligence agents are permitted to do many things that we forbid in civilian life.[3]

Second, espionage must be distinguished from intelligence gathering. Ordinary intelligence gathering need not rise to the level of espionage, insofar as there is much that nation A can learn about nation B simply by collecting information that nation B has made public. More specifically, ordinary intelligence gathering can be carried out without breaking the laws of nation B. Espionage, however, aims to acquire information that nation B has not made public, information that nation B intends to conceal from nation A. Nation B guards its secrets by concealing them, prohibiting their disclosure and prohibiting practices that one might use to discover them. Espionage by nation A therefore involves law-breaking in nation B.

Our final distinction concerns the difference between espionage and war. While espionage involves breaking the laws of the target nation, the aim of espionage *qua* espionage is not to harm the target nation directly; it is merely to obtain the secrets of the target nation. In this way, espionage is different from sabotage, terrorism and warfare. To be sure, espionage will be a regular companion to these other practices – a prerequisite for effective sabotage might be effective espionage. At the same time, the individual practices associated with espionage might involve the perpetration of harm by agents of nation A on agents and citizens of nation B. But espionage is not necessarily linked to harmful intent on the part of nation A towards nation B. Even at the level of individual agents and their targets, the aim is not to provoke violence in nation B's agents and citizens. The functional aim of espionage *qua* espionage is always passive: observation and data collection. That this is the right way to understand espionage as practised in the international community is evidenced by the fact that nations practise espionage (at least in some forms) against those with which they are friendly, as well as those considered rivals or enemies.

Notice here that we have located espionage on a scale that has benign acquisition of information at one end and aggressive, disruptive acquisition of information at the other.[4] My claim is not that espionage constitutes a golden mean between these two, but that espionage represents an imprecise cluster of intelligence-gathering activities that stand in continuum: espionage is far enough up the scale to involve law-breaking in the target country, but not so far that these practices will be seen by the target nation or the international community to constitute a harm justifying a violent response. Espionage is a provocative practice, but it does not intend to provoke.

Espionage and deontology

Deontological approaches to normative ethics place a premium on objective or universal rights. Immanuel Kant, the eighteenth century German philosopher whose work remains central to deontological theories of normative ethics, offers two different starting points for deontological judgment. Here we will focus on his second approach, which is grounded in respect for human dignity. Most commentators see this second approach as a more substantive and applicable starting point than the first. Kant's principle is as follows: 'act that you use humanity, whether in your own person or in any other, always at the same time as an end and never merely as a means' (Kant 1997, p. 38). The idea here is that an action counts as moral only if in acting I respect the dignity of others as autonomous rational agents. In other words, insofar as my actions involve others, I must defer to their judgment about what they themselves should do, rather than induce them to act against that judgment. When I lie to you, for example, I deliberately disrupt your ability to make informed judgments and in this way manipulate your capacity for deliberation and decision-making. I fail to treat you with the dignity that is your right as an autonomous rational agent.

This principle justifies a set of absolute moral duties, including prohibitions on murder, theft and lying as well as prescriptions for beneficence and generosity. At the same time, we must distinguish between 'unremitting' duties and 'meritorious' duties: generally speaking, prohibitions are unremitting duties and prescriptions are meritorious duties (Kant 1997, p. 33). While both types of duty are moral requirements, unremitting duties must always be followed, while meritorious duties may be broken if they conflict with unremitting duties. For example, if the only way for me to carry out a duty of beneficence (a meritorious duty) with respect to a destitute person was to first steal from a rich person (thus violating an unremitting duty), then I should not carry out my duty of beneficence. In other words, actions that aim at some good must always conform to the whole system of rules – one may not violate a rule in order to attain some good.[5]

On this rather brief account, it appears at first glance that espionage is unethical. Practices associated with espionage such as lying, cheating, bribing and blackmailing would be clear violations of Kant's principle. This is the case not only for intelligence agents but also for those who, under the influence of an intelligence agent in one way or another, elect to break the laws of their own nation in order to supply information to an agency. Moreover, these sources treat their fellow officials as means to their own ends. In this way, espionage violates the dignity of others.

One response to this analysis would be to distinguish between espionage motivated by self-defence and espionage motivated by aggression. If my rights and dignity are threatened by my nation, then I might consider aiding my nation's enemy in order to defend myself against this threat. Even Kant allows that a nation may defend itself against aggression committed by another nation (Kant 1996b, pp. 318–19). Moreover, insofar as I may respond not merely to threats against me but also to threats against others, perhaps I have defensive grounds for aiding an enemy of my nation if it is clear that, in my judgment, I would be acting in defence of threatened individuals. In this case, foreign agents would not be using me as a mere means; it would be my autonomous decision to provide them with information.

However, while Kant allows that a nation has a moral right to defend itself against aggression, he is quite clear that moral rules continue to apply in the context of that defence. More generally, whatever good may come from violating our duty to keep our promises, tell the truth and so on, the fact is that a meritorious duty can still never trump an unremitting duty. So even if we are required to prevent harm to ourselves and others, this can never trump the prohibition against lying, cheating, stealing and so on. I am never permitted to lie or steal, no matter what good it might bring about (Kant 1996a).

A second, more sophisticated response to this deontological analysis would be to distinguish between the actions of individuals and the actions of states, arguing that the moral rules that govern states are different from the moral rules that govern individuals. Perhaps acts of espionage are permissible for states and their agents but not for individuals. Justification for this line of response might be drawn from classical Just War theory (following our elaboration of the definition of espionage above), in which the moral rules that apply to soldiers are different from the moral rules that apply to civilians (Fisher 2011, p. 77ff.). But in espionage the actors are states rather than individuals – the individuals involved are merely agents of the state, and their actions must be judged accordingly; they cannot be judged according to a morality of individuals. Perhaps espionage is a permissible state action and its associated practices are permissible for voluntary agents of the state who play the relevant role.

In response, even if we grant that moral rules governing states must be distinguished from moral rules governing individuals, there are still reasons to reject espionage. Kant begins with the assumption that a rational nation is one that seeks to preserve peace between itself and other members of the international community. This, for Kant, is the first principle for the ethical conduct of nation states. War is permissible, but only as a defensive response to aggression on the part of another nation. With this framework in hand, he then writes, '[n]o state at war with another shall allow itself such acts of hostility as would have to make mutual trust impossible during a future peace; acts of this kind are employing assassins or poisoners, breach of surrender, incitement to treason within the enemy state, and so forth' (Kant 1996b, p. 320). The problem with espionage, then, is that it undercuts the possibility of a lasting peace when hostilities cease. Later in the same discussion, Kant explicitly rejects espionage as an appropriate practice during peacetime:

> [T]hose infernal arts, being mean in themselves, would not, if they came into use, be confined for long within the boundaries of war, as for example the use of spies, in which use is made only of others' dishonesty (which can never be completely eradicated); instead, they would also be carried over into a condition of peace, so that its purpose would be altogether destroyed. (Kant 1996b, p. 320)

For Kant, the problem with espionage is that it undercuts the principal aim of interstate relationships, which is the cultivation and preservation of peace. Trust is a necessary condition for achieving this goal, and espionage (as opposed to ordinary intelligence gathering) is, by definition, a breach of that trust.

Espionage and consequentialism

Consequentialist approaches to normative ethics focus on the consequences of our actions: the better the result, the more ethical the action. The standard-bearer for consequentialism, John Stuart Mill, argued that we should define 'good results' in terms of 'happiness' (Mill 1993 [1871], p. 144). In our pursuit of happiness, we do not strive for immediate, individual satisfaction. Instead, the happiness we seek is a long-term, settled happiness for all. Happiness itself is not a subjective assessment of one's mental state, but an objective condition: Mill defined happiness as 'pleasure and the absence of pain' (Mill 1993 [1871], p. 144). For Mill, the highest forms of pleasure are those associated with the exercise of our mental capacities, not those associated with the fulfilment of our appetite for physical pleasure. In this way, moral life in society is based upon removing impediments to happiness (for example, poverty and disease), where individuals can engage in projects that involve reason, imagination and sentiments, which contribute to an overall sense of tranquillity with occasional moments of excitement.

Many commentators argue that the best ethical justification for espionage is consequentialist in nature.[6] Crudely put, insofar as the ends justify the means, the practices associated with espionage – such as theft, bribery, lying and blackmail – can be justified by the fact that these activities contribute to our national interests in security and defence.

Nevertheless, there are two problems with this line of reasoning. First, consequentialist moral judgments require at least some understanding of the various possible consequences of acting or not acting. But espionage aims to gather secret information, which means that the agent and her nation cannot be sure how useful the information they seek will actually be. As a result, it is very difficult to calculate the benefits of obtaining this information, and it is thus difficult to weigh these benefits against the costs associated with obtaining it. We can imagine cases, of course, in which we know that the information we want to acquire will result in a net benefit: for example, we know of an impending attack on our nation and we seek to discover who will carry it out. Nevertheless, the general point here still stands, namely that moral judgment in the consequentialist vein requires information about the consequences of an action that agents, due to the very nature of espionage, do not possess.[7]

Second, and most importantly, every consequentialist normative theory takes as its object the good of the whole, not the good of the part. But espionage in the present structure of the international community aims at the good of an individual nation or subset of nations, rather than the good of the whole. To be sure, improving one's own lot will contribute to the good of the aggregate insofar as each individual is a component of the aggregate. But espionage aims at the good of some particular nation or nations at the expense of the good of some other nation or set of nations. Nations are harmed when their secrets are stolen; nations that obtain secrets gain an advantage at the expense of their rivals. The good of the whole is neither the intended aim nor the expected result of espionage. Of course, espionage could be justified if the good achieved by nation A in practising espionage accrued a net good for the whole. For example, if we accept the premise that Soviet gains during the Cold War meant net losses to the good of everyone, then espionage practices by NATO nations might have been justified on consequentialist grounds.[8]

Both of these objections illustrate the complexity of a moral assessment of espionage under consequentialism. While there might be specific agencies or practices that we could endorse under specific circumstances (in other words, when we know the value of the information that we aim to acquire and when we know that acquiring this information will be of net benefit to the aggregate), there is no obvious or simple way of endorsing everyday espionage as it is practised by intelligence agencies in the modern world.

Espionage and Aristotle

Virtue theory locates moral value in the excellence of the agent. This tradition originates with Aristotle, who argues for the importance of community in relation to this goal.[9] In his view, human beings are 'political animals' (Aristotle 1998, p. 4). As a result, it makes little sense to make ethical judgments with regard to individuals in distinction from the community in which they live. To make sense of Aristotle's approach we must look at the problem from two angles: (i) from the top down with a focus on the common good of the nation or state, and (ii) from the bottom up with a focus on the anthropology of the individual.

Let's start from the bottom up, with the nature and character of the excellent individual agent. Aristotle begins his account of character by looking at the unique function of a thing (Aristotle 1999, pp. 8–9). The excellence of any thing is based upon its excellent performance with respect to its unique function. Just as the excellence of a dolphin relates to it doing whatever it is that dolphins do and doing it well, so the excellence of a human will be found in a person who does what it is that humans do and does it well. Only humans, according to Aristotle, act on the basis of their rational faculties (Aristotle 1999, p. 9). The excellent human is one who exercises this capacity excellently.

Broadly speaking, this capacity is exercised excellently in one of two ways (Aristotle 1999, pp. 17–18). First, we exercise our reason excellently when we pursue knowledge. Second, we exercise our reason excellently when use that knowledge to act well. Excellent actions are those performed by an excellent character. An excellent character, in turn, is one in which our faculty for practical reason regulates our emotions and appetites in accord with the excellences (or virtues) specific to them. For example, when our faculty for practical reason regulates our feelings of fear and does this well habitually, we have the virtue of bravery (Aristotle 1999, pp. 40–5). Too much fear indicates the vice of cowardliness; too little fear indicates foolhardiness. With respect to all of our emotions and appetites, the virtues are found in this 'mean between extremes' (Aristotle 1999, p. 25). When our faculty of practical reason finds the mean, we have the virtue of *phronesis* (prudence or practical wisdom). More generally, *phronesis* is found when, with respect to our emotions and appetites, we are able to feel, desire and act in the right way, at the right time, toward the right person, in the right amount, and so on. In this way, *phronesis* is the virtue of good moral judgment. As Aristotle explains, *phronesis* applies not only to the ways in which reason governs our behaviours *qua* individuals with feelings and appetites, but also to our behaviours *qua* political animals with duties and good habits in our relationships with others. The catalogue of the virtues therefore includes excellences of feelings and appetites (e.g. bravery and temperance) as well as excellences related to our relationships with others (e.g. friendliness and wit). This observation brings us to the second dimension of Aristotle's virtue theory: the flourishing community.

According to Aristotle, the chief good for the community is *eudaimonia*: happiness or flourishing (Aristotle 1999, p. 3). On the one hand, Aristotle's vision of a flourishing community is similar to our own. Common goods include defence, economic progress, social welfare, education and the rule of law. Citizens should be free to pursue lives in which they believe they will flourish; they should also participate in government (Aristotle 1998, pp. 66, 72). On the other hand, Aristotle's vision reflects a deeper commitment to the common good and to each citizen's functional role in her specific community. A citizen's commitments to the common good and to performing her functional role in the community together imply a set of virtues attached to citizenship (Aristotle 1998, p. 71). Some of these virtues are quite general. Aristotle argues that friendliness, for example, is a virtue associated with our ordinary dealings with others in the community. Other virtues are relevant only if one occupies the relevant role or has the relevant capacities in the community. A virtue like magnificence (the excellence of the wealthy person) will be relevant only to wealthy citizens of the community. Considered structurally,

Aristotle idealises human community as a set of nested groups: each citizen is part of a family; each family is part of a village; and each village is part of a single, unified nation-state (Aristotle 1998, pp. 2–5, 81). Nations cannot be components of a further unity in the strictest sense; international groupings are too large and diverse to have a common good that could provide a basis for unity.[10] Aristotle does allow for the possibility of treaties, leagues and other alliances among nations. But none of these arrangements subsumes its member states in the way that the nation subsumes the villages of which it is composed. Even so, we can describe relations among nations according to an Aristotelian ideal.

Two dimensions of this ideal are important for our investigation. First, in international relations, nations will pursue foreign policies aimed at securing conditions for their own flourishing. In other words, Aristotle is an instrumentalist when it comes to international relations: our activities in the international community are a means for achieving our national ends, not ends in themselves. To be clear, Aristotle is not a realist in the same sense as Hans Morgenthau: Aristotle's 'national interest' is the common good of my particular nation, but this good is objectively determined and bears a family resemblance to the common goods that other nations have established for themselves. Our common humanity secures this family resemblance just as surely as it rules out social or political evolution toward a single world government. The second dimension of Aristotle's ideal is the recognition that our relations with other nations and their citizens demarcate functional roles related to additional virtues. In the ancient world, for example, hospitality was a virtue that governed one's relationship with a foreigner. By extension, our initial disposition towards foreign nations and foreign nationals should be one of respect, accommodation and generosity.

Taken as a whole, Aristotle's account paves the way for an ethical defence of espionage. In the first place, intelligence gathering appears to be a necessary part of international relations in Aristotle's model. International relationships are an essential part of life on our small planet. If we are to engage in these relationships with an eye toward improving the flourishing of our nation, it will be important to understand the intentions of our international partners. Some of these other nations could be rivals, aggressors or otherwise inimical to our vision of an international community. Intelligence gathering is important in these contexts in order to protect our national security and facilitate the international conditions required for national flourishing.

But must we engage in espionage? Must we intentionally break the laws of other countries in order to obtain their secrets? For Aristotle, this is where *phronesis* becomes important for our political leaders. As with all our activities, espionage must be governed by practical wisdom: we must practise it at the right time, targeting the right nations, using the right methods, employing the right personnel, and so on. It also requires hitting the mean between extremes. The NSA's monitoring of German Chancellor Angela Merkel might be an example of excess, while the CIA's failure to anticipate the rise of ISIS in Syria might be an example of deficiency. To be clear, acts of espionage on the part of a nation are certainly not virtuous as such. Instead, espionage, as a cluster of practices located on a scale of international engagement that has benign intelligence gathering at one end and violence at the other, represents a set of activities that leaders might decide are appropriate for certain circumstances.

Phronesis will be equally important for the agents who perform espionage. Given its nature, no directives from political leaders can sufficiently determine the course of action that agents must take. In other words, since neither political leaders or their agents know exactly what information they will discover or by what means they can best acquire information, agents need freedom to practise their art in a way that befits the excellences they have cultivated. Of course, political leaders may establish boundaries for their agencies in order to protect strategic interests. For example, if it is important for a nation to be – and to be seen to be – a champion of universal human rights, leaders might command their agencies not to use violence to acquire information. But these boundaries do not tell agencies and their agents exactly what they should do. Agencies and agents must therefore develop and cultivate a set of best practices, including an account of the roles, responsibilities and virtues of the intelligence agent.[11] In working out this account, the role of the agent must be seen in the context of an organisation that supports the aims of the state in the context of the international community. This account cannot be too detailed, as we cannot make rules for every possible circumstance in which some form of espionage might be required. Our future relationships with other nations are unpredictable, at least in part. Instead, we augment written guidelines with practices designed to sustain *phronesis* throughout our agents and agencies.

Objections

One might have a host of worries about this Aristotelian justification of the practice of espionage. While we do not have space to consider all of these in detail, we can briefly consider two important ones: the problem of bifurcated identity and the problem of abuse.

Bifurcated identity

One natural worry is that practices associated with espionage will corrupt the intelligence agents who practise them. These activities are unacceptable (and often illegal) in civilian life, and yet all agents also live as civilians with roles and responsibilities in their families, villages and cities. The worry here is that the sets of virtues that one must practise in one's different roles conflict, such that agents will have a fractured sense of identity. This is a problem on the Aristotelian view insofar as the flourishing human is one who has a unified sense of identity.

On the one hand, the Aristotelian view can meet this challenge. What must be unified is not the set of virtues that one practises in one's various roles in the community, but instead the good that is common to the community, together with the distinct goods of specific parts that together constitute the community. In this way, one might practise different virtues in different roles, but all of these virtues and roles are unified in that they contribute to the same good. Lots of citizens in ordinary life have virtues in their work life that conflict with virtues in their home life and yet they seem to be able to flourish insofar as their activities in these various roles contribute to the common good.

On the other hand, it is clear that some kinds of bifurcation can be destructive on a personal level. For example, some soldiers returning from deployment or even piloting a drone from afar have trouble reintegrating into civilian life (Galliott 2015, pp. 142–9). The same challenges are likely to face members of the intelligence community. In Aristotelian terms, they might find it hard to transition back into their roles as citizens. The fact that some citizens find these transitions difficult suggests that there is a need for more psychological and sociological research into the conditions that make these transitions difficult and investigation into the ways in which our institutions can help such citizens reintegrate.

Abuse

Another worry about the Aristotelian justification for espionage concerns its reliance on *phronesis*. For *phronesis* to be effective, our political leaders must extend significant latitude to agencies and these agencies must, in turn, extend latitude to their agents. While leaders can provide guidelines, the Aristotelian model requires a significant degree of trust in the moral judgment of individual agents and agencies. But this latitude opens the door to abuses and excesses. As critics of intelligence agencies point out, and as practices that have come to light in the context of the long wars in Iraq and Afghanistan have demonstrated, abuse is a real and persistent problem.

The answer here, in Aristotelian terms, is to recognise that granting agencies the freedom to exercise expert judgment in the practise of espionage is not incompatible with exercising oversight and holding them accountable for their use of this freedom. The actions of agents and agencies should be documented; political leaders should exercise oversight over the programmes and activities of agencies and agents. The key is to regard every operation as an opportunity to improve the craft. Successes become models for future operations, and errors in judgment should not automatically be regarded as reasons to end a practice or dismiss an agent. In Aristotle's view, we become better at moral judgment through repetition under the watchful eye of experts who can step in when our judgment begins to fail. Of course, some mistakes will reveal that an agent or programme is unsuitable for the purposes of the agency. But the Aristotelian goal is to cultivate professional excellence in the craft under the auspices of a clear commitment to the common good. Notice that such a culture is quite different from one that has zero tolerance when it comes to mistakes. The latter is highly dangerous – a culture in which abuses are likely to be hidden, while the former has a built-in capacity for correction and improvement.

Bond vs. Bauer

Finally, let us turn back to the title and close with a pop-culture reference: we can now see, I think, why James Bond is a better agent than Jack Bauer. In the typical adventure, Bond is a well functioning agent from a well functioning agency that is itself part of a well functioning nation. The enemy typically poses an existential threat, such that Bond's activities often go beyond espionage. But the very idea of a small group of specially trained agents with a 'licence to kill' reflects the idea that the international community is not as peaceful as we would like it to be, that we must cultivate in our agencies the expertise required to confront serious threats when they appear. MI6 (Bond's agency) occasionally imposes limits on Bond's actions, but it also grants him a great deal of freedom, reflecting the view that Bond has cultivated the right sort of judgment – moral and practical – with respect to the requirements of the mission. Sometimes things work out because Bond is lucky, but more often things work out because he has excellent judgment and works in tandem with the resources that his organisation provides.

By contrast, a typical day in the life of Jack Bauer is full of ambiguity and excess. He is part of a poorly functioning or corrupt agency that is itself part of a poorly functioning or corrupt nation. He cannot (or should not) trust the people around him and often works alone. At times, he seems to be a slave to excessive fear or anger. In determining what actions to take in order to achieve his ends, he appears to have no moral limits. Moreover, he does not have the kind of reliable support structure that is presupposed in the Aristotelian ideal.

This is not to say, however, that Bauer's actions are wrong or that his decision-making procedures are vicious. The plot device of *24* is that each season takes place in 'real time', over the course of one day. The storyline fitting this structure typically involves a grave and imminent threat; Bauer is compelled by the urgency of the situation to take extreme measures in order to acquire the information he needs in order to respond. In his defence, a justified sense of urgency might correctly prompt an agency or an agent to take drastic steps in order to confront a threat. But justified urgency is not the norm in intelligence gathering. Nor are we convinced that the kinds of threats, intimidation and torture that Bauer often uses are effective ways of compelling sources to give up their secrets. Of course, the writers of *24* intend for us to see Bauer as a patriot; but he is also an antihero. He confronts the threat, but we are not expected to be happy with the way he does it. In fact, his successes seem to depend as much on luck as on his own good judgment. He is therefore not an obvious model upon which we should base a good account of ethical espionage.

Acknowledgements

The views expressed in this article are those of the author and do not necessarily reflect the official policy or position of the US Air Force, the US Department of Defense, or the US government.

Notes

1 For example see Ashley (2004).
2 Cf. Fisher (2011), esp. ch. 4.
3 Some contributors argue that we can provide ethical guidelines for espionage by explicitly adapting the criteria associated with traditional Just War theory. See for example Barry (2006).
4 In this way, my approach tracks Loch Johnson's 'ladder of escalation for covert operations'. See Johnson (2006).
5 Kant appears to assume that conflicts are possible only between unremitting duties and meritorious duties. He says nothing about what we should do if two or more unremitting duties were to be in conflict. On the one hand, it certainly seems hard to think of a case in which one must, for example, steal in order to avoid lying, or cheat in order to avoid committing murder. One alternative that avoids this problem is Robert Audi's neo-intuitionist approach, which is modelled on WD Ross's list of *prima facie* duties. See Audi 2004, pp. 90–101.
6 For example see Johnson (2006, p. 277).
7 Secretary of Defense Donald Rumsfeld's famous comment about the difficulty of 'unknown unknowns' is relevant here. See http://www.youtube.com/watch?v=GiPe1OiKQuk (accessed 13 November 2014).
8 Espionage could also be justified if it were practiced by an agency that aimed at the good of the whole. But insofar as there are no agencies of this sort, this is a moot point.
9 My discussion here is informed by Aristotle's *Nicomachean Ethics* (1999), *Politics* (1998), and Alasdair MacIntyre's elaboration of the two (1999, p. 99ff).
10 One might also worry that modern nation states are too big and diverse to embody the relevant unity.
11 For an example see Johnson (2006, pp. 288–9).

References

Aristotle 1998, *Politics*, trans. CDC Reeve, Hackett, Indianapolis.
Aristotle 1999, *Nicomachean ethics*, 2nd edition, trans. T Irwin, Hackett, Indianapolis.
Ashley, C 2004, *CIA spymaster*, Pelican, Gretna.
Audi, R 2004, *The good in the right*, Princeton University Press, Princeton.
Barry, J 2006, 'Managing covert political action', in J Goldman (ed.), *Ethics of spying: a reader for the intelligence professional*, Scarecrow Press, Lanham.
Brandt, R 1995, 'Some merits of one form of rule utilitarianism', in S Cahn & J Haber, *20th century ethical theory*, Prentice-Hall, Upper Saddle River.
Fisher, D 2011, *Morality and war: can war be justified in the twenty-first century?* Oxford University Press, Oxford.
Galliott, J 2015, *Military robots: mapping the moral landscape*, Ashgate, Farnham.
Hooker, B 1990, 'Rule consequentialism', *Mind*, vol. 99, no. 393, pp. 67–77.
Johnson, L 2006, 'Ethics of covert operations', in J Goldman (ed.), *Ethics of spying: a reader for the intelligence professional*, Scarecrow Press, Lanham.
Kant, I 1996a [1797], 'On the supposed right to lie from philanthropy', in *Practical philosophy*, M Gregor (ed. & trans.), Cambridge University Press, Cambridge.
Kant, I 1996b [1795], 'Toward perpetual peace', Section 1, 3§, in *Practical philosophy*, M Gregor (ed. & trans.), Cambridge University Press, Cambridge.
Kant, I 1997 [1785], *Groundwork of the metaphysics of morals*, M Gregor (ed.), Cambridge University Press, Cambridge.
MacIntyre, A 1999, *Dependent rational animals: why human beings need the virtues*, Open Court, Chicago.
Mill, J 1993 [1871], *On liberty and utilitarianism*, Bantam Books, New York.

2

THE LIMITS OF INTELLIGENCE GATHERING

Gianni Vattimo and the need to monitor 'violent' thinkers

Matthew Harris

This chapter draws upon the philosophy and ethics of Gianni Vattimo to meet the challenges associated with the fallout from intelligence leaks made by Edward Snowden, concerning human intelligence (HUMINT) (mostly online) intelligence operations mentioned by the Government Communications Headquarters' (GCHQ) Joint Threat Research Intelligence Group (JTRIG). The latter has allegedly been involved not only in the profiling, but also (and more controversially) in the infiltrating, distorting and discrediting of individuals and groups online. I use the word 'allegedly' here because GCHQ has refused to comment on the leaks. Concerning JTRIG's methods, suggestions for similar measures were made in 2008 by then Professor of Law at the University of Chicago (and later Obama aide and Harvard professor) Cass Sunstein in collaboration with Adrian Vermeule (Sunstein & Vermeule 2008), as well as by Bergen and Footer for the American Academy of Political and Social Sciences (Bergen & Footer 2008, p. 241). As a result, I will focus on a particular intelligence agency here, but will instead assume the position of a non-defined agency of a Western liberal democracy when making my points. The measures and methods outlined by the JTRIG document and the Sunstein & Vermeule report have been perceived by some in a negative light, ethically speaking (Greenwald 2014), yet I will argue that these practices could be ethically justified. Certain groups should be profiled, infiltrated, and their message distorted because they hold strong views that, whether or not they lead to deeds, are violent in themselves. Confronting these groups, which are extremist, fundamentalist and anti-democratic in character, head-on would turn them into martyrs, furthering their cause. Rather than attempting to overcome groups of this kind, it would be better to distort them, performing a '*Verwindung*' (distortion) of their message, as Vattimo would say. Ethically and operationally, this notion of distortion gets to the heart of the issue about the role of the intelligence officer.

Online HUMINT: controversies and opportunities

Despite its cost and difficulty, HUMINT has made a comeback since 9/11 (Dover, Goodman & Hillebrand 2014, xvii). Due to the ever-increasing amounts of data available online, automated searches using algorithms can be hit or miss in locating a security threat (Bartlett and Miller 2013, p. 34), and then require a further human response in order to deal with the identified threat. Arguably, HUMINT has the most impact of the various forms of intelligence, collapsing the kind of model put forward by Ratcliffe (2003; quoted in Walsh 2011, p. 94), in which the function of intelligence is primarily to interpret, in order to influence decision makers. HUMINT, guided by overarching objectives, can take action through espionage and campaigns of deception. The secret nature of clandestine operations can avoid the public relations problems associated with direct, overt campaigns, such as the rhetoric of the 'War on Terror' that alienated many moderate Muslims in its identification of a clear 'axis of evil' – against which whole nations were placed (Walsh 2011, p. 193). Nevertheless, while the usefulness of 'real-world' HUMINT is in decline, due to the growing importance of social media, online HUMINT is the way forward. Why is real-world HUMINT declining in terms of its usefulness? Robert Dover predicts that, due to soaring use of social media among college students (which is the traditional recruiting ground for undercover agents), the placement of pictures on Facebook pages and the increasing deployment of facial recognition software by governments and other groups, it will be ever more difficult to con-duct clandestine operations (Dover 2014, p. 302). The alternative is to use social media to the advantage of intelligence services.

There has been outcry over JTRIG's 'Four Ds', which are outlined in the document *The Art of Deception: Training for Online Covert Operations* (Greenwald 2014): Deny, Disrupt, Degrade and Deceive. The journalist Glenn Greenwald (2014) has stated that this practice implies that 'agencies are attempting to control, infiltrate, manipulate, and warp online discourse, and in doing so, are compromising the integrity of the internet itself'. Furthermore, Greenwald claims that JTRIG not only targets the 'customary roster of normal spycraft: hostile nations and their leaders', but other potential, suspected threats, such as well known 'hacktivists'. While I would argue that Greenwald's moral stance concerning the 'integrity of the internet' is misplaced for more reasons than we can go into here, his concerns about JTRIG's targets may well be more plausible. The complexity of modern commu-nications technology, the changing locus of social life, and the need to respond to jihadist threats since 9/11 have meant that, as Robert Dover has pointed out, privacy is now perceived by some in the West (more perhaps among younger generations) as less of a right and more of a privilege than it was prior to advent of the twenty-first century (Dover 2014, p. 303). Nevertheless, Dover admits that those over 25, brought up before the advent of the internet, are less inclined to feel this way and would no doubt prefer not to be the targets of 'snooping', let alone character assassination, which can be directed at individuals and groups even if they have never been charged or convicted of a crime. While the profiling of civilians and the use of online HUMINT is inevitable, for reasons I have mentioned above (among others), there needs to be ethical justification for the selection of targets, which will also have the practical benefit of better focusing limited resources. As Greenwald notes, the JTRIG document his website made widely available (via WikiLeaks) mentions that the activity of the group involves 'pushing the boundaries', reaching the limits of intelligence gathering and covert operating.

According to Claudia Hillebrand, a tension exists between the necessary roles and functions of intelligence services and the fundamental values of a genuinely democratic society. For example, there is an apparent conflict between the requirement of secrecy for the sake of security and the belief that democracies should be open (Hillebrand 2014, pp. 305–6). With its role as a tool for clarification, philosophy can provide a way of ethically shaping, explaining and possibly restricting practices such as those undertaken by JTRIG. The writings of the contemporary Italian philosopher Gianni Vattimo will prove useful for these purposes, due to his extensive engagement with issues pertaining to violence, democracy, reality, ethics and communications technology. Moreover, Vattimo's division between 'strong' and 'weak' thought (and, therefore, thinkers) will also help to mitigate the tension mentioned by Hillebrand between the role of intelligence services and the values of democracy.

Gianna Vattimo

On a personal level, Gianni Vattimo (b. 1936), a philosopher working in the postmodern tradition, is an unusual choice when it comes to investigating the ethics of intelligence. This is not to say that Vattimo has not developed a subtle ethical position, but that his own background is far removed from issues surrounding intelligence (these biographical details are taken from Vattimo and Paterlini 2009). To some degree, Vattimo's personal and intellectual trajectory mirrors that of the West over the past fifty years. Growing up in post-war Italy, Vattimo took part in Catholic youth programmes. Nevertheless, during his university years he became intrigued by the philosophy of both Nietzsche and Heidegger. By the time he took up a Humboldt Fellowship in Germany in the early 1960s, he had realised that he was merely a cultural Christian – just before *Time* magazine announced that 'God is dead'. In the 1960s he became increasingly interested in socialism, particularly in 1969 when he convalescing after an ulcer burst, reading Marcuse and Mao. Heidegger was given a back seat during the early to mid-1970s, while Vattimo worked as a professor of aesthetics in Turin. Here he developed a theory of Nietzsche's overman that involved the subject as a revolutionary figure who could challenge the establishment. When some of his students became the target of intelligence even before they could put their revolutionary rhetoric into violent action, their letters from prison made it clear that they had not internalised the subtleties of their master's conceptual distinctions. This experience, along with being himself the target of the feared Red Brigades in Italy (after being outed as homosexual), led Vattimo to develop a philosophy that would oppose violence in all its forms. At the end of the

1970s Vattimo became famous in Italy for his style of *pensiero debole* ('weak thought'). Increasingly, since the late 1980s, Vattimo has drawn links between his work and contemporary themes such as postmodernism, plurality, the return to religion, and even a return to a weakened form of Communism. In recent years he has also been a member of the European Parliament.

Weak thought

What, then, is weak thought? Weak thought is a philosophical style that involves the synthesising of key insights of the German philosophers Friedrich Nietzsche (1844–1900) and Martin Heidegger (1889–1976). Detailed discussion of these thinkers' ideas would be well beyond the scope of this chapter. However, some exposition of what Vattimo takes from their work is necessary in order to understand the ethical importance of profiling, infiltrating and distorting violent thinkers. Nietzsche, for Vattimo as well as for many others, is the thinker of nihilism who announced the 'death of God'. This is not a flat-footed assertion that a being – 'God' – has met his demise. Rather, God is representative of our faith in the West in the 'highest values', in the 'secure foundations' of knowledge, in 'objectivity' in science and ethics (Vattimo 1988, pp. 20–1). What Nietzsche was trying to communicate with this nihilistic announcement was not only that we can no longer believe in the highest values, but also that we no longer feel a need to do so. The reasons for this are many, varied and complicated. One suggestion Nietzsche himself offers is that Christianity elevated the value of 'truth', yet the idea of God himself turned out to be a 'lie' when the natural sciences, the fruit of our enthusiasm for the value of truth, started to flourish as disciplines in their own right; this is why Nietzsche's 'madman', a character he created for the purpose of announcing the death of God in his book *The Gay Science*, says that we humans have killed God (Nietzsche 2001, pp. 119–20). Vattimo frequently cites Nietzsche's argument that there are 'no facts, only interpretations' (Vattimo 2002, p. 49). The death of God de-centres thought, removing the hierarchy of values with 'God'/'Truth' at the top, liberating other discourses, or 'interpretations' as Vattimo – a hermeneutician (a philosopher who theorises the nature of interpretation) – calls them. This understanding of late modernity matches our experience in the West in the past 60 years, where we have seen the constant proliferation of information sources through communication technology, as well as efforts on the part of minority groups to use these means to get their message across in the politics of identity and culture.

Nietzsche tempered his notion of the death of God with the suggestion that the 'shadow' of God would endure for a long time after his death, indicating great prescience on his part (Nietzsche 2001, p. 199). Vattimo recognises this and ties it both to his reading of Heidegger and his understanding of modernity. Heidegger, first and foremost, is a thinker of 'Being', or 'how things are'. One of Heidegger's greatest insights was that the way in which humans have thought of Being has changed throughout history. For a long time, from Plato and Aristotle up to late modernity (approximately since the dawn of the twentieth century), Being was thought of 'metaphysically', that is, in terms of stable, fixed presences. How things 'are' was identified variously with Plato's eternal 'forms' (ideal archetypes of 'goodness', 'beauty', 'truth', 'justice' and so forth), Aristotle's categories, the God of medieval theologians, Kant's autonomous human subject and so on. Vattimo updates Heidegger's thought to imply that now, in late modernity, we cannot think of Being metaphysically but must think of it rather as a series of 'events' or 'openings' that historically condition the way in which we see the world (Vattimo 1988, p. 26). The death of God was one such event. More concretely, some commentators on Heidegger and Vattimo have argued that JFK's assassination was an event, as was 9/11 (Silverman 2007, p. 115). Vattimo attributes the 'end of metaphysics' to technology; the plurality of voices coming through radio, television and the internet, the increasing difficulty of distinguishing 'fact' from 'fake', and the instantaneous reporting of news mean that 'how things are' has lost its metaphysical pretensions of stability and certainty (Vattimo 1992, ch. 1).

To use a Nietzschean phrase, for the past hundred years we have increasingly witnessed the 'fabulisation' of the world; the fixed, immutable world has dissolved into a play of interpretations. While this is nihilistic, Vattimo finds it liberating because he believes that metaphysics is 'violent', since the principle of a fixed, immutable order prevents questioning through the silencing of other people. In other words, metaphysics is incompatible with democracy. A democracy includes many voices, and does not silence questioning. Any kind of 'reactive nihilism' that holds beliefs 'strongly' (that is, metaphysically) is violent. This can take the form of religious extremism, political nationalism or conspiracy theorising, among other forms. These types of thinking react to the event of nihilism by taking the opportunity to emerge into the public space that has been vacated by the dominant metaphysical thinking of the time (which has been either logical positivism or a quasi-Hegelian belief in progress, shattered by the two world wars) and use the end of modernity as an opportunity to re-assert their own extreme beliefs; if all interpretations now have free play, some have taken the opportunity to set theirs up as 'the Truth'. In contrast, Vattimo thinks that such a move repeats the pattern of metaphysics, setting up one more violent, exclusionary way of thinking in place of an older version. Furthermore, one cannot 'overcome' metaphysics in any straightforward way: one cannot wipe the board clean and start again or institute a total relativism of 'anything goes'. One cannot do this because one would simply be repeating the logic of the metaphysics of modernity, of the value of the 'new', of the 'modish' (Vattimo 1992, pp. 1–3). Novelty for its own sake has long been seen as intrinsically valuable, going hand-in-hand with faith in progress, and specifically scientific–technological progress; undoubted progress in the latter was believed to deliver spiritual, moral and cultural progress in particular. The two world wars and the end of ideology at the end of the Cold War put an end to this myth. As such, to attempt to start again with new foundations would not only repeat the logic of metaphysics *per se*, but also re-institute the modern metaphysical value of the new. Instead, Vattimo draws upon Heidegger once more to propose that we can escape the traces of metaphysics that we still find in our language, which binds our horizons of thought ('God's shadow') though a '*Verwindung*' of metaphysics. *Verwindung* is an obscure German term used occasionally by Heidegger that has no straightforward English translation. Broadly, it has connotations of 'convalescence-distortion-alteration' (Vattimo 1988, pp. 172–3). In other words, one can heal oneself (convalesce) from the violence of metaphysics by distorting and altering the traces of metaphysics found in language. One must think in order to live, and one cannot escape the traces of metaphysics found in language, but one should think weakly rather than strongly, like the strong-thinking reactive nihilists. Our duty is to be 'complete nihilists', to think through the logic of late modernity after the death of God and the end of metaphysics in order to perform a *Verwindung* on metaphysical traces in accordance with weak thought.

Applying weak thought to intelligence and espionage

Vattimo's thought can be used to justify practices that are carried out, or are under consideration, by intelligence services. I do not think that Vattimo's thought can help intelligence agencies greatly to refine their targeting procedures, for many of the words associated with 'strong thought' are already 'trigger words' for the interception of communications, such as 'jihad' and 'infidel'. Extremist organisations have been clearly identified online. The issues are, first of all, getting access to information of operational value through their websites and through social media; second, what the intelligence services do with this information; and third, the ethics of this process. As Bartlett and Miller have stated, '[f]or counter-terrorism purposes, and more generally the study of discussions based on socially problematic or stigmatised views, closed forums are often more valuable than open ones' (Bartlett & Miller 2013, p. 45). This indicates that it is important to infiltrate groups online (ideally offline first, although this is far riskier) in order to gain trust to access restricted areas of websites where more important matters are discussed. I explain below why direct confrontation with extremist groups has little effect.

There continues to be a significant amount of discussion about the ethics of targeting individuals and groups for surveillance, infiltration and espionage, with the leak of the JTRIG documents a particularly noteworthy case in point. One assumption is that the people targeted are completely innocent until proven guilty in a court of law, so they should not be monitored and infiltrated. Another assumption seems to be that the 'deceit' and 'lying' on the part of agencies that infiltrate these groups degrades the internet itself. Both of these assumptions can be dispelled on common-sense grounds and through applying Vattimo's ideas about weak thought. Concerning the former, a key task of the intelligence services is to prevent serious crime occurring; one does not wait for the terrorist attack to bring individuals in for questioning. As for lying on the internet, sometimes an end can justify the means. Erskine (2004) foregrounded, in the context of intelligence and national security, concepts commonly used in ethical fields, such as 'consequentialism' and 'deontological', and it could be argued on consequentialist grounds that lying on the internet by pretending to be part of an extremist group in order to infiltrate (and possibly disrupt) actions by that group is justified if they are being violent.

From a Vattimian perspective, the key word here is 'violent'. When it comes to categorising violence, physical attack is only one form. What Vattimo shows is that even violent speech is dependent upon violent thoughts and beliefs. Certain beliefs and thoughts can be violent through their capacity to exclude others and to close down debate – a way of being that is incompatible with genuine democracy. Expressing these thoughts through communications technology indicates that those engaged in the communication are strong thinkers perpetrating violence. Unsurprisingly, Vattimo sees a link between metaphysical violence and physical violence. In a discussion with one of his students, Santiago Zabala, he states that in the Inquisition, '[b]urning heretics was a form of violence defended, in metaphysical terms, by a religion that professed an ultimate truth' (Vattimo & Zabala 2002, p. 455). Numerous other examples could be given, from Nazi ideology to the extremism of fundamentalist Muslims influencing their acts of jihad. As such, while surveillance and infiltration of groups of 'weak' thinkers is unwarranted, there is an ethical case for action of this nature against strong thinkers both with respect to strong thought in and of itself (which is inherently violent) and because there is good reason to believe that it will lead to other forms of violence, such as hate speech and physical harm to others.

The example of the Church raises interesting questions concerning the range of targets of surveillance. Vattimo mentions the issues of women being prevented from becoming priests in the Catholic Church (Vattimo 2007, p. 101) and homosexuality not being morally acceptable as examples of strong thought in the present day (Vattimo & Paterlini 2009, p. 13). Should intelligence services, then, keep the Catholic Church under watch or infiltrate it? Here a key distinction can be drawn between 'closed' and 'open' groups. There has been considerable discussion about the extent to which the Catholic Church has become 'weakened' or is in fact 'weakening itself'. A lot of this discussion addresses a landmark event in the life of the Church, the council Vatican II (1962–5). Key documents, such as *Lumen Gentium*, show a weakening with respect to salvation for non-believers, which is thought to be a key development in the overall process of weakening, albeit one that was by no means resolved during the council or since (Bullivant 2012). One can almost regard it as a *Verwindung* of soteriology. More recently, the current pope, Francis, has been non-committal about the moral status of homosexuals, again potential evidence of weakening (BBC 2013). The key factor is that the Catholic Church is open, it engages in dialogue with itself in terms of relating to its own vast tradition, as well as with other religious and non-religious groups. As an institution it is prepared to 'read the signs of the times', to adapt and listen based on extraneous factors 'in the world'. With 2000 years of history, there are a lot of metaphysical traces that can be weakened, and so the process of secularisation, of weakening, can appear to lag behind the pace of change elsewhere in society. Nevertheless, unless an exceptional piece of intelligence were passed to an agency regarding an individual or small group suspected of criminal activity within the

Church, I see no good reason to expend resources on open communities that are engaged in weakening strong thought.

By contrast, other religious, political and nationalist groups appear to have hardened and grown stronger in their thinking in recent decades, while other extremist groups centred on conspiracy theories have multiplied in number. Charles Townshend mentions that in the 1980s there was a shift towards religious and ideologically motivated terrorism (Townshend 2011, p. 98). Vattimo himself points to non-specific ayatollahs, a thinly veiled reference to the Iranian Revolution in 1979, as a catalysing factor in the return of religion to public consciousness (Vattimo 1999, pp. 26–7). The Iranian Revolution itself was a response to the perceived moral weakness and political corruption of the Western-influenced Iranian state under the Shah (Hashemi 2009, p. 139). As for conspiracy theories, these have flourished and grown in number since both the advent of the internet and the sheer terror of 9/11 (Morello 2004). Whether religious, political, nationalistic or conspiracy-minded, one can see in these groups what Sunstein and Vermeule refer to as extremists' 'crippled epistemologies' and closed nature (Sunstein & Vermeule 2008, pp. 8–9). Focusing mainly on conspiracy theorists, the authors state that overtly external attempts to influence or control such groups will be rejected or perceived by the groups as confirming their own worldview. For example, if the government were to publish scientific data disproving an extremist group's views on what happened to the twin towers on 9/11, the group would see this as confirming their suspicion that there had been a cover-up. Crippled epistemologies process information in this way, as well as relying on limited sources of questionable validity, due in no small part to limited education and reading ability. In these groups, knowledge 'cascades' from influential members down to those with limited abilities and opportunities to access and process information themselves, further restricting the horizons of these group members. It is these closed groups that require surveillance, as they cannot be readily engaged in dialogue to weaken their beliefs.

When a closed extremist community of strong thinkers is identified and yet cannot be engaged in dialogue, other options are available to governments to reduce the group's violence. Military violence against the group would be hypocritical and used only as a last resort; meeting violence with violence would be unjustified. Equally, trying to ban the group, removing its website(s) or arresting its members on ideological grounds would also be acts of violence, forms of 'dialectical over-coming' or *Überwindung*, as Vattimo would put it. Moreover, due to the 'closed' nature of this kind of extremist community, any attempt at an overcoming would reinforce the strong thinking of the group. Rather, I would call for infiltration and an ironic distortion of the group along the lines of a *Verwindung*. This could be achieved in an offline setting. The benefits of online infiltration are greater, as it can lead to Facebook friendship, and studies have shown that people are more honest and forthcoming on Facebook than elsewhere on the internet (Hancock 2013). Facebook friendship would also then quickly expose the agent to a greater network of contacts than offline friendship alone. Nevertheless, offline HUMINT carries significant risks and might not work, for reasons I mentioned earlier.

Whether offline or online, the aim remains the same: performing a *Verwindung*, that is, a distortion of the beliefs, aims and goals of a closed, extremist community. This can be achieved through appearing to buy in to the fundamental narratives and values of the group, but then either (i) ironically distorting them, (ii) exploiting existing minor differences within the community, or (iii) adding to the range of information to cause confusion and a sense of hopelessness.

The introduction of the 'no planes' theory into the 9/11 Truth Movement is an example of (i). The theory bought into the existing narrative of 9/11 being an inside job and there having been a cover-up, and utilised specific features of other parts of the bigger picture (including doubt over whether flight 77 hit the Pentagon and other, unrelated conspiracy theories such as Project Blue Beam). Essentially, the 'no planes' theory created a piece of satire by claiming that the planes that hit the twin towers were not planes, but actually holograms, missiles or photoshopped images. I am unaware of whether the 'no planes' theory was an attempt at infiltration and distortion of the 9/11 Truth Movement, or just a result of a genuine imagination run riot, but the net effect was anger and dissension within the movement. Some members were banned from 9/11 truth websites once the theory began to take hold, and there was a general sense of fear that the movement would lose credibility (Lemons 2007). Interestingly, Lemons mentions that certain ideas, such as the 'no planes' theory, were banned in some quarters of the 9/11 Truth Movement, and he points to this as evidence of the violence of strong thought in action.

With respect to (ii), infiltrating and distorting extremist groups by exploiting differences in their closed communities has already proven to be very effective. Brown and Korff write that:

> Jihadi websites provide much information about their organizations, including core beliefs; ideological divisions; ultimate goals and overall game plan; methods proposed to reach these goals; who makes decisions and how these are made. They often detail ideological splits and identify clerics who will dispute Qu'ranic interpretations who can be co-opted, intimidated or killed, providing a mechanism for intelligence agencies to challenge terror groups' legitimacy and siphon off recruits.
>
> *(Brown & Korff 2009, p. 123)*

I would condone co-opting clerics, but intimidating or killing them in order to gain a foothold in the group would simply perpetuate the kind of violence the agency in question is attempting to reduce. A better plan would be to train one's own 'cleric' in a place that intelligence indicates is a hub for extremism, gaining a reputation 'offline' before using him in both mosques and online forums to split communities along relatively trivial lines. This in turn would weaken the power of individual groups in terms of personnel, willpower and technical expertise. This is analogous to the case of the Cuban spy Ana Montes, who studied for a master's degree at Johns Hopkins University and obtained a position as an analyst at the

Defense Intelligence Agency that she held for years, sabotaging plans in the Latin American division (FBI 2011, pp. 4–5). Carrying out a similar plan against extremists would be justified if the targets were 'strong thinkers'. Again, as with (i), the key to infiltration is to be seen to buy into the narrative, but the difference is in not making up a new variation on a common theme, but drawing attention to existing technical differences. An example might be the Islamic interpretation of the thirteenth of *An-Nawawi's forty hadith*: 'None of you [truly] believes until he wishes for his brother what he wishes for himself' (Al-Nawawiyya 1976, p. 56). 'Brother' is interpreted in different ways in Islam, and Oddbjørn Leirvik (2010) has noted that the main fault-line is between whether it points to care for one's fellow Muslims or care for all humans. Careful exegesis of the latter interpretation, skilfully communicated by a respected cleric (whether co-opted or inserted) to a mass audience in a disputed area, could cause division between closed extreme communities of strong thinkers.

Option (iii) would work alongside (i) and (ii) and, to an extent, its effects would be similar. Nevertheless, how one would go about creating confusion and demor-alisation would depend upon the individual or the situation. It would largely depend upon the kind of closed extremist community one was infiltrating. If one were infiltrating a conspiracy community (whether far-right nationalist of the kind responsible for the Oklahoma City bombing, or a more generalised movement such as the 9/11 Truth Movement, which has organised protests), proliferating as many explanations or as much evidence – conflicting, ideally – in support of a conspiracy would be optimal. For example, 'evidence' both for the planes being missiles and being holograms would superficially support the closed group's narrative of a 'conspiracy' yet be mutually incompatible as explanations, causing confusion and gradual disillusionment; it is hard to be passionate to the point of exclusionary violence when one does not know what to believe. Furthermore, a lack of a consistent narrative or the appearance of infighting may well dissuade potential recruits. This approach may not work so well in religious communities that, by the very nature of the concept of religion alone, are less interested in 'details' and 'evidence' and instead hold important tenets on faith alone. Nevertheless, option (ii) falls into this category to some extent, although the key difference is that this option focuses on different *interpretations* of a single *point*, whereas option (iii) per-tains to different *explanations* and pieces of evidence for the development of a *narrative*.

Conclusion

How can 'monitoring', 'infiltration' and 'distortion' of groups not yet convicted of crimes be ethically justified? I have advocated a way of dealing with extremism that causes neither physical nor metaphysical violence to anyone. Admittedly, it is a teleological, consequentialist ethical approach to intelligence operations, and one in which the intelligence officer takes an active, operational role in a form of espionage (as I have had no legal training, I have avoided looking at the legal side of the issue). Military action leads to physical violence, whereas outright banning and overt prohibition cause defiance, further reinforcing extremism. I have suggested the criterion of being open or closed as a way of identifying communities of 'strong-thinking' extremists that should be monitored, infiltrated and distorted. This could prevent undue invasions of the privacy of the vast majority of the populace, including 'strong-thinking' groups that are in the process of weakening, however slow this process might be in some cases. Furthermore, I have outlined ways in which a *Verwindung* of closed groups of strong thinkers could take place that is compatible with Vattimo's programme of weak thought: strong, violent positions are to be weakened by introducing more plurality into closed narratives in order to de-centre their thinking and to take their foundations out from underneath them. In an online world that is far from transparent, in the midst of an irreducible plurality of interpretations, it is simply baffling to talk about the 'integrity' of the internet. Thus use of the whole range of tools open to a twenty-first-century intelligence service – for the purpose of reducing violence without inflicting physical harm or dialectical overcoming (that is, repeating strong thought) – should be encouraged rather than censured.

References

Al-Nawawiyya, Al-A 1976, *An-Nawawi's forty hadith*, trans. E Ibrahim & D Johnson-Davies, Holy Koran Publishing House, Damascus.

Bartlett, J & Miller, C 2013, *The state of the art: a literature review of social media intelligence capabilities for counter-terrorism*, Demos, London.

BBC 2013, 'Pope Francis: Who am I to judge gay people?' *BBC News*, 29 July, www.bbc.co.uk/news/world-europe-23489702

Bergen, P & Footer, L 2008, 'Defeating the attempted global jihadist insurgency: forty steps for the next president to pursue against Al Qaeda, like-minded groups, unhelpful state actors, and radicalized sympathizers', *Annals of the American Academy of Political and Social Science*, vol. 618, pp. 232–247.

Brown, I & Korff, D 2009, 'Terrorism and proportionality in internet surveillance', *European Journal of Criminology*, vol. 6, no. 2, pp. 119–134.

Bullivant, S 2012, *The salvation of atheists and catholic dogmatic theology*, Oxford University Press, Oxford.

Dover, R 2014 'Communications, privacy and identity', in R Dover, MS Goodman & C Hillebrand (eds), *Routledge companion to intelligence studies*, Routledge, London and New York, pp. 297–304.

Dover, R, Goodman, M & Hillebrand, C 2014, 'Preface', in R Dover, MS Goodman & C Hillebrand (eds), *Routledge companion to intelligence studies*, Routledge, London and New York, pp. xvi–xvii.

Erskine, T 2004, '"As rays of light to the human soul?": moral agents and intelligence gathering', *Intelligence and National Security*, vol. 19, no. 2, pp. 359–381.

FBI 2011, *Higher education and national security: the targeting of sensitive, proprietary and classified information on campuses of higher education*, White Paper prepared by FBI Counterintelligence Strategic Partnership Unit, US Department of Justice, Federal Bureau of Investigation, Washington, DC, https://www.fbi.gov/about-us/investigate/counterintelligence/higher-education-and-national-security

Greenwald, G 2014, 'How covert agents infiltrate the internet to manipulate, deceive, and destroy reputations', *The Intercept*, 24 February, https://firstlook.org/theintercept/2014/02/24/jtrig-manipulation

Hashemi, N 2009, *Islam, secularism, and liberal democracy: toward a democratic theory for Muslim societies*, Oxford University Press, Oxford.

Hillebrand, C 2014, 'Intelligence oversight and accountability', in in R Dover, MS Goodman & C Hillebrand (eds), *Routledge companion to intelligence studies*, Routledge, London and New York, pp. 305–312.

Hancock, J 2013, 'Social media makes us more honest', *CNN*, 13 January, http://edition.cnn.com/2013/01/13/opinion/hancock-technology-lying

Leirvik, O 2010, '"Aw Qāla: 'Li-Jārihi"': some observations on brotherhood and neighbourly love in Islamic tradition', *Islam and Christian–Muslim Relations*, vol. 21, no. 4, pp. 357–372.

Lemons, S 2007, 'The yoda of 9/11', *Phoenix New Times*, 9 August, www.phoenixnewtimes.com/2007-08-09/news/the-yoda-of-9-11/5

Morello, C 2004, 'Conspiracy theories flourish on the internet', *Washington Post*, 7 October, www.washingtonpost.com/wp-dyn/articles/A13059-2004Oct6.html

Nietzsche, F 2001 [1882], *The gay science*, J Nauckhoff & B Williams (ed. and trans.), Cambridge University Press, Cambridge.

Silverman, HJ 2007, 'Can the globalised world be in-the-world?' in S Zabala (ed.), *Weak thought: essays in honour of Gianni Vattimo*, McGill-Queen's University Press, Montreal/Kingston, London/Ithaca, pp. 110–116.

Sunstein, CR & Vermeule, A 2008*Conspiracy theories*, Public Law & Legal Theory Research Paper Series no. 199, University of Chicago Law School, http://ssrn.com/abstract=1084585

Townshend, C 2011, *Terrorism: a very short introduction*, Oxford University Press, Oxford.

Vattimo, G 1988, *The end of modernity*, trans. J Snyder, Polity Press, Cambridge.

Vattimo, G 1992, *The transparent society*, trans. D Webb, Polity Press, Cambridge.

Vattimo, G 1999, *Belief*, trans. D Webb & L D'Isanto, Polity Press, Cambridge.

Vattimo, G 2002, *After Christianity*, trans. L D'Isanto, Columbia University Press, New York.

Vattimo, G 2007, 'A prayer for silence', in JW Robbins (ed.), *After the death of God*, Columbia University Press, New York, pp. 89–113.

Vattimo, G & Paterlini, P 2009, *Not being God: a collaborative autobiography*, trans. W McCuaig, Columbia University Press, New York.

Vattimo, G & Zabala, S 2002, 'Weak thought and the reduction of violence', *Common Knowledge*, vol. 8, no. 3, pp. 452–463.

Walsh, PF 2011, *Intelligence and intelligence analysis*, Routledge, New York and Oxford.

3

THE EPISTEMOLOGY OF INTELLIGENCE ETHICS

Alexander Fatić

The focus of this chapter is on the argument that the use of intelligence in security policy is rarely predicated upon the need to find out the truth about events (and much less any comprehensive truth about the conflict that intelligence collection arises from or is intended to prevent). It is, rather, predicated upon a rights game, where the protection of a set of rights (arising from sovereignty, citizenship or other forms of belonging to a political or moral community) is the real objective. Such a shift in focus, from finding out the truth to using what appears to be the truth in order to advance competing sets of rights, allows controversial methods of intelligence collection, processing and operational use to purport to a moral justification where, if the focus was the truth, no such justification would be possible. This chapter thus deals with an epistemology of intelligence ethics, showing that such ethics will depend on the type of epistemology projected onto intelligence work.

The chapter argues that any type of intelligence is best understood as a quasi-epistemic game, rather than a truth-driven process that is subject to a morality dictated by a truth-driven epistemology. This has significant consequences for the professional ethics of intelligence work, as well as for the status of intelligence in the security policy of a democratic state.

Introduction: epistemological and quasi-epistemological intelligence games

Epistemology is crucial to intelligence gathering as much in the instrumental as in the moral sense. Intelligence gathering is fundamentally geared towards attaining knowledge of things that would otherwise remain hidden. Epistemology, on the other hand, is a theoretical perspective that examines the conditions for gaining knowledge, including questions of what it is to know something, what counts as reliable knowledge and, to an extent, what the relationship between knowledge and the truth might be.

The traditional understanding of intelligence gathering is of a system of methods for discovering important facts that would otherwise remain hidden, where these facts are crucial to the protection of national interest, public policy or, in the case of criminal intelligence, for reaching a just and legitimate verdict in a criminal trial. In this chapter I will call all the actions that contribute to the traditional idea of learning hidden truths through intelligence 'the epistemological game'. While in this understanding of the goal of intelligence the ultimate value is the truth of the affairs one inquires about, the process of gaining this truth is itself is a game: it is subject to certain rules that are not always straightforward and that may appear to be militating against the truth. For example, the epistemological game of intelligence, while striving to uncover the truth of things, routinely includes spreading misinformation, disguising other truths and creating the illusion that the ultimate object of the game is something else. Thus deceit is a legitimate tool in pursuing the truth through intelligence.

There are, however, uses of intelligence that are not geared to finding out the truth, though they appear otherwise. These I call 'quasi-epistemological games'. Many operations that are typically described as 'special warfare', including intelligence actions whose main aim is to instil fear in a population or in policymakers, as well as those 'intelligence' operations that are such only in name and include assassinations of key figures in various opponent structures, tend to be justified in terms of 'clearing the ground' or removing obstacles to proper truth-finding. Quasi-epistemological games are also used to find out information, rather than the truth as a whole, in order to use such information to achieve some goal that is not the truth. This is why in quasi-epistemological games a proper intelligence product is not always sought: normally, in order to lead to actionable knowledge, or to a truth based on which legitimate actions in national defence or criminal justice might be founded, raw intelligence material (or information) must be processed, evaluated and interpreted. Only such properly interpreted intelligence material can be considered a final intelligence product. In quasi-epistemological games such care is unnecessary. Information that arises from any phase of the intelligence process can be considered actionable, depending on its content and on what might be achieved by using it. This is why the use of electronic, especially signals intelligence (SIGINT), is so prevalent in modern intelligence: intercepting an electronic signal often leads to seemingly convincing information that can be readily used to convince or disturb someone without verifying, checking or creatively interpreting such material (Fatić 2011). Quasi-epistemological intelligence games include many manipulative intelligence strategies intended to cause a particular type of reaction in the recipient, rather than to find out the actual state of affairs with respect to legitimate security or other policy concerns. For example, among standard quasi-epistemological games are deliberate leaks of partial, misleading or simply false information to other intelligence services or to the public, in order to produce a favourable policy result or public mood.

The conservative British government of Margaret Thatcher was famous for its use of 'leaks' to the press to prepare the public for the introduction of controversial policies. Often this included the leaking of an 'insider story' that a particular, often quite outrageous, public policy was being introduced, such as the abolition of all unemployment benefits. Once the public was sufficiently alarmed that the benefits would disappear, the government came forward with reduced benefits, to give but one example: a policy which, while obviously unpopular, looked far more reasonable than the abolition of benefits altogether. Issues of immigration, which most governments used to understand primarily as issues of economics and demographics, are now routinely described as security problems, and all sorts of connections with various security threats (predominantly with militant Islamism) are used to justify what Ole Weaver calls 'securitisation' of the immigration discourse – a term that has since achieved considerable prominence in public policy studies (Higgott 2004). The essence of this strategy is to present as many general policy issues as security-relevant in as dramatic a form, as possible, in order to elicit a maximum of willingness by the population to bear sacrifice, or to justify the curbing of traditional civil rights (Weaver 2008). As a result, immigrants are held in guarded and barbed-wired detention camps that at least physically resemble concentration camps, and their immigrations status is decided using procedures that increasingly militate in principle against their human rights (Latour 2014). The American government has also extensively used a policy of securitisation.

All of these strategies methodologically belong to the intelligence operations of quasi-epistemological games. Just as in any other aspect of human relations, actions that appear to relate to truth-seeking might and often do aim at something rather different, and often have little to do with truth or knowledge themselves.

The rights game as a quasi-epistemological game

A principal shift in emphasis from the truth to 'rights' has been particularly effective in justifying quasi-epistemological games in general policy as well as in intelligence gathering. It is worth taking some time to understand how the 'rights' discourse is used to securitise public policy, before moving on to show how rights are becoming an increasingly fundamental pillar to intelligence policy rather than the truth (Fatić, Korać & Bulatović 2013, pp. 14–20).

The shift from conceptualising intelligence gathering as seeking hidden truths to the task of interpreting is based on the idea that there are certain rights, typically political rights, that are so important to the political community that the goal of advancing them warrants forfeiting the truth. By my lights, this idea is morally problematic and deserves elaboration. It is basically rooted in consequentialist moral thinking which, however, is not entirely consistent: it assumes that there are certain classes of rights that are so valuable that their maximisation justifies sacrificing other rights without letting those whose rights are sacrificed even know that the trade-off is being made. This means that, for example, the right to the truth about public policymaking may be deceitfully undermined in the putative interest of citizens' right to protection from various security threats. This type of thinking is consistent with the newest arguments to the effect that the state is primarily bound by the so-called 'duty to protect', and that this duty morally justifies the state's otherwise controversial actions, including the trampling of traditional liberal political rights such as those related to the transparency of public policymaking (Kasher and Yadlin 2005).

The consequentialist perspective on rights in this context can naturally spill over the initially conceived bounds and turn into a perceived licence for the government to pursue whatever policies it may deem beneficial for its capacity to fulfil its 'duty to protect', more or less regardless of its other duties to citizens. Richard Falk wrote about the initial 'necessity' for the US to provide a sense of security for its citizens after 9/11 by attacking someone, regardless of whether or not it could actually establish that that group or country was behind the attack on the World Trade Center. Thus Falk argued (he later revised this stance, however) that it was psychologically necessary for the US to attack Afghanistan, even if (or even though) Washington had known that the Afghan government had little to do with the attacks and/or that the attacks would not help remove the threat of Islamic terrorism. This psychological necessity, according to him, constitutes in part a legitimacy for the action; it is easy to see how Falk's argument dovetails with the 'duty to protect' doctrine: if the state has the duty to protect as its paramount moral duty to its citizens, it is justified in starting an otherwise unjust war with another state if doing so is likely to increase the overall security, or sense of security, of its citizens (Falk 2003).

The rights discourse, when it is used to replace the discourse focused on the truth, easily lends itself to the moral justification of particularly intrusive and controversial methods of gathering and using intelligence. The Snowden case illustrates a typical situation that can arise from the rights discourse: the idea that the rights of citizens to protection by the state are so strong that they justify the suspension of their other rights, including, importantly, the right to know the truth about the extent to which they are subject to surveillance by their own state (Gurnow 2014). Theoretically, if the 'duty to protect' as the foundation for a moral justification of intelligence collection is pushed far enough, limitless surveillance of a state's own citizens might be considered legitimate. Where a reference to the truth might heal the abuses of democratic values, the replacement of the truth discourse with a rights discourse provides a virtual *carte blanche* for the introduction of a fully fledged security state, with all of its nightmarish uses of intelligence.

What then is 'quasi-epistemological' about the rights discourse? Well, such discourse, while obviously overemphasising some rights while underemphasising others, tends to retain a quasi-epistemological aspiration: typically, intelligence services that conduct intrusive and apparently unwarranted data gathering policies *vis-à-vis* their own citizens verbally assume that one of the important goals of their work is learning the truth. While the discourse itself is dominated by 'rights' and 'duties', there is never an explicit statement of the irrelevance of the truth, because such an acknowledgement would instantly delegitimise the intelligence service:

people continue to think that truth is the ultimate criterion for judging the value of intelligence. Conversely, public opinion would rightly perceive an intelligence service that openly disparaged the truth in favour of rights as manipulative and threatening. Thus the American policymakers never admitted that they knew that attacking Afghanistan (or later Iraq) would not only fail to bring the jihadis to heel, but would in fact aggravate the problems with Islamic terrorism. Even after it became clear that Iraq, once a secular country that in no way presented a terrorist threat, had become one of the most dangerous hotbeds of Islamic terrorism worldwide, the American government did not fully acknowledge that erroneous intelligence had been used to justify the invasion. In fact, what the US government would have had to acknowledge is something far more sinister for traditional democratic rights: it was not merely 'erroneous', but deliberately abused intelligence, whose aim was not to establish the truth but rather to provide a pretext for the invasion (Jervis 2006). Similarly, combined intelligence and foreign policy efforts to remove the Assad government in Syria by aiding armed Islamic opposition groups have already ricocheted dramatically through the rise of the so-called 'Islamic State of Iraq and the Levant' (ISIL) in Syria and its sweeping offensive to conquer large parts of Iraq and Syria (McQuaid 2014).

From a traditional point of view of intelligence as an epistemological game, all of the above actions would be considered seriously detrimental policies, arising from deeply flawed intelligence work and resulting in untruthful intelligence products. It would of course be naïve to think that epistemically flawed intelligence could be responsible for successive, yet strategically highly consistent, military and foreign policy campaigns resulting in an array of new conflicts and the opening of new 'civilisational' fault-lines. It is at least reasonable to assume that the US government was able to conclude that, after the upsurge of Islamic extremism following the invasion of Afghanistan, the same would occur after the invasion of Iraq and after the destabilisation of the Middle-Eastern regimes of Egypt and Syria – through the strangely consistent and well organised series of 'Arab Springs' that started in 2010. If one assumes that policymakers are at least as intelligent as the average observer of foreign policy, it is reasonable to conclude that the intelligence games that preceded and facilitated these detrimental developments across much of the Islamic world were not epistemological, but in fact quasi-epistemological games. Their aim was not far removed from what has in fact been achieved, and the current outcomes are not simply a result of gross incompetence on the part of intelligence services coupled with policy incompetence on the political level: the actual aim was to achieve the results that have in fact transpired, which means that intelligence was not used in order to uncover the truth but rather to manipulate and prejudice a desired course of events. Quasi-epistemological intelligence games are manipulative uses of intelligence that are potentially dangerous for democratic process and government accountability.

One of the main problems with the swapping of truth-based discourse on intelligence with a rights-based discourse is that the diminution of truth as the guiding light of intelligence gathering inevitably leads to a diminution of public trust in the intelligence and security services more generally. Once public trust is sufficiently undermined, political legitimacy is questioned as well (Hough et al. 2010). An intelligence policy that is guided by appeals to various rights, while openly acknowledging that it is indifferent to the truth of the events it seeks to interpret, would inevitably be distrusted by the public. The discourse based on rights, without an anchor in the truth, readily lends itself to all kinds of abuse and manipulation which, in the end, result in more rights being violated than protected. Although quasi-epistemological games of intelligence such as those described are never followed by open acknowledgements of indifference to, and much less of open disdain for, the truth, the clearer it is that their actual workings are motivated by a desire to prejudice specific policies and actionable intelligence products – rather than finding out the truth – the greater the public reprimand of such intelligence will be. Thus the quasi-epistemological use of intelligence is a way in which intelligence services may delegitimise themselves.

The cultural context for modern intelligence

Despite the multicultural norms that have been adopted as part of politically correct language in multicultural democracies, modern intelligence is based to some extent upon discriminating in terms of nationality and race, characterised by a propensity to engage in explicit or implicit ethnic profiling and predicated upon the prejudice connected with perceptions of dominant security threats today. Until the most recent developments in 2013 and 2014, caused by the escalation of the Ukrainian crisis, which revitalised Cold War sentiments between the Russian Federation on the one hand, and the US and the EU on the other, the trend in the development of security threats has been towards non-state entities and informal groups as the main belligerents. More often than not the threat is now seen to come from relatively marginal social groups with strong religious beliefs and unorthodox organisation and motives, which makes fighting them effectively very difficult. After all, one of the main facets of terrorism is that it is fundamentally incongruent with the traditional sides in military conflict: the calculation of risks is different and the readiness to sacrifice is disproportionately higher than in conventional military conflicts. This makes 'unorthodox' security threats particularly frightening for intelligence services: any intelligence failure readily translates into large numbers of civilian victims with immense political fallout, as was the case with 9/11. In turn, such a threat to the integrity and status of intelligence services leads them to adopt exceedingly discriminating cultural views and operational guidelines.

A good illustration of such views is given by a Swedish intelligence officer and member of the Swedish National Defence College, Lars Ulfving:

> There are two lines of development worth commenting on in this context, particularly when they can be made to interact. The first is the emergence of new warrior castes, or classes and warrior societies … and also streetfighter nations which do not need to be nation-states.

These consist of individuals who are psychologically separated from Western thinking in ethical questions. The young generation is being raised for combat, to believe that combat itself is honourable and that killing in war is glorious. In their most primitive form they may consist of larger youth gangs. The members of the castes have acquired a taste for blood; they do not behave with human rationality according to western definitions, and are completely ruthless. ... Consequently, no politically or economically rational motives in the western sense are to be found among these groups.

(Ulfving 2003, p. 22)

The above lines, which come from a textbook on intelligence published by the national defence college of one of the most tolerant and inclusive nations on Earth today, show very clearly the extent to which the tendency has developed to almost dehumanise the informal groups that are seen to present the dominant threat. The idea that those who present security threats tend to be removed from the recognisable ethical standards that we supposedly share implies that the treatment required by those same ethical standards, including proper recognition of their interests, kindness and mercy, is not due to them. It was this thinking that made possible (and still makes possible) the Guantanamo detention camp, the scandalous treatment of 'terror' prisoners in Iraq in the American Abu Ghraib prison, the use of 'waterboarding', sleep-deprivation and so-called 'intensive interrogation tactics', as well as many other abuses both of wartime justice and intelligence. Such dehumanising makes it natural to 'stress ... the ageless importance of good intelligence, deception, disinformation and propaganda to subdue an opponent, preferably without resistance' (Ulfving 2003, p. 38).

Obviously one of the main problems with views like the above one is that deception, disinformation and propaganda simply cannot be considered 'good intelligence', and much less are they morally justified types of intelligence work. The fact that most intelligence services use such quasi-epistemic games is no more a confirmation of their legitimacy than the fact that governments occasionally invade foreign countries is a foundation for the legitimacy of aggressive wars. The developing interest in intelligence ethics since the 1980s bears witness to a sense widely shared by the public of threat from the intelligence services, which are not held in check by a degree of professional ethics and institutional integrity like other public services. This particularly concerns the work of the intelligence services in peacetime – while in the times of war deception might be a necessary and indeed legitimate form of engagement for intelligence as well as for any other part of the military, in peacetime the use of wartime methods is highly problematic. As most intelligence worldwide is collected during peacetime, and since the very mission of the intelligence service is primarily preventative, the normal context in which the ethics of intelligence are considered is the operation of intelligence services in peacetime.

Obviously the lines quoted above suggest a blurred line between wartime and peacetime: once we are willing to label those who do not agree with our values as belligerent moral degenerates with 'a taste for blood', which is essentially Ulfving's suggestion, it is very easy to make the additional step of declaring a perpetual state of war against them regardless of whether countries and/or armies are engaged in any type of recognisable warfare. Thus the declaration of the 'war on terror' by George W Bush after 9/11, which preceded the actual expansion and dramatic intensification of the terrorist threat worldwide, served to allow intelligence and other security services to adopt highly aggressive wartime tactics as their normal modes of operation during peacetime.

One of the problems with the declaration of cultural wars has become very clear in the Western 'war' on Islamic extremism. This is that they quickly turn into real wars. Initially conceived as legitimising (or quasi-legitimising) tools to support essentially punitive actions against potential terrorist threats in distant theatres of engagement, such wars tend to 'come home' unexpectedly: punitive strikes lead to radicalisation of members of the targeted communities at home, and before long bombs start to explode at urban marathons, soldiers are killed while walking around their barracks or mowed down by cars on freeways (Sky News 2013; CNN 2014; Montreal Gazette 2014).

The blow-back effect of punitive strikes against Islamic targets, and the increasingly open stereotyping of Muslim identity, especially in large urban Western communities, seems to mark a trend of Islamic radicalisation of Western-born Muslims – even of recent converts to Islam with little or no experience with Muslim cultures (Murshed & Pavan 2009). The phenomenon known colloquially as 'Londonistan', after the influential book by Melanie Phillips (2006) – the trend of radicalisation of young Muslims, especially in mosques in East London, where most of these young men have never been to the Middle East, do not speak Arabic, and have spent all of their lives and undergone all of their socialisation in British society – bears powerful witness to the potency of this ricochet effect of cultural wars.

Intelligence ethics is closely connected with the epistemology of intelligence. This is because the cognitive ambitions of intelligence services tend to guard it against abuses that typically arise when such ambitions are forfeited in exchange for quasi-epistemic games dealing in 'rights'. If the citizens of modern Western cities have the right to be secure, then the best way to provide them with a maximum of security from terror attacks might well be to stick to truth as the main aim of intelligence. Finding out the truth about what motivates Islamic militants in the Middle East, however, might be uncomfortable for the powers of the international arena. As Ted Honderich argues, the exceedingly uneven distribution of power and wealth worldwide, which sees an increasingly large majority of the world's population, especially that concentrated in the Middle East and Africa, deprived not only of basic commodities necessary for life but also of political power and basic rights arising from proper and effective political representation, leads to revolt, including terrorism (Honderich 2002). Truthful intelligence on the existence of weapons of mass destruction in Iraq would have prevented the forceful removal of Saddam Hussein's government, and in all likelihood there would have been no Islamic terrorism in Iraq today, just as there had been none during Hussein's reign (simply because the secular Iraqi government had kept the extremists in check).

Truthful intelligence, instead of manipulative quasi-epistemic games, would probably have prevented Western governments from instigating the 'Arab Spring' in Egypt with the removal of Hosni Mubarak from the Egyptian presidency in 2011. Had Mubarak not been brought down, the Muslim Brotherhood would not have taken power in Egypt, and no further instigation of a military coup against them would have been necessary for the West in Egypt. As a result of 'playful' rather than truthful intelligence, the US and Europe became involved in a series of rights-breaking, highly risky and deeply illegitimate policies in the Middle East, some of which backfired so badly that covert interventions had to be conducted repeatedly, first to bring down an establishment, and then to remove the group that had come to power in place of the initial government, such as in Egypt. The end result of such experiments is the least desirable state of affairs, where a state with a civil government ends up being governed by the military, such as has been *de facto* the case in Egypt under the populist general Abdel-Fattah el Sisi (Economist 2014).

All of the instrumental uses of intelligence I have mentioned here that were not intended to lead to the truth, but rather to obscure the truth in order to legitimise preconceived political and military actions, could be explained in two ways. These relate to two separate contexts for the cultural interpretation of modern intelligence. One has already been briefly described in terms of the use of intelligence in order to target 'high-risk' cultures, such as Muslim culture is seen to be. The detrimental consequences of this type of instrumental use of security apparatus generally, including the intelligence services, unfortunately seem quite obvious.

The second cultural context specifically concerns the culture of the intelligence service itself. One of the main problems of intelligence services throughout history has been their lack of stable identity, proper self-perception of professional dignity and a democratically tested, quality standard of ethics.

Most of the current discussions about organisational culture of intelligence services tend to simply question-beg from the point of view of how the intelligence services perceive themselves and their status in the society. Such discussions tend to focus on what I would consider a highly impoverished concept of 'organisational culture', which is reduced to perceptions of the way in which intelligence officers discharge their duties, how effective they are, and how they conceptualise periodic organisational reforms of intelligence-gathering methods (Bean 2009). While issues of intelligence reform and responsibility in the discharge of duty are by no means irrelevant for intelligence culture, they are only a small part of it. The larger question here is whether intelligence services perceive themselves as organisations that gather together dignified professionals who are bound by professional ethics, or as structures that exist in total conformity with the wishes of the government. This, I feel, is the key issue for the ethics of intelligence, which allows for the interpretation of such ethics in terms of the epistemology of intelligence efforts. The perspective that this question opens is the same as for any other public service: to what extent is such a structure's identity self-sufficient and independent from the will of the government? And, conversely, to what extent it is inherently tied to following government decisions unquestioningly? Compared with other parts of the government apparatus, it seems that these questions, while structurally the same for all public services, are particularly dramatic and controversial where intelligence services are concerned.

A number of the circumstances that characterise intelligence work contribute to tensions over the identity of the intelligence service and its relationship to the contingent will of the government. Intelligence officers are routinely expected to make highly discriminative decisions with regard to the increasingly large amounts of fragmented information with which they work. Any failure by the intelligence service is increasingly political and generates serious fallout for the government, especially since the 'war on terror' brought casualties to the very hearts of Western capital cities – in North America and Europe in particular. As a result, intelligence services face escalating tensions with regard to the so-called crying-wolf syndrome: situations where numerous indications that an adverse event might occur appear over a course of time and, while none is decisively falsified, nothing appears to happen. The overload of potential alarms that later appear false or exaggerated thus forces the intelligence service to lift the threshold for reaction. In practice this means that, if several similar warnings have not proven valid, the intelligence apparatus will not react to every warning of the same kind with the same vigilance as though it was a new warning. Logically this widens the possibility of a security crisis resulting from any of the discrete warnings that might be ignored. The quality of discretionary decision making thus remains an irreducible and crucial element of intelligence, and there is increased pressure on the exercise of such discretion, which has become more political in nature (Fatić et al. 2013, pp. 20–2). Such decisions are obviously heavily influenced by cultural factors, both within the service and outside it: the status and self-perception of the intelligence service within the community largely determine the extent to which the intelligence officer will act on the basis of her moral judgment as opposed to pure organisational conformity.

While there are approaches to intelligence culture today that consider themselves 'postmodern' in that they question the relevance of culture *per se* and insist on the individual accountability of intelligence officers for their actions, regardless of organisational and political expectations, this is of course much easier said than done (Bean 2009). In order to be able to exercise moral judgment within their official discretion, intelligence personnel require specific ethical prerequisites in terms of standards and accepted ways of moral thinking within the service.

Examples of intelligence officers blowing the whistle on irregularities within the service are replete. However, most intelligence services still lack firmly embedded formal institutional ethics.

The role of virtue in the intelligence service

In intelligence, some virtues may be highly dangerous, and thus the development of professional intelligence ethics that would be based on specific virtues is a challenging demand. Virtues such as loyalty alone, without the possession of broader social insights and a moral 'compass' that points beyond the interests of the profession and even of one's state, could and do lead to intelligence services acting detrimentally when it comes to important rights and moral expectations – even in democratic states. The possession of broader socially oriented virtues has made possible cases such as Edward Snowden and others' whistleblowing with regard to widespread, even rampant, practices within the intelligence services that challenge not only the legal but civilisational norms of democratic life and state behaviour.

The crucial role of virtues in the ethics of intelligence is fundamentally connected with the pitfalls of democratic procedure when it is devoid of substantive values. So-called 'proceduralism' in democratic theory takes it that the democratic procedure is what matters rather than the substantive outcomes of such procedures: as long as the integrity of the procedure is unimpaired, the process conveys validity on the substantive outcome (Peter 2007). One of the obvious problems with proceduralism is that it is consistent with substantively appalling outcomes as long as they are brought about by proper process. It is imaginable that what David Hume called 'incorrigibly corrupt' people might make up a community within which a perfectly procedurally democratic process could yield morally unacceptable results (Hume 1963 [1777]). This is why authors such as David Estlund emphasise the role of 'background consensus', against which democratic procedures receive their full legitimacy (Estlund 2009). Of course, Estlund's idea is only one way in which the internal value-vacuum of proceduralism can be addressed; another could be the positing of certain affirmative values without which procedural democracy is simply not a democracy in the full sense. While the problem of proceduralism in democratic theory is not the primary emphasis of this chapter, it generates important equivalences in the context of virtue within the ethics of intelligence.

An uncritical insistence on proceduralism characterises most current efforts to institute professional ethics for intelligence: it is believed within most government bureaucracies that as long as there are sufficient procedural restrictions and oversight, which more or less guarantee that such procedures are observed by intelligence officers, major moral controversies might be avoided. Thus there exist restrictions, for example those that require warrants in order to enact intrusive surveillance such as electronic interception of communications; similarly the existence of parliamentary committees for the oversight of intelligence services based on positivistic rules of engagement. The problem with such procedural guarantees is that many rules that govern intelligence are classified themselves, which means that it is quite possible for various problematic intelligence strategies to be made entirely legal and procedurally justified while nevertheless threatening fundamental rights and being substantively morally controversial. For example, assuming that the mass surveillance of citizens by the National Security Agency (NSA), which Edward Snowden revealed, is completely legal, this does not change the fact that it is at stark odds with what American citizens had reason to expect based on the founding values of American society, including fundamental rights and freedoms such as those of privacy, free speech and freedom of political association (Bojanić 2013).

In fact, in intelligence services procedures are less powerful in terms of being a deterrent for ethical impropriety than they are in most other fields of institutional action. Given the secrecy that makes up the cultural context of intelligence gathering, procedures tend to be either hidden from the public or limited in terms of public access to data. This places the onus of moral decision making on the intelligence officer and their conscience: only the clear concepts of virtue and values on which such virtue is based can provide adequate motivation for intelligence staff to make valuable moral decisions in intelligence gathering. At the same time, virtue ethics appears to be under-represented in the ethics of intelligence. The ethics of intelligence too often appears in generally functionalist and utilitarian forms − though utilitarianism is not meant to be a disqualification here, as in its broad understanding it is compatible with a variety of methodologies of moral thinking (Kordig 1974). What utilitarian reasoning obscures is the dramatic character of moral decision making on the part of the intelligence officer, which arises from various layers of their conscience. The general emphasis in utilitarianism is on the calculation of the most beneficial consequences in a variety of terms, ranging from direct 'utility' for the state to goods perceived as the observance of rights (rights utilitarianism) or the promotion of the rule of law and other legitimate rules in society (rule utilitarianism). All aspects of utilitarianism purport to provide a legitimation framework that eliminates the personal drama of decision making against the backdrop of the secrecy and considerable discretion that characterise the intelligence service. This drama, however, should not be eliminated or reduced − it should be encouraged.

The instilling of specific professional virtues in the intelligence service could prevent professional burnout in moral decision making, known as 'moral numbing'. Such psychological anaesthetised states are often deliberately encouraged in the military: the best researched cases include psychological work to render soldiers willing to kill members of their own species, which is contrary to fundamental moral intuitions (Grossman 1996). Work on the development of professional virtues might also prevent moral relativism arising from rationalisations about the 'higher interests' of the state, which creates problems in the moral judgments of police and military officers when they switch their official roles for private ones and *vice versa* (Tilley 1995).

Professional virtues can be identified upon reflection on the problems and dilemmas that occur in the process of switching between the roles of private citizen and intelligence officer. The idea of intelligence virtue is based on the prospect of reconciling state interests and the functional imperatives of intelligence (including secrecy, loyalty and the execution of orders) with the broader social conscience of the intelligence officer. It is this conscience, and the values inherent within it, that makes possible resistance to the overwhelming and progressively threatening culture of the state's dominance over civil society via its intelligence functions, both abroad and domestically.

It is of course unlikely that the political authorities will be motivated to encourage a culture of broader social conscience in intelligence services. There are two main reasons for this. First, intelligence is one of the most powerful tools of the political establishment in furthering a variety of public and less public agendas. Second, in the minds of political elites the effectiveness of the intelligence service depends on its more or less full instrumentalisation by the government. At the same time, resistance on the part of intelligence services to overbearing governments that perceive intelligence as merely a tool, rather than a public service in its own right, is the most effective barrier to serious abuses.

The moral dimension of intelligence collection does not principally differ from that of the public services in general. Just as public services take pride in their own ethics and consider themselves a guild of sorts, intelligence services are not merely a tool for the achievement of war- or peacetime agendas set by political authorities. One virtue of intelligence officers is the ability to judge such agendas – in particular the means proposed for their pursuit. Such virtues should be incorporated into a formalised ethics of intelligence, which will help turn intelligence gathering into a fully recognised profession in its own right, with its own concepts of integrity and social responsibility.

Acknowledgements

This chapter arose from work on project no. 179049, funded by the Serbian Ministry of Education and Research and implemented by the Institute for Philosophy and Social Theory, University of Belgrade, 2010–15. Parts of the text also come from my previously completed research on the problem of truth in the context of war crimes trials, which was published in co-authorship with Aleksandra Bulatović (Fatić and Bulatović 2012). The parts of the text that derive from this previous research have been partially argumentatively re-developed to suit the context of intelligence, but my views remain fundamentally the same, in particular on the general issue of quasi-epistemological games in the criminal trial and in intelligence. A part of the argument presented here also derives from equivalent considerations of the truthfulness of criminal trials for war crimes, developed separately in Bachmann and Fatić (2015).

References

Bachmann, K & Fatić, A 2015, *The UN international criminal tribunals: transition without justice?* Routledge, London.

Bean, H 2009, 'Organizational culture and US intelligence affairs', *Intelligence and National Security*, vol. 24, no. 4, pp. 479–498.

Betts, RK 2007–8, 'Two faces of intelligence failure: September 11 and Iraq's missing WMD', *Political Science Quarterly*, vol. 122, no. 4, pp. 585–606.

Bojanić, P 2013, 'Pacifism: equipment or accessory of war?' *Philosophia*, vol. 41, no. 3, pp. 1037–1047.

CNN 2014, 'Boston marathon terror attack fast facts', *CNN*, 26 September, http://edition. cnn.com/2013/06/03/us/boston-marathon-terror-attack-fast-facts

Economist 2014, 'As-Sisi ascendant', *The Economist*, 20 September, www.economist.com/ news/middle-east-and-africa/21618908-general-has-good-first-100-daysat-cost-political-freedom-al-sisi

Estlund, D 2009, 'Epistemic proceduralism and democratic authority', in R Geenengs & R Tinnevelt (eds), *Does truth matter: democracy and public space*, Springer, Frankfurt.

Falk, R 2003, *The great terror war*, Olive Branch Press, New York.

Fatić, A 2011, 'Metode i tehnike kriminalističko-obaveštajne analize u svetlu pitanja o integritetu analitičara' ('Methods and techniques of criminal-intelligence analysis in light of the analyst's integrity'), *Revija za bezbednost (Security Review)*, vol. 5, no. 1, pp. 24–38.

Fatić, A & Bulatović, A 2012, 'The problem of truth in war crimes trials', *International Problems*, vol. LXIV, no. 1, pp. 34-52.

Fatić, A, Korać, S & Bulatović, A 2013, *Etika kriminalističko-obaveštajnog rada (Ethics of criminal intelligence)*, Institute for International Politics and Economics, Belgrade.

Grossman, D 1996, *On killing: the psychological cost of learning to kill in war and society*, Back Bay Books, New York.

Gurnow, M 2014, *The Edward Snowden affair: exposing the politics and the media behind the NSA scandal*, Cardinal Publishers Group, Indianapolis.

Higgott, R 2004, 'US foreign policy and the "securitization" of economic globalization', *International Politics*, vol. 41, pp. 147–175.

Honderich, T 2002, *After the terror*, Edinburgh University Press, Edinburgh.

Hough, M et al. 2010, 'Procedural justice, trust and institutional legitimacy', *Policing*, vol. 4, pp. 1–8.

Hume, D 1963 [1777], *Essays: moral, political and literary*, Oxford University Press, Oxford.

Jervis, R 2006, 'Reports, politics the intelligence failures: the case of Iraq', *Journal of Strategic Studies*, vol. 29, no. 1, pp. 3–52.

Kasher, A & Yadlin, A 2005, 'Military ethics of fighting terror', *Journal of Military Ethics*, vol. 3, pp. 14–21.

Kordig, K 1974, 'Structural similarities between utilitarianism and utilitarianism', *Journal of Value Inquiry*, vol. 8, no. 1, pp. 52–56.

Latour, V 2014, 'The securitisation of British multiculturalism', in R Garbaye & P Schnapper (eds), *The politics of ethnic diversity in the British Isles*, Palgrave Macmillan, Basingstoke, pp. 38–54.

McQuaid, J 2014, Reviving the Caliphate: fad, or the future?, CNA Analysis and Solutions, Arlington, http://stabilityinstitute.com/governancd/religion/modern-caliphate-fantasy-or-trend

Montreal Gazette 2014, 'Attack on soldiers an act of violence against Canada, Quebec: public security minister', *Montreal Gazette*, 21 October, http://montrealgazette.com/news/local-news/soldier-dies-after-being-run-down-in-st-jean-sur-richelieu

Murshed, M & Pavan, S 2009, Identity and Islamic radicalization in Western Europe, MICROCON Research Working Paper, MICROCON, Brighton, www.microconflict.eu/publications/RWP16_MM_SP.pdf

Peter, F 2007, 'Democratic legitimacy and proceduralist social epistemology', *Politics, Philosophy and Economics*, vol. 6, no. 3, pp. 329–353.

Phillips, M 2006, *Londonistan*, Encounter Books, New York.

Sky News 2013, 'Woolwich trial: "killer nearly beheaded soldier"', *Sky News*, 30 November, http://news.sky.com/story/1175452/woolwich-trial-killer-nearly-beheaded-soldier

Tilley, J 1995, 'Two kinds of moral relativism', *Journal of Value Inquiry*, vol. 29, no. 2, pp. 187–192.

Ulfving, L 2003, *Wilderness of mirrors: operational–strategic intelligence – theory, empiricism, and methodology*, Swedish National Defence College, Stockholm.

Weaver, O 2008, 'The changing agenda of societal security', *Globalisation and Environmental Challenges: Hexagon Series on Human and Environmental Security and Peace*, vol. 3, pp. 581–593.

PART II

Interrogation, torture and terrorism

4

THE HUMAN COSTS OF TORTURE

Matthew Beard

Much modern debate about torture has focused on the question of whether torture can ever be justified. Torture, in every serious moral treatment of the subject, is thought to be a bad thing. Some argue, however, that it may be morally permissible to practise torture because the benefits outweigh the moral costs. This places the moral requirement to treat every human being with justice, in direct competition with the responsibility of statesmen and intelligence officers to make decisions that protect their citizens (Allhoff 2003). In this chapter I will largely ignore that debate. Instead, I will focus on the ethical consequences of performing acts of torture or being subjected to torture, whether or not the actions themselves are morally justifiable.

Torturers are asked to perform acts that degrade, mock, traumatise or objectify other human beings. It is therefore reasonable to ask whether institutions that employ torturers are cultivating character traits in those men and women such that they are unlikely to make good citizens or to flourish as persons. That is, whether the deeds torturers perform lead to the formation of character vices such as insensitivity to the suffering of others, manipulative attitudes toward relationships or difficulty in trusting other people; and whether, even if torturers are able to retain some form of virtue during acts of torture, their ability to flourish as human beings is compromised. Even virtuous people can suffer emotional and psychological harms that render them unable to excel to the extent they otherwise would. If institutions require people to become torturers, it behoves them to make sure those people fully understand the toll that torture will have on their souls.

Acknowledging the moral costs of becoming a torturer requires an understanding of what torture is and what it does. In the concluding section of this chapter I summarise some of the literature on the phenomenology of torture–victimhood, and – in keeping with the theme of this volume – how one particular technology, namely unmanned aerial vehicles (more frequently called drones), might be capable of causing very similar kinds of character damage to those that torture aims to generate.

Torture: definitional debates

The United Nations Convention Against Torture and Other Cruel, Inhuman or Degrading Treatment or Punishment[1] defines torture as:

> [A]ny act by which severe pain or suffering, whether physical or mental, is intentionally inflicted on a person for such purposes as obtaining from him or a third person information or a confession, punishing him for an act he or a third person has committed or is suspected of having committed, or intimidating or coercing him or a third person, or for any reason based on discrimination of any kind, when such pain or suffering is inflicted by or at the instigation of or with the consent or acquiescence of a public official or other person acting in an official capacity.
>
> *(United Nations 1987, Article 1.1)*

This is a helpful starting point, but it is not without its shortcomings. For example, as Michael Davis (2008, p. 189) observes, 'an illegal organization, such as the mafia, is, without official "consent or acquiescence" as capable of torture as any government'. Even though Mafiosi or gang thugs will never be brought before the International Criminal Court for their actions, they are still capable of torture. The crime of torture is not determined by *who* performs the action, but by qualities inherent to the action itself. Thus we must ask *which* qualities of the action constitute torture. The UN definition suggests that what constitutes torture is the *severity* of the pain or suffering that is inflicted, in combination with the *reasons* for which the pain is inflicted – reasons that may include intelligence gathering, punishment, intimidation and coercion or any reason based on discrimination. However, not *all* pain or suffering for these purposes can constitute torture. After all, criminals suffer a loss of freedom when they are imprisoned as punishment for their crimes, but criminal imprisonment should not be considered torture. The amount or intensity of the pain and suffering must meet a certain threshold before the label of torture can be applied.

So emerges a deeper difficulty with the UN definition: the fact that by identifying torture as the intentional infliction of *severe* pain or suffering, one implicitly condones inflictions of *less than severe* pain or suffering. Here we enter a realm stifled by ambiguity. For example, how serious is the suffering inflicted on a prisoner who is forced to sleep naked on a cold floor? This treatment, although inhumane and painful, may not fit the legal definition of torture and therefore may not violate an individual's 'right not to be tortured'. How should 'severe pain and suffering' be understood? Two possibilities emerge: first, the *degree* of suffering inflicted; second, the *quantity* of pain one endures. Under the first conception, certain types of suffering will always constitute torture regardless of how long they go on for. This approach sees torture as a line in the sand that delineates a set of actions that are so severe in the level of pain and suffering they inflict that they necessarily constitute torture. The second approach is more flexible as to the manner in which pain and suffering are meted out, but is more interested in terms of quantifying how much a person has suffered over time. For instance, waterboarding may be considered a type of suffering severe enough to constitute torture, but a particular detainee might prefer fifteen minutes of waterboarding to a fortnight of sleep deprivation. Under the first conception, sleep deprivation may be a sufficiently moderate form of suffering and therefore fall below the torture threshold; under the latter, even tickling a person for an indefinite period of time may constitute torture – the longer it goes on, the more torturous it becomes.

Michael Gross (2010, p. 123) argues that it is important to distinguish between 'moderate physical pressure or "torture light" and cruel or vicious torture'. Gross rejects torture on the grounds that it is ineffective, but also holds that 'there is no overwhelming evidence that the costs of torture in a democracy are intolerable' (2010, p. 146). By torture, Gross means 'moderate physical pressures' such as extreme temperature exposure, sleep deprivation, minor assault (slapping, pushing) and waterboarding (2010, pp. 127–8). These are distinguished from more brutal measures (i.e. rape) because the suffering is less extreme and its duration shorter than other measures (2010, p. 128): the short duration and comparably diminished amount of pain suggest that while these kinds of pressures do qualify as torture, they are not cruel or vicious. However, as I suggested above, moderate pressures do not remain moderate forever. An analogy can be drawn here to the sufferers of medical symptoms: pins and needles that last for five to ten minutes can be irritating, or even amusing to some, but if those symptoms did not subside for many years, the suffering would be severe indeed. In fact, one of the most famous methods of torture – Chinese water torture – rests on this exact premise. It takes something minorly irritating – a drip on the forehead – and repeats it over an indefinite period of time, where the person has no ability to stop it. The success of the torture in this case relies on the denial of freedom, the powerlessness to stop the discomfort, and the uncertainty as to when – or if – it might end.

A better definition of torture is offered by Patrick Lee, who focuses not on the acts or outcomes of torture, but on the intention behind it. Lee (2006, p. 132) defines torture as 'acts of mutilation or acts that attempt to reduce the detainee to a subhuman, dis-integrated state, for the ulterior purpose either of interrogation, deterrence, revenge, punishment, or sadistic pleasure'. This definition identifies the 'type of choice and execution of choice' (Lee 2006, p. 132) that is involved in torture; specifically the reduction of a human detainee to something less than human. Thus, placing soiled female underwear on the faces on detainees with strict sexual sensitivities, as occurred at Abu Ghraib prison, is likely to constitute torture. It also explains why the UN Convention's distinction between torture, cruel treatment and degrading treatment is mistaken: any kind of treatment that aims to dis-integrate a person's psyche is torturous. Under this framework, torture is better understood as an adjective: particular kinds of treatment are torturous when they have the aim of undermining integrated personhood. For Lee, torture is not an act, but an intention. This explains how, in the above cases, tickling, pins and needles, or water dripping on one's forehead can constitute torture, just as much as sleep deprivation, waterboarding, or de-nailing. Torture does not require the *experience* of extreme pain or suffering by victims, but merely that such an experience be intended.

Lee's account also helps us to draw an important distinction between torture and interrogation. Torture, as Lee explains, is defined by (i) the objective, which can be punishment, intelligence or even sadistic gratification; and (ii) the means of bringing about the objective, namely the dis-integration of a human being, resulting in his becoming sub-human. Interrogation, by contrast, is always aimed at obtaining intelligence (and thus has a more narrow aim than torture), but more importantly is distinguished by the *means* employed to obtain information. Interrogation uses a host of different methods, many of which are unpleasant: exploitation of close relationships, manipulation of facts, or more coercive measures such as blackmail. However, these methods all aim at making the detainee *choose* to offer the information she possesses. By contrast, torture *forces* the information out by destroying a person's ability to resist. The distinction lies in the interrogator or torturer's attitude to her victim, and whether she is willing to accept the possibility that her victim will not volunteer information. Interrogators will accept that possibility; torturers will not.

Thus far, we have seen theorists try to distinguish torture from interrogation, torture-lite (a softer version), and cruel or vicious torture (a more extreme form). We can also distinguish between different types of torture based on the purpose of the torture – interrogational torture should be distinguished from punitive or sadistic torture, at least for the sake of discussion. Indeed, it is interrogational torture that is most relevant to those within the military and intelligence communities, and which therefore deserves (and receives) most focus. Following Lee, we can define interrogational torture as interrogation whose methods for soliciting the truth from an individual aim to dis-integrate the victim, or reduce her to a sub-human state. This is what Hollywood scriptwriters have in mind when they describe torture as attempts to 'break people'. They envision a point at which a person's psychic and bodily integrity are so diminished that any will they had to retain information disappears, and the truth flows from them like a stream. The question, many argue, is what could justify 'breaking' a person in such a way, if anything? And are there certain types of treatment that break a person beyond repair, and should therefore never be performed? Put another way, when and to what extent can degrading a person to sub-human levels be justified?

Amongst a host of possible answers is that of the pragmatist, who responds with 'never' – not because he is morally opposed to torture, but because it does not work. This fact was acknowledged by former US General David Petraeus (2007, ch. 4) in a letter to US service personnel in Iraq in 2007:

> Some may argue that we would be more effective if we sanctioned the use of torture or other expedient methods to obtain information from the enemy.

They would be wrong. Beyond the basic fact that such actions are illegal, history can show that they are frequently neither useful nor necessary.

Empirical debates regarding the efficacy of torture are ongoing.[2] However, even if these questions are answered and torture were shown to be ineffective, we would still face debate as to whether 'torture-lite' was morally acceptable. To this debate, Michael Davis responds that:

> To debate whether a certain way of treating a person 'amounts to torture' is to admit the treatment in question is well within the domain of the inhumane and therefore prima facie among the most serious of moral wrongs.
>
> *(Davis 2008, p. 197).*

Discussions about whether various forms of coercive interrogation can be justified dwell in a moral shadowland: simply being there may be enough to find oneself lost in the dark. In what follows, I argue that when it comes to the effects of coercive interrogation on the character of the interrogator, the distinction between torture and torture-lite is unimportant: the moral costs in either case are devastating.

Torturous characters

In what follows I will broaden the torture debate beyond justification or definitional issues regarding the distinction between torture, torture-lite and interrogation. Instead I will consider how torture affects one's moral character, asking questions such as *what does it mean to be a torturer?* And is the character of the interrogator who performs 'torture-lite' affected differently from the more brutal torturer?

This second question has been touched upon by Jessica Wolfendale (2009, p. 49), who notes that '[t]he distinction between the methods referred to as torture lite and so-called real torture serves a further aim: it is sometimes used to distinguish not only between types of torture methods but also between the moral character of torturers and their motivations.' The difference between torture and torture-lite seems to be (at least in part) that the latter does not intend to dis-integrate person-hood in the same way as the former. This is obviously a contentious claim, since for Lee torture is concerned with the intention, not the act itself, and it seems that torture and torture-lite differ only in the *quality* of suffering they aim to inflict, not in their having different intentions with regard to the infliction of suffering.

Whilst non-anaesthetised surgery to save a life might involve the same kind of acts as certain forms of brutal torture without being torturous, it seems more difficult to distinguish the permissibility of different types of torture, such as waterboarding and de-nailing. Wolfendale asks whether torture-lite actions *demonstrate* a corrupt moral character (in the way that torture does), but it is worth continuing that line of questioning and considering whether they can *create* one. This, I believe, is a more important line of questioning given that most interrogators will not take any pleasure in what they are required to do, even where what they do does not amount to the legal definition of torture. However, we would do well to ask whether over time those same people may come to enjoy what they do, whether their interrogation methods are likely to escalate, or if the actions they are required to perform are detrimental to their character in other ways. Let's begin with the following case from Brian Orend's discussion of torture:

> [At Abu Ghraib] the world saw some shocking photos of American troop conduct … Some of it – like deliberate, prolonged sleep deprivation, and using dogs to attack or threaten already prone and naked people – clearly violated the Geneva Conventions. Others might have been visually disturbing but do not obviously count as human rights violations, such as forcing the prisoners to wear dog collars, or having American women ridicule their private parts, or putting female panties on their faces temporarily.
>
> *(Orend 2006, p. 111)*

Orend disapproves of both clear violations (torture) and less obvious cases (torture-lite) as 'a violation[s] of both the letter and the spirit of the principle of benevolent quarantine' (2006, p. 111), but is not willing to completely condemn torture-lite: 'I suppose we might condone efforts at psychological pressure … when the goal is getting information which might save innocent lives' (2006, p. 111). Orend's approval is unusual given that he simultaneously holds that '[t]orture hardens the heart and corrupts the character of the torturer' (2006, p. 112). If torture has such calamitous implications on the torturer, why would she ever choose to do it?

One common and popular claim is that the torturer is, as Nolen Gertz describes in a critical exposition, 'both a monster and … an agent of morality' (Gertz 2014, p. 71). The popularity of this claim does not demonstrate its truth, however – it ignores the possibility that the torturer 'does not see himself as a *torturer who happens to save lives* but as a *lifesaver who happens to torture*' (2014, p. 71). This strikes me as basically true, and undermines the full extent of Orend's critique of torture as heart-hardening. The torturer who interrogates reluctantly, and out of a genuine belief that torture is necessary to achieve the goals of war, or to save a huge number of lives, may not find his heart hardened or his character corrupted. However, *routine* torture – of the kind that might emerge if torture was to become institutionalised as a matter of official (or unofficial) government policy – is likely to harden the heart (c.f. Gertz 2014; Gordon 2014). But it is not clear that Orend's concerns are exclusive to the torturer – they are also likely to apply to the interrogator (or the 'torturer-lite'). If the infliction of severe pain and suffering cause dispositions that 'harden the heart', so too may the infliction of less severe pains and sufferings. If willingness to mock, insult, lie and threaten is likely to damage the character of the interrogator, cannot this alone serve as a basis to condemn such behaviour? Nancy Sherman's work on the moral psychology of warriors is informative here. She argues that:

> The nearly exclusive focus on torture has silenced a more general debate about the moral shadowland in which the interrogator dwells, even when he does

not practice torture. ... [T]he space the interrogator inhabits has its own special moral demands. And with it comes a distinct set of moral and psychological vulnerabilities.

(Sherman 2010, p. 117)

Sherman suggests that even 'interrogation-short-of-torture' entails ethical difficulties for the interrogator. The detainee's vulnerability, loyalty and trust are exploited by the interrogator for specific ends, and the skills needed to do so are not compatible with the overall flourishing of a life. In cases such as torture, merely determining whether a deed is *justified* or not is insufficient to appreciate the full moral scope of the situation; a more robust account of the morality of torture should explore the effects that performing such deeds has on the torturer's character. For example, occasionally soldiers will kill one of their own in training mishaps, through technological malfunction or simple human error, but most of the time will be free of moral or legal fault for their actions.[3] In such situations, those who are responsible are usually only causally so; most of the time no moral or legal culpability can be attributed. But still there are profound implications for that soldier's future flourishing and character. He or she may face, as a product of the calamitous mistake, guilt, shame, regret and so forth – experiences that may ruin her character (c.f. Shay 1994). If we are to delimit a complete ethics of espionage, we must accommodate the aretaic into discussion, appreciating that the deeds operatives perform will infiltrate their character and shape their flourishing by way of memories, trauma, changed character traits or psychological scars. Indeed, if it were ever possible to show that a person *could* forfeit his right not to be tortured, it may nevertheless be wrong for any individual to commit torture if doing so would foster character traits that are contrary to his ability to be a good citizen or live a fulfilling life. Pope Paul VI demonstrated an understanding of this in the Pastoral Constitution *Gaudium et Spes*:

[W]hatever is opposed to life itself, such as any type of murder, genocide, abortion, euthanasia or wilful self-destruction, whatever violates the integrity of the human person, such as mutilation, torments inflicted on body or mind, attempts to coerce the will itself; whatever insults human dignity, such as subhuman living conditions, arbitrary imprisonment, deportation, slavery, prostitution, the selling of women and children; as well as disgraceful working conditions, where men are treated as mere tools for profit, rather than as free and responsible persons; all these things and others of their like are infamies indeed. They poison human society, but they do more harm to those who practice them than those who suffer from the injury.

(Pope Paul VI 1965, sec. 4)

Torturers do risk corrupting their character in doing what they do, but so too do interrogators. However, a broader understanding of the costs of torture may not prove sufficient for everyone to reject torture entirely. Some may argue that we simply *need* people to corrupt their souls for the greater good. I believe they are wrong, nevertheless it behoves me to address that possibility by examining which type of person might be best for conducting torture in the event that a state does sanction it. This will also serve as a description of the character traits that might be best in an interrogator, whose character is also at risk (although less so than the torturer), and whose profession is more easily justified.

The best, for the worst

Darrell Cole (2012, p. 39) argues that torture should never be legal (for it would be too easily abused), but that it might be morally justified. He bases his argument on the belief that there is no substantial moral difference between the type of harm inflicted in torture and the type of harm inflicted on the battlefield on enemy combatants. If, Cole contends, intentional killing is justifiable under some circumstances, torture must also be justifiable. After all, the torture victim is at least left alive.

Cole's error is in seeing a straight similarity between killing and maiming on a battlefield, and maiming in an interrogation room. There are obvious differences between the two. First, soldiers' on the battlefield can be motivated by a host of different things: anger, justice, self-defence and so on. Torturers are, as I have discussed, motivated by the dis-integration of personhood in their victims. This may indeed be the motivation of some soldiers, but it is certainly not the intention of all of them. Second, contemporary Just War theory usually defines legitimate targets of killing as those 'engaged in harming' (Orend 2006, p. 107). In reality, however, most victims of torture present no immediate threat (although the information they possess may, in fact, be used to save lives). However, what Cole does note is that torturers and interrogators are not the only people whose responsibilities can be hazardous to their moral character; soldiers also perform tasks that are morally treacherous. Thus, in trying to delimit the type of character that would serve an interrogator or torturer well, we should look at general soldiers (an area that has received far more philosophical attention).

Shannon E. French's book *The code of the warrior* focuses on how soldiers past and present developed codes of honour, or 'warrior codes' – a commonly held standard of what the ideal warrior does and does not do that bears normatively on each warrior within the culture (French 2003, p. 3). The work focuses largely on how warrior codes assist in preventing the commission of atrocities, not only because they entail horrific abuses to the innocent, but also because in committing them, warriors begin to erode their own humanity. French argues that '[a] warrior's humanity is most obviously at risk when he or she participates in an atrocity. Vile actions such as rape, the intentional slaughter of civilians, or the torture of prisoners of war dehumanise the victims and degrade the perpetrators' (French 2009, pp. 121–2). One means of defending against the erosion of a warrior's humanity is to ensure that warrior identities incorporate values and virtues as integral aspects of the vocation of soldiering. Thus soldiers come to understand excellence within their vocation to mean not only proficiency in arms, but courage in defending the innocent, restraint against anger and respect for the dignity of even one's enemies.

If these insights are applicable to interrogators and torturers, it would seem that they should be applied in a slightly different way. After all, torturers in particular cannot be required to simultaneously respect the dignity of their victims whilst trying to degrade them to a sub-human level, can they? But Cole argues that they can, seeing torture as a manifestation of the virtue of charity. For Cole (2012, p. 29), 'charity demands that, even though we love our enemies, in the sense that we desire their eternal good, we must come to the aid of our innocent neighbors who are being threatened by our unjust neighbors'. However, Cole ignores the fact that for an *act* to be charitable requires more than its being motivated by charity – it must actually *intend to do something charitable*. As the Catholic moral theologian St Thomas Aquinas (1920, II–II Q. 64, Art. 1) noted, charity cannot justify doing evil so that good may come of it.

If, then, torture cannot be a manifestation of virtue, the best we can do is to ensure that it is not a manifestation of *vice*. This will entail – as we observed in the case of soldiers – that torturers and interrogators restrain themselves against emotions such as hatred and anger. The environments in which many interrogations (torturous or not) are conducted are conducive to extreme emotions. Cole describes the environment as 'one in which it is believed (with good reasons) that the prisoner has some knowledge about the plans of a terrorist group. What sort of plans, when they are to take place, how far developed they are, and who exactly is involved will usually be unknown variables' (Cole 2012, p. 40). Neil Altman points out that such an environment is likely to lead to knee-jerk reactions based on emotion rather than rational decisions:

> It is naïve to think that panic and sadism would not be driving cognition and choices of action in [ticking bomb scenarios], not to mention less clear-cut situations such as those facing interrogators at Guantanamo Bay and Abu Ghraib when faced with an unspecified but plausibly horrific threat from nameless and faceless people, and confronted with a person who may or may not have specific information about those threats.
>
> *(Altman 2008, p. 663)*

Given this, we should be concerned not only about torturers, but about whether the extremity of the environment is likely to lead to interrogators escalating their methods to include torture in times of great stress. Because of this, Cole argues that interrogators must be required to deploy a Stoic resistance in high-stress situations.

> In order to avoid torture, the interrogator, ideally, will be the kind of person who possesses the sort of character that makes them immune to the temptation to torture unnecessarily, and at the minimum this means persons who have proven that they can think clearly and act well under pressure, persons who can see into the essential nature of the circumstance that is tempting of torture.
>
> *(Cole 2012, p. 45)*

So the type of person who makes an ideal interrogator is one who is disinclined to resort to torture in extreme situations. The ideal interrogator-cum-torturer (for Cole, they are one and the same) is one who will only torture when it is absolutely necessary. The professional duty to use force only when necessary is also shared by torturers and soldiers: St Augustine, the so-called 'father of Just War theory', argued that soldiers must fight with a sober and virtuous disposition, taking no joy in what they are required to do (Augustine 2003, 19.7). As David Perry (2009, p. 217) notes, 'anyone who hopes to remain a person of integrity – an admirable person – would not use more than the minimum degree of force necessary to obtain vital information'.

Perhaps the most we can ask of torturers is that they not indulge in or enjoy their craft. As we have noted consistently throughout this chapter, torturers dwell in a moral shadowland. At the very least, we ought to ensure that torture is never used when interrogation will do, and that the type of people who perform torture are never the type who would enjoy it, and thus that they will avoid the temptations of the situation, as Cole (2012) describes above.

However, if the most we can ask of interrogators or torturers is that they not perform their deed where unnecessary because of the moral toll this can have, this is good cause to ask whether torture is ever worth perpetrating. Furthermore, the limitation of torture to where it is necessary heightens the need to determine whether torture is ever effective; if it cannot be proven to work, it is never necessary.

'Broken people' and accidental torture

Gertz (2014) is expressly critical of accounts of torture that fail to consider the perspective of the torturer. Failing to do this means assuming that 'there is no one else involved in the torture and hence no one to be found culpable' (2014, p. 72). The reality, Gertz argues, is that regimes and institutions develop torturers, and failing to recognise this fact is to ignore the reality of torture. A similar critique might be levelled against the (admittedly fewer) accounts of torture that fail to address precisely what is wrong with torture, and what it feels like to *be* tortured. This omission is guilty of the same kind of 'groundless hypothesizing' of which Gertz is so critical (2014, p. 72). For this reason, I will devote the final section of this chapter to understanding precisely *what it means to be 'broken'* – in Lee's terms, dis-integrated. I will also argue that torture is not the only way to dis-integrate a person, and that the widespread practice of drone warfare is also capable of producing similar dis-integration, which should have important policy implications.

In an important article, David Sussman (2005, p. 3) argues that:

> there is a core concept of what constitutes torture that corresponds to a distinctive kind of wrong that is not characteristically found in other forms of extreme violence or coercion, a special type of wrong that may explain why we find torture to be more morally offensive than other ways of inflicting great physical or psychological harm.

This core concept that sets torture apart, according to Sussman, is twofold. First, it involves 'a profoundly asymmetric relation of dependence and vulnerability between the parties. The victim of torture must be unable to shield herself in any significant way, and she must be unable to effectively evade or retaliate against her tormenter' (2005, p. 6). Second, 'the torture victim must see herself as being unable to put up any real moral or legal resistance to her torment' (2005, p. 7). These two characteristics conspire to produce, as Rebecca Gordon (2014, p. 29) describes, 'an isolated, broken human being'.

This isolation is crucial to torture. The victim of torture is alone with his or her tormentors, and what begins as physical pain begins to transform beyond power-lessness and into perversion. The victim, subject to arbitrary pain at unknown times, is almost entirely divested of control, and the control that remains is per-verse. For instance, a victim may retain some sense of control by being able to predict when and how he or she will be tortured. However, for this prediction to succeed, 'the victim must trust in the sincerity of people who have already shown that they have no scruples about how they treat her' (Sussman 2005, p. 8).

The victim of torture is dis-integrated, in part, because torture corrupts the victim's mind such that foundational attitudes such as trust and hope are simultaneously necessary and self-destructive. Torture aims to create what the United States' *KUBARK Counterintelligence Interrogation Manual* describes as 'DDD', debility, dependency and dread (Farber, Harlow & West 1957). Eventually, the combination of these three Ds leaves the victim as 'little more than a point of pure receptivity, having the most basic forms of agency effectively at the command of another' (Sussman 2005, p. 32).

Recall Lee's account of torture as an intentional disposition. *Acts* of torture are simply acts performed with torturous intention. They tend, under Lee's account, to produce the effects discussed, but this is incidental (or, perhaps, supplementary) to the actual evil of torture, which lies in the disposition of the torturer. Under this account, torture would be evil whether or not it succeeded in breaking, or even harming, another human being. Similarly, there might be actions that unintentionally subject people to dis-integration without being torturous in Lee's intentional sense. Consider, for example, this testimony from a participant in the NYU and Stanford University study *Living under drones*:

> I have been seeing drones since the first one appeared about four to five years ago. Sometimes there will be two or three drone attacks per day ... We see drones hovering 24 hours a day but we don't know when they will strike ... Children, women, they are all psychologically affected. They look at the sky to see if there are drones. Firoz told us, 'The drones make such a noise that everyone is scared.'
>
> *(Stanford Law School & NYU School of Law 2012, p. 151)*

Note the similarities: a perpetually present tormentor, an asymmetry between tormentor and victim, and an inability to resist. At least two of the three

Ds – debility and dependency – are present in the ever-looming threat that drone strikes pose to civilian populations. The chronic fear posed by ever-present drones (who locals call *machar* – mosquitoes – because of the constant humming) means that civilians are caught in a perpetual state of waiting. Waiting for the next attack and for the possibility of their own death. The constant presence of drones results in civilians living in a state of perpetual potential victimhood.

This is paradoxical, given that one of the most frequent arguments in favour of drones is their potential to alleviate civilian suffering by reducing collateral damage (Strawser 2010, pp. 351–2). If one of the consequences of a drone *policy*, as opposed to individual uses of drones (which is the focal point of recent discussion) is character dis-integration in innocent civilians, this may be an unacceptable side-effect of their use.

Notes

1   The Convention is in fact only effective as a convention against torture, because 'other cruel, inhuman, or degrading treatments' are mentioned only in the title of the document and are never defined.
2   Jean Maria Arrigo offers a summary of much of the empirical debate, arguing that the outcomes of torture interrogations make it unjustifiable (Arrigo 2004).
3   Sherman tells the story of one man, responsible for providing security for a position in Iraq, who authorised a replacement battery for a Bradley gun. The replacement battery, as it turned out, had different amperage, and the gun fired, killing a US Private (Sherman 2010, pp. 96–7).

References

Allhoff, F 2003, 'Terrorism and torture', *International Journal of Applied Philosophy*, vol. 17, no. 1, pp. 105–118.
Altman, N 2008, 'The psychodynamics of torture', *Psychoanalytic Dialogues: The International Journal of Relational Perspectives*, vol. 18, no. 5, pp. 658–670.
Aquinas, T 1920, *Summa theologica*, trans. Fathers of the English Dominican Province, New Advent, www.newadvent.org/summa/index.html
Arrigo, JM 2004, 'A utilitarian argument against torture interrogation of terrorists', *Science and Engineering Ethics*, vol. 10, no. 3, pp. 543–572
Augustine 2003, *City of God*, trans. H Bettenson, Penguin, Victoria.
Cole, D 2012 'Torture and just war theory', *Journal of Religious Ethics*, vol. 40, no. 1, pp. 26–50.
Davis, M 2008, 'Justifying torture as an act of war', in L May (ed.), *War: essays in political philosophy*, Cambridge University Press, Cambridge.
Farber, IE, Harlow, HF & West, LJ 1957 'Brainwashing, conditioning, and DDD (debility, dependency, and dread)', *Sociometry*, vol. 20, no. 4, pp. 271–285.
French, SE 2003, *The code of the warrior: exploring warrior values past and present*, Rowman & Littlefield, Lanham.
French, SE 2009, 'Sergeant Davis' stern charge: the obligation of officers to preserve the humanity of their troops', *Journal of Military Ethics*, vol. 8, no. 2, 116–126.
Gertz, N 2014, *The philosophy of war and exile: from the humanity of war to the inhumanity of peace*, Palgrave Macmillan, Basingstoke.

Gordon, R 2014, *Mainstreaming torture: ethical approaches in the post-9/11 United States*, Oxford University Press, Oxford.

Gross, ML 2010, *Moral dilemmas of modern war: torture, assassination, and blackmail in an age of asymmetric conflict*, Cambridge University Press, Cambridge.

Lee, P 2006, 'Interrogational torture', *American Journal of Jurisprudence*, vol. 51, pp. 131–148.

Orend, B 2006, *The morality of war*, Broadview Press, Peterborough, Canada.

Perry, DL 2009, *Partly cloudy: ethics in war, espionage, covert actions, and interrogation*, Scarecrow Press, Toronto.

Petraeus, DH 2007, Letter dated 10 May 2007: 'APO AE 09342–01400', www.washing tonpost.com/wp-srv/nation/documents/petraeus_values_051007.pdf

Pope Paul VI 1965, *Gaudium et Spes*, www.vatican.va/archive/hist_councils/ii_vatican_council/ documents/vat-ii_cons_19651207_gaudium-et-spes_en.html

Shay, J 1994, *Achilles in Vietnam: combat trauma and the undoing of character*, Atheneum, New York.

Sherman, N 2010, *The untold war: inside the hearts, minds, and souls of our soldiers*, W.W. Norton, New York.

Stanford Law School & NYU School of Law 2012, *Living under drones: death, injury, and trauma to civilians from US drones in Pakistan*, International Council for Human Rights and Conflict Resolution Clinic at Stanford Law School and Global Justice Clinic at NYU Law School, https://law.stanford.edu/publications/living-under-drones-death-injury-a nd-trauma-to-civilians-from-us-drone-practices-in-pakistan

Strawser, BJ 2010, 'Moral predators: the duty to employ uninhabited aerial vehicles', *Journal of Military Ethics*, vol. 9, no. 4, pp. 342–368.

Sussman, D 2005, 'What's wrong with torture?', *Philosophy & Public Affairs*, vol. 33, no. 1, pp. 1–33.

United Nations 1987, *Convention against torture and other cruel, inhuman or degrading treatment or punishment*, http://treaties.un.org/doc/Publication/UNTS/Volume%201465/volume-1465- I-24841-English.pdf

Wolfendale, J 2009, 'The myth of "torture-lite"', *Ethics & International Affairs*, vol. 23, no. 1, pp. 47–61.

5

THE IMPLICATIONS OF SPYING AND TORTURE FOR HUMAN FREEDOM FROM A SARTREAN POINT OF VIEW

Martine Berenpas

In 2002, the media began to report that Americans were engaging in torturing a large number of prisoners at the Guantanamo Bay naval base. At first the American government denied that torture methods were being used on prisoners, but soon they had to admit that some torture was used as an 'enhanced interrogation technique' to obtain information from terrorists and other prisoners (Fletcher 2008, p. 4). The Justice Department advised the White House that torture 'may be justified' in interrogations conducted as part of the war on terror (Washington Post 2002).

In this chapter, I unravel the nature of torture and show its close relation to spying. By using the phenomenology of Jean-Paul Sartre, I argue that torture is a reaction to the look of the other who reveals my bodily existence. Sartre unfolds his account of the recognition of the other as a sort of voyeurism that is motivated by the possibility of the other's looking at me.

Sartre argues in *l'Etre et le néant* (1943) that humans are ontologically inclined to use strategies such as masochism and sadism in reaction to the gaze of the other. However, Sartre argues that these attitudes are all 'acts of bad faith' because they have their origin in the human being's refusal to take up her existence as *for-itself* (*pour-soi*). In this chapter, I argue that spying and torture are rooted in human beings' denial of their nature as *for-itself* and their desire to be *for-itself-in-itself*. The human cogito is inclined to mask its nature as absolute freedom, which results in a violation of the other's freedom as well as one's own. Torture not only harms the victims' freedom, but also prevents the torturer from unfolding her absolute freedom.

Sartre's ontology of bad faith, which he outlines in *l'Etre et le néant*, shapes his theory of the recognition of another human freedom. Sartre describes the encounter with the other as an objectifying event in which the look (or gaze) of the other alienates the human from her absolute freedom and makes her dependent on the other for her self-awareness.

Human beings can react in two different ways to their objectification by the gaze of the other. They can either appropriate that which the other reveals of them, or they can deny that the other is able to look at them and reveal their bodily existence. In relation to torture, I will concentrate on the second attitude in reaction to the gaze. Sartre argues that the denial of the capacity of the other to reveal something of a human being leads to 'distinct acts of hate, sadism and indifference' (Sartre 1943, p. 420). I will argue that torture can be better understood through Sartre's analysis of sadism and needs to be seen as a reaction to the look of the other.

Sartre's account of intersubjective experience shows us that strategies to control the other, such as torture, have their origin in the gaze of the other. Spying and voyeurism are a relation to the other as another subjectivity, and are a direct result of the objectification of one human being by another. In this chapter, I will outline the way in which torture should be seen as a concrete reaction to the look of the other and how it is grounded in the struggle for absolute freedom. Spying and torture are, in Sartre's analysis, closely related, and are one of the more violent outcomes of the troublesome experience of the encounter with the other.

Sartre's analysis of the recognition of the other shows us furthermore that acts of torture and violence all fail because they limit the absolute freedom of the victim as well as the offender. The culprit is humankind's ontological tendency to mask human nature as *for-itself*, which makes human beings prone to acts of bad faith. The torturer denies the victim's subjectivity and treats him as a mere object. This attitude is bound to fail, because we can never escape the look.

For Sartre, acts of bad faith such as torture are rooted in the human being's fear of dealing with its own nature as *for-itself*. Sadism and torture are grounded in existential fear and are a reaction to the power of the look of the other. Torture is therefore more than a mere method for obtaining information; it reveals the nature of humankind and its natural tendency to fall into acts of bad faith.

The structure of the human cogito

Husserl made it possible to take the cogito as the starting point of philosophical enquiry without falling into the pitfall of idealism. He argued that the human cogito was intentional: being conscious is being conscious *of* something. The cogito can go beyond itself and can direct itself to that which is outwards: the *phenomena*.

Sartre's ontology is inspired by Husserl's intentionalism and deals with the fundamental difference between the human cogito and a mere thing. In line with Husserl, Sartre defines the human cogito as intentional, which to Sartre means that the cogito is 'the activity of directing itself at something which is different than it' (Sartre 1943, p. 25).

In *l'Etre et le néant*, Sartre unfolds the idea of consciousness, which, due to its intentionality, is a *not-being* or a *nothingness*. For Sartre, consciousness is essentially a negating activity because it experiences that which it is conscious of always as *something-which-it-is-not*. Even being conscious of the fact that one's being conscious is a non-identity. The distinctive characteristic of the human cogito is that it is a nothingness with the negating activity as its core: 'the being through which nothingness enters the world needs to negate nothingness in its being' (Sartre 1943, p. 57).

By negating that of which it is conscious, the human cogito can transcend the phenomena because it is always something that it is not. Sartre interprets this ability as absolute freedom: 'We are *always* free, Sartre argues, to determine by the direction of our focusing which elements of our perceptual (or conceptual, or imaginary) field will be elevated to the status of figure and which will sink into the ground. Thus, all conscious acts, whether they are acts of looking, thinking, imagining, or what have you, are free' (Detmer 2008, p. 69).

Sartre's ontological account of the negating human cogito leads to a sharp distinction between consciousness (defined as a *for-itself*) and a mere thing (defined as an *in-itself*). The human cogito is a nothingness that never coincides with what it is conscious of, while the mere thing lacks intentionality and is as such 'full' of being (Sartre 1943, p. 72).

The absolute freedom of the human cogito means that it can become anything it wants to be. Sartre denies that human consciousness has fixed qualities or a specific inner nature. Human existence is to Sartre nothing more than the negating activity of the cogito:

> Human reality cannot receive its ends, as we have seen, either from outside or from so-called inner 'nature'. It chooses them and by this very choice confers upon them a transcendent existence as the external limits of its projects. From this point of view – and if it is understood that the existence of Dasein precedes and commands its essence – human reality in and through its very upsurge decides to define its own being by its ends. It is therefore the positing of my ultimate ends which characterizes my being and which is identical with the sudden thrust of freedom which is mine.
>
> *(Sartre 1943, p. 443)*

Sartre presents the human being in *l'Etre et le néant*, but also in his novels, as the creature that is doomed to be free. The human being cannot escape from his endless task of giving himself significance and direction. He bears the full responsibility for every choice he makes and for everything he becomes. Sartre even argues that the human being needs to take up her facticity as her own choice. This means accepting one's body, gender and social environment as part of one's own projects.

The absolute freedom and the total responsibility that humans have for their actions and choices is something that is very difficult for them to bear. They will try to mask their absolute freedom by denying their facticity or by pretending that they have fixed qualities or characteristics that they cannot change. The origin of these 'acts of bad faith', as Sartre calls it, is consciousness' attitude to its nothingness. Consciousness tends to understand its nothingness as a lack of being, and yet it 'desires to be'. The human being therefore becomes a 'useless passion' who is anguished over their own absolute freedom and longs for the stability of the *in-itself* (Sartre 1943, p. 65).

The human desire to be *in-itself-for-itself* leads to acts of bad faith and prevents it from unfolding its absolute freedom. Bad faith appears when the human being, for example, pretends that the situation in which he finds himself makes it impossible for him to make a free choice. This '*homme sérieux*', as Sartre calls him, acts like he is a determined thing that cannot give himself direction.

Sartre argues that the man who denies that his facticity affects him is also of bad faith. In *l'Etre et le néant*, he gives the example of a young woman who has a romantic dinner with a man. The man lays his hand on the woman's hand, but the woman refuses to respond to this gesture. She pretends the man's hand touching her hand doesn't affect her. She acts out of bad faith because she refuses to take responsibility for her body, and for her facticity as such.

Sartre's conception of self-determination and responsibility is unique because he incorporates the 'necessity of contingency' (Sartre 1943, p. 327). It is necessary that human beings determine themselves, but this determination is ultimately contingent and has no definite meaning. The man who acts out of bad faith acts from an impossibility to choose and refuses to assume his facticity as his own. Furthermore, Sartre argues that bad faith is linked to the other as other consciousness. It is the other who reveals my objectivity and confronts me with my facticity.

The look and the nature of spying

For Sartre, consciousness is radically transformed when it encounters another consciousness. The encounter of the other challenges my ontological structure by introducing a new structure that is beyond my own experience. The encounter with the other reveals the structure of *being-for-others*, which is ontologically related to *being-for-itself*.

Sartre shapes his ontology in such a way that he does not need to be bothered by the problem of solipsism. One of the fundamental problems in philosophy of other minds seems to arise from the disparity that exists between my own consciousness and that of others. It is claimed that the individual has a special access to the content of her mind in a way that she does not have to anyone else's.

For Sartre, this disparity does appear, because of the way he posits the human cogito. To Sartre, the individual does not have special 'privileged knowledge' about his own mind that he lacks with regard to others. In Sartre's ontology, consciousness is a nothingness; it has no personality or an interiority that can be classified as 'me'. Rather, Sartre constructs that which can be identified as a 'me' as a series of acts that can be an object for each consciousness. The self is nothing more than the sequence of acts, and these acts are as accessible to me as they are for the other. For Sartre, all egos are tentative objects that are fallible and open to discussion. My own self is to Sartre therefore no more tied to me than it is to you (Sartre 1943, p. 44). Furthermore, Sartre does not seem to need to justify the individuality of the human cogito. For Sartre, each consciousness is embodied and as such already individuated. The embodied existence of each consciousness is revealed by the look of the other.

Sartre's account of intersubjective experience is grounded in the 'look' or 'gaze' of the other as another human consciousness. Sartre takes the look of the other as the origin of the relation to the other. The other is to Sartre first and foremost recognised as another human consciousness because he can see me. Human beings can only experience the subjectivity of the other by becoming an object for the other. Sartre's main concern, however, is not the other's existence as such, but rather the role that the other plays in acquainting me with my own objectivity.

In *l'Etre et le néant*, Sartre devotes a long chapter to the 'look' or 'gaze' of the other. The most striking characteristic of the other is that she forms a threat to our absolute freedom. According to Sartre, the look of the other disputes the presumed self-sufficiency of my pre-reflective consciousness and challenges the transcendence–facticity structure of my consciousness as *for-itself*. When a human being encounters the other, she experiences this other as a consciousness that is not her consciousness. This experience thus already assumes the recognition of the subjectivity of the other. The experience of the other as another consciousness is, however, introduced by the other's ability to *look* at me.

Through the look of the other, the human being not only will become aware of the subjectivity of the other, but will also be confronted with the fact that, to the other, the human is a determinate being. The look of the other sees the human being in a way that he can never see himself. The other therefore reveals something of humankind that cannot be reconciled with the structure of his *for-itself*:

> But in order for me to be what I am, it suffices merely that the other looks at me. It is not myself, to be sure; I myself shall never succeed at realizing this being-seated which I grasp in the Other's look. I shall remain forever a consciousness. But it is for the other ... for the other I *am seated* as this inkwell is *on* the table; for the other, *I am leaning over* the keyhole as this tree is *bent* by the wind. Thus for the other I have been stripped of my transcendence.
>
> (Sartre 1984, p. 351)

For Sartre, human reality is the absolute freedom of forming projects and goals. It is the encounter with the other that disrupts this absolute freedom because the other fixes my situation and reveals to me events that cannot be traced back to my *for-itself*. The gaze of the other is a threat to humankind's absolute freedom, because the human being has to accept that the other reveals something of her that she cannot reconcile with her *for-itself*. That which the other reveals of her can never become an object of her own consciousness. The human being can never see himself as the other sees him. It is the fascinating structure of *being-for-the-other* and the ability of the other to reveal my embodied existence that makes Sartre's account of the other so valuable in understanding the nature of spying.

Sartre argues that *voyeurism*, or spying, is 'a pure process of relating to the instrument to the end to be attained, a pure mode of losing myself in the world, of causing myself to be drunk in by things as ink is by a blotter' (Sartre 1984, p. 433). The origin of the word 'voyeurism' can be traced back to the psychoanalytical theory of Freud. Freud links voyeurism to his concept of 'scopophilia', which is the 'joy of looking'. Sartre seems to pick up on this joy of staring at others. For both Sartre and Freud, voyeurism is subjecting the other to the 'curious' and 'controlled' gaze (Sartre 1943, p. 298; Freud 2000, p. 66).

Sartre describes voyeurism using the example of a voyeur caught looking through a keyhole. Before being caught, the experience of spying is a pure pleasance that is motivated by curiosity and the possibility of the human cogito as *for-itself*. Before being caught, consciousness is unselfconsciously experiencing these emotions because it is only through the look of the other that consciousness becomes self-aware. Once the voyeur is seen, or has the impression that he has been caught spying, he is turned into something else. The voyeur realises that the other can see him spying through the keyhole and this awareness makes him no longer 'master of the situation' (Sartre 1943, p. 304).

Through the gaze of the other, the human being not only becomes aware of the subjectivity of the other, but is also confronted with the fact that her consciousness is not only a perspective, but also an object within the world. The gaze of the other makes us aware of what we are at a particular moment in our facticity and is the origin of self-awareness. It is the self-awareness that the look of the other triggers that gives rise to emotions such as shame or pride. Shame and pride are, for Sartre, special modes of non-positional consciousness (Sartre 1943, p. 312). Non-positional consciousness is open to reflection. When we reflect on our own emotions of shame or pride, we realise that this sort of *being-conscious-of* is an intentional self-apprehension. Intentional self-apprehension realises an intimate relation between me and myself. It is, however, a relation that is ultimately mediated by the presence of the other; I can never feel ashamed without the self-awareness the other's gaze provokes. I cannot deny, however, that the other reveals something of me that does not belong to me. Shame is therefore 'a recognition that I am as the other sees me' (Sartre 1943, p. 317).

Sartre argues that the gaze of the other alienates the human being from his absolute freedom, because it forces him to take responsibility for that what the other reveals of him. This confrontation with his own embodied existence, which he cannot change, is difficult for the human being. The other's apprehension of me is both mine and not mine. It is mine in the sense that it would be absurd to claim that what the other reveals of me is not part of me. But on the other hand, that which she reveals of me cannot become an object to my own consciousness. It is not mine because it does not originate from my own consciousness. The encounter with the other reveals 'my being without *being-for-me*' (Sartre 1943, p. 312). In looking at me, the other objectifies me and forms a threat to my consciousness as being *for-itself*.

I think we are justified in generalising these ontological outlines that stand between individuals to the relation between states. In order to do so, I assume that whatever rights that states can legitimately be said to have must derive from the rights of their individual citizens.

When we apply Sartre's ontological account of the power of the look to the threat of spying, we can conclude that spying is seen by societies as a severe threat because it is related to a self-awareness that alienates the human cogito from maintaining her nature as absolute freedom. Spying is a potential danger not only because of the secret information that might be disclosed, but also because of the fundamental threat to the self-determination of a nation. Spying aims at the very heart of a political nation as a self-governing, self-determining unity. I think this is the reason why espionage in every part of the world leads to severe punishment for the spy.

Torture and sadism as reactions to the look

Sartre establishes a close relation between the look of the other and the threat to human freedom. In the previous paragraph it became clear that spying is a mode of *being-for-the-other* that alienates the human being from his absolute freedom. In looking at me, the other reveals my facticity and forces me to accept a part of myself that does not originate from my *for-itself*.

The distance between me and the other is, for Sartre, a given that cannot be dissolved. To Sartre, 'no totalitarian and unifying synthesis of "others" is possible' (Sartre 1984, p. 339). The distance between the other's free endeavour to give meaning and significance to the world and my own endeavour cannot be bridged.

The look of the other challenges my subjective constitution of the world and is something I have to deal with. To Sartre, my objectification by the look of the other demands a response, which will ultimately result in a struggle for freedom. Sartre distinguishes two attitudes that can follow in response to the look. The first is an effort to integrate that which is revealed by the other with my absolute freedom. This reaction results in the concrete relations of love, language and masochism. The second reaction Sartre distinguishes is of particular interest to this chapter, because it results in relations of hate, indifference, sadism and desire. I will argue that these concrete relations can be seen in torture. The concrete relations of desire, hate, indifference and sadism are grounded in a denial of the other's subjectivity by objectifying the other in turn.

It's important to note that Sartre is not interested in morally justifying these concrete relations or the attitude to the gaze of the other. The question of whether human actions are morally justified is beyond the scope of ontology. Ontology is a purely descriptive analysis of human consciousness and its particular place in the world; it is free from moral justifications or prescriptive conditions.

To Sartre, the two attitudes both initiate a struggle with the other to regain one's absolute freedom. The look of the other reveals something of humankind's being that does not originate from the human being's own consciousness. The other sees the human being in a way that he can never see himself and transforms the human cogito into a *being-for-the-other* that he has to accept as his own.

The look triggers two distinct reactions that are related to the concrete relations of love, masochism and language; and hate, indifference, desire and sadism. Sartre argues that all these concrete relations result in the alienation and suppression of human freedom. Sartre's ontological account does not seem to provide a synthesis of human freedoms in which both freedoms can live as *for-itself*. In the encounter with the other there is always a loss of freedom. Iris Murdoch even argues that 'the lesson of *l'Etre et le néant* seems to be that personal relations are usually warfare, and at best represent a precarious equilibrium, buttressed as often as not by bad faith' (Murdoch 1959, p. 59). Sartre himself argues that 'the essence of the relation between consciousness is not *Mit-Sein*' – as Heidegger claims – but is characterised by oppression and conflict (Sartre 1943, p. 433).

The two attitudes result in a struggle for control of human freedom and are all characterised by violence. In love, for example, the human being will try to be the person the other thinks he is. He will try to appropriate the being that the other reveals of him and he will try to live up to the other's expectations. Sartre argues that these efforts towards appropriating the being that the other reveals of me are grounded in the human desire to appropriate the other's freedom. In love, language and masochism, human beings will try to make the other's freedom the foundation of their own being. In love this results in the effort to 'incorporate that transcendence within me without removing from it its character as transcendence' (Sartre 1943, p. 417).

The effort of trying to appropriate the other's freedom by making her freedom the foundation of my being is bound to fail. The assumption that human beings can *be* what the other attributes to them is an illusion. As absolute freedom, or *for-itself*, the human being never is, and yet always is, a *becoming-to-be*. Human beings cannot ground themselves, nor can they take the other's freedom as the foundation of their being. In the concrete relations of love, language and masochism, the human is trying to force the other to love him. The lover 'wants to be loved by another freedom and demands that this freedom is no longer free' (Sartre 1943, p. 407).

Indifference, hate and sadism are the result of a different attitude to the gaze of the other. The distinct characteristic of these concrete relations is the human denial of the fact that the other is another freedom who reveals part of one's being. In this attitude, human beings try to 'transcend the other's transcendence' by denying the look of the other and objectifying the other in turn. In this reaction, the human being refuses to take full responsibility for the facticity of her situation.

The United Nations General Assembly defined torture as:

[A]ny act by which severe pain or suffering, whether physical or mental, is intentionally inflicted on a person for such purposes as obtaining from him or a third person information or a confession, punishing him for an act he or a third person has committed or is suspected of having committed, or intimidating or coercing him or a third person, or for any other reason based on discrimination of any kind, when such pain or suffering is inflicted by or at the investigation of or with the consent or acquiescence of a public official or other person acting in an official capacity.

(Davis 2005, 163)

In an essay on torture entitled 'The moral justifiability of torture', Michael Davis argues that this definition falls short and offers a more specific description of torture. Davis defines torture as: 'the intentional infliction of extreme physical suffering on some non-consenting defenseless other person for the purpose of breaking his will' (Davis 2005, p. 161). In Davis' definition there is a distinct echo of Sartre's analysis of sadism, which can thus be seen in torture.

Davis distinguishes several features of torture, one being the vast inequality between the tortured and the torturer (Davis 2005, p. 164). This characteristic seems to overlap with Sartre's definition of sadism as 'passion', 'drought' and 'perseverance' (Sartre 1943, p. 439). Sartre gives an extensive analysis of the nature of sadism, in which the inequality between the sadist and the victim is highlighted.

Sartre argues that 'sadism is the failure of desire' (Sartre 1943, p. 438). The sadist does not want to deal with the look of the other and refuses to acknowledge the other as another human freedom. The sadist has reduced the other to a mere object by inflicting pain on his body. In sadism as well as in torture, there is an inequality between abuser and victim. The sadist as well as the torturer uses the other as a 'mere instrument' in an 'effort to control the other by bodily violence' (Sartre 1943, p. 439); or, as Davis argues, 'for the purpose of breaking his will' (Davis 2005, p. 161).

In his analysis of torture, Davis emphasises the physical helplessness of the victim as well as his intellectual helplessness, in the sense that the victim does not know exactly what the torturer is after or when the torture will end. Just as in sadism, torture has no clear, well defined goal. It seems that in both cases it is up to the abuser when the acts of violence will end. The goal of sadism seems to be the fulfilment of the sadist's desire to inflict pain on the other's body; in the case of torture it seems to be sharing specific information or confessing. It is, however, seldom clear to the victim when these goals will be met. In torture, for example, victims seldom have a clear idea of how much and what information they would have to confess for the torture to stop.

The main shared feature of both sadism and torture is that the abuser has absolute control over the victim's body; while the difference between the two seems to be the abuser's motivations to engage in violating the other's body.

When we take Davis' definition of torture, however, the difference between the goals of sadism and torture seems to be more closely related, in that torture is directed at breaking the victim's will. Although it might be that the sadist, more than the torturer, is exhilarated by the emotional distress of the victim, it is surely not the case that torture is motivated only by a wish to obtain information or a confession. Both actions are directed at denying the subjectivity of the other by reducing the other to pained, contingent flesh.

Another striking resemblance between torture and Sartre's analysis of sadism is the harming of another subjectivity by inflicting pain on her body and as such reducing her to an object. For both the sadist and the torturer, it is enough that the victim can bear physical suffering against her will. Both the sadist and the torturer are first and foremost indifferent to the welfare of the victim, and persevere in their violent actions.

In one of Sartre's essays, translated as 'A victory' (1958), Sartre discusses the status of torture in the light of French colonisation of Algeria. Sartre took a firm stand against practices of torture that were used in the Algerian war. He claims that this violent strategy ultimately failed, arguing that torture was used by the French to 'convince us of our impotence'. To Sartre, torture is not an atrocity that could be blamed on a particular set of brutal individuals. He sees it inherent in 'the whole logic of colonial warfare' (Sartre 1958, p. 442).

When we relate Sartre's justification of violence for a political cause to his ontological account of the recognition of the other, it seems that violence in society is grounded in the encounter with the other and the subsequent struggle for absolute freedom. Torture is therefore not something used randomly, or an unexplainable excess of human behaviour, but one of the concrete outcomes of the violent structure of personal relations.

The concrete relations that Sartre distinguishes in his work, that we also have recognised in torture, do not allow the human being to regain her freedom and remain the absolute foundation of her self-realisation. The two attitudes that Sartre outlines in reaction to the look of the other result in a struggle that has no end. The attitudes are bound to fail because they don't allow for two freedoms to maintain a relation without harming their freedom as *for-itself*.

Spying, torture and bad faith

Sartre's analysis shows that torture is a doubtful method of intelligence collection for protecting citizens, not only because of its practical failure, but also because it restricts human freedom rather than protecting it. Sartre argues in 'A victory' that torture 'costs human life and does not save any' (Sartre 1958, p. 73). Not only does torture fail practically, due to the fact that many people refuse to talk under torture or disclose false information in a desperate effort to make the pain stop, it is also bound to fail from an ontological point of view. Torture is grounded in the refusal to accept the objectification of oneself by the look of the other, and is therefore a refusal to take responsibility for one's own facticity. Acts of torture are as such acts of bad faith.

Acts of bad faith are characterised either by a refusal to accept the nature of the human cogito as *for-itself* or a refusal to assume one's own facticity. In torture I try to deny the freedom of the other and reject the objectification of myself. I reduce her in turn to an object, but these actions never contribute positively to my being, in the sense that they cannot help me to realise myself more fully. Neither does it contribute to the self-realisation of the other, whose free activity I am restraining.

It's interesting to relate the observation that torture is an act of bad faith to the nature of spying more generally. When concrete relations such as torture are grounded in the violent structure of human recognition, it seems that the interpersonal relations in Sartre's ontological account all result in acts of bad faith. Sartre rejects the possibility of any action in common with the other and rejects the possibility of any healthy concrete relations between myself and the other.

If the concrete realisation of the ontological relation is the domain of bad faith, it seems that the ontological account of the other is already inauthentic in nature. The way the human cogito approaches the other sets them up for violence and struggle rather than empathy and cooperation.

Returning to the nature of spying, the human cogito will function as a free endeavour until the individual realises that he or she can be seen. The realisation of the existence of the other seems to transform the cogito and seems to be the origin of bad faith. Spying is as such a limitation of human freedom, because the very nature of spying is that the spy is very much aware of the fact that she can be seen (or identified) by the other.

When we read *l'Etre et le néant* closely it seems, however, that the mere presence of the other does not in itself constitute the problem of bad faith. The problem of bad faith seems to be grounded in the human cogito's inauthentic attitude towards itself as *for-itself*. Sartre argues that the human cogito understands itself as a *lack of being* rather than as *otherwise-than-being*. This lack of being motivates the cogito's desire to be, which leads to the violent struggle with the other. It is the desire to be that motivates the concrete relations of love, masochism and language; in these relations the human being tries to take the other's freedom as the foundation of his own being. In the relations of sadism, desire, hate and indifference the desire to be leads to an instrumental appropriation of the other. The desire to be leads to the desire to unite the *in-itself* and the *for-itself*. It is the desire to become the object of my own continual choice and creation that motivates sadism and torture.

When the origin of bad faith is already grounded in the way the human cogito understands itself, it can be said that Sartre's whole ontology, outlined in *l'Etre et le néant*, is an ontology of bad faith. The ontological structure of intersubjectivity is plausibly consistent with an ontology characterised by violence, oppression and bad faith. Sartre's ontological analysis can be seen as the basis for an investigation into the moral nature of human relations. Having outlined the origin of the violent structure of human relations, to which spying and torture are related, it seems important to investigate how individuals might escape from these violent structures and whether they are capable of respecting each other's freedom as *for-itself*.

References

Davis, M 2005, 'The moral justifiability of torture and other inhumane treatment', *International Journal of Applied Philosophy*, vol. 19, no. 2, pp. 161–178.

Detmer, D 2008, *Sartre explained: from bad faith to authenticity*, Open Court, Chicago.

Fletcher, G 2008, *Tort liability for human rights abuses*, Hart Publishing, Oxford.

Freud, S 2000 [1905], *Studienausgabe. Band V. Sexualleben. Drei abhandlungen zur sexualtheorie*, Franz Deuticke, Leipzig.

Lacan, J 2004, *Ecrits: a selection*, trans. A Sheridan, Routledge, London.

Murdoch, I 1959, *Sartre: romantic rationalist*, Yale University Press, New York.

Sartre, J-P 1943, *l'Etre et le néant*, Gallimard, Paris.

Sartre, J-P 1958, *The question*, trans. J Calder, Calder, London.

Sartre, J-P 1984 [1943], *Being and nothingness: a phenomenological essay on ontology*, trans. HE Barnes, Washington Square Press, New York.

Washington Post 2002, 'Memorandum for Alberto R. Gonzales Re: Standards of Conduct for Interrogation under 18 U.S.C. §§2340–2340A', August 1, Office of the Assistant Attorney General, www.washingtonpost.com/wp-srv/nation/documents/dojinterrogation memo20020801.pdf

6

PREDICTION MARKETS AS AN ALTERNATIVE TO ONE MORE SPY

Dan Weijers

Real-world policy decisions involve trade-offs. Sometimes the trade-offs involve both the efficacy and morality of potential policies. In this chapter, the morality and likely efficacy of hiring one more spy to help anti-terrorist intelligence gathering efforts is compared to the morality and likely efficacy of implementing a prediction market on terrorism. Prediction markets on terrorism allow registered traders to buy and sell shares in predictions about terrorism-related real-world events. The comparison at the heart of this chapter is based on the assumption that it would cost about $5 million to bankroll the prediction market project – or to establish another spy, including equipment and head office support, for 15 years. The comparison reveals that implementing a prediction market on terrorism is likely to be more efficacious and less morally problematic than hiring one more spy.

The chapter is organized as follows: the first section introduces prediction markets on terrorism and offers some reasons to think that they might be effective. The second section addresses objections to the effectiveness of prediction markets, including the concern that participants in the market will not have the requisite knowledge to enable the market to produce reliable predictions, and the worry that the market will produce bogus predictions due to manipulative trading. The third section considers two moral objections to prediction markets on terrorism, both related to the use of the markets as a form of insurance. The fourth section introduces two further moral objections to prediction markets on terrorism: that the markets will (but should not) reward informants, and that the markets involve the repugnant act of betting on death. The fifth section completes the comparison of implementing a prediction market on terrorism with funding one more spy, concluding that implementing a prediction market is the preferable policy.

Prediction markets on terrorism

Prediction markets allow registered traders to buy and sell shares in predictions about real-world events (Weijers 2013, para. 1). For prediction markets on terrorism, those real-world events are always related to terrorism, and will likely include predictions about terrorist attacks (Hanson 2006a, pp. 264–5). For example, shares in the prediction 'There will be a fatal terrorist attack on the US Embassy in Egypt during January 2015' might be for sale at around $1 in a market that pays out $10 for each share in a prediction that turns out to be true. When acting rationally, traders with the belief that there is a 20 per cent chance of there being a fatal terrorist attack on the US Embassy in Egypt during January 2015 will purchase any share offers that are cheaper than $2 (20 per cent of the $10 pay-out). At any given moment, the price of shares in a prediction can be understood as the market's prediction of the likelihood of the predicted event actually happening.

While it may seem counterintuitive that the predictions of (mostly) non-experts could be aggregated into something useful, prediction markets have been demonstrated to do exactly that in many domains (Surowiecki 2004, p. 77–83). Moreover, Wolfers & Zitzewitz (2004, p. 1) point out that prediction markets have produced better calibrated (i.e. more accurate) predictions than 'moderately sophisticated benchmarks' in several domains, including domestic politics, sales of consumer goods and box-office takings. Green, Armstrong & Graefe (2007) have also demonstrated that prediction markets can perform comparably with, or better than, Delphi methods, which pool the views of relevant experts.

Weijers explains the remarkable success of prediction markets like this:

> Most of us have some genuine information about the topics in question as well as some randomly incorrect information. When all of this information is aggregated in the right way, the random incorrectness tends to cancel out (because it's random) and the genuine information accumulates into the basis of an accurate prediction.
>
> *(Weijers 2013, para. 5)*

Furthermore, in prediction markets, the incentives are in the right place. Participants are rewarded for their accuracy, and participants with more knowledge can trade many times. In these ways, prediction markets are quite unlike polling, which doesn't reward accurate information and gives everyone an equal 'vote' regardless of their level of knowledge. It is the success of prediction markets in a diverse range of domains, and the broad applicability of their underlying logic, that has led several authors to suggest using prediction markets to gain anti-terrorist intelligence (e.g. Hanson 2006a; Looney 2004; Surowiecki 2004, p. 77–83; Weijers & Richardson 2014a, 2014b; Yeh 2006).

The general justification for setting up a prediction market on terrorism is that it is likely to produce some knowledge relevant to counter-terrorism efforts that would not have been gathered through existing intelligence-gathering means, at least not in as timely a manner. This was one of the many goals of the prediction market, Policy Analysis Market (PAM), being developed by Richard Hanson and his colleagues before the project was dramatically halted due to government intervention (Hanson 2006a, 2006b, 2007). The aspect of PAM focusing on gathering anti-terrorism intelligence was the focus of concerted criticism from many people. Nobel laureate economist Joseph Stiglitz criticised the project on both moral and efficacy grounds, commenting that it represented 'market fundamentalism descending to a new level of absurdity' (Stiglitz 2003, para. 8). His criticisms are notable because he offers such a broad range of them, and because he is an expert on prediction markets. Since the full range of his criticisms has not yet been adequately addressed, the rest of this chapter deals with them all.

Prediction markets on terrorism can't generate useful information

Participants won't have new knowledge

In his previous work on prediction markets – which he refers to as futures markets – with Sanford Grossman (Grossman & Stiglitz 1976, 1980), Stiglitz identified the importance of traders bringing relevant information to prediction markets:

> We focused on competitive markets in which we assumed participants had some relevant information. For instance, a farmer knows something about his own crop, so if he participates in a futures market he will bring his knowledge to bear on that market. Voters who participate in a futures market also bring relevant information – whom they and their friends are voting for – and that is why futures markets may predict presidential elections reasonably well.
>
> *(Stiglitz 2003, para. 5)*

However, Stiglitz expressed doubt that a prediction market on terrorism would attract traders with this kind of relevant knowledge, since he found it hard to believe that 'there is widespread information about terrorist activity not currently being either captured or appropriately analyzed by the "experts" in the FBI and the CIA', and perhaps harder still to believe that traders in a prediction market on terrorism would have that information (Stiglitz 2003, para. 10).

Whether prediction markets on terrorism could attract traders with relevant information is an empirical question that seems unlikely to be completely answered without a real-world test. Nevertheless, there seems to be good reason to think that the right kind of prediction market on terrorism could indeed attract traders with relevant information. Consider an anonymous prediction market on terrorism that was actively promoted to a wide range of potential participants from around the world (except, of course, for allied intelligence agency operatives, since then the market would not be one among many distinct sources of information, and would possibly provide too much information to terrorists). Several groups of participants

TABLE 6.1 Characteristics of the potential user groups of a prediction market on terrorism.

Group	Size	Relevant direct private information	Relevant ambient private information	Location	Incentive	Power over event
Ordinary civilians	large	none–low	low	mainly in allied countries	mainly interest/fun	none
Connected civilians	small	low–moderate	low–high	mainly in or nearby suspected 'terrorist host' countries	mainly financial or informative	none–low
Allied security force members	small	none–low	moderate	diverse	mainly financial or informative	none–low
Allied intelligence agents	tiny	moderate	high	diverse	mainly financial	low–moderate
Terrorists	tiny	very high	very high	mainly in 'terrorist host' countries	financial or mis-informational	moderate–high

of different sizes and with different kinds of information and incentives to invest could be expected, as outlined in Table 1.

Contrary to what several writers on this topic have suggested (e.g. Posner 2004, pp. 175–6; Stiglitz 2003), even some ordinary citizens with little chance of ever crossing paths with a terrorist or terrorist supporter might have useful private information about the likelihood of particular types of terrorist attack. For example, as Hanson (2006a, p. 265) points out, these completely unconnected ordinary citizens might still have useful private information about the relative vulnerability of certain potential terrorist targets. Furthermore, if these unconnected ordinary citizens worked as security guards, or as janitors, or in certain other roles, then they might have information about the vulnerability of potential targets that intelligence agencies do not.

Regardless of whether ordinary citizens will bring relevant knowledge to the market, the most likely traders to bring relevant information to the market are connected civilians. Connected civilians are people who come into contact with terrorists and their supporters, but do not support terrorism themselves. Posner (2004, pp. 175–6) denies the possibility that this group exists, but surely not everyone sharing a geographical location with terrorists approves of their methods. The contact might be direct (connected civilians could know someone and suspect or know that person to be a terrorist) or indirect (they might have overheard snippets of conversation because they live or work in places that terrorists and their supporters frequent). Connected civilians who live in known 'terrorist host' countries might hold both direct private information and a high level of ambient private information related to terrorist activities, particularly if they live in an area that at least partially supports the terrorist activity in question (since terrorist activity might be discussed more openly there). Ambient private information is the aggregate of the indirect information held by an individual, such as information from television news, opinion polls and hearsay. Furthermore, different individual connected citizens are likely to hold different private information; one might hear about a timeframe, another about a location, and so on.

Why wouldn't these connected citizens simply alert intelligence agencies instead of using a prediction market to get their message out? There are lots of potential reasons. Some connected citizens would have financial motives for participating in the market. They would have little reason to approach the authorities. A payment might be offered for further information, but the informer may be investigated, constantly followed, or even tortured. Even if the informant had anti-terroristic motives, getting in touch with intelligence agencies is risky for the same reasons; raising the heat could result in reprisals from terrorist supporters, and the act of informing could result in being tortured for further information. The informant might also worry about not being taken seriously, or being ignored. It might also be difficult or impossible for some informants to contact the right agencies. There might not be the right kind of embassy nearby, and they might not have the resources to find the number for, and make the call to, the Pentagon. On the whole, it seems much more likely that the majority of connected civilians who desire to relay anti-terrorist intelligence, and especially those in 'terrorist host' countries, would prefer to use an anonymous prediction market than to risk direct personal contact.

So, if a prediction market on terrorism had enough connected civilians, and it played its aggregating role effectively, a lot of relevant information that was previously unavailable to intelligence agencies might be elicited. Now, compare this new knowledge to the knowledge that might be created by one more spy. The CIA already employs 1600 spies (Miller 2012, para. 3). Is it reasonable to think that a radically different method of gathering intelligence will produce less novel information than increasing the number of spies by 0.0006 per cent?

Manipulation dilemma

Even if a prediction market on terrorism could attract traders with relevant information, Stiglitz cites a further issue that might prevent it from being effective – the manipulation dilemma:

> If trading is anonymous, then it could be subject to manipulation, particularly if the market has few participants – providing a false sense of security or an equally dangerous false sense of alarm. If trading is not anonymous, then anyone with information about terrorism would be, understandably, reluctant to trade on it. In that case, the market would not serve its purpose.
>
> (Stiglitz 2003, para. 11)

It seems unarguable that if participation in the prediction market required the registration of a lot of personal details, then many would-be participants would be deterred. Some would doubtless worry about being tracked down and investigated, harassed or tortured. Therefore the 'manipulation by anonymous traders' problem seems to be the best horn of the dilemma to tackle. Hanson (2006a, pp. 266–8) has discussed some ways to deal with this problem, but the most useful solution would be a *mainly* anonymous model. The market would be set up to be anonymous and advertise itself as such. However, authorities could gain access to whatever general information is collected through the market. For example, the CIA would know whether suspicious trades are made from the same account, or from the same geographical area. Furthermore, given the right warrant, some financial institutions or intermediaries involved with the transactions might be able to provide more detailed information.

The main worry with anonymous traders manipulating the market, expressed by Posner (2004, p. 175), is that the genuine relevant information gathered by the market will be swamped by the purposefully deceptive trades made by terrorists. Whether manipulative trades will regularly, occasionally, or ever swamp the genuine information is hard to discern theoretically. Nevertheless, several mathematical models indicate that prediction markets can still perform just as well, or even better, when some of the participants are attempting to manipulate the price (Hanson 2006a, pp. 266–8; Wolfers & Zitzewitz 2004, pp. 16–17). The models show that, in order to survive manipulation, a prediction market needs a sufficient number of participants with some relevant private knowledge and the money and inclination to trade on that knowledge (Hanson 2006a, pp. 266–8; Wolfers & Zitzewitz 2004, pp. 16–17).

For example, imagine that a group of terrorist participants were selling stock in a particular prediction short so as to reduce the price of that prediction, and thereby reduce the possibility of interference with their planned attack. Cases like this can be referred to as 'diverting cases' because the terrorists are attempting to manipulate the market in a way that diverts attention away from the prediction that might warn intelligence agents about their planned attack. In diverting cases, the connected citizens might think that, based on their private information about a planned terrorist act, the price is a bargain because it does not reflect the probability of the event happening and so they would buy as much of the under-priced stock as they could. As a result, the attempted manipulation of the market would have failed and, rather than create a diversion, the terrorists would merely have wasted their money. Even if terrorists could keep the price down, the increased activity in the market, with the traders pushing the price down all coming from the same geographical area, would be a clear sign that terrorists might be attempting a diverting manipulation, and thereby provide the same signal to intelligence agencies that a high price would.

The reverse kind of case, which can be referred to as a 'disrupting case', is trickier, however. Terrorists might attempt to buy all the stock in a particular prediction so as to make it look like a terrorist attack is imminent. Possible motives for this include disrupting and scaring their enemies (hence the name), and possibly undermining confidence in the prediction market. If terrorists did buy all the stock of a particular prediction for these reasons, very few participants are likely to have the kind of direct private information required to give them reason to correct the market. It's close to impossible for connected citizens to have information to the effect that *all* of the main terrorist cells around the world *will not* attack a certain place at a certain time. There is, however, a slim chance that some connected citizens have information about a terrorist plot to artificially inflate that prediction. Most likely, when connected citizens see the price of a stock in the prediction steadily rise, they might assume that other participants have some relevant private information that they do not, and therefore view the price change as genuine. On the other hand, it seems plausible that all genuine participants in the prediction market have the default assumption that any particular terrorist attack is very unlikely. Indeed, this default consideration, in combination with their ambient information, could lead them to see the price rise as attempted manipulation or inept trading by inexperienced participants. If they did see it this way, then the genuine traders might try to sell stock in the prediction until the price returned to relatively normal levels. Given the broad range of factors that may be at work here, it would be presumptuous to claim to know how most, or even many, real-world prediction markets on terrorism would react to attempted disruptive manipulations. Indeed, only a formal real-world trial seems likely to resolve this worry to any significant degree of satisfaction.

Importantly, a prediction market's ability to prevent disrupting cases of terrorist misinformation is not nearly as significant as its ability to prevent diverting cases. The consequences of successful disrupting manipulations are mainly inconveniences and slight economic costs. The consequences of diverting manipulations, however, could be the calamitous death and destruction that successful terrorist attacks can cause. And, as was just argued, a prediction market on terrorism is much less likely to be successfully manipulated in diverting cases.

So, while some doubts remain, an intelligently designed prediction market on terrorism – with a broad range of traders from around the world – appears to have a relatively good chance of being effective. 'Relatively' is important here, since the likely effectiveness of such a market should be compared with the likely effectiveness of one more spy. Since, as has been argued, there are no clear reasons why a prediction market on terrorism could not produce useful information, as it does in so many other domains, and one more spy using the same old methods seems relatively unlikely to produce more than a little new anti-terrorist intelligence, it seems reasonable to conclude that prediction markets are likely to be more effective than one more spy.

Insurance

However, more effective policy options are not always chosen, especially when they produce more moral issues than the alternatives. Stiglitz (2003) raises two moral issues based on the use of prediction markets on terrorism for insurance.

Perverse incentives

Stiglitz explains the moral hazard problem of insurance this way: '[B]y providing "insurance" for participants, futures markets can also create the long-noted "moral hazard" problem – the notion that insurance can alter incentives. Someone who has insured his house for 110 per cent of its value has an incentive to set it afire' (Stiglitz 2003, para. 11). The implication is clear: traders who stand to profit if a terrorist attack occurs have an incentive to bring out such a terrorist attack. However, while the moral hazard problem does seem to pose real ethical problems in certain domains in which the benefits may outweigh the costs (e.g. life insurance, property insurance), prediction markets on terrorism is not one of them.

The vast majority of people in the world, and potential participants in a prediction market on terrorism, try to avoid harming others, and abhor the thought of killing an innocent person. Imagine that hundreds of normal people bought some stock in there being a terrorist attack because the price was low and they thought that an attack was more likely than the price indicated. It seems exceeding unlikely that any people in that situation would suddenly get the idea that they should plan and carry out a terrorist attack just to reap the financial rewards. First, how much money would it take to convince a normal person to commit an act of indiscriminate killing? I suspect no amount would be enough. Second, even if someone could be swayed to kill innocents by a multi-million-dollar payday, they might not have the knowledge, connections and financial resources to carry out the attack. Third, there is no point being rich if you are caught planning or carrying out an act of terrorism because money is not so useful if you are in prison for the rest of your life or dead, shot by security forces. And being thwarted in this way is likely because by betting heavily on a predicted attack (which is required to substantially profit from it), the trader would alert the CIA to their intentions. Fourth, as Hanson (2006a, p. 269) has suggested, the markets should be set up with an upper limit so that it would be impossible to make more than several thousand dollars, in which case money can be more easily made elsewhere. Would someone who is not already a terrorist become one, and risk their life in doing so, just to kill innocent people for an amount of money that they could make by working another shift or investing in the regular stock market (Hanson 2006a, pp. 268–70)? Surely not; the benefits are swamped by the likely costs.

That just leaves traders who already are terrorists – people who think there is also some other benefit to carrying out a terrorist attack. It makes sense that an *arsonist* would set fire to her house if it was over-insured. Similarly, it makes sense for a *terrorist* to commit an act of terror if he could gain financially as well as furthering his other aims. But terrorists are those who plan to, and do, carry out terrorist attacks anyway. So no new acts of terror are encouraged by the existence of prediction markets on terrorism. Furthermore, if terrorists attempt to make money from the prediction market in this way, then they are doing exactly what will enable the prediction market to help prevent terrorism; they will be sending a clear message of their intentions, allowing the CIA to thwart and possibly capture them.

Therefore the moral hazard problem does not apply to prediction markets on terrorism; the notion that the markets would encourage more of the behaviour they are designed to protect people from is implausible.

Further inequities

Stiglitz also raises the insurance-related issue that a prediction market on terrorism would allow 'those with the sophistication and money to "hedge" against the threat of terrorism, financially at least, leaving the rest of Americans fully exposed!' (Stiglitz 2003, para. 12). Stiglitz sees this as a problem, stating, 'the U.S. government should be concerned with the exposure of all Americans to terrorism' (Stiglitz 2003, para. 12). This argument is flawed in two important ways.

First, note that one of the most harrowing features of terrorism is that it involves indiscriminate killing (Khatchadourian 1998, p. 24). As a consequence, terrorism exposes *everyone* to the threat of being indiscriminately killed. Rich and poor alike were killed in the 9/11 attacks. Rich and poor alike lost loved ones. Rich and poor alike experienced grief and terror for months and years afterward. No amount of insurance could have hedged against that suffering because money cannot fix those problems. Money cannot shield people from the grief caused by losing a loved one to an indiscriminate attack. So attempting to hedge against terrorism seems misguided, something that will only achieve the narrowing of the wide gap between how much money and sense they have (not by increasing their 'sense').

Second, yes, the government should be concerned with the exposure of all Americans to terrorism. But rather than being a reason for banning prediction markets on terrorism, this seems a better reason for implementing them. The exposure of Americans to terrorism gives the government reason to investigate every potentially useful strategy to increase anti-terrorist intelligence-gathering efforts. Indeed, this is the main reason for setting up a prediction market on terrorism – to protect everyone from the risk of terror, grief and death.

So, while insurance does raise moral concerns, Stiglitz has given no good reason to think that the attempted use of prediction markets on terrorism as insurance poses any moral concern at all. This conclusion places prediction markets on terrorism on an equal footing with one more spy – neither poses any moral issues related to insurance.

Other moral problems

Stiglitz (2003) and others (e.g. Dorgan 2003) have also presented two further potential moral problems with prediction markets on terrorism – rewarding informants and betting on death.

Rewarding informants

Stiglitz has argued that traders with genuine information about terrorist attacks should be investigated, rather than given a pay-out for their correct predictions:

'shouldn't these people be investigated rather than rewarded?' (Stiglitz 2003, para. 10). However, it is not obvious that we could or should investigate such people.

First of all, without the prediction markets, it is unclear how spies would know who to investigate. Second, it seems likely that this kind of 'investigate everyone' thinking deters innocent would-be informers. Worries about being investigated are probably seriously restricting the amount of useful intelligence the CIA is currently gathering. And, as for rewarding the participants whose predictions are correct: why not? The participants who make money trading on the prediction market will have been lucky, or they will have knowingly contributed useful information. The lucky ones are probably innocent, and their reward will probably be used to fund the pay-outs of other traders on future predictions (their luck will likely run out soon). Of the other participants who are financially rewarded, some will be innocent, others guilty, and still others somewhere in between. Rewarding the innocent participants, who bring useful information, seems like the right thing to do. Rewarding the not-so-innocent traders, who bring useful information, is not ideal, but neither are the alternatives.

The important comparison here is between rewarding possibly less-than-saintly traders in the prediction market, and spies rewarding clearly less-than-saintly informants by paying them to provide novel intelligence on terrorists' plans. These alternatives are similar, but the key difference between the two is the correct alignment of reward and useful information. Using the old-fashioned method of paying informants, we do not always know whether the informant is lying to us. But we pay them anyway. Now consider prediction markets on terrorism – only those traders who provide useful information are rewarded by participating in prediction markets. Lying or not, if someone won money on a prediction, then they were right and they provided useful anti-terrorist intelligence. Therefore, while neither prediction markets on terrorism nor one more spy would get a clean pass on this issue, the prediction market seems preferable because it avoids the morally and informationally worst outcome of paying bad people for misleading information.

Betting on death

Perhaps the most discussed potential moral issue regarding prediction markets on terrorism is that the trades they require to be effective can be seen as a form of betting on death. In reference to PAM – the prediction market with anti-terrorism aspects designed by Hanson and colleagues – Stiglitz said this: 'Under the proposal ... participants would [be] betting, in effect – and perhaps profiting – on such potential events as an attack by North Korea or an assassination of Yasser Arafat' (Stiglitz 2003, para. 9). Democratic senator Byron Dorgan was more expressive:

> This betting parlor on the Internet ... [this] Internet casino ... is unbelievably stupid ... It will be offensive to almost everyone. Can you imagine if another country set up a betting parlor so that people could go in ... and bet on the assassination of an American political figure ...? ... It is offensive.
>
> *(Dorgan 2003, paras 8–11)*

However, it is far from clear how offensive the idea really is, especially when compared with the relevant alternatives.

A prediction market on terrorism would be nothing like a casino. Profit motives are in play, but, as mentioned above, many traders will have more altruistic motives as well. Furthermore, making wagers on matters of life and death is not always immoral. Consider buying shares in a company that is involved in death, like a coffin-making company, a weapons manufacturer, or a life insurance company. Or simply consider buying life insurance. These transactions are all essentially wagers on matters of life and death, but they are generally considered to be morally permissible. A prediction market on terrorism would be no online 'death pool' – a website that encourages participants to make lists of famous people who might die during the next year, and then pays them real money if they correctly predict the most celebrity deaths. The point, and likely effect, of prediction markets on terrorism is to respect life by helping prevent terrorist attacks, not to be disrespectful of matters of life and death (Weijers & Richardson 2014b).

Surely some people will find the very idea of betting on terrorist attacks highly offensive. But all policy decisions are about trade-offs. Lives could doubtless be saved by lowering the speed limit on freeways, but that would inconvenience many. Implementing a prediction market on terrorism would effectively be trading off some offence, and a modest financial outlay, against the likely chance of helping to prevent terrorist attacks. Consider how offensive and costly the 9/11 terrorist attacks were. Even helping to prevent one terrorist attack like that would make it worth offending some people and spending a few million tax dollars. Given that a prediction market on terrorism could help prevent many attacks, this trade-off should be a relatively easy one to make.

The final analysis

Of course, the most important trade-off for the purposes of this chapter is between funding a new spy and a prediction market on terrorism. Both options were assumed to have the same financial cost and, erring on the side of caution, both might be said to have at least a slim chance of generating novel anti-terrorism intelligence during any given period. Indeed, it was argued that, mainly because of its novelty as an approach to intelligence gathering, a prediction market seems likely to be more useful as an intelligence-gathering tool than one more spy. However, if prediction markets on terrorism are offensive, then the right policy decision might still be to fund one more spy. But that would not be the right decision, since the behaviour required of spies is morally worse than the offence that prediction markets on terrorism might cause.

It would be a mistake to think that spies are politely handed novel intelligence on terrorist activity from reputable sources. If a spy is going to produce any useful information, she likely has to extract it. To have any reasonable chance of being effective, spies must lie, cheat, steal, bribe, trespass, forge documents, invade privacy, threaten, coerce, blackmail, detain, incapacitate and possibly torture. Naturally, these activities are at least offensive, and in most cases clearly immoral. Whether torture is usually, or even *ever*, effective is still debated (e.g. Blakeley 2011, pp. 546–50; Dershowitz 2002, ch. 4; Koh 2004, p. 653). But even if we assume that torture is effective and thereby justified in a very select group of cases, it is still morally problematic. Even when torturing someone in an attempt to prevent a terrorist attack, the act of torture may also harm the torturer. As Weijers and Richardson (2014b, p. 38) have argued, having to inflict cruel suffering on another human being might psychologically and morally scar the torturer in a way that gives even morally permissible torture a stark moral downside (see Chapter 4 in this volume).

The moral depravity of torture and the other immoral actions required of effective spies are not easily overlooked, especially once they are out in the open. Even the President has admitted that CIA agents have continually resorted to torture in this post-9/11 period, *even though this runs contrary to our considered moral values* (Dilanian 2014, para. 2). Furthermore, torture and some of the other immoral acts to which effective spies must occasionally resort cannot easily be recast as inoffensive. However, the same is not true of prediction markets on terrorism. If the public first hears about prediction markets on terrorism as a kind of casino in which they can bet on when and where innocents will be slaughtered by terrorists, then of course they will find it offensive. Alternatively, if the public first hears about an anti-terrorism tool that financially incentivises people to share relevant information that they would have otherwise kept to themselves, they are likely to applaud the government for doing all they can to prevent the scourge of terrorism.

On balance, then, implementing a prediction market on terrorism will produce some offence, with the amount varying based on the presentation of it to the public, but clearly less than any widespread advertisement of the various immoral activities that spies must engage in to extract useful information. Indeed, what sounds more offensive: trying to prevent a terrorist attack by encouraging people to bet on whether a terrorist attack will occur, or by sticking pins under their fingernails and subjecting them to long periods of waterboarding?

All things considered, implementing a prediction market on terrorism is likely to be more efficacious, given its novelty, and less morally problematic, given its moral issues are limited to offence, than hiring one more spy. Therefore, in pursuit of anti-terrorism intelligence, implementing a prediction market on terrorism is preferable to hiring one more spy.

References

Blakeley, R 2011, 'Dirty hands, clean conscience? The CIA inspector general's investigation of "enhanced interrogation techniques" in the war on terror and the torture debate', *Journal of Human Rights*, vol. 10, no. 4, pp. 544–561.

Dershowitz, AM 2002. *Why terrorism works: understanding the threat, responding to the challenge*, Yale University Press, New Haven.

Dilanian, K 2014, 'Obama admits US tortured detainees', Associated Press, 2 August, www. stuff.co.nz/world/americas/10340771/Obama-admits-US-tortured-detainees

Doherty, B 2012, 'Intrade prediction market targeted by our commodity futures trading commission (for absolutely no good reason)', *Hit & Run Blog*, 26 November, http://reason.com/blog/2012/11/26/intrade-prediction-market-targeted-by-ou

Dorgan, B 2003, 'Senators Ron Wyden and Byron Dorgan hold news conference on a terror financing scheme', George Mason University, 28 July, http://hanson.gmu.edu/PAM/govt/senator-wyden-dorgan-pressconf-7-28-03.txt

Green, KC, Armstrong, JS & Graefe, A 2007, 'Methods to elicit forecasts from groups: Delphi and prediction markets compared', *Foresight: The International Journal of Applied Forecasting*, vol. 8, no. 8, pp. 17–21.

Grossman, SJ & Stiglitz, JE 1976, 'Information and competitive price systems', *American Economic Review*, vol. 66, no. 2, pp. 246–253.

Grossman, SJ & Stiglitz, JE 1980, 'On the impossibility of informationally efficient markets', *American Economic Review*, vol. 70, no. 3, pp. 393–408.

Hanson, R 2006a, 'Designing real terrorism futures', *Public Choice*, vol. 128, no. 1, pp. 257–274.

Hanson, R 2006b, 'Decision markets for policy advice', in AS Gerber and EM Patashnik (eds), *Promoting the general welfare: new perspectives on government performance*, Brookings Institution Press, Washington, DC.

Hanson, R 2007, 'The policy analysis market (a thwarted experiment in the use of prediction markets for public policy)', *Innovations: Technology, Governance, Globalization*, vol. 2, no. 3, pp. 73–88.

Khatchadourian, H 1998, *The morality of terrorism*, Peter Lang, New York.

Koh, HH 2004, 'A world without torture', *Columbia Journal of Transnational Law*, vol. 43, pp. 641–662.

Looney, RE 2004, 'DARPA's policy analysis market for intelligence: outside the box or off the wall?', *International Journal of Intelligence and Counterintelligence*, vol. 17, no. 3, pp. 405–419.

Miller, G 2012, 'DIA to send hundreds more spies overseas', *Washington Post*, 1 December, http://articles.washingtonpost.com/2012-12-01/world/35585098_1_defense-clandestine-service-cia-spy-agency

Posner, RA 2004, *Catastrophe: risk and response*, Oxford University Press, New York.

Stiglitz, J 2003, 'Terrorism: there's no futures in it', *Los Angeles Times*, 31 July, http://mason.gmu.edu/~rhanson/PAM/PRESS2/LATstiglitz-7-31-03.htm

Surowiecki, J 2004, *The wisdom of crowds*, Doubleday, New York.

Weijers, D 2013, 'Technology: prediction markets', Observatory for Responsible Research and Innovation in ICT, http://responsible-innovation.org.uk/torrii/resource-detail/1181 [URL no longer available].

Weijers, D & Richardson, J 2014a, 'Is the repugnance about betting on terrorist attacks misguided?', *Ethics and Information Technology*, vol. 16, no. 3, pp. 251–262.

Weijers, D & Richardson, J 2014b, 'A moral analysis of effective prediction markets on terrorism', *International Journal of Technoethics*, vol. 5, no. 1, pp. 28–43.

Wolfers, J & Zitzewitz, E 2004, *Prediction markets*, No. w10504, National Bureau of Economic Research, Cambridge, MA.

Yeh, PF 2006, 'Using prediction markets to enhance US intelligence capabilities', *Studies in Intelligence*, vol. 50, no. 4, pp. 137–149.

PART III

Spying as war:
classificatory problems

7

PERSONS, PERSONHOOD AND PROPORTIONALITY

Building on a just war approach to intelligence ethics

Kevin Macnish

There are a number of different approaches that one can take to intelligence ethics. In recent years, Michael Quinlan, Ross Bellaby and David Omand have each argued that the principles of the Just War tradition can be usefully employed to assess the ethics of intelligence (Bellaby 2012; Omand 2012; Quinlan 2007) from a deontological perspective. I have elsewhere argued that Just War principles are helpful in assessing surveillance (Macnish 2014), which has obvious overlaps with intelligence work. In this chapter I defend the approach of employing the principles of the Just War tradition to intelligence and develop these principles further than Quinlan, Bellaby and Omand have done so far. First, I consider the benefits of this approach. I then look at the challenges it faces, and in so doing present a comprehensive list of those challenges, answering each in turn. Finally, I accept that one challenge in particular (that of a lack of real guidance) holds particular weight. I address this challenge through a consideration of the Just War principle of proportionality as it applies to coercive techniques of intelligence collection. When weighing proportionality, it is tempting to see the assault in coercive intelligence as solely against the individual. I argue that the assault is also against personhood and the wider community, and goes both deeper and wider than an assault 'merely' against a single person. I conclude that coercive practices in intelligence are not *mala in se*, but that they are justifiable only in rare cases.

Just intelligence

The Just War tradition, which is an attempt to recognise and place moral limits on the declaration and prosecution of war, can be dated back at least as far as Cicero (Cicero 2006); and there are elements, such as the principles of last resort and discrimination, that can be found in the Bible (Deuteronomy 20:10–14). Over the course of history, a number of principles have emerged that are often grouped together and today referred to as the 'Just War theory'. The Just War approach distinguishes between a war that is just in its declaration (*jus ad bellum*) and a war that is just in its prosecution (*jus in bello*). One can be just from the perspectives of *ad bellum* and *in bello* (although it is hard to find an actual case of this), just from the perspective of *ad bellum* but not *in bello*, or just from the perspective of *in bello* but not *ad bellum*. Finally, of course, a war can fail to be just from the perspectives of either *ad bellum* or *in bello* considerations. In recent years there has also been a push to focus on the morality both of ending a war and of conduct in the aftermath of fighting (*jus post bellum*), although this discussion is sufficiently immature to have yet developed any broadly agreed principles (Bass 2004).

There is no absolute agreement as to precisely which principles should be included in Just War considerations (O'Donovan 2003, pp. 13–14). The principles of *jus ad bellum* most commonly accepted include a just cause (the reason for going to war); a correct intention (the intention for going to war is the same as the just cause); the authority to declare war (to avoid private conflicts escalating); a formal declaration of war; a chance that the war will be successful in achieving the just cause; the stipulation that the war must be necessary, or a matter of last resort and a requirement that war is a proportionate response to the occasioning cause. Given that these relate to the decision to enter into war, they are generally directed at the leaders of a state. The *jus in bello* principles, by contrast, are directed more towards those who do the actual fighting (although they also have a bearing on those leaders who might direct soldiers to pursue certain policies). The number of *in bello* principles is similarly disputed, although there are two on which there is universal agreement and that have been enshrined in international law through the Additional Protocols to the Geneva Convention (ICRC 1977). These are proportionality of military acts and discrimination in targeting between combatants and non-combatants. Further principles sometimes included are the necessity of military actions (if this is not included in the proportionality consideration); treatment of prisoners (to encourage surrender over fighting to the death and so limiting bloodshed); and means *mala in se* (the banning of certain weapons or actions as evil in themselves, most typically seen in terms of chemical and biological weapons).

The application of the above principles to intelligence work has clear appeal. The principles are well established and understood within the philosophical and military traditions; they have been tried, tested and refined over centuries into a robust approach to an ethics of war, and they can be transposed into intelligence work without much modification. Taking *jus ad bellum* principles first (to which Quinlan refers in the case of intelligence as *jus ad intelligentium*), it seems correct that espionage should have a just cause, be carried out by a correct authority, and be a proportionate response to the occasioning trigger. Furthermore, the intention of surveillance should be the same as the just cause, the espionage should have a chance of success, it should be necessary (in that the alternatives to meeting the just cause are either exhausted or morally worse options), and there should be, if not a formal declaration, at least an understanding that espionage is a likely response to the occasioning trigger.

Furthermore, when looking at the *jus in bello* principles (Quinlan's *jus in intelligentia*), the parallels continue: intelligence officers (IOs) *should* act in a manner that is proportionate and they *should* discriminate between legitimate and illegitimate targets. Comparisons can also be drawn between IOs and soldiers. Both are agents of the state, and how they act reflects on the state they represent. Both engage in a degree of deception – soldiers through camouflage and ambush, IOs in adopting false identities or masking their 'real' work. There is an apparent degree of moral equivalence between IOs as there is between soldiers: whatever the ideology of 'their masters', they are essentially just 'doing their job'; and a mutual respect can arise across international barriers based on tradecraft and irrespective of ideology.[1] Finally, when caught, IOs and soldiers are typically neutralised and repatriated (for IOs in peacetime this is usually fairly immediate, for soldiers in war repatriation occurs at the conclusion of the war). 'It is generally agreed that spies, when captured, are not to be summarily executed without trial; spymasters are usually allowed diplomatic status ... to the extent that the "spy" may be thwarted but not destroyed' (Hulnick & Mattausch 1989, p. 517).

They also fit intuitively. The principles seem to apply well in both cases, and also to limit more extreme actions such as torture in an IO's rules of engagement. They also bring the advantage of centuries of discussion with regard to the relative merits of each principle, its precise meaning and its application in a variety of settings. This alone is a valuable contribution to the debate.

While there are advantages to applying the Just War principles to intelligence, these are not unfettered. There are challenges too. Tony Pfaff, for example, points out that threats to the military are those already existing, whereas in intelligence threats are merely potential. Pfaff suggests a check such that 'for intelligence gathering activities in peacetime to be justifiable, there needs to be an analogous "act of aggression" that gives the nation that seeks to obtain these secrets, in some sense, a "right" to them' (Pfaff 2006, p. 76). That is, we should not be spying on our friends. Of course, as Pfaff recognises, intelligence threats are not always *merely* potential (intelligence collection is carried out in wartime as well as in peacetime, while that carried out against terrorists falls between the two), and military threats may be potential rather than actual (e.g. the Panzer divisions sitting on the German side of the Ardennes in 1940 prior to the *blitzkrieg* of France). These qualifications aside, Pfaff's condition would hold in the majority of cases.

A further challenge can be levelled against the Just War approach by rejecting key elements in the analogy between IOs and soldiers. While this does not undermine the use of Just War principles, it does show that they deserve further consideration. One disanalogy becomes particularly clear when we consider IOs who have no official cover (NOC), rather than those with diplomatic cover. As noted by Arthur Hulnick and Daniel Mattausch (1989), those with diplomatic cover fall under the purview of international laws, which set out how these individuals may be treated. This is not because they are spies, but because they are diplomats. NOCs are seen and treated somewhat differently: they are not neutralised through automatic repatriation but more typically through imprisonment, sometimes for years. Furthermore, when captured in times of war, soldiers are imprisoned as prisoners of war and are, or should be, treated as neutralised threats and afforded food, shelter and basic privileges for the duration of the war. However, spies, and especially NOCs, are more often shot. In times of war the spy is essentially a non-uniformed combatant often living in urban areas. This muddies the already murky waters between combatants and non-combatants and risks putting non-combatants' lives at risk: if combatants (spies) masquerade as non-combatants, then reprisals for the actions of spies could be visited on non-combatants in general. When Reinhard Heydrich was assassinated in Czechoslovakia in 1940, for example, in response the Germans attempted to remove the village in which the assassination took place from the map, irrespective of who had actually taken part.[2]

A pertinent question also arises as to who, in intelligence work, constitutes a legitimate target and who does not. Pfaff argues here that anyone who knowingly 'enters the game' (i.e. works for an intelligence organisation or for an entity that is likely to be subject to foreign intelligence interests such as a nuclear weapons laboratory) is a legitimate target (Pfaff 2006, pp. 82–3). However, this strikes me as a little too easy. Not everyone who 'enters the game' does so through giving free, informed consent, and an IO may not know whether certain people are even aware that they are at risk of being targeted by foreign intelligence. What of the husband of an IO with diplomatic cover? Did he know that his wife was involved in intelligence when they married? Does he support her activities, and to what extent (is his support moral or physical)? At what stage, if ever, then, could he become a legitimate target? Is it ever legitimate to target him (for example, through a honey trap or planting goods in his pocket so that he might be detained for 'shoplifting') in order to apply pressure on his wife?

A further area in which the Just War tradition has been brought to bear on intelligence ethics is in the application of the doctrine of double effect (DDE). The DDE is used to deal with scenarios in which an action will lead to both a good and a bad outcome, and argues that to intend the good outcome is justifiable but to intend the bad outcome would be blameworthy. Further qualifications stipulate that the good outcome cannot come about as a result of the bad outcome and that the respective outcomes must be in proportion, such that a great deal of harm isn't caused to achieve a modicum of good. In his discussion of the ethics of intelligence, Pfaff considers the problem of deception on the part of IOs when it comes to their family and friends, who are not allowed to know about the IO's true job for reasons of national security, their own safety and the safety of the IO. He applies the DDE to an IO's lying to friends and family, such that this renders the act justifiable if the intention is to protect the friends and family (and not to deceive them), if they are not protected purely by the deceit, and if the harm of the deceit is outweighed by the harm that would result from them knowing the truth.

This is an interesting if controversial approach. Judith Jarvis Thomson, Thomas Scanlon and Frances Kamm have all rejected the DDE from a deontological perspective (Kamm 2008; Scanlon 2008; Thomson 1991), while others, notably Jeff McMahan (2009), continue to defend it. Were the DDE to hold, it would be an effective means of resolving the problem of deceiving friends and family. However, it might also justify too much: could the targeting of an IO's unwitting wife be legitimated in the same way if the intention were to gain information of importance to national security? If so, then she could thereby become a legitimate target despite never having given informed consent to her part 'in the game'.

A further challenge can be raised to the Just War approach by noting that war occurs in times of exception, whereas intelligence gathering does not. During wartime, normal standards of morality are suspended for combatants in favour of standards set by the Just War position. In war, soldiers engage in activities that would not be acceptable for an ordinary citizen to perform; and so there is a need to find the limits of what a soldier should be permitted do. However, the activities of soldiers in wartime, even within the confines of the Just War tradition, are not acceptable activities for those same soldiers to undertake in peacetime. *Only* during war (and some very exceptional occasions of national emergency) is it acceptable for a soldier to shoot and kill someone or to aim artillery and missiles at another state's buildings. In peacetime these activities are rightly condemned as murder and/or as initiating a conflict. By contrast, intelligence gathering happens around the clock, 365 days a year. It never ceases, and so cannot be classed as occurring in a state of exception. Rather, intelligence gathering is the norm. Hence when special dispensation is granted to soldiers, in times of war, to commit what would otherwise be criminal acts, this happens because the agent is a soldier *and* the context is exceptional. When we think about giving special dispensation to IOs to act in a manner that under other circumstances would be morally unacceptable, and usually illegal in the countries in which they are practising, this is based purely on the fact that the agent is a spy. There is no mitigating exceptional circumstance. As such, this approach seems very close to a case of special pleading.

One possible response to this challenge is to confront the separation between *jus ad intelligentium* and *jus in intelligentia*. As noted above, the Just War analogues are treated as distinct, with *jus ad bellum* applying to leaders, classically the sovereign, while *jus in bello* applies to soldiers. The sovereign therefore announces the parameters of war within which the soldier can operate under the conditions of *jus in bello* (i.e. killing other combatants with impunity). A simple application of the Just War analogy would suggest that the sovereign can still set the parameters of intelligence within which the IO operates. Yet this is precisely the problem: wars end, while intelligence work often does not, and so the *in extremis* conditions become positively quotidian. An alternative involves the rejection of the sovereign/spy separation in the case of intelligence. This could lead to each act of intelligence being required to meet the full conditions of *jus ad intelligentium* and *jus in intelligentia*. Rather than seeing intelligence gathering as a series of operations carried out under exceptional conditions, such as war, each act of intelligence gathering is seen as its own exceptional condition and required to meet every principle of the just intelligence canon. This is *not* to say that the IO should be the final arbiter of whether or not intelligence gathering is morally acceptable in a particular circumstance; just as the sovereign is not the final arbiter in the case of war. The implication is that the IO is able to decide whether an act of intelligence gathering is permissible, like the sovereign in the case of war, but she nevertheless remains accountable for her actions to the state and, in democratic regimes, the people. The principles by which the IO can expect to be judged, therefore, are those of both *ad intelligentium* and *in intelligentia*. [3]

Finally, Hulnick and Mattausch argue that the Just War principles offer 'only nominal consolation to the conscientious intelligence professional' (Hulnick & Mattausch 1989, pp. 515–16), although they do not elaborate on this or justify the position with much vigour. Overall, while there is an intuitive fit between the principles of Just War and the ethics of intelligence, this fit is not perfect. The challenges that I have outlined above have focused more on *jus in intelligentia* than *jus ad intelligentium*. The latter seems to fit more easily: correct authority, proportionality, necessity, just cause, etc. are all sensible principles to follow when determining whether to engage in intelligence work. However, it is in the *undertaking* of intelligence work that, arguably, the more serious ethical problems arise. By more serious ethical problems I mean those that directly challenge the autonomy of the agent through acts of coercion. Examples would include inducing people to lie, engaging in blackmail, conducting acts of torture to extract information, or treating agents as expendable. Here the principles of *jus in intelligentia* provide less obvious guidance, and yet it is precisely here that the IO needs help in determining which actions are permissible and which are not. This is true even when the principles of *ad intelligentium* and *in intelligentia* are combined, as I have suggested above. When considering proportionality, for example, we can ask: what is *not* justified when one is acting in the interests of the security of one's country? In this regard, then, and especially when one considers coercive activities such as torture, blackmail, inducement to betray and the expendability of agents, Hulnick and Mattausch's sentiment that the principles offer 'only nominal consolation to the conscientious intelligence professional' carries some weight.

The problem of proportionality

I take Hulnick and Mattausch's critique to present a serious challenge to the application of Just War principles to intelligence. I also think that this is particularly true in the case of the principle of proportionality, which in traditional Just War discourse applies to both *ad bellum* and *in bello* considerations. Proportionality involves a balancing of costs and benefits. Do the benefits clearly outweigh the costs? Then the action is proportionate. Do the costs clearly outweigh the benefits? If so, then the act is disproportionate. Inevitably there is a grey area between the two in which the one does not 'clearly' outweigh the other, but, while important, that need not concern us here. [4] As it stands, this might appear to be a matter of straightforward consideration of consequences. However, Thomas Hurka has argued convincingly that not all benefits should be weighed in the balance (Hurka 2005). He points out that war can have a rejuvenating impact on a national economy, but that to consider this as a *benefit* of engaging in war would be morally corrupt. We should not go to war, or engage in a particular battle, because it might help our economy.

Instead, Hurka argues that proportionality should be a matter of weighing the costs of an action against the just cause for undertaking that action. If a state goes to war to defend a group from persecution, then it is against this that all military actions should be measured. This Hurka describes as a 'sufficient just cause'. He also talks of 'contributing just causes', namely those that would not in themselves justify going to war though they are nevertheless worthy of consideration as a benefit of war (for example, the good that can come from disarming an enemy to prevent a return to aggression (Hurka 2005, p. 41)). These are contrasted with a third category (that I have elsewhere described as 'peripheral benefits': Macnish 2015) which, as with economic benefit, should not be weighed.

These legitimately considerable benefits are to be weighed against all reasonably foreseeable costs of the action. By reasonably foreseeable I mean the consequences that a person could reasonably predict will follow from the action at the time the decision is made. Hence the deaths of civilians following the dropping of atomic bombs over Hiroshima and Nagasaki could have been foreseen. The subsequent radiation sickness, and particularly the impact on future births, arguably could not.

As suggested above, when an IO is charged with protecting national security, the fate of one individual can seem insignificant as a part of the broader picture. What, she might rhetorically ask, are one person's injuries when considered against the saving of millions from a terrorist or missile attack? Seen in this way, coercive acts such as blackmail and torture can easily be seen as proportionate. If the IO is happy that the person undergoing torture is a legitimate target, then the stated *jus in intelligentia* principles are met and so the act is justified. However, this strikes me as counter-intuitive. Leaving aside the efficacy of coercive acts for the purpose of this discussion, this approach seems to provide ready justification for those coercive acts. While I am not prepared to rule those acts impermissible in all circumstances (I do not, as I argue below, see them as evil in themselves), I do want to make them harder to justify than the approach above seems to suggest.

Persons and personhood

The existing proportionality consideration seems to say that the coercion of one person (cost) weighed against national security (benefit) means that the person will always lose. However, this seems to be a counter-intuitive state of affairs. As such, a resolution will lie either in decreasing the weight of the benefits or increasing the weight of the costs. I intend to do the latter, demonstrating that the coercion of the individual has wider ramifications than merely harming that individual. Through this I will argue that the coercion of an individual is an acceptable manoeuvre in intelligence gathering only in rare cases.

It is perhaps natural to see the cost of the coercion of an individual to fall on that individual. In the case of a honey trap, we may condemn that person for getting into bed with someone other than their spouse. The impact on her family is rarely considered, or if it is, the responsibility falls squarely on the shoulders of the philanderer. This, though, is at least sometimes overly simplistic. While it may be that the individual really does look to leap into bed with whomever he can find, this is by no means always the case. The target might have been sent great distances from her family and be struggling to find a sympathetic ear in her temporary location, she might be struggling to save a failing relationship, or she might have been drugged. While I am not condoning adultery, honey traps (and blackmail in general) are typically carefully thought-through attacks on vulnerable individuals and can have devastating effects on them and their families.

Torture has an even clearer detrimental impact on the individual, whether it involves physical beatings or forced stress positions, or even disorientation through kidnapping and enforced lack of sleep. We tend to be more sympathetic to the victim of torture than we are to the victim of a honey trap or other form of blackmail, and with good reason. The latter exercised at least some autonomy in getting themselves into a compromising situation, whereas the victim of torture did not. However, both cases exemplify coercive attacks not only on the individual person and their immediate family, but also on the wider community, and ultimately on what it means to be a person.

I have already referred to a number of arguments put forward by Tony Pfaff in his consideration of ethical intelligence. Pfaff's overall position is that ethical parameters should be introduced using Kantian principles – in particular the Categorical Imperative, which would have us respect the dignity of other people, refusing to use others as mere means (Pfaff 2006, p. 73). This has some interesting implications for intelligence work. There may be a level of concern about the individuals targeted by the IO to release secret documents, but ultimately those individuals are important to the IO because of the documents, not for their own worth. Granted that this is not *necessarily* the case (the agent may also be valued as a person by the IO), it is more readily identifiable in cases of coercion. In these cases the autonomy of the would-be agent is directly overridden by the coercive act in order to gain the information that the would-be agent can provide.

As noted above, Pfaff suggests that this becomes tolerable when that individual knowingly 'enters the game'. However, if we can overcome the Categorical Imperative through informed consent, then the Kantian principle ceases to act as a universal moral limit, and we are back to a more basic scenario of weighing one person's wellbeing against national security, where the conclusion of that decision is virtually predetermined.

While I have problems referring to espionage as a 'game' in any context (I find this vocabulary unpleasantly reminiscent of nineteenth-century militarism and schoolboy pranks, both of which fail to take seriously the real and potentially devastating impact coercive espionage can have on the lives of those affected), I do think that the Categorical Imperative can provide a way of understanding the value of an individual in the proportionality consideration of *jus in intelligentia*. The Categorical Imperative places a high value on the individual as one who cannot be used as a mere means. If this is right, then no coercive measures would be tolerable for the IO as long as they treat the agent as a mere means to the information he may be able to obtain. Passive surveillance and the gathering of intelligence freely offered might be justifiable, other conditions of just intelligence-gathering pertaining, but torture, blackmail and other means of coercion would not.

Employing the Categorical Imperative adds significant qualitative weight to the value of the person on whom such coercive measures will be carried out. Such measures are an assault not just on a person but on person*hood*, on what it means to be a person (at least in Kantian terms) in terms of autonomy. There is also significant quantitative weight in the value of the person who is similarly overlooked in the 'one person versus national security' argument. This quantitative weight derives from the fact that the assault on the individual through the application of coercive means does not end with the person herself. Nor does it extend merely to her family and friends but rather, I want to suggest, to the broader community.

In recent years, a similar move has been made in discussions concerning the value of privacy. Daniel Solove and Priscilla Regan have both argued that attacks on privacy tend to be viewed as an attack on the individuals whose privacy is violated. However, this oversimplifies the situation. Privacy has a value to the wider community that goes beyond the individual. As Solove writes,

> the problem with framing privacy solely in individualistic terms is that privacy becomes undervalued. Often, privacy receives inadequate protection in the form of damages to compensate individual emotional or reputational harm; the effects of the loss of privacy on freedom, culture, creativity, innovation, and public life are not factored into the valuation.
>
> *(Solove 2008, p. 89)*

He goes on: 'privacy harms affect the nature of society and impede individual activities that contribute to the greater social good' (Solove 2008, p. 92). It is not difficult to see how the debate over privacy, while involving a less coercive harm than the forms of intelligence under discussion here, has nonetheless suffered from a similar lack of imagination on the part of those considering the extent of the relevant harms.

Looking at these social harms in greater depth, Priscilla Regan has argued that there are at least three social values apparent in privacy: a common value, a public value and a collective value. The common value is the shared perception of value in a particular good; the public value lies in the value of that good to the democratic political system; and the collective value is found in the fact that it is difficult for one person to enjoy that good without all having a similar level of access to the same good (Regan 2002, p. 399; Regan 1995).

Following Solove and Regan, a similar position can and should be taken regarding autonomy-challenging coercive measures applied for the purposes of intelligence gathering. Coercive measures are therefore an assault not just on the individual, but on the community at large. As with privacy, there are at least three social values that are harmed through intelligence gathering by coercive means.

There is a common value in that we all value our autonomy and our freedom to choose our own futures. There is a public value in that our autonomy is of pivotal importance to the democratic political system. Without individual freedom to choose and vote, democracy collapses, along with the society that it protects. Finally, there is a collective value in that we share a common interest in participating in a society in which coercive practices are not tolerated. We rightly shrink from the prospect of a police state, no matter the amount of protection it may offer from criminals. The more we tolerate such coercive practices in society, the greater the likelihood that they will continue to be practised, and potentially practised more widely. Rather than being a society that condones such practices, we risk becoming a society that is typified by them. Heeding the words of Martin Niemöller, if we do not speak out for those with whom we do not associate, we risk there being no one left to speak out for us when our turn comes (as cited in Ishay 2008, p. 217).

If I am correct in these assertions, then there is a qualitative and a quantitative value to autonomy that is overlooked in the 'individual vs. national security' proportionality equation outlined above in cases of coercive intelligence gathering. The implication is that the harms involved in enacting coercive measures on an individual go far wider and far deeper than merely harming that individual person. Rather, they go to the root of what we take a person to be, and they extend to the community of persons at large. As such, these harms can be justifiably inflicted far less often than might previously have been thought.

It is worth stressing that while these harms can be justified less frequently than the individual vs. national security equation might suggest, it does not follow that coercive measures can never be justified. They are not *mala in se*. The approach that I take remains a consideration *within* the principle of proportionality, and so it can be overridden in particular circumstances. While these circumstances are by no means frequent, they are not inconceivable. This is especially true in cases such as wars fought against totalitarian regimes which, by their very nature, seek to dehumanise and denigrate what it means to be a person (Arendt 1968).

It might be countered that in cases of wars against totalitarian states we should not depart from treating the IO as a representative of the state. An IO from a liberal democracy could therefore be seen to have a special duty to uphold the values of democracy in the face of totalitarianism, which would imply maintaining the high value of personhood. At the same time, however, there is a pressing need to protect that democracy from collapse and prevent the ultimate devaluing of *all* persons living therein. In such circumstances I believe it not unfeasible that coercive measures may be justifiably employed. That is not to say that this should ever be undertaken lightly, and the remaining conditions of just intelligence should also all be met.

The conclusion is that coercive measures are tolerable as a means of intelligence only during times of war or severe national emergency, and not always even then. Coercive practices are, I believe, less justifiable in intelligence work than is often taken to be the case. In times of peace, and between allies, coercive means of intelligence are simply not justified. During war, by contrast, and particularly wars in which the value of personhood is challenged, such means may be justified.

Conclusion

Using the Categorical Imperative as a guiding principle within the proportionality consideration provides a valuable development to the existing literature, which applies the principles of Just War thinking to intelligence ethics. It leads to a more intuitive conclusion when considering the justifiability of coercive means of intelligence gathering. As a means of weighing the value of a person, this approach raises the worth of an individual so that considerations of blackmail or torture become more than a matter of one person's pain weighed against the security of a nation. It is rather the value of autonomy, in itself and as a social value, that is weighed against the security of a nation. This is a far stronger consideration than the wellbeing of one individual, albeit still not an absolute prohibition.

I will end by stressing that the conclusions to my argument are not in any way deleterious to human intelligence gathering, although they do apply more obviously to HUMINT than to SIGINT or OSINT. Human intelligence is an important aspect of the state's intelligence apparatus, and I have no problem with members of foreign states who wish to defect and bring their secrets with them. This was certainly true of many brave agents in the Cold War, who willingly risked their lives to inform the West about Soviet intentions and capabilities. The challenge I am raising relates to *coercive* methods used in intelligence. In such cases the harms visited, irrespective of whether those on whom the harms are visited see themselves participating in some great game, are often simply too great to justify.

Notes

1 It is important to note that the theory of the moral equivalence of soldiers has been strongly challenged by Jeff McMahan (2006; see also Walzer 2006 for a response to McMahan). While interesting and undeniably pertinent to the intelligence debate, I shall not develop the implications for IOs if McMahan is correct in his assertions here.
2 In saying this I am not arguing that the Nazi response to the assassination was justified, but remarking that by carrying out the assassination in the guise of Czech non-combatants, the assassins foreseeably put the lives of genuine non-combatants at risk.
3 I am grateful to Helen Morley for pointing this out to me as a possible solution.
4 For those interested in pursuing this question, I recommend Thomas Hurka's 'Proportionality in the morality of war' (Hurka 2005) or my own 'An eye for an eye: proportionality and surveillance' (Macnish 2015).

References

Arendt, H 1968, *The origins of totalitarianism*, Harcourt, New York.
Bass, GJ 2004, 'Jus post bellum', *Philosophy & Public Affairs*, vol. 32, no. 4, pp. 384–412.
Bellaby, R 2012, 'What's the harm? the ethics of intelligence collection', *Intelligence and National Security*, vol. 27, no. 1, pp. 93–117.
Cicero, MT 2006 'On duties', in GM Reichberg, H Syse & E Begby (eds), *The ethics of war*, Blackwell, Oxford.
Hulnick, AS & Mattausch, DW 1989, 'Ethics and morality in united states secret intelligence', *Harvard Journal of Law & Public Policy*, vol. 12, p. 509.

Hurka, T 2005, 'Proportionality in the morality of war', *Philosophy and Public Affairs*, vol. 33, no. 1, pp. 34–66.

ICRC 1977, *Protocol additional to the Geneva Conventions of 12 August 1949, and relating to the protection of victims of international armed conflicts (Protocol I)*, International Committee of the Red Cross, Geneva.

Ishay, MR 2008, *The history of human rights: from ancient times to the globalization era*, University of California Press, Berkeley.

Kamm, FM 2008, 'Terrorism and intending evil' *Philosophy & Public Affairs*, vol. 36, no. 2, pp. 157–186.

Macnish, K 2014, 'Just surveillance? towards a normative theory of surveillance', *Surveillance and Society*, vol. 12, no. 1, pp. 142–153.

Macnish, K 2015, 'An eye for an eye: proportionality and surveillance', *Ethical Theory and Moral Practice*, vol. 18, no. 3, pp. 529–548.

McMahan, J 2006, 'Liability and collective identity: a response to Walzer', *Philosophia*, vol. 34, pp. 13–17.

McMahan, J 2009, 'Intention, permissibility, terrorism, and war', *Philosophical Perspectives*, vol. 23, no. 1, pp. 345–372.

O'Donovan, O 2003, *The just war revisited*, Cambridge University Press, Cambridge.

Omand, D 2012, *Securing the state*, Hurst, London.

Pfaff, T 2006, 'Bungee jumping off the moral highground: ethics of espionage in the modern age', in J Goldman (ed.), *Ethics of spying: a reader for the intelligence professional*, Scarecrow Press, Oxford.

Quinlan, M 2007, 'Just intelligence: prolegomena to an ethical theory', *Intelligence and National Security*, vol. 22, no. 1, pp. 1–13.

Regan, P 1995, *Legislating privacy: technology, social values, and public policy*, University of North Carolina Press, Chapel Hill.

Regan, P 2002, 'Privacy as a common good in the digital world', *Information, Communication & Society*, vol. 5, no. 3, pp. 382–405.

Scanlon, TM 2008, *Moral dimensions: permissibility, meaning, blame*, Harvard University Press, Cambridge, MA.

Solove, DJ 2008, *Understanding privacy*, Harvard University Press, Cambridge, MA.

Thomson, JJ 1991, 'Self-defense', *Philosophy and Public Affairs*, vol. 20, no. 4, pp. 283–310.

Walzer, M 2006, 'Response to Jeff McMahan', *Philosophia*, vol. 34, pp. 19–21.

8

JUST WAR, CYBERWAR AND CYBER-ESPIONAGE

Matthew Beard

This chapter will deal, almost exclusively, with the ethical framework known as Just War theory (JWT), and show how it can be relevantly applied to matters of espionage and cyber-espionage. However, to begin with we will have to engage with a seemingly obvious question: why talk about war in a volume about espionage? Although there are connections between the two – the most obvious being their shared concern for national security – war seems to occupy a very different moral space from espionage. The former is widespread, public, involves soldiers and killing; the latter is discrete, targeted, and involves spies and deception. What is the connection between the two?

One connection is that each is a practice justifiable only when performed by states and political communities as a means of relating to other states and political communities. There may be exceptions to this, especially given the increasing number of large-scale non-state actors involved in political action. In the main, however, the right to engage in war or espionage is reserved for states or large political communities. Furthermore, both espionage and war are justified by the same duty: the duty of states to defend the rights of their citizens (Gendron 2007, p. 402; Pfaff & Tiel 2004, p. 4).

Each practice is also connected in that, when either war or espionage is justified, it seems that certain behaviours that are ordinarily prohibited are made permissible (Pfaff & Tiel 2004, p. 1). There may be a number of reasons *why* killing or deception is made permissible: the culpability of the victim, the right of killers or deceivers to defend themselves by such means, the greater good that such indiscretions might bring about, or the shared acceptance of victimhood that comes with being a soldier or a spy. What is consistent, however, is that practices of war and espionage seem to justify the violation of state and individual rights to freedom from attack, self-determination, property and privacy (to name but a few examples).

In ethical discussions of war, the questions of why, when and how sovereign or individual rights – specifically, rights against being attacked or killed by another person – no longer apply in a morally compelling sense are usually answered with reference to JWT. As Seth Lazar (2014) has noted, many just war theorists have seen war as a morally *exceptional* space in which different moral principles can be said to apply. This has led, in both academic and political discourse, to a dichotomy being identified between states of war and states of peace. However, such a claim can only be logically upheld if the exceptional principles that are said to apply to war apply *exclusively* to war (and of course, if – as Lazar argues – war is not an exclusive space, then the claim cannot be upheld).

Thus we should be scrupulous in detecting modes of thinking that treat international relations as if they could be divided between states of 'war' and 'not-war' (peace). As John Courtney Murray argues:

> I am not sure that one should talk today in these categories, 'war and/or peace,' leaving unexamined the question just what their validity is as moral and political categories. The basic fallacy is to suppose that 'war' and 'peace' are two discontinuous and incommensurable worlds of existence and universes of discourse, each with its own autonomous set of rules, 'peace' being the world of 'morality' and 'war' being the world of 'evil,' in such wise [*sic*] that there is no evil as long as there is peace and no morality as soon as there is war.
>
> *(Murray 1959, p. 54)*

This categorical approach to morality and international politics is visible in the fact that whilst international law has clearly addressed the matter of espionage in times of war, it has entirely ignored the practice of peacetime espionage (Demarest 1996, p. 330). However, this distinction is no longer helpful, since 'intelligence activities are now accepted as a common, even inherent, attribute of the modern state', and 'the success of international peace operations, and the positive contribution of non-governmental organizations to conflict resolution often depend upon timely, accurate intelligence' (Demarest 1996, p. 321). Tony Pfaff and Jeffery Tiel (2004, p. 2) argue that 'any discussion of proper intelligence operations in wartime requires an understanding of the justification and moral limits of intelligence operations in peacetime'. Intelligence is not, and ought not to be, restricted to times of war.

The strict and arbitrary distinction between war and peace is further challenged when one considers cyber-operations – the subject of this chapter. The relative ease with which both state and non-state actors can use technology to conduct espionage today means that peacetime espionage is increasingly likely. In addition, the distinction between what constitutes war and what constitutes espionage is less clear in the cyber-realm. For example, Thomas Rid (2012) argues that possible acts of cyberwar can be categorised into three different kinds: sabotage, espionage and subversion. This suggests that, at least when it comes to cyber-operations, the distinction between espionage and war is not a particularly powerful one.

In this chapter I will treat Rid's arguments regarding cyberwar's relationship to cyber-espionage as basically right, but will make some clarifications about the ways in which cyberwar and cyber-espionage are also dissimilar. I will also treat the distinction between war and peace as one not of category, but of degree. However, one need not share these views to accept the possible applicability of JWT to cyber-espionage (or to espionage more generally); other arguments (Gendron 2007; Perry 2009; Gregory 2014) exist that make similar claims without relying on the same foundational beliefs as I do here.

In what follows, I respond to critics who have suggested that JWT is not, in its present form, a remotely adequate framework through which to consider the ethics of cyberwar. I will argue that these criticisms do not hold true for cyberwar, but that, even if they were true of cyberwar, there are relevant differences between cyberwar and cyber-espionage which mean that these critiques of JWT do not hold. Thus I argue that JWT *can* be used as a means of evaluating the morality of cyber-espionage.

In the growing literature on the ethics of cyberwar, one of the few points of consensus is that cyberwar poses a new challenge for those interested in the intersection of war and ethics (De George 2003; Lin, Allhoff & Rowe 2004; Shackleford 2009; Dipert 2010; Rowe 2010). Some (Rowe 2010) think that cyberattacks are incompatible with ethics, whilst others are more positive about the prospects for the moral use of cyberwar (De George 2003; Dipert 2010). However, whichever position one takes, issues seemingly emerge from cyberwar that – at least on the surface – challenge traditional conceptions of JWT. These issues contribute to the view of cyberwar as a new type of war in itself: 'cyberwar signifies a transformation in the nature of war' (Arquilla & Ronfeldt 1993, p. 31).

Part of the transformation appears to stem from what Christian Enemark describes, in his treatment of drone pilots, as 'disembodiment' – 'activity [...] in the absence of physical risk' (Enemark 2014, p. 77). The ethical and vocational virtues and responsibilities of military service, Enemark argues, are connected to the risks taken by military personnel; in the absence of these risks, normative considerations of war ought to change. Given that cyber-espionage also disembodies its operatives in the same way, we ought to consider whether or not disembodied spying represents so radical a departure from traditional espionage as to require an entirely new ethical framework. I consider this question first, before moving on to explore how JWT's applicability to cyberwar suggests that it will be equally applicable to cyber-espionage.

Is cyber-espionage different from espionage proper?

Thomas Rid (2012) argues that possible acts of cyberwar can be categorised into three different forms: sabotage, espionage and subversion. Espionage, importantly, 'is an attempt to penetrate an adversarial system for purposes of extracting sensitive or protected information' (2012, p. 20). Sabotage involves a 'deliberate attempt to weaken or destroy an economic or military system' (p. 16), whilst subversion entails 'the deliberate attempt to undermine the authority, the integrity, and the constitution of an established authority or order' (p. 22). What distinguishes the cyber-versions of these forms of war from their conventional alternatives are the weapons or instruments used in conducting the operation: cyber-versions utilise cyber-instruments.

Rid's argument is that none of these practices alone, nor a combination of all three, can reach a level that would warrant describing the operation as an act of 'war.' Borrowing Carl von Clausewitz's (1997) criteria for war, Rid observes that typical cyber-operations have not, and probably will not, ever be able to fulfil the criteria for war (Rid 2012). I believe Rid to be wrong – mainly because his argument relies on induction in an area of rapid technological innovation and in which one cannot be assured that the future will even remotely resemble the past – but that does not matter for our purposes here. What does matter is that Rid explicates three different activities, in which states, non-state actors and individuals might all engage against one another, that are, at least some of the time, independent of war. But, importantly, these are simultaneously (and perhaps paradoxically) defined as acts of cyber-war.

Rid believes cyber-espionage to be a distinct category of cyber-operation, dedicated specifically to gathering intelligence as opposed, for instance, to destroying enemy systems (sabotage). Although there is some argument that espionage is a broader practice that includes covert action, political subversion and assassination (Perry 2009), for the purposes of this discussion, I will follow Geoffrey Demarest's definition of espionage as 'the consciously deceitful collection of information, ordered by a government or organization hostile to or suspicious of those the information concerns, accomplished by humans unauthorised by the target to do the collecting' (Demarest 1996, pp. 325–6), with cyber-espionage being the extension of these practices by way of information communication technology (ICT) systems.

Note that Demarest's description refers to the conscious and deceitful collection of information. For this reason I will not be discussing widespread cyber-surveillance policies such as the infamous PRISM program of the United States, nor related proposals of Australia and the United Kingdom. Rather, I will limit my focus to those activities in which operatives aim to collect information to which they are not entitled from specific targets.

Cyberwar and Just War theory

In a seminal article, Randall Dipert argues that cyberwar 'differ[s] from previous forms of warfare' (2010, p. 384)[1] in such a way that traditional principles of military ethics – which he argues are best represented by JWT – cannot be relevantly applied. Dipert (2010, pp. 385–95) presents three arguments in support of this position.

1. Cyberwar, unlike traditional war, does not require that permanent damage, violence or lethal force to be perpetrated in order to be used as a necessary means of conduct.

2.   Cyberattacks will not usually fit the traditional 'aggression' criteria that JWT uses. The JWT model is redundant in an age of non-physical attack, and must be reconsidered in order to account for cyberwar.
3.   JWT, being focused on distinguishing legitimate and illegitimate targets of attack, cannot adequately deal with the 'attribution problem' within cyberwar.

I will begin by discussing (1), but in so doing, will also develop an argument for (3), which is informed by (1). Dipert notes that JWT has been motivated by concerns about 'the lethality and massive destructiveness of war'. This makes cyberwar a curious case, because 'cyberwar often will not be like that' (p. 386). In fact, as Dipert's taxonomy of cyberharms shows, cyberattacks may be neither lethal nor broadly destructive. This useful taxonomy relies on a distinction in computer science between different entities: data, algorithms, the algorithm's application to the data and the hardware (p. 398). Only the latter – the damage of hardware – counts as damage that might be called 'widespread destructiveness'; harm to digital systems or data is not incorporated in existing international law or principles of Just War.[2]

Dipert examines the United Nations (UN) Charter's definition of aggression as 'the threat or use of force against the territorial integrity or political independence of any state' (UN Charter 1945, ch. 1 art. 2 sec. 4) and Walzer's (2006, p. 52) similar definition of it as '[e]very violation of the territorial integrity or political sovereignty of an independent state', observing that both of these seem to place 'armed' attack at the heart of their accounts. Obviously, whether we ought to consider a cyberattack an 'armed attack' is controversial at best. Dipert argues that it is 'not obvious' why we should consider them armed attacks as this seems 'literally understood, to designate soldiers using 'arms', roughly, as artifacts for inflicting injury or death, or causing physical destruction of objects' (Dipert 2010, pp. 395–6). Existing theories of *casus belli* limit the type of attack worthy of response by war to those that are physical. How, then, should we respond to cyberattacks? Can we ever respond to a cyberattack with a conventional strike? These are questions that JWT struggles, Dipert alleges, to answer.

The next – related – concern is that cyberharms are not physical in nature. How can JWT deal with cyber when, for instance, '[a] cyberattack does not involve intrusions into the territory or airspace by soldiers or even by physical objects' (p. 397) Such an incursion does not look like the paradigmatic form of aggression (which for Dipert is Pearl Harbor). The Russian cyberattack on Estonia prompted the Estonian Prime Minister to ask: 'What's the difference between a blockade of harbors or airports of sovereign states and the blockade of government institutions and newspaper websites?' (Rid 2012, p. 7). JWT's response, Dipert seems to think, would be the presence of military forces.

Dipert's contention is that JWT's interest in physical attack and aggression makes its application to cyberwar at best unclear. He asserts that most Just War theorists tend to follow a 'view of aggression or attack as invasion or destruction' (2010, p. 396–7), citing Nicholas Fotion as evidence of this. However, this is to misrepresent Fotion, who actually posits a new (and controversial) view of *casus belli* called the 'multiple reasons process', which allows 'wars triggered by a series of small acts of aggression, assassinations, sabotage, systematic harm done to people' (Fotion 2007, pp. 76–7). Fotion, who Dipert takes to be representative, actually holds that there are just causes for war beyond aggression.

However, it might be argued that few Just War theorists subscribe to Fotion's 'multiple reasons process', and therefore Dipert's assessment of JWT still holds, even if his description of Fotion does not. This objection fails to be convincing though, as more traditional theorists – including Michael Walzer (2006) and Brian Orend (2006), both of whom Dipert cites – are more interested in aggression *vis-à-vis* a breach of states' rights (or, as classical theorists such as di Vitoria would put it, 'a wrong received' (di Vitoria, Pagden & Lawrence 1991, p. 319) than in aggression *vis-à-vis* physical attack. This is the key fact that Dipert overlooks: armed attack is *not* the key condition of aggression; it is the breach of the crucial state rights of territorial integrity and/or political sovereignty that constitutes aggression in both international law and Walzer's JWT. This broad attack on the suitability of JWT, based on the non-physical nature of cyberharm, is insubstantial because JWT already has a 'general notion of harm' centred on states' rights. What matters is (1) that harm – of any kind – is unjustly inflicted; (2) that it is great enough to justify military response (this is what JWT refers to as the 'proportionality condition'); and (3) that it is harm against either the citizens of a state or the state as a whole.

These two ideas – proportionality and (more importantly) defining aggression relative to states' rights – give a means of defending JWT against Dipert's grievance. In responding to the Estonian Prime Minister, a Just War theorist might suggest the following: there may be no difference, in principle, between these two types of blockade. Indeed, both breach the rights held by every state. However, the duration of the 'blockade' was roughly three hours and 30 minutes; a conventional blockade that lasted less than a day would not warrant military action, and neither does this 'cyberblockade'.

This third charge – the attribution problem – is not a problem for JWT and is certainly not new. Aquinas (1920, II-II, q. 40, art. 3) argued that the laying of ambushes is a justifiable strategy in war, stating that 'a soldier has to learn the art of concealing his purpose lest it come to the enemy's knowledge'. This seems to me to be true concerning anonymous attacks *during* war. Prior to war, cyberattacks will be forbidden by the *jus ad bellum* condition, which requires that war be declared publicly. Thus JWT is equipped to respond to the question of whether – and under what conditions – an anonymous attack might be justified.

A second question concerns how a state might respond to an anonymous attack. The attribution problem, that is, stems from a deeper epistemic question: 'How much justification or evidence is necessary in terms of a threshold for morally going to war?' This question, Dipert alleges, '[has] been ignored by most theorists of the morality of war' (2010, p. 393). However, ignorance of the question on the part of Just War theorists does not reveal the inadequacy of the theory itself. Indeed, JWT *can* confront – and some theorists have already considered – this very question. For instance, Grotius argues that in cases of uncertainty about the justice of one's cause, one should err on the side of peace (Grotius 2006, Bk. II, XXII.V) – meaning, in short, that one ought not to go to war.

Neither is this epistemic concern unique to cyberwar: indeed, the 'fog of war' – the inherent uncertainty of dealing with military issues – has been acknowledged by a number of theorists (Bethke Elshtain 2003, p. 102; Orend 2006, pp. 44, 114; Walzer 2006, p. 281). Another issue in which it is particularly prevalent is discussions of the morality of preventive war; a point that Dipert acknowledges (2010, p. 393). Debate continues in this area, but international law seems to require that an impending attack be certain before a response can be legitimised (Bothe 2003, p. 232; Zedalis 2005, p. 214), and certainly classical just war theorists maintain that one must be certain of a forthcoming attack before military action can be justified (di Vitoria et al. 1991, p. 316; Grotius 2006, Bk. II, I.I). Even Walzer (2006, p. 81), who permits some preventive actions ('anticipations'), requires that an enemy show 'manifest intent to injure', indicating that without at least near-certainty, one's cause will not be just.

The point here is simply that JWT is not ill-equipped or inadequate for dealing with the attribution problem from a theoretical standpoint. It will, no doubt, be very difficult for states wanting to act well in response to secretive cyberattacks, just as it is difficult for those same states to respond justly to terrorism. However, to say that JWT cannot fit the attribution problem within its theoretical framework seems incorrect. Certainly, the relative anonymity of cyberattacks is problematic, and suggestions for solutions are required, but the important point is that these solutions can come from *within* the logic of existing JWT.

The above discussion is also informative regarding cyber-espionage. Dipert expressly excludes cyber-espionage from his discussion, but cannot escape the fact that war and espionage are not easily distinguished in the cyber realm. For instance, he includes within his description of cyberattack 'intrusive cyberattacks', wherein 'malware gains access to sections of a computer's software or stored data through a site' (Dipert 2010, p. 388–9). There are a range of things that an attacker may do once he or she has access to a system, including damaging or destroying sensitive information. Similarly, instead of destroying information, one might steal it – a practice that seems consistent with at least part of what cyber-espionage entails given that, as discussed above, in cyber-espionage actors utilise ICT in order to consciously and deceitfully collect information without the knowledge of those who own that information. This is to say, in short, that a crucial element of cyber-espionage is cyberattack.

Dipert, who defines espionage as the gathering of enemy information, notes that '[t]raditionally, mere espionage has not been viewed as a *casus belli*' (2010, p. 393). He is right, but his claim that cyberattacks *can* constitute a *casus belli* if they threaten 'extensive damage to the well-being of a populace' (2010, p. 405) seems to suggest that a cyberattack that leads to an act of cyber-espionage in which critically sensitive information is stolen and the populace made vulnerable *may* constitute *casus belli*. Cyberwar and cyberespionage are not as easily to separate as many suggest.

Cyberespionage and Dipert's critiques of JWT

Above I have responded to Dipert's attack on JWT's applicability to cyberwar and suggested some ways in which cyber-espionage and cyberwar are conceptually and practically linked. However, I am also aware that not everyone will be persuaded by my response to Dipert, and I therefore want to demonstrate why, *even if* my responses to Dipert are not found compelling, Dipert's criticisms of JWT and cyberwar do not affect the possible applicability of JWT to cyber-espionage.

Much of the strength of Dipert's argument stems from the claim that cyberwar, according to many theorists, marks such a radical departure from conventional war that existing modes of ethical reasoning about warfare cannot be usefully applied to it (Dipert 2010). A similar claim is advanced by Enemark (2014) with regard to drone pilots and military practice. However, the same is not true of cyber-espionage. Espionage taking place in digital space does not radically depart from existing intelligence practices, and therefore does not demand the development of entirely new ethical frameworks for evaluation. Thus, even if my response to Dipert in defence of JWT's applicability to cyberwar fails, it holds true for cyberespionage. I will demonstrate this with reference to each of Dipert's three objections in turn.

The first of Dipert's objections concerns the non-kinetic dimensions of cyberwarfare. The moral framework of JWT is designed to govern the ethics of killing and causing physical harm – something that is not necessary to cyberwar. Traditional discussions of the morality of going to war, or morality in war, understandably have been motivated by the lethality and destructiveness of war. But cyberwarfare will not often display these same qualities, although in some cases it could be both lethal and physically destructive (Dipert 2010, 386).

Considerations of the morality of war begin with the recognition that killing people is *prima facie* wrong (Carrick 2008, p. 195) and then explore the conditions under which killing might, nevertheless, be justified. Traditional JWT's assessment of possible justifications for killing do not fit well with cyberwar, where killing is (although possible) not an intrinsic aspect of the practice (which is, primarily, the use of computer software and technology by one nation to attack the governmental or civilian information systems of another nation). Because the moral challenges that underpin cyberwar are different from those that underpin traditional war, Dipert argues that JWT, in its current form, is not a suitable moral framework.

However, even if Dipert's charge is plausible, the same charge cannot be levelled against cyber-espionage because, as Peter W. Singer explains, 'cyberespionage is the use and targeting of computers to obtain a secret of some sort (Singer 2014, p. 93)'. What is different about traditional and cyber-espionage is not – as Dipert claims of cyberwar – the act itself, but simply its means. Singer's discussion continues by noting that 'much like other forms if espionage [cyber-espionage] is clandestine [...] and usually involves a government agency' (2014, p. 93). That is to say, cyber-espionage simply *is* the next stage in the evolution of espionage practices.

Consider an example: the leadership of a nation X wants to know if members of the ruling party of its rival, Y, intend to order a sudden invasion in response to growing tensions in the region. Fifty years ago, they would have ordered intelligence operatives to infiltrate Y's infrastructure (in fact, X would probably already have 'sleeper' agents in place) and search records in order to find formal evidence of an intention to invade, to eavesdrop on conversations that might be relevant and exploit the lax security practices of low-level employees that might have important information.

Today, if X had the same desire, they would take similar steps. They would begin by penetrating the digital infrastructure of Y's government departments – most likely through vulnerabilities caused by non-vigilant employees. Following this, they would search records in order to find formal evidence of an intention to invade and eavesdrop on email and webcam conversations, amongst other things. The only difference lies in the means. In this sense, cyber-espionage is no different from wire-tapping, in the sense that this technology allowed one to overhear a conversation without being within earshot.

Although access to the means of conducting espionage has broadened and, in many senses, spying has become much easier due to the ubiquity of ICT (Singer 2014, p. 93), it is not true that cyber-espionage is a staggeringly different practice altogether, even if the same cannot be said of war. This accounts for the first of Dipert's three objections.

Dipert's second argument regards the 'aggression-centric' model of JWT, whereby aggression – a 'violation of the territorial integrity or political sovereignty of an independent state' (Walzer 2006, p. 52) – is understood as the primary, if not only, just cause for war. A necessary condition for just war, on prevailing understandings, is that the aggression constitutes an 'armed attack' (Orend 2006, p. 32). By armed attack, Brian Orend (who is representative of a consensus in this respect) refers explicitly to physical violence. Trade embargoes, for instance, cannot – no matter how severe – constitute aggression because the means by which this type of violence (vis-à-vis 'rights-violating action') is inflicted does not require the expenditure of physical force. It is unclear, for instance, whether purely digital incursions constitute aggression to which a state might ever justifiably respond with physical force, or whether they could ever be dire enough to warrant war as a response.

Dipert rightly highlights some problems with this definition for JWT generally, but in particular for cyberwar:

> An unprovoked cyberattack by one nation on the civilian or military infrastructure of another nation is thus not very much like traditional, paradigmatic forms of aggression or attack. A cyberattack does not involve intrusions into the territory or airspace by soldiers or even by physical objects.
>
> *(Dipert 2010, p. 397)*

However, this second objection also fails when it comes to espionage, because the distinction between the physical and the non-physical is simply not relevant to spying. This is because spying is not aggression-centric in the way that war is, as evidenced by recent claims that more work is required in the area of *peacetime* espionage. Furthermore, whatever justifies espionage, it is certainly not actual physical damage. As Angela Gendron (2007, p. 418) argues, it is unrealistic in the extreme to think that espionage might only be justified in the same circumstances that war is justified. Rather, espionage constitutes what Michael Walzer (2006, xv) describes as *jus ad vim* – force short of war – and therefore requires a lower threshold of justification.

Furthermore, spying is not about damage, it is about knowledge – which means that the distinction between the physical and non-physical is largely spurious. All knowledge is ultimately non-physical. Prior to the emergence of widespread ICT, spying consisted in stealing or copying documents, tapping phones to eavesdrop on conversations, converting individuals into 'false-flag' agents by means of coercion or blackmail, and so on. Perry (1995) describes the activities of intelligence agents as being characterised by (amongst other things) persuasion, coercion, deception and manipulation. Each of these activity-types aims at learning something about the enemy or potential enemy. Ethical espionage will set moral limits on who, for instance, can be deceived, coerced or manipulated, but these standards are about potential targets *vis-à-vis* their culpability and rights; not in regard to their physical embodiment. Whether I am blackmailed with information that was stolen from an envelope or stolen from my hard drive does not matter; by contrast, whether I am attacked by a computer virus or by the payload of an air strike matters a great deal.

The third challenge Dipert lists is the so-called 'attribution problem'. The problem, put simply, is that cyberattacks are usually undertaken under the guise of anonymity. The use of proxies, dummy computers and masked IP addresses means that it can be incredibly difficult for victims of a well constructed cyberattack to determine who it is that perpetrated the attack, or worse, who is presently attacking them. This poses a challenge for Just War theory because, as we will see, the theory is predicated on the belief that those who are demonstrably culpable of serious ethical transgressions can be met with armed and forceful attack if necessary; if the source of an attack cannot be identified, one of Just War theory's foundational premises is undermined. Furthermore, the 'spirit' of the Just War tradition invokes the notion that war is, in an important sense, public. For example, historically, most versions of Just War theory have insisted that for a war to be justified it must, amongst other things, have been publicly declared. Where there is the possibility of attacking one's enemy without leaving evidence of one's attack, it becomes more difficult for states and individuals to be held to the other moral standards that Just War theory posits and defends. Thus difficulties in identifying the source of an attack do represent real and problematic challenges to the direct application of Just War theory to war waged in cyberspace.

However, here too (perhaps especially so) the analogy does not extend to espionage. Espionage is intended to be secret and therefore has always intentionally been about obfuscation. This is to say that when it comes to espionage, the attribution problem is implied and inescapable. For some, such as Immanuel Kant (1983 [1795], p. 110), the inherent dishonesty of spying might mean that it is justifiable in wartime, but a slippery slope leads inescapably to the use of spies in peacetime. This seems to me to be an acceptable view; but if we are to claim, as I think we can, that espionage can be a morally acceptable practice, then we have to accept that anonymity, whether through false passports or false IP addresses, is acceptable in practice.

I have shown that arguments against a moral continuity between war and cyberwar, on which Dipert's critique of JWT rests, are not applicable to cyber-espionage. In fact, cyber-espionage is teleologically analogous to traditional forms of espionage in the sense that each is ultimately concerned with knowledge and information. Although espionage is, in important senses, grounded by the moral importance of the state and the need to secure it against possible threats, its aspirations are epistemological: to obtain information about the activities of others, and to provide mis-information regarding one's own activities. The question that remains is how we ought to think about activities aimed at collecting information or spreading mis-information when they are performed online.

Discussions of espionage and cyber-espionage call into focus the foundational premise of the ethics of espionage – namely that (amongst other things) state-sanctioned deception, fraud and theft of information can be morally justified by the state. This claim is tested at length elsewhere in this volume, and can also be viewed through the lens of JWT (c.f. Perry 2009), but I do not have time to address it here. Rather, I wish to suggest that *if* such an evaluation of either espionage or cyber-espionage was to be undertaken, the examiner might consider JWT a viable framework within which to evaluate it.

Acknowledgements

A version of this chapter was originally published as Beard, M 2013, 'Cyberwar and Just War theory', in Center for Applied Ethics and Philosophy (ed.), Applied ethics, risk, justice and liberty, Centre for Applied Ethics and Philosophy, Hokkaido.

Notes

1 All references to Dipert are – unless specified otherwise – from this 2010 article.
2 There is, however (as I understand it), a sense in which this type of damage is physical in nature: although software changes do not correlate to the destruction of any physical object, they do cause a change in the storage systems of that object, where the data are physically manifest in magnetic signals on the hard drive. Thus the deletion or alternation of data does correlate to a physical change. One can destroy data from within a computer, but also by exposing the hard drive to substantial magnetic energy. I do not think this undermines Dipert's argument, but it is worth noting that there is a physical component to the harm here. Cyberattacks are a nuanced type of attack, but they are not entirely non-physical. The equivalent would be perhaps to say that psychological harms are not non-physical insofar as they correspond to changes in parts of the victim's brain/mind.

References

Aquinas, T 1920, *The summa theologica of St. Thomas Aquinas*, trans. Fathers of the English Dominican Province, New Advent, www.newadvent.org/summa

Arquilla, J & Ronfeldt, D 1993, 'Cyberwar is coming!', *Comparative Strategy*, vol. 12, no. 2, pp. 141–165.

Beard, M 2013, 'Cyberwar and Just War theory', in *Applied ethics, risk, justice and liberty*, Centre for Applied Ethics and Philosophy, Hokkaido.

Bethke Elshtain, J 2003, *Just war against terror: the burden of American power in a violent world*, Basic Books, New York.

Bothe, M 2003, 'Terrorism and the legality of pre-emptive force', *European Journal of International Law*, vol. 14, pp. 27–240.

Carrick, D. 2008, 'The future of ethics education in the military', in P Robinson, N De Lee & D Carrick (eds), *Ethics education in the military*, Ashgate, Aldershot.

von Clausewitz, C 1997, *On war*, trans. JJ Graham, Wordsworth, Ware.

De George, R 2003, 'Post-September 11: computers, ethics and war', *Ethics and Information Technology*, vol. 5, pp. 183–190.

Demarest, Lt Col. GB 1996, 'Espionage in international law', *Denver Journal of International Law and Policy*, vol. 24, pp. 321–348.

Dipert, RR 2010, 'The ethics of cyberwarfare', *Journal of Military Ethics*, vol. 9, no. 4, pp. 384–410.

Enemark, C 2014, *Armed drones and the ethics of war: military virtue in a post-heroic age*, Routledge, London.

Fotion, N 2007, *War and ethics: a new just war theory*, Continuum, London.

Gendron, A 2007, 'Just war, just intelligence: an ethical framework for foreign espionage', *International Journal of Intelligence and Counterintelligence*, vol. 18, no. 3, pp. 398–434.

Gregory, E 2014, 'What do we want from the just war tradition? New challenges of surveillance and the security state', *Studies in Christian Ethics*, vol. 27, no. 1, pp. 50–62.

Grotius, H 2006 [1625], 'The rights of war and peace' in G Reichberg, H Syse & E Begby (eds), *The ethics of war: classic and contemporary readings*, Blackwell Publishing, Victoria.

Kant, I 1983 [1795], *Perpetual peace and other essays*, trans. T Humphrey, Hackett, Indianapolis.

Lazar, S 2014, 'Political philosophy and war' in H Frowe & S Lazar (eds.), *Oxford handbook on the ethics of war*, Oxford University Press, Oxford.

Lin, P, Allhoff, F & Rowe, N 2004, 'War 2.0: cyberweapons and ethics', *Viewpoints*, vol. 55, no. 3, pp. 24–27.

Murray, JC 1959, 'Remarks on the moral problem of war', *Theological Studies*, vol. 20, pp. 40–61.

Orend, B 2006, *The morality of war*, Broadview, Toronto.

Perry, DL 1995, '"Repugnant philosophy": ethics, espionage, and covert action', *Journal of Conflict Studies*, vol. 15, www.scu.edu/ethics/publications/submitted/Perry/repugnant.html

Perry, DL 2009, *Partly cloudy: ethics of war, espionage, covert action, and interrogation*, Scarecrow Press, Lanham, MA.

Pfaff, T & Tiel, JR 2004, 'The ethics of espionage', *Journal of Military Ethics*, vol. 3, no. 1, pp. 1–15.

Rid, T 2012, 'Cyberwar will not take place', *Journal of Strategic Studies*, vol. 35, no. 1, pp. 5–32.

Rowe, N 2010, 'The ethics of cyberweapons in warfare', *International Journal of Cyberethics*, vol. 1, no. 1, pp. 20–31.

Shackleford, S 2009, 'From nuclear war to net war: analogizing cyber attacks in international law', *Berkley Journal of International Law*, vol. 25, no. 3, pp. 193–251.

Singer, PW 2014, *Cybersecurity and cyberwar: what everybody needs to know*, Oxford University Press, Oxford.

UN Charter 1945, *Charter of the United Nations*, www.un.org/en/documents/charter/chapter7. shtml

di Vitoria, F, Pagden, A & Lawrence, L 1991, *Vitoria: political writings*, Cambridge University Press, Cambridge.

Walzer, M 2006, *Just and unjust wars*, 4th edn, Basic Books, New York.

Zedalis, R 2005, 'Circumstances justifying pre-emptive self-defense: thoughts prompted by the military action against Iraq', *Nordic Journal of International Law*, vol. 74, pp. 209–230.

9

A DILEMMA FOR INDISCRIMINATE PRE-EMPTIVE SPYING

Nicolas Tavaglione

Spying takes many forms. One may spy on specific individuals or groups on the basis of prior intelligence, in order to verify some specific suspicions or to accumulate more evidence: this is discriminate reactive spying. Standard espionage novels for the most part utilise discriminate reactive spying and this is how the term 'spying' is widely understood in popular culture. At least since Gary Marx's classical study of undercover police surveillance (Marx 1989), moreover, discriminate reactive spying has attracted a great deal of scholarly attention.

But one may also spy indiscriminate targets *en masse* on the basis of no prior intelligence, in order to identify suspect individuals. This is 'PRISM-style' indiscriminate pre-emptive spying. Somehow combining the old-fashioned logic of dragnet police operations with the contemporary trend towards 'preventive justice' (Ashworth & Zedner 2014) and the new potential of Big Data (Mayer-Schönberger & Cukier 2013), indiscriminate pre-emptive spying was brought to public attention by the Snowden revelations in 2013. Until that point, indiscriminate spying was considered a means of totalitarian intimidation on the Stasi model (Los 2006), not as an element in the pre-emptive toolkit developed by liberal democracies after 9/11. Thus the concept of indiscriminate *pre-emptive* spying, as distinguished from indiscriminate *intimidative* spying, is an offspring of the Snowden revelations. Being some sort of novelty, it has not yet received much scholarly attention.

In this chapter I focus on indiscriminate pre-emptive spying (henceforth IPS) and develop the following argument. At first glance we have very strong reasons to condemn IPS: it violates moral and legal prohibitions against invading privacy, and it thus wrongs its targets – namely whole populations around the globe – even if they do not know that their privacy is being invaded. (And if the schemes of NSA leaders had been successful, we would still have no such clue.) Such a preliminary verdict, however, draws on some very strong assumptions. First, moral and legal prohibitions may never be violated: this is *absolutism*. Second, being wronged without being harmed is possible. Since the targets of IPS do not know that they are being spied upon, espionage has no effect on them. And since it has no effect, it causes no harm to them. Therefore, if there is something morally problematic with IPS, it must be a wrong without a harm. Let us call that *pure-wrongism*.

My argument starts from assumptions that are far more favourable to IPS. Let us give up both absolutism and pure-wrongism. First, let us admit that moral principles are defeasible: on some occasions, it may be morally justified not to abide by them. Second, let us grant for the sake of argument that pure-wrongism is false: there is no such thing as a wrong without a harm. Maybe there are occasions where prohibitions against invading privacy are defeated by stronger countervailing reasons. Perhaps spying on innocent targets is morally justifiable provided we make sure that they do not suffer any harm. From this morally cooler viewpoint, it is therefore not clear that IPS is (always and everywhere) condemnable.

I shall argue that in order for IPS to be morally acceptable, even if we give up absolutism and pure-wrongism, two conditions (at least) must be met. First, IPS ought to be necessary – as is the case each time one envisions violating some well established moral presumption. For example, if I want to violate the presumption against killing in a situation of self-defence, my using lethal force ought to be necessary to repel the attack. Second, IPS ought to follow as far as possible the model of 'perfect voyeurism' – i.e. 'covert watching or listening that is neither discovered nor publicized' (Doyle 2009, p. 181), where I accumulate masses of information about a person's private life without ever imposing any harm on that person.

From this perspective, however, it appears that IPS is caught in a dilemma. Either it conforms to the model of 'perfect voyeurism', and in such a case it cannot be necessary for it cannot even be useful in the first place. Or it gives itself the means of being useful and thus potentially necessary, but then it cannot conform to the model of 'perfect voyeurism'. Either way, it cannot be morally acceptable. As a consequence, there is no hope of justifying PRISM-style surveillance.

The argument will proceed as follows. In part 1, I present the first horn of the dilemma – the necessity condition. In part 2, I defend the second horn of the dilemma – the requirement of 'perfect voyeurism'. In part 3, I discuss the dilemma and examine whether supporters of IPS could find some way out.

Moral presumptions and the necessity condition

If we give up absolutism, then standard moral principles are best seen as general moral presumptions: they hold as long as they are not defeated by stronger countervailing reasons. I ought not to lie; but it may be the case that some particular lie is justified by the need not to hurt someone or to avert some preventable disaster. I ought not to kill; but it may be the case that some particular killing is justified by the need to defend myself or someone else against an unjust attack. I ought not to steal; but it may be the case that some particular theft is justified by the need to save a life – as in Peter Unger's thought experiment where I have to steal a yacht from its legitimate owner in order to sail off the coast to save a woman in danger of drowning (Unger 1996, pp. 63ff). On the same model, I ought not to invade your privacy by collecting personal information about your religious, sexual or political life. But in certain circumstances, such a prohibition may be defeated: if I am a detective and I have specific suspicions about your having committed a murder, I may be justified in wiretapping your phone in order to collect evidence. Defeasible moral presumptions are commonplace in applied ethical reasoning.[1]

Equally commonplace, however, are constraints on defeasibility. Constraints on defeasibility have been elaborated with utmost clarity in relation to self-defence in the face of both the law and morality (e.g. Fletcher 1988; Rodin 2002). We admit a legal and moral presumption against killing other human beings. This presumption is notoriously defeasible when it comes to defending oneself against the potentially lethal attack of an unjust aggressor. But defeasibility is subjected to strict constraints. Suppose A is victim to a potentially lethal attack by B. According to the standard logic of self-defence, A may fight back with potentially lethal force provided among other things that: (i) A's use of force is causally efficient in repelling the attack; (ii) A has no less violent means to escape the assault; and (iii) the amount of force used by A is proportionate to the attack by B (if B only pinches A, A may not shoot B in the head). It thus appears that self-defensive force ought to be *necessary*, where 'being necessary' means 'being a non-substitutable means (to a given end)'. If condition (i) is violated, then A's use of force is useless and cannot be seen as a *means* to the end of self-preservation. If condition (ii) is violated, there are less problematic routes to self-preservation and A's use of force is a *substitutable* means. If condition (iii) is violated, finally, there are equally efficient routes to self-preservation, and A's use of that specific amount of force is *substitutable* again.

The defeasibility of the prohibition against killing is thus strictly codified. And that should come as no surprise, since the issues at hand – life and death and peaceful social coexistence – are of particular importance. But my point here is that such constraints on defeasibility are not exclusive to self-defence. Imagine that I envision doing act *a*, where there is a moral principle P according to which *a* is forbidden. To conclude that P is defeasible and that I may do *a*, it is not sufficient to mention another principle, Q, according to which *a* is permitted or obligatory. Suppose act *a* is a lie, and it thus falls under the moral presumption against lying. To conclude that the presumption against lying is defeated in this particular case, it is not sufficient to mention the principle of non-malevolence commanding that one should minimise harm done to others and to add that on some occasions non-malevolence justifies lying. I need to make sure that *this particular lie* is necessary in order to minimise harm. My lie *a* could fail to be necessary in order to minimise harm in one or several of three possible ways. First, my lie *a* could fail to be necessary because it has no causal efficacy: *a* does not cause any reduction in harm. Second, my lie *a* could fail to be necessary because there are other less costly ways to minimise harm (I could remain silent, for example). Third, my lie *a* could fail to be necessary because it is disproportionate: lying about event *e1* would be sufficient, but I lie about events *e1, e2* and *e3* – such that my lie is overreaching. Or suppose that act *a* is a theft, and it thus falls under the prohibition against stealing. But this particular act of theft could make it possible for me to help my friend Mafalda to pay for some expensive medical treatment of which she is in dire need. And I take seriously the principle of friendship according to which one ought to help one's friends as much as one can. Act *a* is thus condemned by one principle and recommended by another. May I conclude that the prohibition on stealing is defeated in those circumstances? Not exactly. I would first have to make sure that (i) my theft was causally efficient (will Mafalda accept the money?); (ii) there were no other less costly ways to help Mafalda with her predicament (could I not borrow the money from a rich cousin of mine?); and (iii) my booty was proportionate to Mafalda's needs (is it necessary to steal £10,000 when Mafalda's medical treatment only costs £2,000?). What I shall call the *necessity condition of defeasibility* is the conjunction of these three requirements of causal efficacy, absence of less costly alternative means, and proportionality.

Of course, the necessity condition does not exhaust all constraints on defeasibility. Classically, the main constraint bears on the relative weight of the goods protected by the conflicting principles: I may not kill someone in the name of etiquette or for the sake of making a good joke; good manners or a sense of humour, while valuable, do not outweigh the preservation of human life. Weighing goods is a tricky business (e.g. Hurka 2005). But that should not preoccupy us here, for we will admit without further ado, for the sake of argument, that the good aimed at by IPS, namely security, is of sufficient importance to compete with the good of privacy. And we shall accept that balancing security and privacy does not raise an epistemic problem.[2] For our present purposes, the necessity condition is sufficient.

Let us take a look at IPS, then. Since we have given up absolutism, the prohibition on invading privacy is nothing but a moral presumption and as such it can be defeated. But its being defeated is subject to the necessity condition. There is nothing very original in this claim. For instance, Persson and Hansson, in relation to privacy in the workplace, admit that 'employees have a prima facie right to privacy, but this right can be overridden by competing moral principles' (Persson & Hanson 2003, p. 59). In my own terminology, they admit that employees are protected by a moral presumption against invading their privacy that can be 'overridden by competing moral principles'. But such a defeat is subjected to four constraints, three of which are of direct interest to us. First, 'the means chosen are efficient to obtain the required information' – this is the requirement of causal efficiency. Second, 'the least intrusive means to obtain the required information are chosen' – this is the requirement of the absence of less costly alternative means. Third, 'the resulting intrusion into the employee's privacy is not so severe as to outweigh the employer's interests' – this is the requirement of proportionality (2003, p. 66). Taken together, these three conditions offered by Persson and Hansson impose the necessity condition on workplace invasions of privacy.

IPS consists in deploying high-tech means in order to record mediated communications between hundreds of thousands of individuals on an indiscriminate basis. It may be the case that protecting the security of American citizens and

American interests defeats the presumption against invading privacy, and defeats it with regard to innocent citizens and denizens who have done nothing to specifically forfeit their 'right' to privacy. If that is the case, however, proponents of IPS must make it sure that IPS satisfies the necessity condition. They should ascertain, therefore, that (i) IPS will have causal efficacy in thwarting terrorist plots, preventing attacks and arresting enemy combatants; (ii) there are no other less costly ways to achieve the same goal; and (iii) the amount of surveillance deployed is proportionate to the goal. Here is the first horn of the dilemma.

Perfect voyeurism

Among the common presumptions of ordinary morality we not only find the prohibition against invading privacy, but also the prohibition against wronging innocent people. IPS, like more garden varieties of surveillance, may by hypothesis defeat the first; but how does it fare regarding the second? In contrast with discriminate reactive spying, it concerns virtually anyone in the target population. And 'virtually anyone' implies 'many innocent persons' – in any case, many more innocent persons than malevolent terrorists and mischievous criminals. Whereas discriminate reactive spying – say, wiretapping – may be justified by the demands of a criminal investigation and authorised by competent judicial overseers provided there is a reasonable suspicion of criminal behaviour or intent, indiscriminate preemptive spying cannot be so warranted. Because it is indiscriminate, it targets unsuspected individuals in order to ascertain that, so to speak, they are legitimately unsuspected. Data mining is supposed to discover suspect behavioural patterns or suspect communication networks among *ex ante* unsuspected targets. Therefore any requirement of reasonable suspicion would be irrelevant with regard to IPS. Technically and until proven otherwise, therefore, IPS targets are innocent.

If this is so, however, IPS targets are protected by the fundamental common presumption against wronging innocent people. Therefore IPS ought not to wrong any of its targets. But how can that be possible, since by definition IPS invades their privacy? It is possible because pure-wrongism has been rejected for the sake of argument. According to pure-wrongism, it is possible to wrong people without causing them any tangible harm: harmless wrongs are possible. Imagine I am a Jehovah's Witness and on Monday I clearly told my doctor that I would refuse a blood transfusion whatever the circumstances. On Tuesday I crash my car and am severely hurt. During the subsequent operation, it becomes clear to the doctor that I urgently require a blood transfusion. Since I am under anaesthesia, I won't know about what happens during the operation. The doctor thus decides to transfer blood against my explicit will, and does not inform me afterwards. In such a case, it does not sound absurd to claim that I have been wronged – after all, an autonomous choice I made has been deliberately disregarded. But I did not suffer any harm; quite the contrary: my autonomy being violated contributed to my interest in staying alive being promoted. The story thus neatly illustrates the possibility of harmless wrongs – and we could imagine many more such stories.

It may even be the case that rejecting the possibility of harmless wrongs is doomed to absurdity. Consider the following case of causal overdetermination imagined by Parfit (1984, p. 70): 'X and Y simultaneously shoot and kill me. Either shot, by itself, would have killed.' If X had not shot, I would still have been killed. If Y had not shot, again, I would still have been killed. From a causal viewpoint, it thus appears that neither X nor Y made a difference. Therefore neither X nor Y has caused me any harm. And we seem bound to conclude that none of them wronged me. Which is absurd. Yet one natural way to eschew absurdity, though not the only one, is to admit the possibility of harmless wrongs: even if neither X or Y caused me any harm, each of them wronged me. Thus the idea of harmless wrongs has some solid credentials and pure-wrongism is far from odd (for an extensive discussion of harmless wrongs, the *locus classicus* is Feinberg 1986). This idea has been put to use to criticise invasions of privacy such as voyeurism, which can be defined as a kind of spying motivated by personal psychological drives. What is wrong with voyeurism? This question has been posed by Nathan (1990). His answer strives to go beyond the consequentialist focus on potential harm. For the consequentialist approach to voyeurism, Nathan convincingly argues, leads to the following conclusion: when kept genuinely secret, voyeurism does not cause any physical or mental harm to its victim. From a consequentialist viewpoint, therefore, undetected voyeurism cannot be considered objectionable. It follows that 'the more 'careful' a spy one is, the less morally culpable one becomes' (Nathan 1990, p. 368). Such a conclusion is absurd, says Nathan. The perfect voyeur whose spying goes 'undetected and unpublicized' is not harming anyone; but we should acknowledge that wronging without harm is possible; this way, we can resist the conclusion that the perfect voyeur is less culpable than the clumsy one. And Nathan's analysis of the harmless wrongdoing of perfect voyeurism is germane to the case of the Jehovah's Witness above. Purposively deceiving his victims, the perfect voyeur deprives them of the possibility of assenting to 'what is going on' (1990, p. 370) thus treating them as a mere means and violating the Kantian Formula of Humanity. In Nathan's words, 'such deception violates the obligation to treat humanity as an end in itself by failing to take seriously the victim's capacity for autonomous choice' (1990, p. 370).

Now IPS can be seen as a kind of non-pathological political voyeurism. According to Nathan's pure-wrongism, then, IPS necessarily wrongs innocent targets by deceiving them, depriving them of the possibility of assenting or dissenting with regard to their being closely observed and failing to treat them as ends in themselves. And this is true whether or not IPS is in addition harming them. It follows that IPS cannot meet the necessity condition because it violates the requirement of proportionality: in order to catch a handful of actual or potential terrorists, it wrongs hundreds of thousands – possibly even millions of innocent people.

But I have decided to reject pure-wrongism under the principle of charity. So we shall henceforth reflect on the issue as if pure-wrongism were false. It follows that while IPS necessarily invades its targets' privacy, it does not necessarily wrong them: let's admit that if I am not aware of my privacy being invaded, I incur no harm and therefore am not wronged. If I am aware of being spied upon, I know that my interest in privacy is being frustrated; I may start to worry about how the personal data collected about me will be used and with whom they will be shared; I may be afraid of being the object of so much state attention; I may come to feel the 'chilling effect' of surveillance and to alter my natural behaviour out of fear of upsetting the authorities. Surely no average person would want to attract suspicion from Washington. Nobody wants a US drone in his or her backyard. Thus it seems beyond dispute that detected and publicised IPS harms its targets. And it also seems beyond dispute that harming innocent people entails wronging them. For the sake of proportionality, such a massive wrong cannot be morally acceptable. Henceforth, for IPS to be morally justifiable it must follow the model of perfect voyeurism according to Doyle (2009): it must remain undiscovered, unpublicised and unexploited. It must be flawless spying without effect. And the spies involved must be on 'Mars, or 100 light years away' (Doyle 2009, p. 181). Here is the second horn of the dilemma.

The dilemma

We can now see why IPS is caught in a dilemma. In order to be morally justified, IPS must satisfy the two following requirements:

i   *necessity*: IPS must be necessary – i.e. it must be causally efficient, there must be no other less costly alternatives and it must be proportionate;
ii *perfect voyeurism*: IPS must follow the model of perfect voyeurism – it must remain undetected, unpublicised and unexploited.

But these two requirements cannot both be met at the same time. On one hand, for IPS to be causally efficient, it cannot remain unexploited. Furthermore, if it is exploited, it runs the risk of being detected – the Snowden revelations are a case in point. Satisfying the requirement of necessity thus entails violating the requirement of perfect voyeurism. On the other hand, for IPS to be perfect voyeurism, it cannot be causally efficient. Satisfying the requirement of perfect voyeurism thus entails violating the requirement of necessity. Either way, IPS fails to satisfy one of the two constraints on moral justification. We must conclude that IPS cannot be morally justified. PRISM-style surveillance is thus necessarily immoral.

For IPS, this is very bad news. Indeed this conclusion, it must be stressed, is based on four highly charitable concessions. First, the argument works without assuming either moral absolutism or pure-wrongism. Hence it cannot be rebutted as biased against surveillance in general or IPS in particular. Because it does not rely on some form of privacy-absolutism, it easily escapes the charge of 'civil-libertarian panic'. And because it does not rely on pure-wrongism and its largely Kantian underpinnings, it cannot be accused of deontological squeamishness. Second, the argument also concedes that security is an undisputable good, *pace* Zedner (2003) for instance, and that the idea of striking a balance between security and civil liberties is not a meaningless piece of neoconservative propaganda, *pace* Waldron (2003) and Holmes (2009) among many others. Third, the argument does not take into consideration all constraints on defeasibility that can be reasonably contemplated. For example it does not dwell on Bellaby's 'Just Intelligence' principle of discrimination between legitimate and illegitimate targets. According to Bellaby (2012, p. 116), one should distinguish 'between those individuals without involvement in a threat (and thereby protected), and those who have made themselves a part of the threat (and by so doing have become legitimate targets)'.

Obviously, such a principle would condemn IPS right from the start. Finally, the argument is purposively neutral with respect to a vast array of potential political objections against IPS. For example, it remains silent about citizenship issues and democratic accountability (Applbaum 1992; Kutz 2009; Sagar 2007). The stage is thus set for IPS to obtain victory. In spite of that, it loses. But does it really? Let us examine three possible objections.

(i) To begin with, one may question the validity of the requirement of perfect voyeurism. There is no problem with the necessity condition, for it is closely linked to basic instrumental rationality. But why on earth should we admit the requirement of perfect voyeurism if it makes IPS incompatible with efficiency? Of course, we have good reasons to keep IPS secret – for unsuspicious targets will probably give out more information than suspicious ones. Yet this is merely an instrumental consideration. Since invading privacy may be justified on the grounds of security, let us only examine whether a given act of spying is necessary to promote security. Yet unfortunately, that will not do. For if a given act or programme of spying involves wronging one million innocent people in exchange for catching three, ten or even a hundred terrorists, then the requirement of proportionality gets frustrated. Henceforth the act or program of spying under consideration does not satisfy necessity. The only way to escape this proportionality problem is to make sure that the act or programme of spying does not wrong, and hence does not harm one million innocent people. As such, we fall back on the requirement of perfect voyeurism.

(ii) But maybe the case for perfect voyeurism is overstated. In a scenario of successful IPS, only suspect individuals or groups will be harmed. IPS proceeds and data mining reveals that Doctor Mephisto is a suspect from an NSA viewpoint: His 'social graph' has worrying connections to Waziristan, he often visits radical Salafi websites and we know from his Amazon account that he bought seven chemistry handbooks in the past few months. So we decide to start spying on *him* more closely and we ask all the required judicial authorisations to intensify surveillance. Doctor Mephisto thus becomes the target of discriminate spying. The suspicion is confirmed, Doctor Mephisto is arrested on charges of terrorist conspiracy, and the story ends here. Apart from Doctor Mephisto, nobody suffered from IPS. There is no need, then, to keep IPS unexploited – as the model of perfect voyeurism would have it. Provided the use of intelligence is discriminate enough, there is no reason to insist that IPS be unexploited. But here comes the press, asking disturbing questions. Why has Doctor Mephisto has been arrested? What are the charges against him? Where does the evidence come from? The only way to keep IPS secret now would be to thwart the process of free public information. And this, surely, harms the body politic: citizens have an interest in knowing what the state is doing, and this interest is frustrated (for an excellent analysis of the conflict between state secrecy and democratic accountability, see Sagar 2009). Conversely, if the free press does its job, then IPS cannot remain undetected. The general public discovers that privacy has been massively invaded and the many harms caused by the awareness of being spied upon now enter the stage. The optimistic story above is therefore far too simplistic. The only realistic way to make sure that IPS does not harm innocent people is to keep it unexploited, even against the bad guys.

(iii) There may be a logical flaw in the argument. As is well known, 'ought' implies 'can'. And my argument has the following structure: IPS ought to respect two requirements, X and Y; but it is impossible to respect both X and Y at the same time; therefore IPS cannot respect both X and Y. As a consequence, it is false that IPS ought to respect both X and Y. As a first rejoinder, one may first take a critical look at the ought–can principle. Some authors (Gowans 1994, p. 140; Stocker 1990, pp. 95–6) invite us to think about cases like the following: I borrow £10,000 from my friend Jimmy, promising him to repay my debt on the first of July. But I am pathologically unable to manage a budget and on 30 June I am completely bankrupt. On 1 July I cannot repay my debt. If the ought–can principle is true, then it is false that I ought to repay my debt. Yet this conclusion sounds grossly counterintuitive: 'It would be at best a bad joke for me to suggest that since I have squandered my money, I ought not to repay my debts now' (Stocker 1990, p. 96). Therefore there may be something wrong with the ought–can principle. But such a claim goes against the grain of every good ethics handbook, so it is a dangerous move to make. Hence a second rejoinder is in order: my argument does not infringe the ought–can principle. It seems to do so, but that is an illusion stemming from the highly specific action-description involved in the concept of IPS. Let us consider an act of spying *tout court*. Is such an act morally justifiable? Well, since it violates the presumption against invading privacy, it has to satisfy the necessity condition. Maybe it does satisfy it, maybe not, and much depends on further information about the precise kind of spying it is. And, as is the case for every action one may envision, that particular act of spying is submitted to the moral presumption against wronging innocent people. Maybe it abides by it, maybe not, and much depends on further information about what precise kind of spying it is. So let's be more precise. Working in some intelligence agency, Max contemplates spying on an innocent teenage girl in the hope of finding out information that would allow him to wreak havoc on her father – an important foreign official – by destroying his family life. This is discriminate spying, not in Bellaby's normative sense of 'discriminate', but in the sense of 'targeted': it is no IPS. Does the intended act of spying satisfy the presumption against wronging innocent persons? No, it does not: if successful, Max's scheme is bound to harm the daughter, not only the father – for destroying someone's family life is detrimental to every family member. The only way Max could improve his scheme, on this point, would be for him to turn into a perfect voyeur: he may spy on the girl as long as the spying remains flawless and without effect. But if Max turns into a perfect voyeur, then his spying becomes useless and thus fails with respect to the necessity condition. Given the content of his intentions, Max *cannot* satisfy both the presumption against wronging innocent persons and the necessity condition. But this is not the fault of the moral requirements themselves. It is due to the wicked content of Max's intentions. And we can argue, in Stocker's parlance (1990, p. 20), that Max is 'culpably unable' to meet the relevant moral requirements: by contemplating an intrinsically wicked plan, Max himself is 'the creator of the situation that necessitates the choice' between violating the first requirement and violating the second (1990, p. 21). Fortunately, he has a way out: give up the plan. The same is true of IPS. Given its nature, it cannot satisfy two reasonable and rather charitable moral requirements. Like Max, promoters of IPS are the creators of a situation that necessitates an impossible choice between disregarding the requirement of necessity and disregarding the requirement of perfect voyeurism. Like Max, they are culpably unable to achieve their schemes. The lesson to be drawn is that we should be cautious when invoking the ought–can principle: in many cases, the fault lies with the act and the actor, and not with the moral requirement. IPS is a highly specific kind of spying; and such a specific kind of spying can never be justified, because of its nature. Blame it on IPS.

Conclusion

If the argument presented here is sound, as I think it is, then IPS is inescapably wrong. Even when we make charitable concessions, PRISM-style surveillance does not pass the test of moral justification. The conclusion is straightforward. But it may have some disquieting implications. Think of Edward Snowden: he denounced a case of IPS at great personal risk and is now confined to Russia, having been refused asylum by twenty-one different countries. Yet he may be considered a hero. At first sight, every friend of liberalism, democracy and privacy ought to show him the most sincere gratitude. But here comes a paradox. According to the argument presented in this article, IPS ought to remain as hidden as possible – due to the requirement of perfect voyeurism. The less hidden IPS is, the more harmful. It follows that by publicising IPS, Snowden made a major contribution to the harms caused by PRISM-style surveillance. So our judgment of him must be ambivalent. On one hand, Snowden gave US citizens and denizens all over the globe better information about the extent of public surveillance. Given our legitimate interest in knowing what our government is doing and what other states are doing to us, Snowden rendered us (targets of IPS) an invaluable service. On the other hand, Snowden made IPS much more harmful than it would have been had he kept silent. Because of Snowden, friends of privacy came to be seen as having legitimate concerns and the 'chilling effect' of surveillance was given a boost.

This paradox reveals that IPS is trapped in a second, more general dilemma. From one angle, the paradox helps us to see why IPS is not only wrong, but also morally corrupting. From a liberal and democratic viewpoint, it is no doubt laudable to publicly denounce state immorality: when it concerns violations of major civil liberties, whistleblowing is admirable or imperative. But according to the requirement of perfect voyeurism, whistleblowing produces wrongness. Seen from this perspective, IPS achieves a quasi-alchemical transformation, namely turning virtue into vice. This is *moral corruption*. From another angle, the Snowden paradox shows above all that applied ethics should not reject the possibility of harmless wrongdoing. It is such a rejection that leads to the requirement of perfect voyeurism. And it is the requirement of perfect voyeurism that leads us to think that whistleblowing produces wrongness. If we admit the possibility of harmless wrongdoing, then the paradox dissolves. By publicly denouncing IPS, Snowden did not harm us; he only made us aware that we were being wronged without noticing it. IPS deserves *no charity*.

So friends of IPS are faced with a hard choice. They can insist that IPS be approached with charity, as I have done here, and in that case they can hope to escape outright condemnation. Because without the charitable concessions made here, IPS is a non-starter. Or, they can resist the charge of moral corruption. But they cannot have it both ways. For the charge of moral corruption precisely derives from the charitable concessions made in this article. In sum, one must conclude that, from a moral viewpoint, IPS is a lost cause.

Notes

1   What I call 'moral presumptions' are generally discussed under the term 'prima facie rules'. I prefer talking about 'moral presumptions', however, distancing the discussion from meta-ethical talk about the epistemic role of moral principles – as exemplified e.g. by Shafer-Landau (1997).
2   These are only charitable concessions that do not suppose anything regarding the truth of the matter. Indeed we may have serious doubts that security really is a good, for the concept of 'security' is far too vague not to arouse suspicion (Zedner 2003). And we may be sceptical about the prospect of striking a balance between security and freedom or privacy on solid grounds (Waldron 2003).

References

Applbaum, AI 1992, 'Democratic legitimacy & official discretion', *Philosophy and Public Affairs*, vol. 21, no. 3, pp. 240–274.
Ashworth, A & Zedner, L 2014, *Preventive justice*, Oxford University Press, Oxford.
Bellaby, R 2012, 'What's the harm? the ethics of intelligence collection', *Intelligence and National Security*, vol. 27, no. 1, pp. 93–117.
Doyle, T 2009, 'Privacy and perfect voyeurism', *Ethics and Information Technology*, vol. 11, pp. 181–189.
Feinberg, J 1986, *Harmless wrongdoing*, Oxford University Press, Oxford.
Fletcher, G 1988, *A crime of self-defense*, University of Chicago Press, Chicago, IL.
Gowans, C 1994, *Innocence lost: an examination of inescapable wrongdoing*, Oxford University Press, Oxford.
Holmes, S 2009, 'In case of emergency: misunderstanding tradeoffs in the war on terror', *California Law Review*, vol. 97, no. 2, pp. 301–355.

Hurka, T 2005, 'Proportionality in the morality of war', *Philosophy and Public Affairs*, vol. 33, no. 1, pp. 34–66.

Kutz, C 2009, 'Secret law and the value of publicity', *Ratio Juris*, vol. 22, no. 2, pp. 197–217.

Los, M 2006, 'Looking into the future: surveillance, globalization and the totalitarian potential', in D Lyon (ed.), *Theorizing surveillance: the panopticon and beyond*, Willan Publishing, Oxford.

Marx, G 1989, *Undercover: police surveillance in America*, University of California Press, Oakland, CA.

Mayer-Schönberger, V & Cukier, K 2013, *Big data: a revolution that will transform how we live, work and think*, John Murray, London.

Nathan, DO 1990, 'Just looking: voyeurism and the grounds of privacy', *Public Affairs Quarterly*, vol. 4, no. 4, pp. 365–386.

Parfit, D 1984, *Reasons and persons*, Oxford University Press, Oxford.

Persson, AJ & Hansson, SO 2003, 'Privacy at work – ethical criteria', *Journal of Business Ethics*, vol. 42, pp. 59–70.

Rodin, D 2002, *War and self-defense*, Oxford University Press, Oxford.

Sagar, R 2007, 'On combating the abuse of state secrecy', *Journal of Political Philosophy*, vol. 15, no. 4, pp. 404–427.

Sagar, R 2009, 'Who holds the balance? A missing detail in the debate over balancing security and liberty', *Polity*, vol. 41, pp. 166–188.

Shafer-Landau, R 1997, 'Moral rules', *Ethics*, vol. 107, no. 4, pp. 584–611.

Stocker, M 1990, *Plural and conflicting values*, Oxford University Press, Oxford.

Unger, P 1996, *Living high and letting die: our illusion of innocence*, Oxford University Press, Oxford.

Waldron, J 2003, 'Security and liberty: the image of balance', *Journal of Political Philosophy*, vol. 11, no. 2, pp. 191–210.

Zedner, L 2003, 'Too much security?' *International Journal of the Sociology of Law*, vol. 31, pp. 155–184.

10

THE MORALITY OF UNCONVENTIONAL FORCE

Thomas Simpson

Are there moral limits on what spies may do? And if so, what are they? The task of this chapter is not to set out a list of prohibitions or requirements, at least not in the first instance. Rather, it is to articulate and justify a moral framework that will result in such requirements. The framework faces the interesting and tricky problem that, for all practical purposes and with some limited exceptions, non-practitioners cannot identify any such list. Moreover, practitioners cannot do so non-mutably. One has to enjoy the epistemic privileges that come from currently being a spy in order to contribute. This is frustrating for philosophers who would like to exercise *ex cathedra* moral authority. But there is a more serious implication: the juridification of policy for spies should be resisted.

The conclusion for which I argue is well summarised in the following slogan: spies play by big boys' rules. The framework that I defend does not apply only to spies; it also applies to other practitioners of unconventional force, such as special forces or cyber-spooks, who likewise enjoy the permissions and restrictions that come from rule-governed practices.

This form of enquiry is important. The years since 9/11 have seen an increasing desire among policymakers to use unconventional force in pursuit of national security objectives. The reasons for this are various. There is an accepted practice of governmental denial when it comes to unconventional operations. Oversight procedures are not public. The organisations involved are more agile and more often able to avoid the media limelight. Most importantly, non-state actors now pose a degree of threat that was arguably not present in previous years, but war is neither a proportionate nor an effective means by which to conduct operations against these targets. Indeed, some think that the human rights violations consequent on war are so serious that there is moral imperative to seek forcible alternatives in countering threats (Dill 2014, 2016). Yet the kinds of activities in which the CIA, in particular, has been engaged, such as waterboarding and extraordinary rendition, have raised significant controversy. We lack a clear account of the morality of these practices in both popular and academic discourse.

My argument proceeds as follows. I first identify the kinds of activities in which I am interested. I then outline how existing views on the ethics of force have been taken to apply to espionage. In particular, the *ad bellum* and *in bello* strictures of Just War theory are readily taken to apply directly to spies. This approach is compelling given some currently widespread views about the ethics of force. The approach is mistaken, however, for it misconstrues the status of Just War principles. Rightly understood, at least some of these principles have compelling force because of their status as mutually beneficial conventions. I then apply this view to espionage and other forms of unconventional force, outlining the tricky policy implications of my thesis.

Intelligence work

My interest is in force that is unconventional because of the social, moral or legal context in which it occurs. Specifically, I am interested in force used by a state outside its sovereign territory but not during declared war between nations. I use 'force' in a capacious sense, defined extensionally by the activities stated below. Such uses fall outside the two paradigmatic contexts for the legitimate use of force, viz. the international work of the military in times of war and humanitarian intervention, and the intra-national work of the police and criminal punishment system.

Unconventional force – in the forms I am concerned with – is used for two principal purposes. First, it is used to gain intelligence, in support of national security. Security relates to the severity of possible harm and the likelihood of harm. Intelligence helps achieve security by detecting likely threats, enabling steps to be taken actively to deter the threat, or to interdict it, or to mitigate the severity of harm. It also helps to reduce uncertainty regarding both severity and likelihood. The activities that take place in the pursuit of this goal include several varieties of '-INT': the recruiting and deployment of agents (HUMINT); eavesdropping on communications (SIGINT); observation of activities through satellite imagery and other image-gathering platforms (IMINT), and so forth. Learning what adversaries are saying, and what they are doing, allows analysts to assess and evaluate likely intentions and capabilities. Much of what is said and done can be learned from open sources (OSINT), where no force is required. But adversaries that pose a genuine threat are likely to wish to conceal their intentions and capabilities as much as possible. Countering this requires secret intelligence. Discovering adversaries' intentions and capabilities may be achievable, indeed only achievable, through force. This will certainly involve gaining access to private spaces, to either physical or digital property. At its most dramatic, it may involve interrogation or even torture.

Force may also be used directly, to interdict and disrupt enemies. At the soft end of the spectrum, I count sowing false information about one's own intentions as a form of force, as it deceives enemies about the extent of one's own knowledge. The means by which this is achieved may be various; sometimes it may consist merely in deceitful speech, but it may also involve more direct forms of action. More forcible measures may include the blackmail or bribery of individuals whose compliance is useful to one and detrimental to one's adversary. At the hard end of the spectrum is physical force used against property and people: sabotage and destruction; and assassination, targeted killing, rendition and detention. I use 'intelligence work' as a catch-all label for activities conducted in pursuit of the twin aims of learning about an enemy's intentions and capabilities and disrupting their activities, but not in the context of war. Paradigmatically, it is spies who undertake intelligence work. They are assisted in this work by special forces and communications specialists.

Targets of unconventional force are various. The target may be an enemy state, achieved through targeting their military, industrial, political or covert capabilities, and both personnel and physical hardware. Terrorists, from individuals to internationally coordinated networks, are now firmly on the list.

Reductivism

How should the morality of unconventional force be evaluated? A natural line of thinking is the following. We have an extensive body of theory regarding the morality of the use of force in war, namely that articulated by the Just War tradition. Rejecting both pacifism and a crass form of realism, Just War theory acknowledges the necessity of the use of force but sets boundaries on what may be done. Unconventional force differs from conventional force – that exercised by the military and the police – in its institutional context. It is conducted by the CIA, for instance, not the Pentagon. But force is force. Given the validity of Just War theory, at least in its outline terms, it is plausible that the same moral strictures it places on conventional force apply to unconventional force. At the very least, the same tension is discernible between the pragmatic necessity of intelligence and the inescapability of its moral evaluation. The philosopher's job is to explain how the criteria for *jus ad bellum* and *jus in bello* apply in this new context. The corollary practical task is to ensure that appropriate regimes of legal accountability are created, so that those who exercise unconventional force comply with the strictures of morality.

This is the approach most favoured by current and former intelligence professionals. It usually results in the re-statement of Just War principles to the form of unconventional force in hand. An example is David Omand (2009). His guidelines for the use of force recapitulate, in modestly revised terminology, those of *jus ad bellum* and *in bello*: sufficient cause, integrity of motive, proportionality, right authority, reasonable prospect of success (Omand 2009, also 2014, pp. 286–7). The principle of public declaration is naturally absent; more strikingly absent is that of distinction (see also Bellaby 2012; Glendron 2007; Quinlan 2007). Kevin McNish likewise takes this approach to the ethics of a specific intelligence practice, viz. surveillance (2014; see also Chapter 7 in this volume).

I reject this approach. But it is worth noting how compelling it is, given some currently widespread views about the ethics of war. Traditional Just War theory is based on what Michael Walzer called 'the domestic analogy' (2006, p. 58). On this view, states are viewed as sovereign individuals that are morally analogous to individual persons. As such, they possess rights of self-defence that entitle them to go war in defence of their people and territory. Michael Walzer rejects the domestic analogy, seeking to ground the ethics of war solely on the rights of self- and other-defence that individuals hold (2006, p. 54). He reaches largely traditional conclusions about the ethics of war. Since then, scholars have adopted his premises, but questioned his conclusions. Jeff McMahan, for instance, has argued that these premises cannot justify the traditional views that combatants do not wrong if they fulfil the requirements of *jus in bello*, regardless of the *ad bellum* justice of their cause; that liability to attack arises if one is a combatant and that it arises *only* if one is a combatant (McMahan 2004, 2009). Likewise, David Rodin has argued that nations are not justified in defending their territory or political institutions against aggressors that would not kill were their aims not to be resisted (Rodin 2002, 2014). Cécile Fabre has argued that subsistence wars are justified, in which economically destitute nations invade rich neighbours for material resources (Fabre 2012, pp. 97–129).[1] These revisionary conclusions are argued on the basis of the following shared central premise: ethical permissions and prohibitions on the use of force derive solely from what individuals are permitted and prohibited to do to each other. Call this *reductivism* about the ethics of force. It has the implication that the best way to learn about the ethics of force is to examine possible encounters between individuals where there is as little distracting information as possible. It has the further implication that there are no unique moral considerations that arise from social context.

Given this reductivism, it follows that there is no substantial difference between the ethics of force in the conventional context of war and the unconventional context of intelligence work. The attempt to apply the principles of Just War theory to unconventional force finds its grounding not just in there being a useful analogy between the two contexts (see e.g. McNish 2014, p. 146). Rather, it is grounded in there being no moral difference between the two. It is important to note that the application of the Just War criteria to the unconventional context does not depend on one's view about what the correct principles are. One may be a Walzerian traditionalist or a McMahan-esque revisionist regarding its content. So long as traditionalism or revisionism is based on the reductivist premise, then we learn the ethics of unconventional force by looking at those of conventional force. This is so not because of any logical priority, but merely due to historical contingency: scholars started reflecting on the conventional context prior to and in a more sustained way than they have done for the unconventional. According to one's views on the correct account of the principles of Just War, one derives the content of principles for just intelligence work. As it happens, most prior accounts of the ethics of intelligence work have incorporated traditionalist views about the conditions of Just War. But that is inessential to the methodology.

Reductivism provides a ready critique of attempts to identify moral considerations that are unique to unconventional contexts. Daniel Brunstetter and Megan

Braun (2013) aim to do the latter for force that falls short of war, and which is subject to evaluation under '*jus ad vim*'. They propose that force short of war is morally permissible in situations where war would not be, with certain kinds of *injuria* or threat – such as the bombing of embassies, kidnapping of citizens or the prospect of a state failing which possesses nuclear weapons – meriting a forcible response, but one that falls short of war. They propose that a necessary condition for the just use of force short of war is that there be limited prospects of escalation. Brunstetter and Braun's position is highly plausible. But the reductivist reply comes quickly. The moral significance of the prospect of escalation is already expressed by the *jus ad bellum* criterion of proportionality. The deeper point is that the category of *jus ad vim* is redundant, because the categories of *jus ad bellum* and *in bello* are also redundant. Or rather, the utility of each of the terms is given purely in terms of their extension; each picks out a certain category of acts that it is useful to be able to talk about discretely (Helen Frowe makes this argument; see Frowe n.d.). In sum, the ethics of force is not domain-specific. As McMahan puts it, the 'conditions of war change nothing at all; they merely make it more difficult to ascertain certain facts' (2006, p. 47).[2]

An alternative view, to which I subscribe, takes the social context of force to be morally significant. I shall now develop this in more detail.

Conventions of force

The reductivist premise is false. The principles of Just War have a different structure of justification from that deriving from permissions held by individuals *qua* individuals. As such, permissions and prohibitions regarding the use of force may be sensitive to prevailing social practices. Call this *exceptionalism* about the use of force. Exceptionalism about force is the tacit assumption underlying the traditional view of the ethics of war, and it accounts for why permissions to kill are present in war that are extraordinarily absent in civilian life. But there is no plausible reason to suppose that it applies only to war. If it applies at all, I argue, exceptionalism also applies to unconventional force. I do not aim to provide here an all-things-considered defence of the position; that task would be too large. Rather, my aim is to provide a statement of the position and outline how a justification of it would proceed. I do so by examining a disagreement between Jeff McMahan and Henry Shue, and drawing an unnoted conclusion from Shue's position.

McMahan – arguably the most prominent reductivist – distinguishes sharply between the 'deep morality' of war and the laws of war. The former assumes the reductivist premise, from which he derives revisionary conclusions. The latter serves to regulate the actual conduct of war. The laws of war have 'to be formulated to take account of the likely effects of its promulgation, institutionalization, and enforcement' (McMahan 2008, p. 33). He acknowledges the practical discrepancy between the two. It is 'entirely clear that the laws of war must diverge significantly from the deep morality of war as I have presented it' (McMahan 2004, p. 730). Given the possibility of discrepancy between morality and law, McMahan then considers possible forms of conflict between the two. He concludes that individuals must follow the dictates of either law or morality where one forbids or requires; that doing so is consistent with a permission from the other; and that one must follow the prohibitions of morality in defiance of the law's requirements (2008, pp. 37–9).

The account is puzzling. McMahan's enquiry can be understood as investigating the permissions and prohibitions that individuals enjoy in the state of nature, so to speak – that of Locke, not Hobbes. It is pre-societal. But given the existence of society, we can ask what the best rules are that would enable us to interact, and perhaps even to cooperate. As Henry Shue notes, one ought to aim at the morally best rules. But we do not have to choose:

> between what the morally best laws permit and require and what morality permits and requires, because morality requires that, where we need laws, we formulate the best laws and then follow them where they apply. We can take the morally best action by obeying the morally best law, where we ought to follow a law. We may of course have to choose between the actual laws and what morality requires the law to be, but that is because, and when, the actual laws are not the best laws.
>
> *(Shue 2008, p. 91)*

Shue's account does not pit morality against law. Rather, in morality's requiring obedience to legitimate law, morality 'is all of a piece: the fundamental moral considerations are the fundamental moral considerations' (2008, p. 88; see also Dill & Shue 2012). McMahan's enquiry focuses on an unduly restricted subset of fundamental moral considerations, viz. desert and liability to attack. But there are other fundamental moral considerations, such as the minimisation of loss of life, which also weigh in the balance when it comes to the formulation of law. The moral obligation to follow the best law – or even just a reasonable, legitimate one – is an all-things-considered obligation. Desert is not the only moral consideration.

My sympathies in this disagreement are with Shue. In support of his position, just think what its denial would entail. Law, on McMahan's picture, becomes a solely pragmatic interest, albeit pervasively present. But this cannot be right. Law claims the moral authority when it comes to action-guidance; it is not merely a practical incentive to avoiding punishment. Rather, punishment is expressive of the public's moral judgment of the criminal. Very often, when laws are good, the responsible person also views herself as under an obligation to accept that authority. To forestall objection, it is also important to note what Shue is *not* committed to. He is implicitly committed neither to consequentialism, on which a right action is one that maximises the greatest goodness, nor contractarianism, on which one ought to follow the rule that a reasonable person would agree to under fair bargaining conditions (contractarianism readily gives rise to exceptionalism about the use of force; see Benbaji 2009, 2014). No doubt his view is amenable to both these positions. But all he is committed to is the claim that fundamental moral considerations include more than desert-relations; that the last do not trump; and that law derives part of its moral force from other such considerations. There is one implication of his view, however, that he does not draw and which I wish to highlight.

The fundamental moral considerations that Shue identifies are not only served by law. They are also served by tacit conventions. In David Lewis's analysis, a convention arises when there is mutual interest in arriving at a regularity of behaviour in a repeated interaction, but where there is more than one possible regularity that each would prefer, and in which it becomes common knowledge which regularity of behaviour has been settled upon (1969, p. 76). Whether one drives on the right or the left is an example. It does not matter which side is settled upon, but it matters very much that a side is adopted. In other situations, it matters which regularity is settled upon, but it matters to everyone that a regularity is settled upon more than that their favoured regularity is arrived at. A convention is thus a stable equilibrium. Conventions *could* be set by a central authority. But equally often, they arise through a certain regularity of behaviour's having a degree of salience and thereby being settled upon by a number of people. Or it could be simply a historically contingent matter, a result of someone finding a good resolution of the coordination problem, and the social influence that they had, the networks of which they were members, and so on. In the latter case, a convention is tacit. In the former case, where it is set by a central authority, a convention is formal. Indeed, there is a compelling understanding of part of the origin of law – and thus part of its justification – on which the law is a formal, centralised means of setting beneficial conventions (see Marmor 2009).

It is often a tricky empirical question whether a convention holds in a particular domain, but it does so if and only if there is a regularity of behaviour that is followed, and if it is common knowledge that it is followed, by people who face a particular interaction situation. A convention exists only under generally sustained conditions of reciprocity. Conventions are morally significant. Where they exist, and are beneficial, there is moral reason to follow them. But they are morally significant only in the domains of interaction in which they hold. Where they do not hold, one has to fall back on other sources of moral direction.

Conventions exist in war. What counts as a legitimate target for attack, for instance, could have been construed very differently. The convention of counting all and only those in uniform as legitimate targets has the merit of being simple, symmetrical and mutually beneficial in its limitation of war's destructiveness. This also applies to conventions around care for prisoners of war; the exemption of medical and religious personnel from targeting; the prohibition of poisoning; protection of parliamentarians and so forth. Each of these limits the destructiveness of war, without strict regard for the moral permissiveness of attacking individuals that arises in virtue of the unjustified threat they either caused or now pose. All of this serves to illustrate Thomas Schelling's remark that 'the possibility of mutual accommodation [in war] is as important and dramatic as the element of conflict. Concepts like deterrence, limited war, and disarmament, as well as negotiation, are concerned with the common interest and mutual dependence that can exist between participants in a conflict' (Schelling 1960, p. 5; for longer discussion see Mavrodes 1975).

Noting the moral significance of conventions is important. For one, it explains how international humanitarian law could have arisen through a gradual process of development, in which conventions evolved, rather than being created *ex nihilo* in an act of law-making. For another, it suggests how someone can be justified in following not the letter of the law, but a rule of behaviour that is actually complied with by participants in an activity.

Practices of surrender illustrate both of these points. Various conventions and nationally self-binding documents state that an enemy soldier is considered *hors de combat* if they clearly indicate their intention to surrender (see ICRC 2005, pp. 161–9), and quarter must therefore be given. Undoubtedly so. But throughout history, very different moments at which quarter must be accepted have been adopted. In early modern European warfare, for instance, it was thought that besieged cities had the right to surrender while attackers were investing the walls. Upon indicating a desire to surrender, the expectation was of a parleying for terms, with the garrison's worst prospect being that of being taken prisoner. Depending on the strength of their position, they may very well have been allowed to walk away with their arms, ceding only the town. But a breach of the walls constituted a point of no return. Once the attackers had forced a hole in the walls or had committed to the assault, the defenders forfeited the right of surrender, and no quarter could be expected. Although attackers could still accept an attempted surrender if they chose, they did not wrong the defenders if they refused. The seizure of most cities resulted in a lot of bloodletting.

The justification for this practice was mutual self-interest. The horrendous costs in blood incurred by an attacker in seizing a defended city were to be avoided if at all possible. In raising the expected costs of continued defence, the convention ensured that defenders had to make a clear-headed decision about the likelihood of success. Changing the strategic structure of the choice resulted – it was believed – in fewer deaths overall, and less destructive patterns of warfare. Nor is this style of thinking restricted to the early modern period. In the Falklands campaign, British paratroopers adopted a *de facto* 100 metre or so threshold. They declined to accept the surrender of Argentine soldiers who fought while the paras were in the exposed and vulnerable advance, and then put their hands up as the assaulting troops jumped into the trenches. 'Too late' was the thought (for such cases, see Fraser 1973; Jennings & Weale 1996).

Categoricity

Conventions are not morally limitless. There are some actions that cannot become morally permitted, even if there were a convention according to which they had. This is as true of rules of warfare as it is in other areas. I take the prohibition on torture to be an example. To mark the contrast, distinguish *categorical requirements* from conventional rules, whether tacit or formal. Because some moral norms are categorical requirements, rather than conventional ones, the principles (for example) of Just War have multiple justifications. This is marked, roughly, by the distinction between *mala in se* and *mala prohibita*. The former generate categorical requirements.

Against juridification

The basic case for exceptionalism about force has been made. I now apply it to unconventional force, and draw a key policy implication.

Given exceptionalism, the rules that govern the use of force in the unconventional context may be substantively different from those governing the conventional context. Moreover, they may be different in ways that grant moral permissions – as well as prohibitions – that are not found elsewhere. This is not true of all moral norms, for some are categorical requirements. But it is true of those that are conventional – although it may turn out that analogues of the principles of Just War theory are generally thought to apply to espionage, at least by intelligence practitioners, which would be an interesting and surprising outcome. But this is probably not the case. Instead, spies, special forces and cyber-spooks refrain from certain kinds of actions on the grounds that their own people and property will be liable to the same treatment if they do not restrain themselves, such that it serves the purposes of all in that community, internationally, to restrain from those actions.

More significantly, intelligence practitioners may undertake certain kinds of action on the understanding that their own people and property are *already* reciprocally liable to such treatment. In this case, an existing regularity of behaviour may create permissions that pre-social morality would deny. There are limits to what permissions may be created, namely those constituted by the categorical requirements of morality. These categorical requirements need not be trivial. Targeting those who are uninvolved in the affairs of state or in political activity may well be prohibited. But outside of these prohibitions there may be considerable lassitude. Spies, and other practitioners of unconventional force, play by big boys' rules.

The conventional rules that govern intelligence work are tacit. Through repeated operations between adversaries, regularities of behaviour emerge that render some actions permissible and others forbidden. Reciprocity is a necessary condition for these to emerge. They have an awkward consequence. Given liberal nations' standing suspicion of the intelligence services, there is a continual demand for greater oversight. The demand is invariably for juridification: the establishment of oversight procedures based on the creation of law to govern intelligence agencies, and its application by the judiciary. This is in contrast to oversight exercised by the executive which is politically accountable to the electorate. I reject this view because it relies on moral norms that go beyond the categorical requirements of morality. As well as being self-defeating, the juridification of intelligence work is neither required nor possible.

Juridification is self-defeating because it undermines the conditions of the possibility of intelligence work. For Shue, the laws of war ordinarily take the form of black-letter law. Black-letter law, however, is peculiarly inapposite to intelligence work. It is of the essence of law that it be public. But public declaration of which methods are prohibited, and by implication which are permitted, renders one's techniques transparent to adversaries. It thereby thwarts the very point of having an intelligence capacity – the possession of which is itself permissible, by the criterion of reciprocity.

Juridification is not required morally. The parameters of legitimate action by intelligence practitioners are substantially dependent on what is accepted practice between adversaries. Self-binding oneself to an articular code of conduct, from which adversaries have reneged, is plainly imprudent; nor is it required.

Finally, juridification is not possible. Partly as a result of the problem of self-defeat, the conventions that govern intelligence work are forced to remain tacit rather than formal. As such, non-practitioners cannot gain the epistemic standing that would allow them to learn about the regularities of behaviour that govern force in the unconventional contests between nations and networks. Furthermore, accepted practice is mutable and susceptible to development and change – as all mores are. One must be a current practitioner to know what the current conventions are. Only big boys get to know what the rules are, but it is by those rules that they must be morally evaluated.

Notes

1 It is disputed how revisionary some of these conclusions are, or whether they constitute a return to views espoused by the medieval jurists. See Reichberg 2008 for discussion.
2 I owe the reference to Helen Frowe.

References

Bellaby, R 2012, 'What's the harm? the ethics of intelligence collection', *Intelligence and National Security*, vol. 27, no. 1, pp. 93–117.
Benbaji, Y 2009, 'The war convention and the moral division of labour', *Philosophical Quarterly*, vol. 59, no. 237, pp. 593–617.
Benbaji, Y 2014, 'Distributive justice, human rights, and territorial integrity: a contractarian account of the crime of aggression', in C Fabre and S Lazar (eds), *The morality of defensive war*, Oxford University Press, Oxford.
Brunstetter, D & Braun, M 2013, 'From jus ad bellum to jus ad vim: recalibrating our understanding of the moral use of force', *Ethics and International Affairs*, vol. 27, no. 1, pp. 87–106.
Dill, J 2014, *Legitimate targets? Social construction, international law and us bombing*, Cambridge University Press, Cambridge.
Dill, J 2016, 'Forcible alternatives to war', in J Ohlin (ed.), *Theoretical boundaries of armed conflict and human rights*, Cambridge University Press, Cambridge, in press.
Dill, J & Shue, H 2012, 'Limiting the killing in war: military necessity and the St. Petersburg assumption', *Ethics and International Affairs*, vol. 26, no. 3, pp. 311–333.

Fabre, C 2012, *Cosmopolitan war*, Oxford University Press, Oxford.

Fraser, A 1973, *Cromwell: our chief of men*, Weidenfeld & Nicolson, London.

Frowe, H n.d., 'The use of drones and the ethics of defensive force', podcast, Stockholm University, www.elac.ox.ac.uk/podcasts

Glendron, A 2007, 'Just war, just intelligence: an ethical framework for foreign espionage', *International Journal of Intelligence and Counter-Intelligence*, vol. 18, no. 3, pp. 398–434.

ICRC 2005, *Customary international humanitarian law: Vol. 1 Rules*, J-M Henckaerts & L Doswald-Beck (eds), Cambridge University Press, Cambridge.

Jennings, C & Weale, A 1996, *Green-eyed boys: 3 para and the battle for Mount Longdon*, Harper Collins, London.

Lewis, D 1969, *Convention: a philosophical study*, Harvard University Press, Cambridge, MA.

Marmor, A 2009, *Social conventions: from language to law*, Princeton University Press, Princeton, NJ.

Mavrodes, G 1975, 'Conventions and the morality of war', *Philosophy and Public Affairs*, vol. 4, no. 2, pp. 117–131.

McMahan, J 2004, 'The ethics of killing in war', *Ethics*, vol. 114, pp. 693–733.

McMahan, J 2006, 'Killing in war: a reply to Walzer', *Philosophia*, vol. 34, no. 1, pp. 47–51.

McMahan, J 2008, 'The morality of war and the laws of war', in D Rodin & H Shue (eds), *Just and unjust warriors*, Oxford University Press, Oxford.

McMahan, J 2009, *Killing in war*, Oxford University Press, New York.

McNish, K 2014, 'Just surveillance? Towards a normative theory of surveillance', *Surveillance and Society*, vol. 12, no. 1, pp. 142–153.

Omand, D 2009, 'Ethical guidelines in using secret intelligence for public security', in C Andrew, RJ Aldrich & WK Wark (eds), *Secret intelligence: a reader*, London: Routledge, pp. 395–410.

Omand, D 2014, *Securing the state*, Oxford University Press, Oxford.

Quinlan, M 2007, 'Just intelligence: prolegomena to an ethical theory', *Intelligence and National Security*, vol. 22, no. 1, pp. 1–13.

Reichberg, GM 2008, 'Just war and regular war: competing paradigms', in D Rodin & H Shue (eds), *Just and unjust warriors*, Oxford University Press, Oxford.

Rodin, D 2002, *War and self-defense*, Oxford University Press, Oxford.

Rodin, D 2014, 'The myth of national self-defence', in C Fabre and S Lazar (eds), *The morality of defensive war*, Oxford University Press, Oxford.

Schelling, TC 1960, *The strategy of conflict*, Harvard University Press, Cambridge, MA.

Shue, H 2008, 'Do we need a "morality of war"?', in D Rodin & H Shue (eds), *Just and unjust warriors*, Oxford University Press, Oxford.

Walzer, M 2006, *Just and unjust wars: a moral argument with historical illustrations*, Basic Books, New York.

PART IV

Remote surveillance and killing

11

I, SPY ROBOT

The ethics of robots in national intelligence activities

Patrick Lin and Shannon Ford

The ethics of military robots is marching ahead, judging by recent news coverage and academic research. Yet there has been little discussion concerning robots in the service of national intelligence and espionage, which are omnipresent national security activities. This is surprising, because most military robots are used for surveillance and reconnaissance, and their most controversial uses can be traced back to the Central Intelligence Agency (CIA) in targeted strikes against suspected terrorists (O'Connell 2012, p. 270).

In this chapter, we examine the key moral issues for the intelligence community with regard to the use of robots for intelligence collection. First, we survey the diverse range of spy robots that currently exist or are emerging, and examine their value for national security. This includes describing a number of plausible scenarios in which they have been (or could be) used, including: surveillance, attack, sentry, information collection, delivery, extraction, detention, interrogation and as Trojan horses. Second, we examine several areas in which spy robots present serious ethical and legal challenges. We conclude by examining some moral concerns with shifting from intelligence collection to action, as enabled by robotics technology.

Emerging robotics technology

This first section surveys existing robotic surveillance and the emerging technologies. Military robots are arguably more effective than their human counterparts in completing national security tasks that are dull, dirty and dangerous. But note that robot–human interaction is likely to remain a potential weakness. We examine cases where the overuse of robots might also create problems. Finally, we briefly examine emerging civilian applications for surveillance robots.

Rise of the spy robots

Robotics has been a game-changer in national security and intelligence, particularly in the development of military capability. We now find military robots in just about every domain including, air, land, sea and space. These robots come in many sizes: from tiny insect-like robots to aerial drones with wingspans greater than a Boeing 737 aircraft. Some robots are fixed to battleships, while others patrol national borders. There has been research into micro-robots, swarm robots, humanoids, chemical bots and biological–machine integrations. As we might expect, military robots have warlike names such as TALON SWORD, Crusher, BEAR, Big Dog, Predator, Reaper, Harpy, Raven, Global Hawk, Vulture, Switchblade and so on. But not all military robots are designed to function as weapons. For example, the purpose of the Battlefield Extraction Assist Robot (BEAR) is to retrieve wounded soldiers on a battlefield (Rutherford 2009).

Military robots prove themselves useful in the service of national security because they are more effective than their human counterparts in completing dull, dirty and dangerous jobs (known as the three Ds). The military often have dull jobs such as extended reconnaissance, patrols or standing guard over perimeters. Military robots can perform these functions well beyond the limits of human endurance. Dirty jobs include such military tasks as working with hazardous materials or cleaning up after nuclear or biochemical attacks. Military robots can operate in environments unsuitable for humans, such as underwater and outer space. Dangerous jobs that can be performed by military robots include searching for enemy combatants inside cave networks, controlling hostile crowds, or clearing improvised explosive devices (IEDs).

Arguably, there is a fourth D that needs to be considered. This is the military robots' ability to act with 'dispassion'. The claim here is that military robots are better at seeing through the 'fog of war' to reduce unlawful and accidental killings (Arkin 2010, p. 333). Robots do not act with malice, hatred or other emotions that may lead to war crimes and other abuses, such as rape. Robots do not have an instinct of self-preservation that causes them to act out of fear. They are unaffected by emotion, adrenaline and hunger. Where an ordinary soldier's judgment is undermined by sleep deprivation, low morale and fatigue, the military robot continues to operate at the same level. They are objective, unblinking observers. So the argument is that robots can perform many standard military tasks better – that is, more effectively and more ethically – than humans in the high-stress environment of the battlefield.

The weakest link?

Robots can replace humans when it comes to certain tasks but, in most situations, humans will still be in control. Humans either will have significant input in terms of the robot's actions or will maintain the capacity to veto a robot's course of action. The 'human factor' is likely to remain a significant issue for the use of robotic technology, with robot–human interaction a potentially weak link in practical applications. For example, unmanned aerial vehicles (UAVs) such as Predator and Global Hawk can stay in the air far longer than a normal human being. But human operators must still be awake to the activities of such vehicles. Some military UAV operators may be overworked and fatigued, which can lead to errors in judgment. But even in the absence of these factors, humans still make wrong decisions, either through incompetence or bad motivation.

A second worry is that UAV operators – who might control drones from the other side of the world – are more likely to become detached and care less about killing. Royakkers & Van Est (2010, p. 295) argue that UAV operators are more likely to morally disengage from their task and that this disengagement 'limits, or even eliminates, proper reflection among cubicle warriors on the life-and-death decisions they make'. The concern is that this might lead to a greater number of unjustified strikes and collateral damage. But other reports indicate that UAV pilots become hypersensitised, not desensitised. Controllers have an intimate view of their targets via video streaming, following them for hours and even days. They can also see the aftermath of a strike, which may include strewn body parts and dead children. Some reports indicate that operators are, in fact, more likely to suffer from post-traumatic stress disorder (PTSD) than soldiers in the battlespace (Strawser 2013, p. 16).

A third question about robot–human interaction concerns the programming of robots in cases where they have access to better decision making information than their human masters. In some cases, robots will have better situational awareness because they are fitted with advanced sensors that allow them to see in the dark, through walls, to be networked with other computers and so on. This raises the following problem: if a robot knows better, should it ever refuse a human order? Following orders is the bedrock for a chain of command and accountability. Let's consider a scenario where a human orders a robot to fire a missile at a house that is thought to belong to enemy combatants. The robot, however, uses its superior sensors to identify that the house is occupied by non-combatants. Should the robot refuse the order to attack the house? Given that we already rely on the technical capacities of UAVs to enable more precise strikes, are we also obliged to use their superior information-collection capabilities to minimise collateral damage in this way?

It might also be the case that robots themselves are the weakest link. For one thing, robots can effectively replace humans in physical tasks – such as heavy lifting or working with dangerous materials – but it does not seem likely that they will be able to take over more psychologically nuanced jobs such as gaining the confidence of an agent, which involves humour, mirroring and other social skills. So the less technologically dependent area of human intelligence (HUMINT) will still be important in the foreseeable future.

The extensive use of military robots might bring tactical benefits, but it can also undermine strategic goals. We have already heard that the use of technology in war or peacekeeping missions is not helping us win the hearts and minds of the relevant local populations (Kilcullen & McDonald Exum 2009; Sluka 2011, p. 76). Sending robot patrols into politically sensitive environments to keep the peace can send the wrong message about our concern for residents. Human diplomacy is still required for such tasks. Furthermore, the extensive use of UAVs in war might also backfire if enemy combatants come to believe that we are cowardly for not engaging with them face-to-face. They may also conclude that we are not committed to the fight (Enemark 2013, p. 6). This undermines strategic goals by making the enemy more resolute and fuelling their propaganda and recruitment efforts, which could then lead to a new crop of determined terrorists.

Finally, without defence, robots could be targeted for capture. This presents a problem in that they are likely to contain both critical technologies and classified data. Clearly we should not allow robots to be captured. But self-destruction could be triggered at the wrong time and place, injuring people and creating an international crisis. So do we give them defensive capabilities, such as evasive manoeuvres or non-lethal weapons like repellent spray, Taser guns or rubber bullets? Such 'non-lethal' measures might also become deadly. In running away, for example, a robot might run down a child or a group of non-combatants. And we already see frequent news reports about unintended deaths caused by Tasers and other supposedly non-lethal weapons (Black 2013).

Civilian applications

Civilian applications for surveillance robots are also emerging. These include robots that watch for suspicious behaviour in public places, such as children's playgrounds or major sporting events. It is likely that current and future biometric capabilities will be used to create robots that can detect faces, drugs and weapons at a distance and underneath clothing. Robots can also be used for alerting people, in tasks such as providing information, reciting laws or issuing warnings. Such capabilities will almost certainly provide an opportunity for intelligence gathering on an unprecedented scale. For example, the K5 Autonomous Data Machine has enough camera, audio and other sensor technology to produce 90 terabytes of data a year per unit. It also runs behavioural logarithms that analyse multiple data points simultaneously to predict when a situation may be on the verge of becoming dangerous (Statt 2013, para. 8).

In delivery applications, special weapons and tactics (SWAT) police teams already use robots to interact with hostage-takers and in other dangerous situations. So robots could be used to deliver other items or to plant surveillance devices in inaccessible places. Likewise, they can be used for extractions, too. As mentioned earlier, the BEAR robot can retrieve wounded soldiers from the battlefield. In the future, an autonomous car or helicopter might be deployed to extract or transport suspects and assets, thereby reducing the risk to personnel.

Robots can also be used for the purpose of detention. Robot sentries are already being used to guard buildings, and recently have been guarding people too (Pasculli 2013, p. 8). One benefit of this is that it eliminates the types of prisoner abuse that were perpetrated by the human guards at Guantanamo Bay Naval Base in Cuba and Abu Ghraib prison in Iraq. But the unemotional and dispassionate nature of robots also makes them well suited to performing interrogation and torture. Robots can monitor vital signs of interrogated suspects as well as a human doctor can, but without the entanglement of the Hippocratic Oath to do no harm. They could also administer injections and even inflict pain in a more controlled and perhaps more effective way.

Ethical and legal challenges

This section examines some of the key ethical and legal challenges for using spy robots. First, I examine some responsibility and compliance issues related to the use of spy robots, including who takes responsibility for serious accidents, e-waste environmental problems, legal obligations and privacy concerns. I then discuss the use of spy robots to manipulate, coerce and deceive our adversaries. Finally, I consider the impact of spy robots on the capabilities of the institutions that use them, and the potential for proliferation.

Responsibility and compliance

First of all, we should note that robot errors could plausibly cause serious accidents. We all know that technical faults are a fact of life and that they happen all the time in the technology we use daily. So it would be naïve to think that something as complex as a robot would be immune to such problems. For example, in 2011 an RQ-Shadow UAV collided with a military cargo plane in Afghanistan, forcing it to make an emergency landing (Hodge 2011). In 2010, a software anomaly caused operators to lose control of an MQ-8B Fire Scout helicopter UAV for about half an hour, whereupon it strayed into restricted airspace over Washington, DC (Cavas 2010). And in 2007, a South African robotic anti-aircraft weapon (an Oerlikon GDF-005) malfunctioned, emptying its twin 250-round auto-loader magazine of high-explosive 0.5 kg 35 mm cannon shells, killing nine soldiers and wounding fourteen more (Shachtman 2007). Regardless of whether or not harm is caused accidentally or intentionally, the autonomy of such robots leads to questions about who (or what) is responsible for their actions. Can we attribute responsibility to the robot itself or should we hold the operator responsible (or perhaps even the programmer)? Will manufacturers insist on a release of liability – such as the standard end-user licensing agreements (EULA) we agree to when we use software? Or should we insist that such products be thoroughly tested and proven safe?

A second issue is the legal obligations of robots. As robotics become more pervasive in our everyday lives, it is likely that they will share our roads, airspace and waterways. So it is necessary that they should comply with domestic laws. This includes spy robots in the service of national intelligence, since – along with autonomous cars, domestic surveillance robots and rescue robots – they will interact with society at large. But what about complying with something like a legal obligation to assist others in need, such as required by a Good Samaritan Law or basic international laws that require ships to assist other vessels in distress? Would an unmanned surface vehicle, or robotic boat, be legally obliged to stop and save the crew of a sinking ship? This was a highly contested issue in the Second World War (e.g. the Laconia incident), when submarine commanders refused to save stranded sailors at sea, as required by the governing laws of war in place at the time. It is not unreasonable to claim that this obligation should not apply to submarines, because stealth is their primary advantage and surfacing to rescue gives away their position. Could we therefore use similar reasoning to release unmanned underwater vehicles (UUVs) and unmanned surface vehicles (USVs) from this obligation?

A third issue is the environmental, health and safety problems created by the extensive use of robots. E-waste is already a major health and environmental hazard across the globe, with an estimated 50 million tonnes of e-waste produced each year in the US alone (Kaushik 2014, para. 6). The increasing use of robots will add to this problem in new and potentially unexpected ways. Microbots and disposable robots can be tiny (e.g. nanosensors) and can be deployed in swarms. If we do not have a process for cleaning them up at the end of their product life cycle, then they could be ingested or inhaled by animals or people. Natural allergens can be harmful to our health, but imagine the damage caused by engineered material that potentially contain toxins such as mercury or other chemicals in their batteries. This is perhaps a problem for any industry that adopts or sells digital technologies, but one that is particularly important in this context.

For the sake of completeness, we should also mention privacy concerns, though these are familiar in current discussions (Calo 2012; Solove 2011). An obvious privacy concern is microbots, which might look like innocuous insects or birds, but can peek into windows or crawl into a house. But another serious privacy issue arises when we consider the ever-increasing biometric capabilities of robots. This includes technology to recognise faces from a distance or in a crowd, detect drugs or weapons under clothing, or detect contraband substances inside a house from the outside. These technologies blur the important legal distinction between 'surveillance' and 'search', which is intended to protect the right to privacy. The difference here is that, at least in some key nations, law enforcement officials are legally obliged to obtain a judicial warrant before conducting a search. The presumption is that a search infringes an individual's right to privacy and so law enforcement officials must justify their actions by proving reasonable suspicion. In contrast, surveillance does not require the same legal standard. So as technology allows surveillance to be more intrusive, there may be a legal gap that puts privacy at risk.

Manipulation, coercion and deception

The use of spy robots might also be legally controversial in other ways. For example, we could be tempted to use the capabilities of robots in extraditions, torture, assassinations, transport of contraband substances, and so on.

But more broadly speaking, should we be creating machines that intentionally deceive, manipulate or coerce people? Consider how the CIA bribed Afghani warlords with Viagra for information, which is a less obvious payment than money or weapons (Harnden 2008). Sex is one of the most basic human needs and is a well known resource for manipulation. One disconcerting use of robotic technology might involve providing informants with a sex-robot. Without getting into the ethics of sex-robots here (Levy 2012), such robots could also have secret surveillance and strike capabilities – a femme fatale, of sorts.

Even if not illegal, there are some activities that are unethical, such as the fake vaccination operation in Pakistan that obtained DNA samples with the aim of finding Osama bin Laden. Posing as a humanitarian or Red Cross worker to gain access to enemy territory is an example of perfidy: it breaches what little mutual trust we have with our adversaries, and this is counterproductive to achieving lasting peace. But perhaps robotic mosquitoes could have been deployed instead, thus avoiding the suspicion and backlash that humanitarian workers consequently suffered. Animals and insects are typically not considered to be combatants or anything of concern to our enemies. Even if such acts are not illegal, however, it is still possible for us to act in bad faith, and we should be mindful of that possibility.

Issues of deception also arise in cases where robots are used as Trojan horses. Imagine that we capture an enemy robot, hack into it, reprogram it, and then send it back home to work secretly for us. Would that be any different from masquerading as the enemy by wearing their uniform – another perfidious ruse? Another questionable scenario might be the commandeering of a robotic car or plane owned by the other side. Or perhaps we might commercially manufacture robots with back-door chips that allow us to hijack the machine when it falls into someone else's possession.

Some of these uses for robots might be clever and effective, but the point about deception and bad faith can be related back to a number of criticisms we have so far made about spy robots. The tactical benefits might undermine our strategic goals. They might erode important legal principles. Or such acts might give the impression that we are unwilling to get our hands dirty and make it seems as though we are afraid to commit fully to fighting our battles.

Personnel and proliferation

Another set of concerns with the use of spy robots is the impact they might have on personnel and the capabilities of institutions that use them. For example, we should think about how the use of robotics might impact recruitment in the intelligence community. Modern militaries have demonstrated an increased demand for UAVs that can perform armed attack functions (Sparrow 2009, pp. 169–70; Strawser 2010, p. 342). This will have implications for recruitment and training. Likewise, the increasing use of robots for the purposes of national security intelligence collection will impact the type of people who are recruited and the way they are recruited. Further-more, how do we process and analyse all the extra information we are collecting from our drones and digital networks? If the data flood is not managed effectively by the intelligence community, we risk overloading our decision makers with information, and missing the vital piece of intelligence that can prevent a disaster.

Furthermore, an increased reliance on robots by the intelligence community raises issues of technological dependency and a resulting loss of certain human skills (Carr 2014). We can see this effect when we look at technology that over time has become commonplace. We don't remember as well as we once did, because the development of the printing press means that all our stories can be captured on paper. The widespread availability of calculators means that most of us are not as good at doing arithmetic in our heads as we would once have been. Grammar and spelling skills have deteriorated because we rely on word-processing programs with spell-check functions. This could be a serious problem when highly skilled professions are lost. For example, some are worried that the development of medical robots might cause human surgeons to lose their skills in performing difficult procedures. What would happen if we were in a remote location, or if there was a power cut and we didn't have access to the robots on which we had become dependent? This problem is magnified in the context of national security, since we might be fighting an enemy who is working hard to destroy or disrupt our robotic capabilities. This has led some experts to argue that we should purposefully keep more 'humans in the loop' and reverse the des-killing of human operators through the use of automated machinery (Hagerott 2014).

Finally, the ongoing development of spy robots could create an intelligence arms race. Here we could see a proliferation of spy robots as our adversaries develop or acquire the matching technologies and use them against us. Many nations have already deployed (or are developing) military robots, and the international UAV market is expected to grow from $5.2 billion in 2013 to $8.32 billion by 2018 (Markets and Markets 2013; Zenko & Kreps 2014, p. 7). This will almost certainly lead to the cat-and-mouse games of military capabilities and countermeasures that we have witnessed in the development of nearly every military technology, from crossbows and tanks, to nuclear missiles and stealth technologies. Most recently, the Chinese newspaper *Xinhua* (2014) claimed that China had successfully tested a laser defence system capable of shooting down small-scale drones flying at low attitude.

From intelligence collection to armed attack

In this final section, we examine one particularly important aspect of the use of spy robots: that is, the move from intelligence collection to engaging in an armed attacked on a target. We briefly describe the moral dilemma of national security intelligence collection, which is the tension that exists between a state's duty to protect the political community versus its duty to preserve the rights of individuals. We then discuss the problem with weaponising spy robots. We finish this chapter by examining the (potential) impact of the use of spy robots on international norms.

Intelligence collection

Recently, scholars have been increasingly concerned with the ethics of intelligence collection. Gill (2009), for example, has discussed the way in which the prosecution of the 'War on Terror' has brought up problems to do with intelligence gathering and respect for human rights. Quinlan (2007) has noted that effective intelligence practice means doing things that are contrary to standard moral rules. And Erskine (2010) surveys a number of ethical frameworks that have been employed in assessing actions involved in intelligence collection.

But recent events have brought particular ethical concerns to light, namely 'over the growing ability and tendency of intelligence and security services to intercept, monitor, and retain personal data in an increasingly cyber-dependent world' (Bellaby 2012, p. 94). There are aspects of intelligence gathering, as practised by all major countries, that appear to be morally disreputable. The Snowden leaks, in particular, allowed previously hidden intelligence-collection practices to be revealed to the public, which provoked widespread alarm, condemnation and embarrassment. The concerns raised include the number of people caught up in intelligence collection dragnets, misuses of 'metadata', inadequate protection of confidential personal information, undisclosed 'partnerships' with major telecom and internet companies, and so on (Macaskill & Dance 2013).

We also believe, however, that political leaders have an ethical obligation to act so as to protect their people. National security intelligence is the intelligence collected, analysed and disseminated to decision makers in the task of ensuring the security of the state. This includes the security of individuals within and between states, not just the prevention or prosecution of wars between states. This inclusive definition of security is more accurate in tracing how national security intelligence has evolved and responded since the end of the Second World War, from a pre-occupation with fighting or preventing wars between states to supporting a broader human security agenda (Walsh 2011, p. 10).

In addition, without intelligence collection we would not sufficiently understand the nature of some important threats that we face. The main purpose of national security intelligence is to provide necessary information to policymakers that may help them in making decisions. The presumption is that good (i.e. accurate, comprehensive and timely) information will lead to more effective choices on the part of government officials (Johnson 2010, p. 5).

As such, intelligence agencies face a tension between, on one hand, their duty to protect the political community and, on the other, the reality that intelligence collection may entail activities that negatively affect individuals (Bellaby 2012, p. 94). Clearly it is not viable for intelligence agencies to maintain a permanently shadowy existence, free to act out of sight and out of mind. There is, however, an important distinction between vacuuming up all available technical data for analysis and collecting targeted intelligence for the purposes of national security. The point here is that targeted intelligence collection by spy robots might be morally justified in some cases. But the indiscriminate collection of data is likely to be neither justified nor effective.

A licence to kill?

A further ethical problem for the use of spy robots, on top of the need to justify their use in intelligence collection, is the fact that they are frequently armed and can shift very quickly from surveillance to attack. The tighter coupling of surveillance and the decision to kill in weaponised spy robots has placed a range of unique demands on UAV operators (Asaro 2013, p. 207). For one thing, UAVs have a particularly useful capability for reconnaissance that allows the operator to surveil difficult-to-reach areas for lengthy periods without people being put at risk on the ground. But it is but a short step to arming such UAVs, perhaps as a way of protecting the UAV or to take advantage of the opportunity to hit a terrorist cell. This blurs the line between armed conflict and intelligence collection, a distinction that is getting fuzzier all the time.

If the line between espionage and war is becoming more blurry, and if robots are used for espionage, under what conditions could their use amount to an act of war? Espionage is not considered to be a *casus belli* (i.e. a sufficiently just cause) for going to war. War is conventionally understood to be an armed, physical conflict between political communities. But so much of our modern national infrastructure is dependent on digital or information-based assets that we could potentially be seriously harmed by non-kinetic attacks (i.e. cyberweapons that damage computer systems or steal information). Indeed, the US has declared that, as part of its cyberpolicy, it reserves the right to retaliate with kinetic means to a non-kinetic attack. Or, as one US Department of Defense official said, 'If you shut down our power grid, maybe we will put a missile down one of your smokestacks' (Gorman & Barnes 2011, para. 3; Lucas 2013, p. 369). And what if the spy robot, while trying to evade capture, accidentally harmed a foreign national? Might that also be a flashpoint for armed conflict?

International norms

This leads us to our final area of ethical concern, which is the impact that the use of spy robots has (or might have) on international norms. Some robots – such as the Predator, Reaper and close-in weapon system (CIWS) – already have lethal defensive or offensive capabilities. This creates uncertainty about compliance with International Humanitarian Law (IHL) or the Law of Armed Conflict (LOAC). It might be argued that the use of lethal robots represents a disproportionate use of force relative to the military objective. This refers to the collateral damage, or unintended death of nearby innocent civilians, caused by, say, a Hellfire missile launched by a Reaper UAV. What is an acceptable rate of innocents killed for every bad guy killed: 2:1, 10:1, 50:1? The number has not been agreed upon and it continues to be debated, particularly with regard to asymmetric conflicts.

In contrast to the issue with collateral harm is the opposite problem of a perfectly accurate targeting system. Let's imagine a scenario where we were able to create a robot that targets only combatants and that leaves no collateral damage. Perversely, this might also violate one of the International Committee of the Red Cross's (ICRC) guidelines, which bans weapons that cause more than 25 per cent field mortality and 5 per cent hospital mortality. A robot that kills almost everything it targets could have a mortality rate approaching 100 per cent – well over the

ICRC's 25 per cent threshold. This is possible given the superhuman accuracy of machines. Such a robot would be a fearsome, inhumane and devastating prospect in war, and would go against the infamous Martens Clause in IHL that prohibits unconscionable weapons and tactics (Ticehurst 1997).

There is also a line of argument that suggests we should allow robots to make their own attack decisions (i.e. autonomous robots) (Arkin 2010). Critics argue, however, that robots do not have the human abilities of judgment and interpretation necessary to distinguish combatants from non-combatants (Asaro 2012, p. 693). In other words, robots cannot satisfy the principle of distinction. This principle – which is fundamental to the Geneva Conventions and the underlying Just War tradition – requires that we do not target non-combatants (Begby, Reichberg & Syse 2012, p. 337). But a robot already has a hard time distinguishing a terrorist pointing a gun from, say, a child holding a cane. Even humans have a hard time with this principle, since a terrorist might look exactly like an Afghan shepherd with an AK-47 who's just protecting his flock of goats.

Other developments in robotics technology might have implications for IHL conventions. As we develop human enhancements for soldiers, whether pharmaceutical or robotic integrations, it is unclear whether we have created a biological weapon (Lin, Mehlman & Abney 2013, p. 31). The Biological Weapons Convention (BWC) does not specify that bioweapons need to be microbial or a pathogen. So, in theory, a cyborg with super-strength or super-endurance could count as a biological weapon. Of course, the intent of the BWC was to prohibit indiscriminate weapons of mass destruction (again, related to the issue of discriminate weapons). But what if a soldier became able to resist pain through the use of robotics? What would then count as torturing that person? Would taking a hammer or an electric saw to a robotic limb count as torture?

Conclusion

We know that robotics is becoming increasingly important for intelligence collection because robots are better than humans at completing some national security tasks that are dull, dirty and dangerous. But we also know that the robot–human interaction is a potentially weak link in practical applications. And the overuse of robots can present significant problems. Consequently, we should be wary of the temptation to use spy robots, particularly in ways that are ethically and legally questionable. There are a number of responsibility and compliance issues, including establishing responsibility for serious accidents, e-waste environmental problems, legal obligations and privacy concerns. Spy robots also present a range of new possibilities to manipulate, coerce and deceive our adversaries. In addition, there is likely to be significant impact on the capabilities of the institutions that use them.

A particular ethical concern, however, is the proliferation of spy robots and the implications of weaponising them. The increasing use of spy robot technology certainly highlights the need to justify such enhanced methods of intelligence collection. But also of moral concern is the fact that spy robots are frequently armed and can shift very quickly from surveillance to attack. This capability blurs the line between armed conflict and intelligence collection, which raises a range of additional international legal and ethical problems.

References

Arkin, RC 2010, 'The case for ethical autonomy in unmanned systems', *Journal of Military Ethics*, vol. 9, no. 4, pp. 332–341.

Asaro, P 2012, 'On banning autonomous weapon systems: human rights, automation, and the dehumanization of lethal decision making', *International Review of the Red Cross*, vol. 94, no. 886, pp. 687–709.

Asaro, P 2013, 'The labor of surveillance and bureaucratized killing: new subjectivities of military drone operators', *Social Semiotics*, vol. 23, no. 2, pp. 196–224.

Begby, E, Reichberg, GM & Syse, H 2012, 'The ethics of war. part ii: contemporary authors and issues', *Philosophy Compass*, vol. 7, no. 5, pp. 328–347.

Bellaby, R 2012, 'What's the harm? the ethics of intelligence collection', *Intelligence and National Security*, vol. 27, no. 1, pp. 93–117.

Black, J 2013, 'Are Tasers too deadly to be called "non-lethal"?' *NBC News*, 5 September, www.nbcnews.com

Calo, MR 2012, 'Robots and privacy', in P LinK Abney & GA Bekey (eds), *Robot ethics: the ethical and social implications of robotics*, MIT Press, Cambridge, MA.

Carr, N 2014, *The glass cage: automation and us*, W. W. Norton & Company, New York.

Cavas, C 2010, 'Lost navy UAV enters Washington airspace', *Defense News*, 25 August, www.defensenews.com

Enemark, C 2013, *Armed drones and the ethics of war: military virtue in a post-heroic age*, Taylor & Francis, Abingdon.

Erskine, T 2010, '"As rays of light to the human soul"? Moral agents and intelligence gathering', in J Goldman (ed.), *Ethics of spying: a reader for the intelligence professional, Vol. 2*, Scarecrow Press, Lanham, MD.

Gill, P 2009, 'Security intelligence and human rights: illuminating the "heart of darkness"?' *Intelligence and National Security*, vol. 24, no. 1, pp. 78–102.

Gorman, S & Barnes, JE 2011, 'Cyber combat: act of war', *The Wall Street Journal*, 31 May.

Hagerott, M 2014, 'Limiting automation in a cyber-insecure world', *C4ISR & Networks*, 7 November, www.c4isrnet.com.

Harnden, T 2008, 'CIA give Afghan warlords Viagra in exchange for information on Taliban', *The Telegraph*, 26 December, www.telegraph.co.uk

Hodge, N 2011, 'U.S. says drone, cargo plane collide over Afghanistan', *The Wall Street Journal*, 17 August, http://online.wsj.com

Johnson, LK 2010, *The Oxford handbook of national security intelligence*, Oxford University Press, Oxford.

Kaushik, P 2014, 'Why rising mounts of e-waste jeopardise India's technology-driven growth', *Business Insider India*, 3 November, www.businessinsider.in

Kilcullen, D & McDonald Exum, A 2009, 'Death from above, outrage down below', *The New York Times*, 16 May, www.nytimes.com

Levy, D 2012, 'The ethics of robot prostitutes', in P Lin, K Abney & GA Bekey (eds), *Robot ethics: the ethical and social implications of robotics*, MIT Press, Cambridge, MA.

Lin, P, Mehlman, MJ & Abney, K 2013, *Enhanced warfighters: risk, ethics, and policy*, Greenwall Foundation, New York.

Lucas, GR 2013, 'Jus in silico: moral restrictions on the use of cyberwarfare', in F Allhoff, NG Evans & A Henschke (eds), *Routledge handbook of ethics and war: just war theory in the 21st century*, Taylor & Francis, Abingdon.

Macaskill, E. & Dance, G 2013, 'NSA files: decoded', *The Guardian*, 1 November, www.theguardian.com

MarketsandMarkets 2013, 'Global unmanned aerial vehicle (UAV) market (2013–2018)', Markets and Markets, Magarpatta city, India, www.marketsandmarkets.com

O'Connell, ME 2012, 'Unlawful killing with combat drones: a case study of Pakistan, 2004–2009', in S Bronitt, M Gani & S Hufnagel (eds), *Shooting to kill: socio-legal perspectives on the use of lethal force*, Hart Publishing, Oxford and Portland, OR.

Pasculli, L 2013, 'Genetics, robotics and crime prevention', in *Proceedings of the International Conference on Genetics, Robotics, Law, Punishment*, Padova-Treviso, https://www.academia.edu/4668765/Genetics_Robotics_and_Crime_Prevention

Quinlan, M 2007, 'Just intelligence: prolegomena to an ethical theory', *Intelligence and National Security*, vol. 22, no. 1, pp. 1–13.

Royakkers, L & Van Est, R 2010, 'The cubicle warrior: the marionette of digitalized warfare', *Ethics and Information Technology*, vol. 12, no. 3, pp. 289–296.

Rutherford, M 2009, 'BEAR robot roars to the rescue', *CNET*, 22 August, www.cnet.com

Shachtman, N 2007, 'Robot cannon kills 9, wounds 14', *Wired*, 18 October, www.wired.com

Sluka, JA 2011, 'Death from above: UAVs and losing hearts and minds', *Military Review*, vol. 91, no. 3, p. 70.

Solove, DJ 2011, *Nothing to hide: the false tradeoff between privacy and security*, Yale University Press, New Haven, CT.

Sparrow, R 2009, 'Building a better warbot: ethical issues in the design of unmanned systems for military applications', *Science and Engineering Ethics*, vol. 15, no. 2, pp. 169–187.

Statt, N 2013, 'This crime-predicting robot aims to patrol our streets by 2015', *CNET*, 3 December, www.cnet.com

Strawser, BJ 2010, 'Moral predators: the duty to employ uninhabited aerial vehicles', *Journal of Military Ethics*, vol. 9, no. 4, pp. 342–368.

Strawser, BJ 2013, *Killing by remote control: the ethics of an unmanned military*, Oxford University Press, New York.

Ticehurst, R 1997, 'The Martens Clause and the laws of armed conflict', *International Review of the Red Cross*, vol. 37, no. 317, pp. 125–134.

Walsh, PF 2011, *Intelligence and intelligence analysis*, Routledge, New York.

Xinhua 2014, 'China develops anti-drone laser', *Xinhua*, 2 November, http://news.xinhua net.com

Zenko, M & Kreps, S 2014, *Limiting armed drone proliferation*, Council Special Report No. 69, Center for Preventive Action, Council on Foreign Relations, New York.

12

EMERGING TECHNOLOGIES, ASYMMETRIC FORCE AND TERRORIST BLOWBACK

Jai Galliott

Introduction

In this chapter I consider whether chess still serves as a simulacrum for political and military confrontation. While clearly a metaphor of the highest degree, it embodies a conception of a very particular type of conflict and, moreover, a conception that holds a great deal of significance for our moral and strategic assessment of cyber and unmanned warfare. When we think of chess, we imagine equally configured forces ready to engage in a perfectly symmetrical contest. Each side has clear and distinguishable uniforms. The battle is regulated by robust rules that stipulate how the conflict is to be commenced, conducted and terminated. As David Rodin (2006, p. 153) argued in his exploration of the ethics of asymmetric conflict, this image reflects a moral assessment of conflict in two ways: first, it gives us the idea of war as a fair fight between two combatants; second, because the battle is isolated from all non-combatant elements, it accords with our sense of justice in war by limiting the risk of harm to those directly involved in the conflict. However, as he also points out, there are forms of war that do not embody the sort of symmetry and equality that characterise the contest that is chess (Rodin 2006, p. 153). As modern history confirms, war all too often diverges from the chessboard image of war, and it is the argument of the first section of this chapter that when the degree of divergence reaches a critical point, we begin to experience serious difficulties in interpreting and applying Just War theory. More specifically, it will be argued that distance warfare deployed by technologically powerful states can generate a morally problematic 'radical asymmetry' that sets justice and fairness in conflict or competition with the initial aims of those that aim such wars. In the second section of this chapter, I consider the implications of warfare departing from the sort of transparency that is implicit in the game of chess and earlier forms of conflict. In particular, I suggest that the causal chains that we typically rely upon to attribute responsibility are obscured by the ones and zeros of digital computing and that as defence becomes increasingly computerised and automated, we may need to think more carefully about the implications this has for relations between armed forces.

A brief background to the asymmetry problem

'Asymmetry' and 'asymmetric warfare' are terms that are used and acknowledged widely throughout military, security and policy communities. US Major General Perry Smith puts it well in saying that '[asymmetry] is the term of the day' (Safire 2004, p. 13). The problem is that references to asymmetry and associated terms have become so common and casual – to the point that they are virtually omni-present in scholarly work, government reports and media briefs related to modern military affairs – that there is now a fair deal of confusion and distortion in thinking about asymmetric warfare and this can skew the arguments concerning cyber and unmanned warfare, if not resolved.

While familiar in common parlance, when we begin to apply the terms 'symmetry' and 'asymmetry' to war they take on an additional military meaning such that the definitions and concepts become somewhat less clear. Some argue that asymmetry as a modern military concept did not make its first significant appearance in print until the early to mid-1990s (Safire 2004, p. 13), but detailed references to the same concept can be found at least some twenty years earlier in Andrew Mack's (1975) article 'Why big nations lose small wars: the politics of asymmetric conflict' in *World Politics*. It was in this article that the term 'asymmetric conflict' was described in detail and through which the concept became popularised. As the title implies, Mack was concerned with why large industrial powers failed to achieve victory in conflicts such as those in Aden, Algeria, Cyprus, Indochina, Indonesia, Morocco, Tunisia, Vietnam and others, despite conventional military and techno-logical superiority. To be more precise, he wanted an explanation as to how the militarily powerful could be defeated in armed conflict by the militarily weak. How could the weak win wars? He hypothesised that there must be a range of what he called 'asymmetries' at play. In doing so, Mack acknowledged the work of others who had also written about the role of asymmetries, although in somewhat different terms and with different emphases. For instance, he highlighted that Steven Rosen, E.L. Katzenbach, Johan Galtung and Henry Kissinger have all written about asymmetry in terms of willingness to suffer costs, financial resources, technological resources, goals and strategy (Mack 1975, p. 178). Mack, however, thought that the important asymmetry in the majority of cases was that of public support for political action (1975, pp. 184–6).

This article went largely ignored for many years, but toward the end of the Cold War period it had gained renewed interest among concerned academics because of the changing character of war and military conflict. During the 1990s, research building on Mack's insights began to mature. However, it was not until 11 September 2001 that the notion of asymmetry came to the fore, both in the literature and in common discourse. How could a non-state actor successfully carry out an attack that would cripple the United States for weeks and instil long-lasting fear in its population? In order to make sense of the events of that day and their aftermath, key political figures evoked the concept of asymmetry. The key user at the time was Secretary of Defense Donald Rumsfeld. After noting that the United States was 'going to have to fashion a new vocabulary' to describe this 'new' kind of warfare, he told reporters that he had long been talking of 'asymmetrical threats'. When a savvy reporter pressed the Secretary for further information about what these asymmetrical threats actually were, he could not provide a definition (Safire 2004, p. 13). However, a working definition of 'asymmetric warfare' published by the US Joint Chiefs of Staff states that:

> Asymmetric approaches are attempts to circumvent or undermine US strengths while exploiting US weaknesses using methods that differ significantly from the United States' expected method of operations.
>
> *(US Joint Chiefs of Staff 1999, p. 2)*

From this definition, it is clear that asymmetric warfare is perceived as a strategic threat to the United States and one that may, in theory, be present in any number of different guises and conflict areas. Rumsfeld was able to clarify what he thought to be asymmetric tactics by offering some examples: 'terrorism and ballistic missiles, cruise missiles, [and] cyberattacks' (Safire 2004, p. 13). Others have provided more comprehensive lists. For example, Kenneth McKenzie, again approaching the matter from a US strategic context, identifies six categories of asymmetric tactics. These include the use of or deployment of: (i) chemical weapons; (ii) biological weapons; (iii) nuclear weapons (known collectively in the post-Iraq era as 'weapons of mass destruction'); (iv) information war (such as attacks on key financial, infrastructure or defence systems); (v) terrorism (which is notable because of its focus on non-combatants); and (vi) other operational concepts that may involve guerrilla tactics, the involvement of non-state actors, the commingling of military forces with civilian communities in an effort to complicate weapons use, and the use of primitive weapons in unusual and surprising ways (McKenzie 2000). These US-centric descriptions, when taken in their historical context, reflect the more general fact that the term 'asymmetric warfare' has become synonymous with unconventional attacks which leverage the vulnerabilities of the strong (that are either overlooked or tolerated) in order to avoid conventional military engagements, particularly with Western powers. Rodin (2006, p. 155) confirms this, writing that 'asymmetric tactics are typically the tactics of weakness, not tactics of choice; they are adopted by those who do not have the military capability to engage their enemy on roughly equal terms in conventional war'.

It is wise to take issue with this United States-centric conceptualisation of asymmetric warfare on the basis that it is inappropriately constricting, as will soon be demonstrated. It should first be pointed out that all wars are asymmetric in the sense that perfect equality is highly unlikely to occur in the modern military world and, in any case, it would be practically impossible to verify whether there is perfect equality (Enemark 2014, p. 59). This is not to deny that the definition given earlier is useful in describing the current state of military affairs, i.e. in which there are many conventionally weak but potentially dangerous adversaries prepared to confront world superpowers like the United States with such tactics. However, there remains a need for a sharper and more accurate understanding of asymmetry in warfare. As a bare minimum, a more acceptable conception must establish asymmetry in warfare as a category independent of the perceived power of the actors involved. Let us think back to Mack. While he framed his discussion in terms of how the weak could prevail against the strong, all the asymmetries he identified were simply disparities of some sort between opposing actors in a conflict. The same can be said of those identified by McKenzie. Indeed, effective chemical, biological, radiological and nuclear weapons are only in the domain of the strong, which leads to the thought that asymmetric war is not something that can only be waged by the weak. While weaker actors may have greater reason for waging asymmetric warfare, asymmetric tactics are often a tool of the strong. Furthermore, as Enemark (2014, p. 59) argues, it needs to be recognised that 'asymmetry' can refer to any imbalance in strength that each side in a conflict can bring to bear against the other. Another way to conceive of the matter is to assume that there are positive asymmetries, which involve utilising differences to gain an advantage, as well as negative asymmetries, which might be used by an opponent to gain an advantage (Metz and Johnson 2001, p. 6).

All of this said, the most obvious asymmetry is, of course, technological in nature. This is part of a more general asymmetric relationship generated by information operations, which should, in Mack's terms, be classified as a function of the asymmetry in 'resource power' (1975, p. 182). As will be shown in the next section, an overwhelming asymmetry in technological resource power may also cast doubt over the moral legitimacy of military action. It must also be said that, while technological strength may have guaranteed decisive military victory in earlier years, weaker opponents have since realised that they are not compelled to fight their enemies on the dictated terms and can utilise any of those asymmetries mentioned above.

The concept of radical asymmetry

As already suggested, technological asymmetry is nothing new, at least in the outdated weak-versus-strong sense. Despite this, we can highlight a few conflicts that illustrate humanity's progression along the scale of technological asymmetry. The Battle of Agincourt is often cited as a striking historical example of the sort of effect superior military technology can have on the battlefield. It was at Agincourt that the English achieved victory over the numerically superior French army. It was thought that the English were outnumbered by almost six to one, with the French having troop strength of approximately 30,000 men (Barker 1971, p. 320). Yet what is striking is that due to the longbow, which allowed its users to launch a barrage of powerful arrows at a greater than normal distance, the English suffered only a few hundred war dead, while the French lost many thousands. William Shakespeare later depicted this conflict as ruthless and unchivalrous, a depiction that reflects some of the concerns of this chapter. According to Shakespeare, ruthless and ungallant conflict was essentially one of the paradoxes for the king; something he must wrestle with when protecting his empire (Taylor 1982). Another engagement representative of technological asymmetry was that which took place between well armed colonial forces and an army of traditional African warriors at Omdurman, on the upper Nile, at the end of the nineteenth century (Headrick 2005, p. 275). Under the command of General Horatio Kitchener, the colonial forces fought a vastly larger armed force and managed to achieve a decisive victory, which was critical to the British conquering Sudan. The Egyptian forces under Kitchener's command carried breach-loading rifles and the British carried repeating rifles (which allowed for faster firing), maxims (machine guns) and field cannon. Their opponents, on the other hand, had only spears, swords and muskets (Headrick 2005, p. 275). Unsurprisingly, the Anglo-Egyptian casualties were few and far between, while their opponents lost approximately 10,000 troops (Raugh 2004, p. 257). Showing his concern about asymmetric war, Winston Churchill (1899), who fought in this conflict, later wrote about his disillusionment with modern technology and how dishonourable the Omdurman 'slaughter' was.

The Gulf War was another key point in the progression toward radical techno-logical asymmetry in the more modern sense of the term. Executed by a United Nations coalition force, led by the United States and financed mostly by Saudi Arabia, the Gulf War was waged against Iraq primarily in response to its invasion and annexation of Kuwait. While the Iraq of the 1990s was far from a defenceless state, its weaponry was simply not as advanced as that of the Coalition (Finlan 2008, p. 84). The Gulf War saw the introduction of advanced networked technologies including fighter jets, surveillance aircraft and so on. It was widely portrayed as a 'telepresent' war conducted by 'armchair generals' via satellite (Murphie & Potts 2003, p. 172). There was little contest in this war, with the Coalition achieving a decisive victory with very few losses. The Gulf War essentially served as a template for conducting modern asymmetric warfare, and the Kosovo War was its corollary. This war, aimed at bringing down the Milosevic regime and protecting Kosovo from Serbian aggression, began with several United States ships and a British sub-marine (operating under the North Atlantic Treaty Organization, NATO) firing cruise missiles. Following this, allied aircraft launched a campaign of precision-guided munitions attacks, which were aided by the use of remotely controlled drones (Mahnken 2008, p. 183). Given the technological asymmetry that existed, NATO's aims were met with no military casualties on the allied forces' side (Kemp 2007, p. 60). Accordingly, some theorists have labelled both Kosovo and Iraq as being 'no-risk' wars. In both cases, this is an obvious misnomer. No war that we can conceive of today, even unmanned or cyberwar, can be totally risk-free. War will always pose *some* harm to both combatants and non-combatants. What these theorists mean to convey is that the states that wage this sort of technologically asymmetric warfare are taking significantly less risk, and that such warfare has progressed significantly from the level playing field of the chessboard, which was discussed earlier.

If technological asymmetry is already a common feature of modern warfare as suggested, one might then wonder whether the technological asymmetry generated by today's distance warfare really represents a 'radical' departure from previous levels of asymmetry. Is launching a destructive drone or cyberattack more ethically problematic than dropping a 500-pound bomb at 20,000 feet or pressing a button that launches a cruise missile? The answer is straightforwardly: 'yes'. What makes the former morally repugnant is the ability to target a specific piece of network infrastructure, at great distance, with the knowledge that you are virtually invulnerable to retaliation. Unmanned and cyber warfare make it possible to remove the human actor from the area of conflict – all the while allowing the operators of these systems to target infrastructure more precisely than if they were present in the field themselves – taking us as close to the notion of a 'risk-free' warfare as we are likely to get at any time in the foreseeable future. This is unlike the conflicts with Kosovo and Iraq, in which pilots remained in the air, thus somewhat putting themselves at risk. Objectors to this sort of risk-free war say that an issue arises when distance warfare is used against another force, which does not possess such technology, and when the level of life-threatening risk incurred between the warring parties becomes so imbalanced that we cross a symmetry threshold which makes the fight (and thus the use of the computer as a weapon) intrinsically unjust. To illustrate what people find problematic and to test our moral intuitions, let us consider the following thought experiment.

State X, holding what it thinks is a just cause, decides to engage in conflict with State Y. State X possesses robust unmanned defence and attack technologies. Rather than sending in many traditional human warfighters, State X launches a multi-prong technological attack, starting with the release of a worm aimed at providing intelligence on government network infrastructure. Once this information is transferred across the its network and analysed by super-computers under the control of a well staffed cyber command, State X launches a denial of service attack upon government networks and unleashes swarms of armed drones aimed at destroying the military infrastructure of State Y. State Y, for whatever reason, does not have robust cyber defences and has only conventional armed forces which have no effective way to retaliate against the drone attack, since its enemy has a purely technological in-country presence. So, at the moment when State X commences its remote attack, State Y essentially is doomed to fail in defending itself.[1]

It is this kind of scenario – where one side can inflict damage on the other with virtual impunity – which ethicists find morally troubling. The issue is how such remote conflict could possibly be considered ethical. There are two grounds on which the legitimacy of asymmetrical warfare might be questioned, and these will be considered separately. The first has to do with the notion of fairness and equality in warfare, and how it might be undermined by radical technological asymmetry. The second, which is equally important, has to do with what will be called 'evoked potential': that is, the spontaneous, potentially dangerous and morally questionable alternative asymmetric response/s possibly evoked by the sort of technological asymmetry which is of concern to us. This potential can apply to both state and non-state actors. It is relevant to note here that there are all sorts of unresolved debates concerning the difference between these two sorts of actors, and whether non-state actors can act in accordance with Just War principles in the same fashion as state actors. Here, though, the discussion is restricted primarily to illustrating the moral problem with radical technological asymmetry and makes no claims about this sub-debate.

Fairness in radically asymmetric conflict

Strawser (2010) presents the most comprehensive account of the issues of fairness as they relate to emerging military technologies. Strawser claims that if it is possible for a military pursuing a Just War-sanctioned action to use remote systems in lieu of the manned equivalent, without incurring a loss of capability (by which he means *Just War* fighting capability), then they have an ethical obligation to do so. This contention stems from what Strawser labels the 'principle of unnecessary risk', which holds that in trying to accomplish some objectively good goal, one must, *ceteris paribus*, choose means that do not violate the demands of justice, make the world worse or entail more risk than necessary to achieve the good goal in question (Strawser 2010, p. 344). This principle has a fair deal of *prima facie* appeal. It seems rather uncontroversial to suggest that any technology that *exclusively* minimises harm to warfighters – that is, while imposing no additional 'costs' of another kind – would be morally better. Notwithstanding its *prima facie* appeal, the problem with this principle's application is that, while distance warfare may indeed minimise immediate harm or the risk of it, there may be other unforeseen consequences that countervail the ethical obligation for their use.

Strawser responds to the fairness problem using two arguments, the first of which is perhaps less substantial than the second.[2] His first response is to say that, if the issue concerns whether justified combat should be a 'fair fight' to some extent, this presents no problem because military engagements have been anything but fair for quite some time. He gives the example of a modern-day F-22 pilot killing a tribal warrior wielding a rocket-propelled grenade (Strawser 2010, p. 356). However, this example fails to support Strawser's response. While Omdurman, Iraq and Kosovo all confirm that unfairness is not new, it can be argued that radically asymmetric forms of technological conflict introduce a new, or at least differently disturbing, level of unfairness. In the above example involving the F-22, there is a pilot in the air. Therefore the tribal warrior still has a human to target, regardless of how futile his/her efforts to kill that pilot may be. By contrast, the introduction of unmanned and cyber warfare removes most – if not all – warfighters from the field, and this allows them to overwhelm the enemy at no comparable risk to themselves, using purely technological means.

Strawser's (2010, p. 356) second, and main, line of reply to the fairness objection is that, even if emerging technologies *can* be said to have introduced a new and disturbing level of asymmetry, this still does not present a significant problem for their use. His reasoning appears to be the following: if one combatant is ethically justified in their effort and the other combatant is not, then it is good and just that the justified combatant has the asymmetrical advantage associated with the use of distance weapons. In his view, this is because combatants fighting for an objectively unjust cause have no moral right to engage in violent action, or even defensive action, against combatants fighting for an objectively just cause. There is a moral difference between the two, he would say. Here, Strawser is invoking recent work by Jeff McMahan (2009), which presents a fairly novel reinterpretation of classical Just War theory. While it is not clear whether McMahan's work ultimately has a significant impact on the central issue, it is nonetheless worthwhile working through his response thoroughly. Doing so will provide context for our overall concern with asymmetry, which is a concern regarding the justice of resorting to war in such scenarios. For the ensuing discussion, it will be helpful to briefly recount the traditional theory of Just War and the challenges that McMahan's revision raise for it.

The traditional theory of Just War embodies two main sets of principles that provide a rigorous moral framework. The first concerns the justice of the resort to war (*jus ad bellum*) and the second concerns just and fair conduct in war (*jus in bello*). Under the *jus ad bellum* principles, a state intending to wage war must possess just cause, right intention and proper authority. The war must also be proportional, a likely success and a last resort. Under *jus in bello* principles, activities in war must be discriminate and again, proportional (see Johnson 1981; Walzer 2006a). Under the traditional Just War theory, these two central pillars are considered logically independent from one another. Most importantly for our discussion, this means that it is permissible for a combatant fighting for an objectively unjust cause (an unjust combatant) to fight against a combatant fighting for an objectively just cause (a just combatant), as long as they do not violate the principles of *jus in bello*. In other words, just and unjust combatants are taken to share the same moral status in war. This is commonly referred to as 'the doctrine of the moral equality of combatants' (Walzer 2006a, pp. 34–40). It is essentially a doctrine of battlefield equality. The reason combatants are not held responsible for the decision *to go to war* under this doctrine is because they may, among other things, have been under duress or lacked the requisite information to determine whether their cause was genuinely just, so they are instead judged exclusively on how they fight in the ensuing conflict.

Importantly, Strawser, following McMahan, would reject this notion of equality between combatants. McMahan claims that it seems counterintuitive to say that those pursuing an objectively unjust aim are morally on par with those pursuing an objectively just aim. It is not as though McMahan thinks that we should abandon Just War theory altogether. Rather, he argues that the principles of *jus in bello* should not be considered to be logically independent of those of *jus ad bellum*. Remember that the *jus in bello* convention requires that fighting in war be both discriminate and proportional. McMahan (2009, pp. 15–31) believes that it is virtually impossible to fight in a war, while lacking a just cause, without violating one of these principles. Put most simply, he says that unjust combatants breach the discrimination principle because just combatants are not legitimate targets, since they are innocent in a special sense. Just as a police officer retains their innocence when apprehending a lawbreaker, a just combatant retains her/his innocence in fighting an unjust combatant. Unjust combatants also breach the proportionality principle, because without a just cause, there is no objective good to outweigh any harm done. So, for McMahan, this is why the *jus in bello* principles must be considered in relation to the *jus ad bellum* principles, and also why combatants are not considered to be moral equals in war. Let us label this the 'non-equality thesis'.

Strawser argues from the non-equality thesis that it is good that the just combatant has the asymmetric advantage associated with the use of emerging technologies and is better protected. For Strawser, overwhelming the enemy with a barrage of drones or a devastating cyber attack, and condemning them to what is going to be certain defeat, is not a morally objectionable act. This is because the just combatant is morally justified in taking the life of the unjust combatant, while the unjust combatant is not justified in taking the life of the just combatant, even if the unjust combatant appears to fight in accordance with *jus in bello*. Therefore, according to Strawser, if a particular military force fighting for a justified cause has a better, more advanced and more effective weapons systems than that of their unjustified adversary, they should not refrain from using it because it is seen as 'unfair' or 'unchivalrous'. They are, by the above reasoning, justified in getting that weapons system into the field as quickly as they can to aid in force preservation measures and to improve the likelihood of winning. Thus, responding to the critic's question: 'how can this war be just?', Strawser would say that unjust combatants, who are incapable of fulfilling the requirements of *jus in bello*, are owed no special consideration when it comes to employing a purely remote offensive. This is because they are contributing to a moral wrong, whether or not they are consciously aware of it.

Like Walzer (2006a, pp. 41–3), many will not be convinced by the non-equality thesis, which underpins Strawser's denial that the asymmetry poses a problem for drone employment. The argument proposed is that, in line with traditional thought on the topic, *jus ad bellum* and *jus in bello* should be thought of as logically independent, and that we are correct in making the *prima facie* presumption that there exists moral equality between combatants. As Walzer so eloquently puts it:

> What Jeff McMahan means to provide in this essay is a careful and precise account of individual responsibility in time of war. What he actually provides, I think, is a careful and precise account of what individual responsibility in war would be like if war were a peacetime activity.
>
> (*Walzer 2006b, p. 43*)

These comments highlight the following important point: there is something about war that makes the moral standards that apply to it different from those in normal civilian life. That is, there is something about war which permits soldiers to do things that are normally considered immoral. There are numerous reasons why this

might be so. Many theorists think it fit to talk in terms of the forfeiture of rights –
soldiers waiving rights they would normally hold in peacetime. However, there are
a number of deep problems connected to this approach, particularly concerning the
inalienability of certain rights, namely that to life. Another reason, which follows
from what was said in Chapters 3 and 4, is that there is something in the nature of
the imperfect relationship between individuals and states which allows for those on
both sides to fight justly regardless of the objective justness of their cause. But, for
the moment, let us suppose that this is wrong so that unjust combatants do, in fact,
act wrongly when targeting just combatants, and therefore the just combatants are
entitled to defend themselves against the overall wrong being perpetrated by the
unjust combatants. It is not entirely clear how relevant this actually is to the problem.
In other words, it may be that these questions of fairness and equality – at the *jus in
bello* level at which they are raised by Strawser – are insufficient to explain or deal
with what is fundamentally problematic about the asymmetry in question.

A deeper problem for those advancing the fairness objection consists in pointing
out that using unmanned measures in place of the manned alternative removes an
important element of the justice of resorting to war, an element that seems
important regardless of whether the non-equality thesis succeeds. More specifically,
when the technological imbalance reaches a certain level, it may actually override
any justification for war. To both clarify the fairness objection and draw out the
issues in greater detail, it will be helpful to look briefly at Paul Kahn's (2002, p. 2)
'paradox of riskless warfare'. This paradox is said to arise when the 'pursuit of
asymmetry undermines reciprocity [in terms of risk]'. Kahn (2002, pp. 3–4) says
that any fighting between combatants needs to be qualified in terms of the mutual
imposition of risk. Kahn's paradox occurs at the level of individual combatants or
groups of combatants and is underpinned by a belief in something akin to the
moral equality of combatants, which Strawser refutes. However, for the moment
the reader can put this matter aside, because the aim in discussing Khan's work is
simply to elicit some thought on the general role of risk. Kahn essentially says that,
without the reciprocal imposition of risk, the moral basis for injuring or killing
others is called into question. It is not that he advocates a concept of war of the
chessboard variety, which has equally configured forces. Rather, what he is saying
is that the right to engage in potentially lethal conduct only holds where there is
some *degree* of mutual risk involved. He seems right in using the notion of risk, and
thus threat, as a condition. Sparrow (2011) discusses this idea and deploys it at the
level of individual responsibility. He notes that in wartime, wounded soldiers are
generally considered immune from attack, as they no longer pose an immediate or
near-term threat. Similarly, those who raise the white flag and surrender are also
considered immune from attack, because they likewise pose no threat (Sparrow
2011, p. 127). In both cases, threat (or lack thereof) is at the core of their immunity.

A full account of Kahn's ideas cannot be provided here, but it is evident that the
degree of threat plays an important role in establishing and maintaining any justification to cause harm or kill. This means that if one side's armed forces are incapable,
or rendered incapable, of posing an adequate threat to the other side, the more

powerful side's moral justification for targeting the weaker side's armed forces is void (Kahn 2002). Yet, as mentioned earlier, Kahn's argument is grounded at the individual level. He neglects the role of risk at a higher level, but it is exactly this sort of risk that we need to consider in order to refute Strawser's argument. As noted by Sparrow (2011, p. 128) as well, the kind of asymmetry which is relevant here is that which exists at the macro level, namely at the level of armed forces considered as a whole. This is especially true for our discussion of the use of remote systems. The examples given earlier, of the soldiers who are wounded or have surrendered, perhaps convey the idea that the sort of threat about which we are talking is located at the micro level, that is, between individual combatants. This is the level at which Strawser's discussion takes place. However, with reference to the earlier scenario, the threat that is relevant here is that between State X and State Y considered as a whole, not that between the individual combatants of State X and State Y. This is an important point, because if there is an inadequate level of risk between States X and Y considered as a whole, any reasons that the individual combatants of these states have for taking on any risk will be far less compelling.

In Just War terms, the issue is the following: when the level of asymmetry in war reaches a certain level, a state may be in violation of *jus ad bellum*, the principles of which remain important despite the challenge posed by Strawser's McMahanian argument. Why is this so? Up until this point, we have been talking about the 'deep morality of war'. This is distinct from Walzer's conventional morality of war in that it revolves around the idealistic notion of a system based on objective justice and individual liability. It is this idealistic notion that is responsible for the non-equality thesis and much of Strawser's argument concerning distance weaponry. However, McMahan concedes that there may be laws of war (which embody the traditional Just War principles) to which we should adhere for prudential reasons. These principles will, if consistently and accurately observed, tend to limit the destructiveness of war. This is the reason why the *jus ad bellum* principles remain relevant. Yet McMahan would say that there might be cases in which a given act of violating these *jus ad bellum* principles, when viewed in isolation, might be permitted by the deep morality of war. However, if this act of violation were to lead to other violations, this would make the said act imprudent, because it would fail to limit the destructiveness of war.[3] This two-tiered approach is problematic. Our Just War principles already provide a transitional morality, which will hopefully lead us toward a better state of peace. In granting that we have prudential reasons for adhering to the laws of war, McMahan seems to acknowledge the need for a transitional morality. This seems to mean that his deep morality of war serves little purpose, other than to remind us of the end goal, that is, a better state of peace.[4] His deep morality of war cannot be allowed to constantly trump the transitional morality of war. A full discussion of the reason why we ought to be reluctant to sharply contract prudence with this more idealistic deep morality is beyond the scope of this chapter. The point made here, which is rather uncontroversial, consists in suggesting that, even alongside a deep morality of war and the non-equality thesis and in any warfare, even against the unjust – the just side must adhere to *jus ad bellum* principles. They cannot do whatever they like by appealing to whatever they consider to be the objective justness of their cause.

Having argued that the *jus ad bellum* principles remain important even when fighting an objectively unjust opponent, there are two principles that need to be given particular attention when considering waging a war with remote systems. Both principles are grounded in consequentialist considerations (although one can equally well think of them in deontological terms). The first is the principle of last resort. It is generally recognised that, once war is unleashed, it can often get out of control and take on its own destructive power, with devastating consequences. Therefore war should only ever be fought when necessity demands it; that is, when there is no alternative. However, waging war without any risk to one's own troops (if they can be called that in the case of unmanned and cyber warfare) clearly calls into question one's adherence to this principle. Where there are such high levels of asymmetry created by technology, as in our scenario, war surely cannot be considered a last resort. In most cases, State X would presumably have other, less lethal options available. For example, State X could make clear and obvious to its opponent the fact that it possesses significantly superior technology, perhaps by putting on a non-lethal display of its technological capabilities. This may result in both States reaching some sort of peaceful political negotiation and settlement. Second, there is the principle of proportionality. In the *jus ad bellum* sense, this principle asks us to look at the harm our proposed military action is likely to cause and weigh it against the harm that we hope to avoid. But where the technological imbalance is so radical – that is, where those on the receiving side of an attack are virtually unable to retaliate – it seems that the harm that the technologically superior state hopes to thwart will in many cases be so insignificant that it would present dire problems for the proportionality calculus. In other words, technological war of the sort described in the earlier scenario is rendered unjust. Of course, the deployment of unmanned or cyber force can be more limited in nature and need not cross the symmetry threshold, but the escalation of war poses a constant risk.

Asymmetry and evoked potential/terrorist blowback

For the reasons described above, remote warfare does not necessarily need to be a 'fair' or perfectly symmetrical fight, as represented by the game of chess. But it arguably needs to be *a fight* of some description if it is to have any hope of fulfilling the *jus ad bellum* principles of last resort and proportionality (Enemark 2014, p. 60). Regrettably, it is not immediately clear whether the recent remote attacks meet this description. In fact, in many ways, their employment seems to facilitate the waging of politically motivated violence that, as it turns out, more closely resembles childish retaliation on the part of world superpowers. This section aims to outline a potential counter argument to the asymmetry objection or, more particularly, to the principle relating to proportionality. The other principle, which pertains to matters of last resort, will remain untouched. In pre-empting the asymmetry objection and clarifying what exactly is at issue, it will be shown that we are presented with another potential problem for radically asymmetric remote warfare and thus have a further reason to question its legitimacy.

As we already know, at the *jus ad bellum* level, the principle of proportionality requires that we weigh the harm that the proposed military action is likely to cause with the harm that we hope to avoid. Highlighted in the previous section was the issue that the harm faced was not great enough to justify the attack in question. However, one might object that the only reason the harm was not seen to be so significant was because we failed to look beyond the initial pre-provocation harm and failed to accurately project the longer-term consequences. It might be said that a state contemplating waging war must think more clearly, when projecting the outcomes of a possible conflict, about how its actions will impact and/or provoke the enemy – including how its actions and decisions will influence the enemy's will and response. In other words, the stronger state ought to factor in evoked potential: the spontaneous, possibly dangerous and sometimes morally questionable responses caused by radical technological asymmetry. The problem is, of course, that the extent to which we are required to project consequences under the proportionality principle is not obvious. After all, it is remarkably difficult to predict what the enemy's decisions and responses will be prior to initiating a conflict, and traditionally they have not been given much weight.[5] However, since evoked potential is indirectly linked to radical technological asymmetry, and given that states have an obvious interest in not being subjected to asymmetric tactics, we will, for the sake of argument, entertain the idea that a state should foresee such responses and include them in its calculation of the proportionality of its proposed actions. If nothing else, in dealing with the objection, we should actually demonstrate – presumably to the dismay of those who would object to the earlier treatment of the fairness problem – that evoked potential might tip the proportionality scale too far in the other direction. That is, if we must consider evoked potential, a radically asymmetric cyber- or drone attack may involve so much potential harm that the war will be considered unjust.

Killmister (2008, p. 122) argues that, once we have ruled out the extraordinarily unlikely option of unconditional surrender, there are only a limited number of options open to the weaker state in a situation where there exists a radical imbalance in technological resource power. In the aforementioned example, the vast technological difference means that State X can quite easily locate and attack State Y's core pieces of infrastructure, just because as a developing nation they do not yet have sufficiently robust technological defences in place. The same task is made rather more difficult for State Y because of their enemy's purely technological presence. They cannot attack the other side's soldiers because there are none present. They cannot launch their own cyber- or drone attack because the other side's defences are so robust. This gives rise to an ethically concerning potentiality which Bob Simpson and Rob Sparrow (2013/14, pp. 93–4) have labelled the 'guerrilla problem'. In order to avoid being targeted and possibly killed by their opponents, who have better surveillance and attack capacities, the combatants of State Y may embrace a common asymmetric tactic and decide that they will try to infiltrate their enemy's society, concealing themselves and their weapons amongst the vulnerable civilian population. This tactic has the effect of making it much more difficult and potentially dangerous for State X to abide by the Just War principles of discrimination and proportionality. For conventionally weak states, the aim is often to provoke the enemy and then commingle with the civilian population in the hope that the enemy will be driven to continue with attacks, causing a large number of civilian casualties and other collateral damage. This will, in turn, undermine both local and international political support for the stronger adversary's cause.

At this juncture, it is important to note that the conventionally weak State Y is not alone in utilising this asymmetric tactic and in shifting the burden of risk onto its civilian population. Cyber and drone operators are regularly commingled with civilians. The most well known cyber command centres are based in Washington, and drone operation centres are based around the nearby residential areas. But do distance warriors count as combatants and therefore as appropriate targets for their enemies? This is an important question because, while a good deal has been said about the psychological effects of commingling and protecting those who may be vulnerable to drone and cyber strikes, little has been said about protecting the civilians amongst the perpetrators of remote attacks. A cyber or drone operator who actively tracks and kills enemies is a possible target, because s/he is a participant in combat. However, for a large number of cyber or drone system controllers, their civilian and military worlds are intertwined. Problems about their status arise when an operator finishes her/his shift and goes home. We need to think carefully about whether these operators are targetable when they are eating, sleeping and picking up the children from school. Conventional combatants do not acquire immunity when they eat or sleep and cannot simply 'turn off' their combatant status. But, as we all become more proficient in launching remote attacks and wars become an increasingly part-time endeavour for those engaged in fighting them, we may be forced to reconsider the characteristics and nature of combatant status.

Whether or not we consider State X's distance warriors to be true combatants, any story of the sort of technological asymmetry that accompanies the deployment of remote attack methods and the shielding of military assets will necessarily include those in the civilian realm being exposed to what might be perceived to be an unfair level of risk. This is a recurring theme in Andrew Croome's *Midnight empire* (2012), the main point being that, far from the promise of delivering a safer and more effective remote warfare, emerging technologies may actually bring the battle home by putting those who wage it closer to us than ever before. Over the long term, this may help foster sympathy between the citizens of warring states, but, in the near future, it is likely to inspire hatred. Additionally, although the killing of drone pilots may not be considered a violation of present-day Just War theory, radical asymmetry may come to cause anger and actions that more closely resemble classical domestic terrorism. In fact, the evidence suggests that distance warfare only strengthens the terrorist cause, making the al-Qaeda brand and radical Islam more attractive to vulnerable and disaffected American Muslims, for instance the two young Boston Marathon bombers cited the drone wars in Iraq and Afghanistan as a motivating factor for their terrorist action (Wilson, Miller & Horowitz 2013). Cases like this suggest that we need to take seriously the idea that cyber- and drone warfare may also create more terrorists, outweighing any good derived from these attacks.

Soldiers and statesmen must therefore add a corollary to their defence theorem: if one side uses cyber warfare against which the enemy has no real defence, the victims may reciprocate by utilising tactics that render the technologically superior state comparably defenceless. It is not immediately clear whether these tactics will, in all cases, be contrary to the demands of Just War theory, or unfair on civilians. As mentioned earlier and regarding the first point, there is much debate concerning whether terrorist action can meet Just War requirements (see Held 2008; Nathanson 2010; O'Keefe & Coady 2002). As for the second point, it needs to be admitted that citizens of technologically advanced democratic countries on one hand are the ultimate source of the antagonism towards casualty, but on the other hand are responsible for electing those who authorise war. Citizens may thus be forced to accept that the aforementioned evoked potential is simply a concerning, but necessary, feature of the only sort of warfare they are prepared to sanction. That said, it is the case that, in radically asymmetric conflict, violations of *jus in bello* are much more likely to occur on either side of the conflict. In relation to our scenario, this may tip the proportionality scale against the waging of war in the first instance. That is, if State Y's responses can be foreseen, it may again undermine the *jus ad bellum* justification for State X's actions. If there is reason to suggest that provoking State Y might cause it to appeal to the above-mentioned morally questionable options, State X must think more carefully about what it stands to gain from going to war.

Some might object to the level of foresight required by this account. Let us summarise the argument for simplicity's sake: State Y is doing this bad thing (prosecuting a war with what its opponent sees as unjust aims) and then, because State X utilises cyber- and remote attacks as its means of waging war, State Y does this further bad thing (in this case, harming people near to the place/s from where the remote attack is initiated). It might be said that this is not an argument against State X. The critic might also say that this sort of moral reasoning is pretty strained as an argument against the use of cyber- or drone technologies as a just weapon of war. It has been said that a very high degree of certainty would be required about the fact that launching remote attacks (an action which has other normative advantages) would necessarily cause State Y to do this further bad thing.[6] Furthermore, it has been argued that, even if it can be assured that State Y will do this further bad thing, the moral blame still falls on Y for doing this bad thing, not on X for carrying out a putatively just action via putatively just means. In response to the first section of this argument, it is only necessary to point out that the degree of epistemic certainty involved is already high. History serves as a potent reminder of the fact that technological asymmetry does not preclude enemies with inferior technology from creating and sustaining an impact powerful enough to combat a superpower. In fact, technological asymmetry probably invites such a response from technologically inferior foes, since there are no other options for them.

This does not amount to reassigning blame to State X and absolving State Y of moral responsibility for its actions, nor does it open the door for any state to do bad things in the hope that they might get their enemy to cease efforts against them. Rather, this amounts to acknowledging that the harm generated by such wars comes about for predictable and identifiable reasons. This constitutes the first step toward reaching more amicable resolutions to conflicts in the future. Note that this need not be a big problem for Strawser's main claim *per se*. Recall what his claim was: if it is possible for a military pursuing a *just action* to use emerging remote warfare technologies in lieu of the manned equivalent, without incurring a loss of *Just War fighting capability*, then they ought to do so. Strawser could then simply accept that, *if* cyber or drone capabilities do make military action unjust, they should *not* be used. This may be true in some cases of radically asymmetric conflict. But the answer is not necessarily crystal clear in all cases. These remote systems are not yet beyond control or restriction, so we are left in quite a tricky position as to how we might seek to respond to the problem of radically imbalanced levels of mutual risk, regardless of whether the levels of risk are inadequate or too substantial. We do not want to rule out military operations in every instance. This would also be rather unwise, because to lay down arms could create an even worse asymmetry problem. The relevant question is now how distance warfighting capabilities should be utilised when the levels of risk are significantly imbalanced. It is a question to which we need to devote more of our attention, given the ever-growing technological imbalance between states.

One possible response might be to suggest that the militarily dominant state (possessing cyber or drone capabilities) allows the weaker state a degree of latitude in their application of the Just War principles. However, allowing an enemy to choose an action, which is not as good/ethical as another one, seems counter-intuitive and may lead to serious moral transgressions. For instance, it would be wrong for a strong state to allow its weaker enemy to a carry out a disproportionate attack because of technological asymmetry. Therefore we can say with confidence that giving the weaker state a 'wild card', so to speak, is not the answer. Another much more respectable and less problematic approach, advocated by David Rodin, is for the militarily dominant state to impose stronger requirements on its own application/s or consideration of the Just War principles (Rodin 2006, pp. 161–5). This recommends that the stronger state has to meet higher standards of epistemic certainty when waging war. It seems a sensible ethical option. It does not encourage the stronger state to lower protective measures, nor to 'go easy' on the enemy, nor to lay down its arms, which is good because there is no virtue in taking risk purely for the sake of risk. What, then, might a war that abides by these stronger norms look like? Kahn (2002, pp. 4–5) suggests that, in cases of such high asymmetry, the solution is for the application of any military force to be very restrained and for it to be more like a form of international policing. Such action is based on evidence proving guilt beyond reasonable doubt. De-escalation strategies are also to be preferred; very little collateral damage is tolerable and the death of innocents is strictly prohibited. The effect that policing actions have would amount to giving non-combatants a much higher standing than that of drone operators, and would imply that the number of strikes is to be limited. However, while fewer wars and more international policing-like activity may sound like an admirable goal, some would argue that, as a response to asymmetry, this is too restrictive and we must continue to find the right balance. It may be that if cases of asymmetrical conflict should be governed by standards that are more restrictive than those guiding interstate war, but more permissive than those of domestic law enforcement, we should explore the category of *jus ad vim* (typically concerning justice of force short of war) to assess the ethical use of drones. However, this is ultimately a matter that must be left for discussion by others.[7]

Conclusion

The aim in this chapter has been to show that the use of distance warfighting systems can introduce a morally problematic asymmetry and that, at least in some cases, there are reasons for rejecting the legitimacy of unmanned and cyber engagements on grounds that stem from this asymmetry. Further, it has been argued that it is not so easy to justify an overwhelming asymmetric attack based on the supposed non-equality of combatants. A military with great technological power must thus think twice about the threat that its enemy poses. In considering whether radically asymmetric unmanned warfare really is the best option to achieve a military's desired goal, it must take a long-term and more strategic view of risk, considering all possible evoked responses. On the basis of the evidence and arguments put forward in the previous six chapters, it seems clear that there is a role for drones and other remote weaponry, since they have the potential to offer numerous benefits. However, several questions remain concerning their deployment. In relation to the problem posed by asymmetry, we must ask: in what capacity should distance weaponry be utilised, and to what degree? We must be careful not to miscalculate threat in the 'fog of war' and not to err too far (unjustifiably so) on the safe or dangerous side when faced with a challenge. This is especially true with regard to the political, psychological and time pressures which are often placed on key decision makers in remote warfare. Going forward, we need to think about the effect that asymmetry and other factors can have on enemy populations and the prospects for lasting peace.

Acknowledgements

This chapter is reprinted by permission of the publishers from 'The asymmetry objection', in *Military Robots* by Jai Galliott (Farnham: Ashgate, 2015), pp. 165–86. Copyright © 2015.

Notes

1 Adapted from Killmister (2008).
2 Strawser actually levels three challenges at the 'problem of fairness'. I will look only first two as they contain his main argument, and the third is rendered false by the discussion of the first two.

3 There is a parallel here with the utilitarian argument for torture: if we can torture someone to retrieve information that will save the lives of many people, without anyone finding out and thus setting a precedent for further tortures, then we should do so (under some accounts).

4 For a very interesting discussion concerning McMahan's 'deep morality' and its applicability in our non-ideal world, see Shue (2008).

5 This reflects a more common problem concerning the projection of consequences within broadly consequentialist theories.

6 I am indebted to B.J. Strawser for raising this potential objection.

7 For some ideas stemming from earlier drafts of this chapter, see Braun & Brunstetter (2014).

References

Barker, E (ed.) 1971, *Social contract: essays by Locke, Hume, and Rousseau*, Oxford University Press, Oxford.

Braun, M & Brunstetter, D 2014, 'Rethinking the criterion for assessing CIA-targeted killings: drones, proportionality and jus ad vim', *Journal of Military Ethics*, vol. 12, no. 4, pp. 304–324.

Churchill, W 1899, *The river war: an historical account of the reconquest of the Soudan*, Longmans, Green & Co, London.

Croome, A 2012, *Midnight empire*, Allen & Unwin, Sydney.

Enemark, C 2014, *Armed drones and the ethics of war: military virtue in a post-heroic age*, Routledge, New York.

Finlan, A 2008, *The Gulf War of 1991*, Rosen Publishing Group, New York.

Headrick, D 2005, *Power over peoples: technology, environments, and Western imperialism*, Princeton University Press, New Haven.

Held, V 2008, *How terrorism is wrong: morality and political violence*, Oxford University Press, Oxford.

Johnson, J 1981, *Just war tradition and the restraint of war*, Princeton University Press, Princeton.

Kahn, P 2002, 'The paradox of riskless warfare', *Philosophy and Public Policy Quarterly*, vol. 22, no. 3, pp. 2–8.

Kemp, G 2007, 'Arms acquisition and violence: are weapons or people the cause of conflict?', in CA Crocker, FO Hampson & PR Aall (eds), *Leashing the dogs of war: conflict management in a divided world*, US Institute of Peace Press, Washington, DC.

Killmister, S 2008, 'Remote weaponry: the ethical implication', *Journal of Applied Philosophy*, vol. 25, no. 2, pp. 121–133.

Mack, A 1975, 'Why big nations lose small wars: the politics of asymmetric conflict', *World Politics*, vol. 27, no. 2, pp. 175–200.

Mahnken, T 2008, *Technology and the American way of war*, Columbia University Press, New York.

McKenzie, K 2000, *The revenge of the Melians: asymmetric threats and the next QDR*, National Defense University, Washington, DC.

McMahan, J 2009, *Killing in war*, Oxford University Press, Oxford.

Metz, S & Johnson, D 2001, *Asymmetry and U.S. military strategy: definition, background, and strategic concepts*, US Strategic Studies Institute, Washington, DC.

Murphie, A & Potts, J 2003, *Culture and technology*, Palgrave, London.

Nathanson, S 2010, *Terrorism and the ethics of war*, Cambridge University Press, Cambridge.

Noorman, M 2012, 'Computing and moral responsibility', in *Stanford Encyclopedia of Responsibility*, http://plato.stanford.edu/archives/fall2012/entries/computing-responsibility

O'Keefe, M & Coady, CAJ (eds) 2002, *Terrorism and justice: moral argument in a threatened world*, Melbourne University Press, Melbourne.

Raugh, H 2004, *The Victorians at war, 1815–1914: an encyclopedia of British military history*, ABC-CLIO, Santa Barbara.

Rodin, D 2006, 'The ethics of asymmetric war', in R Sorabji & D Rodin (eds), *The ethics of war: shared problems in different traditions*, Ashgate, Aldershot.

Safire, W 2004, *The right word in the right place at the right time: wit and wisdom from the popular 'on language' column in the New York Times Magazine*, Simon & Schuster, New York.

Shue, H 2008, 'Do we need a "morality of war"?', in D Rodin & H Shue (eds), *Just and unjust warriors: the moral and legal status of soldiers*, Oxford University Press, Oxford.

Simpson, R & Sparrow, R 2013/14, 'Nanotechnologically enhanced combat systems: the downside of invulnerability', in B Gordijn & A Cutter (eds), *In pursuit of nanoethics*, Springer, Dordrecht.

Sparrow, R 2011, 'Robotic weapons and the future of war', in J Wolfendale & P Tripodi (eds), *New wars and new soldiers: military ethics in the contemporary world*, Ashgate, Burlington.

Strawser, B 2010, 'Moral predators: the duty to employ uninhabited aerial vehicles', *Journal of Military Ethics*, vol. 9, no. 4, pp. 342–368.

Taylor, G (ed.) 1982, *Henry V*, Oxford University Press, Oxford.

US Joint Chiefs of Staff 1999, *Joint Strategy Review 1999*, US Government Publishing Office, Washington, DC.

Walzer, M 2006a, *Just and unjust wars: a moral argument with historical illustrations*, Basic Books, New York.

Walzer, M 2006b, 'Response to McMahan's paper', *Philosophia*, vol. 34, no. 1, pp. 43–45.

Wilson, S, Miller, G & Horwitz, S 2013, 'Boston bombing suspect cites U.S. wars as motivation, officials say', *The Washington Post*, 23 April, http://articles.washingtonpost.com/2013-04-23/national/38751370_1_u-s-embassy-boston-marathon-bombings

13

TARGETING THRESHOLDS

The impact of intelligence capability on ethical requirements for high-value targeting operations

John Hardy

Targeted killing is a longstanding feature of war. High-value individuals (HVIs) have been targeted in armed conflicts for much of human history. Current debate about the legality and ethical permissibility of targeted killing focuses largely on the notion that HVIs are known personally by the forces targeting them. In some instances this has historical precedent. Allied operations to kill Reinhard Heydrich and Isoroku Yamamoto during the Second World War are well known examples of one way of targeting specific enemy personnel. These individuals were well known military commanders who played pivotal roles in enemy operations, and their deaths substantially benefited the allies' military campaign. However, current high-value targeting (HVT) operations are considered to be qualitatively different, for two reasons. The first is that current HVT operations take place in an ambiguous conflict setting. The war on terror, broadly defined, does not lend itself to simple comparison with the conventional wars from which most historical examples are drawn. The second is that the type of individual considered to be of high value has changed. While Heydrich and Yamamoto were senior military leaders at or near the head of clear chains of command, many HVIs in the West's ongoing fight against various non-state actors are relatively unknown to the public and are far less senior than their conventional counterparts.

This chapter is concerned more with the second difference than with the first. There is a substantial amount of literature examining the legal and political context of current Western military operations against non-state actors. There is comparatively little dealing with the issue of systematic targeting of specific individuals on the contemporary battlefield. In some ways the two issue are interrelated. Ambiguity of conflict status, enemy organisations and enemy personnel inherently lead to ambiguity in battlefield status and *jus in bello* considerations, such as military necessity, distinction and proportionality. However, in many ways the issue of targeting specific individuals is distinct, because the argument could in principle be moved to a different political context or different conflict type without changing the core issue of who is being targeted and why. This chapter argues that the West's pre-occupation with precision in the application of military force has led to an increasing discrimination of targets, down to the precise identification of specific individuals. HVT operations set an impressive ethical standard. By combining all-source intelligence with pervasive surveillance, the targeting process allows for a degree of distinction never seen before. However, HVT is a victim of its own success insofar as the standard has now been set exceptionally high.

This chapter is formed of four sections. The first examines the long-term trend of precision in targeting and the effect of the revolution in military affairs (RMA) on Western attitudes towards distinction in armed conflict. It argues that enhanced precision has created an expectation in Western societies that risks to civilians are lower in current conflicts than they were for previous generations. The second section argues that the emergence of so-called targeted killings in twenty-first-century counterterrorism and counterinsurgency campaigns is a product of doctrinal innovation and the availability of advanced intelligence and surveillance technologies to military units. The third section examines the integration of targeted strikes, both lethal and non-lethal, and intelligence analysis in HVT operations. It argues that the way HVT is used necessitates a range of intelligence, such as comprehensive pattern-of-life analysis, which substantially improves the precision of targeting. The final section uses current limitations on successfully conducting HVT to identify two important caveats for ethically targeting HVIs within existing surveillance and intelligence capabilities. The chapter concludes that current intelligence standards should be considered minimum requirements for ethical targeting in future operations.

Precision targeting in armed conflict

HVI targeting operations are one result of a broad evolution in precision targeting in Western military practice (Mets 2001). This increased precision in military targeting is largely a by-product of the RMA of the 1990s (Benbow 2004; Sloan 2002). Although such revolutions have been sporadic throughout human history, van Creveld (1991) dubbed the RMA a 'transformation of war'. This was largely due to emerging information and communications technologies that afforded Western militaries an unprecedented advantage in gathering, analysing and disseminating information (Alberts et al. 2001; Perry, Signori & Boon 2004). The enthusiasm for military technology mirrored the increasing popularity of science and technology in Western societies and quickly led to twenty-first-century warfare being characterised by high-technology weapons and communications (Bousquet 2009). Meanwhile, the transformation of war built upon, but did not replace, earlier forms of war (Murray 1997, pp. 70–2). Many of the same challenges remained, while the increasing volume of information available to military commanders complicated their operations and created demand for more intelligence and better analysis to support decision-making processes.

In the aftermath of the RMA, Western warfare was characterised by speed of communication and effective use of precision-guided munitions (Kagan 2006, pp. 258–65). Since the Persian Gulf War, Western military operations have been largely represented in the media by videos of precision weapons advancing towards target buildings and bursting into on-screen static as they detonate (Smith 2002, p. 363). In one famous example, a US laser-guided bomb was guided directly into an open ventilation shaft in an Iraqi Air Force building (Schneider 1997). Standoff weapons became increasingly popular throughout the 1990s, although they raised questions about how practical and ethical long-range targeting processes really were. In some ways this was a new debate, incorporating targeting capabilities well beyond what had been possible only a decade earlier. In other ways it was familiar, taking the form of discussion about the acceptable distance between weapons, operators and targets and what conditions would warrant targeting at standoff range. Johnson (1986) grappled with these issues when discussing cruise and ballistic missile technology and nuclear weapons in the 1980s. A key issue that emerged from this debate was the concept of precision.

Some critics lament the simple correlation inferred between precision and ethicality. For example, Zehfuss (2011, pp. 559–61) contends that precision in targeting is an ambiguous concept and easily confused with accurate targeting in effect, rather than in intention. As such, it is important to examine two distinct aspects of precision: accuracy in identifying a target, and accuracy in striking it. Precision first involves locating and positively identifying a target. This is no small feat on the contemporary battlefield, despite many advances in intelligence, surveillance and reconnaissance technologies. Cutting-edge surveillance technologies are often deployed in armed conflicts, but are only as useful as the intelligence they provide. An important caveat for high-technology intelligence is that the product is not necessarily improved by the quality of technology used in sourcing it. Precision then involves striking a target and limiting the harm caused to non-targeted people and infrastructure to the greatest possible extent (Beier 2003). In the context of HVT, the strike component of the targeting cycle is often a 'kill-or-capture' mission (Alexander 2011). These missions are usually conducted by special operations forces (SOF) or by remotely piloted vehicles (RPVs) – colloquially known as drones.

The objective of enhanced precision is to maintain or improve the military effectiveness of offensive action, while decreasing the risk posed to non-combatants and civilian infrastructure. This mirrors the basic tenets of Just War theory and the Laws of Armed Conflict, which commanders are legally and morally obliged to uphold. The conduct of war, *jus in bello*, has four key principles that underpin the ethics and laws of war. These are distinction, military necessity, unnecessary suffering, and proportionality (Solis 2010, pp. 250–1). Distinction requires combatants to distinguish between military and non-military objectives (2010, pp. 251–4; Sassio 2003). Military necessity is a broad term that encompasses anything within the law that is necessary in order to defeat the enemy (Dinstein 2010, pp. 16–20). However, the action to be taken must relate to a specific military object and must provide clear benefit (Jachec-Neale 2015; Robertson 1997). Commanders cannot engage with targets that have purely speculative value, so they are obliged to identify a materially tangible military value to achieving an objective (Corn & Corn 2012, p. 362). Unnecessary suffering relates to causing harm that is not necessary in attaining the desired military effect (Solis 2010, pp. 269–70). An example of a weapon contravening this rule is the serrated-edged bayonet, where the edge is no more effective at incapacitating an enemy that a standard bayonet, but creates a jagged wound that takes much longer to heal. The principle of proportionality aims to limit attacks on legitimate military objectives that would cause disproportionate unintended harm, particularly to non-combatants (Dinstein 2010, pp. 120–1).

In sum, targeting precision is widely linked to greater adherence to the core ethical principles governing armed conflict. The consequence of this link is that precision has significant political value. Greater precision has reduced the risk of collateral damage without sacrificing the capability to engage with legitimate targets. In some circumstances this can reduce, although not eliminate, the ethical burden of military commanders, who are called upon to weigh up the military necessity of tactical actions against the potential for unintended harm to civilians and non-military infrastructure (Wheeler 2002, pp. 210–12). Despite the essentially incommensurable value of civilian death and injury in calculations of military advantage (Noll 2012, pp. 215–16), the language of precision used by Western governments has been used to validate military actions as ethical. This coincides with increasing expectations that current methods of conducting war will further limit the risk to non-combatants (Thomas 2001, p. 170). In the context of a Western war against international terrorism, precision has led to increasing fusion of intelligence and strike in HVT operations (Flynn & Flynn 2012, pp. 4–7).

Targeting terrorists

In the aftermath of 9/11, the US military was thrown headfirst into what became a protracted fight against an elusive enemy. What started out as an *ad hoc* and often compartmentalised programme of raids in Iraq and Afghanistan quickly transformed into a coordinated large-scale assault on al-Qaeda and its affiliates, local insurgents and hostile warlords. General Retired Stanley McChrystal introduced the term 'industrial counterterrorism' in characterising the network adversaries of the mid-2000s. McChrystal (2011) saw a need to integrate intelligence and strike to a much greater extent than they had been previously. He also saw surveillance- and information-sharing as top priorities in responding rapidly and effectively to the fluid networks the US military was then fighting. McChrystal introduced a range of reforms that placed intelligence at the centre of HVT operations. In keeping with the broader trend in Western militaries to leverage information superiority (Alberts, Garstka & Stein 2000) against less technologically sophisticated opponents, SOF units began more actively pursuing and disseminating intelligence in the operations they shared with conventional forces. Paralleling the 'offensive hunt' strategy proposed for intelligence agencies (Cogan 2004, pp. 315–18), SOF and conventional forces established fusion cells that enhanced the ardent collection and analysis of information fuelling the targeting cycle (Lushenko 2010).

By 2010, Washington was modelling a new approach to network counterterrorism based on a greater understanding of social networks and how the components of a terrorist network operate together and independently of one another (Schmitt & Shanker 2011, pp. 180–94). This process began in the military SOF community, but is widely reported to have been mirrored in the US intelligence community under the Obama administration (Brennan 2012; McNeal 2014). This introduces some difficulties in interpreting the use of force at the *jus ad bellum* level of analysis because there is a strong distinction between targeted killing in war and targeted killing in other circumstances, often considered to be *jus ad vim* (Braun & Brunstetter 2013; Ford 2013). The broader issue of the legitimacy of targeted killing outside the context of war is currently related to individual legal interpretations of the post-9/11 authorisation for use of military force (AUMF) and is beyond the scope of this chapter. It is important to note that there is debate about the legality of targeting HVIs in some parts of the world, but the remainder of this chapter focuses on the principle of operational targeting rather than the political and strategic context of targeting operations.

Targeted killing is a fundamental component of armed conflict. The key organising principle of war is violence, and violence is aimed at killing certain people while sparing others. Current HVT operations are slightly different because specific people are known, nominated for targeting and, when positively identified, are targeted with a kill-or-capture mission. This process is fraught with challenges and faces a great deal of criticism. At the political level some commentators oppose the secrecy of the process (Krishnan 2013), some feel that the naming of targets is immoral (Gross 2003), while others question the legality (Alston 2010) and practical utility (Byman 2006; Carvin 2012) of targeted killing. At the operational level, SOF raids are dangerous (Shea 2011) and sometimes unpopular (Gaston, Horowitz & Schmeidl 2010). RPV strikes are often utilised when raids are not possible (Gertler 2012; Williams 2013), but their appropriateness and effectiveness are also hotly debated (Plaw & Fricker 2012; Strawser 2010). The role of RPVs in current coalition counterterrorism campaigns is poorly understood (Hardy 2014; Taj 2012). Despite potential benefits (McCrisken 2013), they are far less popular than SOF raids (Bergen & Tiedemann 2009; Kilcullen & Exum 2009). UAV strikes are also undesirable in circumstances where HVIs could be captured by ground forces, as the latter provides an opportunity to interrogate the target and exploit the target site for intelligence (Drew 2009; Teson 2012).

The surveillance and intelligence cycle that fuels the targeting process has also been heavily criticised. It is often subject to poorly informed and unhelpful speculation from critics. For example, Wall & Monahan (2011) argue that increased surveillance reduces understanding of subjects because it de-individualises them. Proponents of surveillance reject this reasoning and argue that increased observation of subjects allows for greater differentiation between them and greater discrimination between intended targets and bystanders (Brennan 2012). Another example is the work of activist Medea Benjamin (2012, pp. 25–8), who argues that existing surveillance technologies and weapon systems are not sufficient, but simultaneously opposes the use of improved technologies and the development of more precise weapons. It is difficult to reconcile the military's obligations to correctly identify targets and engage with them with the least possible amount of force with suggestions that it should use less sophisticated surveillance technology and less precise weapons.

Surveillance and intelligence are also ignored entirely in some arguments. For example, HVT operations are often miscategorised as being either personality or signature strikes. Personality strikes refer to the targeting of specific HVIs, while the exact meaning of the phrase 'signature strike' is unclear. From media reports, signature strikes can range from the targeting of mobile phone SIM cards; tracking devices planted on specific, although unidentified, individuals by intelligence officers; and targeting of overtly suspicious activity to groups of men gathering at suspicious locations or large gatherings of people at locations where a lot of signal intelligence has been gathered (Greenfield 2013). Judging from the popular use of the term, signature strikes can be legitimate. For example, the popular website *Liveleak* has released numerous videos showing signature strikes in a range of seemingly legitimate circumstances, such as striking a group of individuals planting roadside bombs where no ground forces were available to interdict. However, these strikes could have been illegitimate, if reports of groups being targeted just for gathering are accurate. In any event, these strikes are more comparable with regular combat operations than with HVT, and will not be considered further here.

Targeting in the context of HVT operations means that an individual was identified and that action was taken to kill or capture that specific individual. Teson (2012, p. 404) notes that the target must be identified for a strike to constitute a targeted killing. Otherwise the term would not differentiate between the 'anonymous intentional killing of enemy combatants in war' and HVT. Teson's argument applies equally well to HVT, the only difference being that individuals are targeted for potential capture and not just killing. Another distinguishing feature of HVT is that targets can have varying levels of utility if captured or killed. While varying degrees of value are associated with the broad label 'high value', HVIs can be ascribed varying levels of utility depending on their intelligence value, importance to friendly operations and importance to enemy operations. The term HVI encompasses both high-value targets, those required by a clandestine network for operational success, and high-payoff targets, which would contribute significantly to friendly operations if captured or destroyed (Headquarters, Department of the Army 2010b, p. B-1).

One way in which the relative value of HVIs can be assessed is by looking at *criticality*. McNeal (2014, pp. 714–7) proposes four factors that can be used to assess a potential target's criticality. The first is value, which measures the importance of an individual to the collective outcomes of a group. The second factor is depth, which measures the time between the effect on a target, generally a capture or kill, and the impact on the group. The third factor is recuperation, which measures the time it takes a targeted group to regain operational effectiveness after a strike. The fourth factor is capacity, which measures a group's current and maximum offensive output over a 24-hour period. In combination, these factors allow analysts to gauge the utility of targeting an HVI in a way that enables commanders to make an informed assessment of military necessity. This information is also useful for prioritising HVIs relative to a commander's available resources.

In some circumstances, the utility of pursuing a target with both high value and high payoff may be necessary to enable further operations, while a target with no payoff value may be deprioritised. The intention to pursue a target in order to engage an adversary may be afforded a higher or lower importance than pursuing a target in order to enable friendly operations, as each can offer different returns on the investment of resources. Similarly, some targets may offer different returns. Capturing bomb-makers or weapons caches may have an immediate tactical effect for coalition forces, while the capture of a high-profile leader might generate a large volume of intelligence as the network communicates in order to coordinate defensive responses. For example, the HVT raid to 'kill or capture' bin Laden may have had a significant effect on the morale on both sides, but it is also likely that valuable intelligence on the network and its central communicators was gathered through site exploitation and captured in reflections.

HVT operations

The primary targeting cycle used in HVT operations is 'Find, Fix, Finish, Exploit, Analyse and Disseminate', F3EAD (Headquarters, Department of the Army 2011b). This process expands on conventional targeting cycles and prioritises the use of intelligence collection, analysis and dissemination at all stages of decision-making. F3EAD uses 'massed, persistent reconnaissance, or surveillance cued to a powerful and decentralized all-source intelligence apparatus' to locate and identify HVIs. The targeting cycle focuses heavily on the exploit and analyse steps 'because these steps provide insight into the enemy's network and may open new lines of operation' (Headquarters, Department of the Army 2010b, p. B-1). HVT operations also incorporate site exploitation to gather information, and fusion cells to analyse and share intelligence. The US Army defines site exploitation as 'systematically searching for and collecting information, material, and persons from a designated location and analyzing them to answer information requirements, facilitate subsequent operations, or support criminal prosecution' (Headquarters, Department of the Army 2010a, p. 1-1). Fusion cells bring conventional and SOF personnel together to aggregate all-source intelligence and create an operational picture of the social and political environment existing within and around the battlespace (Lamb & Munsig 2011).

HVT operations are used to either *pressure, leverage* or *desynchronise* a decentralised enemy network (Hardy & Lushenko 2012). Commanders may *pressure* or harass the network in order to complicate its operations, force errors and delay communications. Pressure is designed to disrupt the enemy's operational capacity and tempo and to stifle its initiative. Commanders may also choose to *leverage* important brokers, including facilitators, financiers and specialists, to degrade a network's functionality and disrupt its operations (Farah 2013; Neumann, Evans & Pantucci 2011). This deprofessionalises the network and imposes training and recruitment costs that further diminish its operational capacity (Wilner 2010, p. 312). Finally, commanders can *desynchronise* the network by killing or capturing visible and symbolic leaders and destabilising the organisation, creating power vacuums and alienating members from one another. Interference with key decision-making processes can also increase the costs of maintaining organisational cohesion by compelling leaders to divert time and resources away from offensive operations to precautionary measures aimed at avoiding detection (Long 2010, p. 20; Luft 2003).

Through these types of HVT operations, analysts gain a rich picture of the social, economic and political networks that underpin and support clandestine networks. This process allows HVT operations to target HVIs with exceptional precision and to reduce the risk to civilians with detailed location knowledge and situational awareness. The sheer volume of analysed data that units conducting HVT possess is astounding. HVT intelligence support involves generating and cross-referencing thousands of data points to construct a comprehensive picture of the network, acquiring holistic pattern-of-life data on targets, tracing logistics and money trails, identifying facilitators and non-leadership persons of interest, and exploiting human and signals intelligence to fuel the targeting cycle (Serena 2011, pp. 115–17). These intelligence requirements demand a sophisticated surveillance and reconnaissance apparatus. Pattern-of-life analysis is particularly demanding in this regard, as it requires constant surveillance of everything HVIs do in daily life, including the places they visit and the people they contact. Analysts examine connections between HVIs' activities, locations and contacts in order to map their social network and role, if any, in a targeted organisation (Headquarters, Department of the Army 2010b, p. B-3).

Due to these competing demands for time and resources, HVT often entails a high operational tempo. In order to capitalise on intelligence gains from SOF raids and intelligence-gathering operations, HVT often requires rapid follow-on raids. These are often informed by *reflections* in targeted networks. Reflections are spikes in communication or 'chatter' in targeted networks that are captured after a raid or airstrike using human, imagery and signals intelligence. These reflections provide real-time information about the effect an operation is having on a network and also identifies the people who are sending and receiving information across the network, the nature of the information they are communicating, and the kind of defensive or reactionary measures they might be planning (Hardy & Lushenko 2012, pp. 422–3). For example, the targeting of Abu Musab al-Zarqawi in 2006, Abu Qaswarah in 2008, and Abu Ayub al-Masri in 2010 resulted from extensive pattern-of-life information on close confidants who regularly delivered information to them (Burns 2006; Ibrahim 2010; Roggio 2008). From high-profile examples such as these, it is clear that many HVIs are well known to the forces that target them. This raises questions about how well known HVIs should be before it is permissible to target them.

Surveillance capabilities and targeting

Western militaries have never had so much information available to them. From the rapid diffusion of situational awareness data across deployed units to the extensive location data collected by RPV pilots while scanning highways and target locations (Barrett 2010), military units are generating, collating and sharing information. In response, forces have had to create sophisticated intelligence-analysis processes to acquire, structure, manage, analyse and disseminate information (Biermann et al. 2004, pp. 3–4). This amounts to a previously unimaginable social sorting capability (Lyon 2005). The targeting cycle results in far better informed decisions prior to strikes precisely because it enables analysts to differentiate between individuals using a range of categorical and intelligence data. This provides numerous benefits, chief among them more effective operations and the potential for more ethical targeting. More discriminate HVT operations are inherently beneficial because accurate targeting is the desired outcome of military action. The added benefit of more effective targeting is that, all other things being equal, the amount of information available to commanders conducting HVT operations allows them to make better-informed distinction and proportionality decisions.

It is important to note two caveats here. The first is that greater potential for improved discrimination will not necessarily lead to reduced risk to civilians. Zehfuss (2011) objects to the inference that greater precision will improve ethical conduct on the battlefield, noting that even the most precise weapon systems have margins of error and are susceptible to human or mechanical error. Moreover, the target area of a 2000 lb bomb is often much smaller than the lethal radius of its blast, meaning that the increased precision of a strike does not necessarily limit civilian casualties in adjacent buildings (Zehfuss 2011, p. 551). Nevertheless, even in this extreme example, precision does reduce the risk to nearby civilians by reducing the likely impact point to a smaller radius and thereby reducing the area affected. While these objections are more relevant to aerial campaigns that employ munitions with larger payloads than HVT operations – which largely rely on ground forces and RPV strikes with the much smaller 100 lb payload of a Hellfire missile – the general caution against complacency in linking precision with ethical outcomes is important.

The second caveat is that the assets required to fully utilise the intelligence and analytical power of targeting operations are in short supply. SOF often don't have their own surveillance and reconnaissance capabilities, and need to coordinate with conventional forces for mission tasks. Forward-deployed units often lack adequate bandwidth to communicate effectively with headquarters. The result is that forward teams have a rich picture of their operating environment, but insufficient global data to provide context and supplementary information to their analyses. Meanwhile, headquarters have a lot of analytical power, in terms of both personnel and computer processing, but have little real-time data from frontline units (McChrystal 2011, p. 69). In addition, the intelligence-collection process required to generate the comprehensive pattern-of-life data used in HVT operations is resource-intensive because the 'enemy is so well hidden that it takes multiple sources of intelligence to corroborate' their location (Flynn, Juergens & Cantrell 2008, p. 57). This means that even units committed to utilising all of the resources available to them may not be able to perform optimally in HVT operations all of the time.

Despite these considerations, the new capacity for highly discriminate targeting alters the standard for the use of force against HVIs. Although operational effectiveness and limiting harm to civilians are often viewed as opposing tensions that tactical commanders must reconcile, HVT offers a methodology that has the potential to enhance both. By ensuring that HVIs are properly vetted and positively identified, commanders can ensure precision in accurately designating a target. By ensuring that the risk to civilian casualties is minimised to the greatest extent possible, commanders can ensure that effective HVT operations are also just. The choice of weapon systems available for HVT operations mirrors this positively reinforcing relationship between operational effectiveness and ethicality. SOF raids are generally preferable for operational purposes because they offer commanders the possibility of capturing and interrogating HVIs while also exploiting the target site. Raids also reduce the risk of civilian casualties by the greatest margin, although even in the most meticulously planned raids, collateral damage remains a risk. Meanwhile, Hellfire missile strikes are effective, although sub-optimal, in terms of combat effect, and may incur a greater risk of collateral damage depending on the situation.

Conclusion

Current methods of HVT have set a high standard for accuracy in designating and engaging with targets. The targeting cycle draws on a capability for robust surveillance and intelligence to identify individuals and examine their surroundings, relationships and general patterns of life before deciding to capture or kill them. This capacity to apply discriminate force in the pursuit of a military objective without sacrificing effectiveness is without precedent. In keeping with the trend that military precision influences popular expectations, the high degree of discrimination and situational awareness characteristic of current HVT operations is likely to become a minimum standard for targeting HVIs. Western societies, in particular, expect risks to civilians to be lower in current and future conflicts than they were for previous generations. The integration of intelligence analysis, rapid strike and site exploitation allow HVT operations to deliver on these expectations now, and will continue to do so in the future: current standards should be considered minimum requirements for ethical targeting in future operations. The current generation of military commanders have set an impressive standard for ethical targeting. It is up to the next generation to improve on it.

References

Alberts, DS, Garstka, JJ & Stein, FP 2000, *Network centric warfare: developing and leveraging information superiority*, US Department of Defense, Washington, DC.

Alberts, DS, Gartska, JJ, Hayes, RE & Signori, DT 2001, *Understanding information-age warfare*, US Department of Defense Command and Control Research Program, Washington, DC.

Alexander, M 2011, *Kill or capture: how a special operations task force took down a notorious Al Qaeda leader*, St Martin's Press, New York.

Alston, P 2010, *Study on targeted killings*, Addendum to the report of the UN Special Rapporteur on extrajudicial, summary or arbitrary executions, 28 May, United Nations General Assembly, Human Rights Council, New York.

Barrett, E 2010, 'Statement of Ed Barrett', in *Rise of the drones: unmanned systems and the future of war*, Hearing before the subcommittee on national security and foreign affairs, House of Representatives, Serial No 111–118, 23 March, Government Printing Office, Washington, DC, pp. 13–18

Beier, JM 2003, 'Discriminating tastes: "smart" bombs, non-combatants, and notions of legitimacy in warfare', *Security Dialogue*, vol. 34, no. 4, pp. 411–425.

Benjamin, M 2012, *Drone warfare: killing by remote control*, OR Books, New York and London.

Bergen, P & Tiedemann, K 2009, 'The drone war: are predators our best weapon or worst enemy?', *The New Republic*, 3 June.

Biermann, J, de Chantal, L, Korsnes, R, Rohmer, J & Undeger, C 2004, 'From unstructured to structured information in military intelligence – some steps to improve information fusion', in RTO SCI Symposium on Systems, Concepts and Integration (SCI) Methods and Technologies for Defence Against Terrorism, NATO Research Task Group on Information Fusion Demonstration, London, 25–27 October.

Benbow, T 2004, *The magic bullet? Understanding the revolution in military affairs*, Brassey's, London.

Bousquet, A 2009, *The scientific way of warfare: order and chaos on the battlefields of modernity*, Hurst & Company, London.

Braun, M & Brunstetter, DR, 2013, 'Rethinking the criterion for assessing CIA-targeted killings: drones, proportionality and *jus ad vim*', *Journal of Military Ethics*, vol. 12, no. 4, pp. 304–324

Brennan, J 2012, 'Efficacy and ethics of the President's counterterrorism strategy', Address to the Woodrow Wilson Center, 30 April, Washington, DC.

Burns, JF 2006, 'U.S. strike hits insurgent at safehouse', *New York Times*, 8 June.

Byman, D 2006, 'Do targeted killings work?' *Foreign Affairs*, vol. 85, no. 2, pp. 95–111.

Carvin, S 2012, 'The trouble with targeted killing', *Security Studies*, vol. 21, no. 3, pp. 529–555.

Cogan, C 2004, 'Hunters not gatherers: intelligence in the twenty-first century', *Intelligence and National Security*, vol. 19, no. 2, pp. 304–321.

Corn, GS & Corn, GP 2012, 'The law of operational targeting: viewing the LOAC through an operational lens', *Texas International Law Journal*, vol. 47, no. 2, pp. 337–380.

van Creveld, M 1991, *The transformation of war: the most radical reinterpretation of armed conflict since Clausewitz*, Free Press, New York.

Dinstein, Y 2010, *The conduct of hostilities under the law of international armed conflict*, Cambridge University Press, Cambridge.

Drew, C 2009, 'Drones are weapons of choice in fighting Qaeda', *The New York Times*, 16 March.

Farah, D 2013, 'Fixers, super fixers, and shadow facilitators: how networks connect', in MJ Miklaucic & J Brewer (eds), *Convergence: illicit networks and national security in the age of globalization*, National Defense University Press, Washington, DC, pp. 75–96.

Flynn, MT & Flynn, CA 2012, 'Integrating intelligence and information: "ten points for the commander"', *Military Review*, vol. 92, no. 1, pp. 4–8.

Flynn, MT, Juergens, R & Cantrell, TL 2008, 'Employing ISR: SOF Best Practices', *Joint Forces Quarterly*, vol. 50, July, pp. 56–61.

Ford, SB 2013, '*Jus ad vim* and the just use of lethal force-short-of-war', in F Allhoff, NG Evans & AH Henscke (eds), *Routledge handbook of ethics and war: just war theory in the twenty-first century*, Routledge, London and New York, pp. 63–75.

Gaston, E, Horowitz, J & Schmeidl, S 2010*Strangers at the door: night raids by international forces lose hearts and minds of Afghans*, Open Society Institute and The Liaison Office, Washington, DC and Kabul.

Gertler, J 2012, *U.S. unmanned aerial systems*, Report for Congress (R42136), 3 January, Congressional Research Service, Washington, DC.

Greenfield, D 2013, 'The case against drone strikes on people who only "act" like terrorists', *The Atlantic*, 19 August.

Gross, ML 2003, 'Fighting by other means in the mideast: a critical analysis of Israel's assassination policy', *Political Studies*, vol. 51, no. 2, pp. 350–368.

Hardy, J 2014, 'Reframing the drone debate', in *Proceedings of the Sixth Oceanic Conference on International Studies*, University of Melbourne.

Hardy, J & Lushenko, P 2012, 'The high value of targeting: a conceptual model for using HVT against a networked enemy', *Defence Studies*, vol. 12, no. 3, pp. 413–433.

Headquarters, Department of the Army 2010a, *Site exploitation operations*, Army Tactics, Techniques and Procedures No. 3-90.15, 8 July, Washington, DC.

Headquarters, Department of the Army 2010b, *The targeting process*, Field Manual No 3-60, 26 November, Washington, DC.

Ibrahim, W 2010, 'Al Qaeda's two top Iraq leaders killed in raid', *Reuters*, 19 April.

Jachec-Neale, A 2015, *The concept of military objectives in international law and targeting practice*, Routledge, London and New York.

Johnson, JT 1986, *Can modern war be just?*, Yale University Press, New Haven.

Kagan, FW 2006, *Finding the target: the transformation of American military policy*, Encounter Books, New York.

Kilcullen, D & Exum, AM 2009, 'Death from above, outrage down below', *The New York Times*, 16 May.

Krishnan, A 2013, 'Targeting individuals: overcoming the dilemmas of secrecy', *Contemporary Security Policy*, vol. 34, no. 2, pp. 278–301.

Lamb, CJ & Munsig, E 2011, *Secret weapon: high-value target teams as an organizational innovation*, Strategic Perspectives 4, Institute for National Strategic Studies, Washington, DC.

Long, A 2010, 'Assessing the success of leadership targeting', *CTC Sentinel*, vol. 3, no. 11–12, pp. 19–21.

Luft, G 2003, 'The logic of Israel's targeted killing', *Middle East Quarterly*, vol. 10, no. 1, pp. 3–13.

Lushenko, P 2010, '"Partnership 'till it hurts": the use of fusion cells to establish unity of effort between SOF (yin) and conventional forces (yang)', *Small Wars Journal*, 20 May.

Lyon, D 2005, 'Surveillance as social sorting: computer codes and mobile bodies', in Lyon, D (ed.), *Surveillance as social sorting: privacy, risk and automated discrimination*, Routledge, London and New York, pp. 13–30.

McChrystal, SA 2011, 'Becoming the enemy: to win in Afghanistan, we need to fight more like the Taliban', *Foreign Policy*, vol. 185, pp. 66–70.

McCrisken, T 2013, 'Obama's Drone War', *Survival*, vol. 55, no. 2, pp. 97–122.

McNeal, GS 2014, 'Targeted killing and accountability', *Georgetown Law Journal*, vol. 102, pp. 681–794.

Mets, DR 2001, *The long search for a surgical strike: precision munitions and the revolution in military affairs*, Research and Education Paper No.12, College of Aerospace Doctrine, Maxwell Air Force Base, AL.

Murray, W 1997, 'Thinking about revolutions in military affairs', *Joint Force Quarterly*, vol. 16, pp. 69–76.

Neumann, P, Evans, R & Pantucci, R 2011, 'Locating Al Qaeda's center of gravity: the role of middle managers', *Studies in Conflict and Terrorism*, vol. 34, no. 11, pp. 825–842.

Noll, G 2012, 'Analogy at war: proportionality, equality and the law of targeting', in JE Nijman and WG Werner (eds), *Netherlands yearbook of international law 2012: legal equality and the international rule of law – essays in honour of P.H. Kooijmans*, vol. 43, TMC Asser Press, The Hague, pp. 205–230.

Perry, W, Signori, D & Boon, J 2004, *Exploring information superiority: a methodology for measuring the quality of information and its impact on shared awareness*, RAND Corporation, Santa Monica, CA.

Plaw, A & Fricker, MS 2012, 'Tracking the predators: evaluating the US drone campaign in Pakistan', *International Studies Perspectives*, vol. 13, no. 4, pp. 344–365.

Robertson, HB 1997, 'The principle of the military objective in the law of armed conflict', *Journal of Legal Studies*, vol. 8, pp. 35–70.

Roggio, B 2008, 'US forces kill al Qaeda in Iraq's Deputy Commander', *Long War Journal*, 15 October.

Sassio, M 2003, 'Legitimate targets of attacks under international humanitarian law', Background Paper, Informal High-Level Expert Meeting on the Reaffirmation and Development of International Humanitarian Law, 27–29 January, Harvard program on Humanitarian Policy and Conflict Research, Cambridge.

Schmitt, E & Shanker, T 2011, *Counterstrike: the untold story of America's secret campaign against Al Qaeda*, Times Books, New York.

Schneider, GR 1997, *Nonlethal weapons: considerations for decisions makers*, Program in Arms Control, Disarmament, and International Security (ACDIS) Occasional Paper, University of Illinois, Champaign, IL.

Serena, CC 2011, *A revolution in military adaptation: the US army in the Iraq war*, Georgetown University Press, Washington, DC.

Shea, N 2011, 'One unit's work illustrates the risks of night raids', *Stars and Stripes*, 23 October.

Sloan, EC 2002, *The revolution in military affairs*, McGill-Queen's University Press, Montreal and Kingston.

Smith, TW 2002, 'The new law of war: legitimizing hi-tech and infrastructure violence', *International Studies Quarterly*, vol. 46, no. 3, pp. 355–374.

Solis, GD 2010, *The law of armed conflict: international humanitarian law in war*, Cambridge University Press, Cambridge.

Strawser, BJ 2010, 'Moral predators: the duty to employ uninhabited aerial vehicles', *Journal of Military Ethics*, vol. 9, no. 4, 342–368.

Taj, F 2012, 'The year of the drone misinformation', *Small Wars and Insurgencies*, vol. 21, no. 3, pp. 529–535.

Teson, FR 2012, 'Targeted killing in war and peace: a philosophical analysis', in C Finkelstein, JD Ohlin & A Altman (eds), *Targeted killings: law and morality in an asymmetric world*, Oxford University Press, Oxford, pp. 403–433.

Thomas, W 2001, *The ethics of destruction: norms and force in international relations*, Cornell University Press, Ithaca, NY.

Wall, T & Monahan, T 2011. 'Surveillance and violence from afar: the politics of drones and liminal security-scapes', *Theoretical Criminology*, vol. 15, no. 3, pp. 239–254.

Wheeler, NJ 2002, 'Dying for "enduring freedom": accepting responsibility for civilian casualties in the war against terrorism', *International Relations*, vol. 16, no. 2, pp. 205–225.

Williams, BG 2013, *Predators: the CIA's drone war on Al Qaeda*, Potomac Books, Dulles.

Wilner, AS 2010, 'Targeted killings in Afghanistan: measuring coercion and deterrence in counterterrorism and counterinsurgency', *Studies in Conflict and Terrorism*, vol. 33, no. 4, pp. 307–329.

Zehfuss, M 2011, 'Targeting: precision and the production of ethics', *European Journal of International Affairs*, vol. 17, no. 3, pp. 543–566.

PART V

Leaks and secrets

14

THE NSA LEAKS, EDWARD SNOWDEN, AND THE ETHICS AND ACCOUNTABILITY OF INTELLIGENCE COLLECTION

Seumas Miller and Patrick Walsh

US National Security Agency (NSA) documents leaked by Edward Snowden, a former NSA private contractor, have catapulted the ethics and accountability of intelligence gathering to the front pages of most major newspapers and media outlets. For more on this case, see Harding (2014). Here there are a range of interconnected ethical issues in need of analysis. Perhaps the most obvious is that of the privacy rights of US and other citizens. Moreover, there is the issue of the ethics of whistleblowing in this area: in the light of national security needs and NSA secrecy provisions, should Snowden have leaked these documents, and should the media have disseminated selected material leaked to them? Further, it is evident that post 9/11 the lines between domestic law-enforcement intelligence gathering and foreign intelligence gathering have become blurred, notably in the legal sphere. For example, under the provisions of the US Patriot Act, law enforcement agencies were arguably only subject to the wiretap provisions of the Foreign Intelligence Surveillance Act (FISA) and, as such, not subject to the normal and broader judicial controls operating in the criminal justice system. Nor is this blurring restricted to the legal sphere. Whatever the moral principles governing intelligence gathering in domestic law enforcement, they surely differ to some degree from those governing foreign intelligence gathering. Moreover, the phenomenon of international terrorist groups that perpetrate attacks on domestic soil muddies the waters; as a result, the specification of appropriate moral principles for the collection of intelligence in relation to such groups is problematic, as it is in other areas of counter-terrorism. This chapter explores these interconnected ethical issues in the context of the Snowden leaks. The issues are interconnected, since the arguments for and against Snowden's leaking of NSA documents (and the subsequent press dissemination of parts of those documents) turn in part on the moral weight to be accorded to individual privacy rights versus that accorded to security post-9/11.

The release by Snowden of a large amount of confidential NSA data to the international press was related for the most part to the so-called Verizon and PRISM affairs. Verizon involved the collection by the NSA of the metadata from calls made within the US, and between the US and any foreign country, of millions of customers of Verizon and other telecommunication providers. Metadata is the unique phone number/internet protocol (IP) addresses of the caller and recipient, the time and duration of the call and the location of the caller and the recipient, but not the content of the communication. PRISM involved agreements between the NSA and various US-based internet companies (Google, Facebook, Skype and so on) to enable the NSA to monitor the online communications of non-US citizens based overseas. Accordingly, PRISM involved the interception of the content of communications and not simply metadata.

Snowden's actions were a major, indeed stunning, breach of institutional confidentiality. They were enabled by ICT and, specifically, the existence of vast amounts of communicable, searchable, analysable, stored data on a computer linked to a network. Given the importance to the integrity of security agencies of compliance with confidentiality requirements, and given the large volume of confidential data released, Snowden's actions surely did considerable institutional damage to the NSA in particular. It is a further question whether the leaks substantially harmed US national security, for example by alerting terrorists to US intelligence-gathering methods.

Nevertheless, perhaps the release of some of this data to the press was morally justified by the public's right to know, for example its right to know that the NSA was engaged in extremely large-scale collection of the metadata of US and other citizens. Certainly, Verizon and PRISM raise important privacy concerns pertaining to both security agencies' collecting and analysing the metadata of their own citizens (Verizon), and their interception of the content of communications between their citizens and foreign citizens and between foreign citizens (PRISM). We note that metadata enables the construction of a detailed profile of a person (for example of the person's associates and activities), especially when combined with financial and other data, and also enables the tracking of a person's movements. Accordingly, it is not necessarily innocuous from a right-to-privacy perspective (Henschke 2013; Lucas 2014).

In so far as such metadata and content collection and analysis has targeted the confidential data and communications of foreign governments and their security agencies, for US national security purposes, it is perhaps best understood as cyber-espionage. In so far as the target has been the data and communications of terrorists, it is perhaps best thought of as cyber-based law enforcement, since terrorism is a crime (including in the context of armed conflict). In so far as such metadata and content collection and analysis has targeted the private data and communication of ordinary citizens (both domestic and foreign), it constitutes an infringement (and in some case, evidently, a violation) of their privacy rights.

The body of this chapter is divided into five sections. In the first two sections, we provide analyses of the key notions of privacy (and, relatedly, confidentiality) and security (bearing in mind the variety of security contexts, for example counter-terrorism versus ordinary law enforcement). In the third and fourth sections, we discuss wiretaps (interception of communicative content) and metadata collection, respectively, in the light of the right to privacy and the need for security. And in the final section we consider the implications of these analyses and discussions for the intelligence-gathering activities of the so-called 'Five Eyes' (US, UK, Canada, Australia and New Zealand). The Five Eyes are a group of historically connected liberal democracies whose intelligence agencies share information and coordinate their activities.

Privacy and confidentiality

The notion of privacy has proven difficult to adequately explicate. Nevertheless, there are a number of general points that can be made. First, privacy is a moral right that people have in relation to other persons with respect to: (i) the possession of information about themselves by other persons; or (ii) the observation/perceiving of themselves – including of their movements, relationships and so on – by other persons.

Second, the right to privacy is closely related to the more fundamental moral value of autonomy. Roughly speaking, the notion of privacy delimits an area, viz. the inner self; however, the right to autonomy relates to the moral right to decide what to think and do, and the moral right to decide *who to exclude and who not to exclude* is an element of this right. So the right to privacy consists of the right to exclude others (right to autonomy) from the inner self (the private sphere).

Third, a measure of privacy is necessary simply in order for people to pursue their projects, whatever those projects might be. For one thing, reflection is necessary for planning, and reflection requires a degree of freedom from the intrusions of others, which is a degree of privacy. For another, knowledge of someone else's plans can lead to those plans being thwarted. *Autonomy* – including the exercise of autonomy in the public sphere – requires a measure of privacy.

In light of the above analysis of privacy, and especially its close relationship to autonomy, we are entitled to conclude that some form of privacy is a constitutive human good. As such, infringements of privacy ought to be avoided. That said, privacy can reasonably be overridden by security considerations under some circumstances, such as when lives are at risk. After all, the right to life is, in general, a weightier moral right than the right to privacy. Thus accessing the financial records of a suspected terrorist, if conducted under warrant, is surely morally justi-fied. We return to this issue below. Let us now turn to some notions that are closely related to privacy, namely anonymity, confidentiality and secrecy.

Individual privacy is sometimes confused with anonymity, but these are distinct notions. Anonymity is preserved when a person's identity in one context is not known in another. Consider the case of Jones, a respectable married man. In another context, Jones might be the anonymous client of a prostitute. Of course, Jones is 'known' to the prostitute, indeed, intimately known. However, the prostitute does not know Jones in his home or work contexts and, likewise, his family and work colleagues do not know Jones in the context of the brothel he visits. Again, consider Smith, a wealthy businessman. In another context, Smith might be an anonymous donor.

Anonymity can be a means to privacy (for example, Smith wants to avoid publicity) or to avoid harm to oneself (for example the reputational damage that Jones might suffer if his visits to the brothel became known). Indeed, anonymity is vital in some situations, for example in the case of a 'tip-off' to police regarding a violent criminal, who would kill the informant if he knew who they were.

These examples demonstrate that anonymity is sometimes an instrumental good. But they also reveal that it is not a constitutive human good. In this respect anonymity is quite different from privacy. But what of confidentiality?

The sphere of individual privacy can be widened to include other individuals who stand in a professional relationship to the first individual, for example a person's lawyer or doctor. Moreover, morally legitimate institutional processes give rise to confidentiality requirements with respect to information, for example committees and tender applications.

Law-enforcement operations give rise to stringent confidentiality requirements, given what is often at stake, for example the wellbeing of informants or the outcome of important investigations that could be compromised by exposure. Military operations might also bear stringent confidentiality requirements, such as 'need to know' principles and legal prohibitions under the Official Secrets Act; again, the stringency of these requirements can be justified given what is often at stake, for example the wellbeing and lives of one's own combatants and the outcome of military missions that might be compromised by being exposed.

At least in the case of security agencies, such as police, military and intelligence agencies, a degree of compliance with principles of confidentiality is a constitutive institutional good in the sense that security agencies could not operate successfully without a high degree of confidentiality.

Another related notion of interest to us here is secrecy. Secret information is not necessarily challenged by the moral right to privacy or by the principle of confidentiality. For, unlike privacy and confidentiality, secrecy is a morally neutral or even pejorative notion. Thus person A can have a moral right to know person B's secrets and B have no grounds for non-disclosure, as might be the case if A is a police officer and B is an offender. Here B has a secret but it has no moral weight *qua* secret.

Secrecy implies that someone possessed of information does not want that information to be disclosed, and that someone else has an interest in finding out the secret information. Secrecy is at home in contexts of conflict and fierce competition, for example wars, organised criminality and market-based companies. More generally, secrecy is at home in contexts of security (see next section).

Excessive secrecy undermines operational effectiveness, for example the 1980 helicopter incursion by the US into Iran to rescue hostages failed because secrecy prevented various helicopter crews from coordinating their activities. Moreover, high levels of secrecy can mask incompetence, for example when it was erroneously thought that Saddam Hussein possessed weapons of mass destruction. High levels of secrecy can also mask corruption, illegality and human rights abuses, for example in authoritarian regimes. Accordingly, in contrast with confidentiality, secrecy is not a constitutive institutional good.

We have distinguished privacy, anonymity, confidentiality and secrecy, and argued that whereas privacy is a constitutive human good and confidentiality a constitutive institutional good, neither anonymity nor secrecy is a constitutive good. A final point concerns the relative moral weight of privacy and confidentiality. Here we make the point that sometimes confidentiality requirements can be overridden by the right to privacy, and sometimes the reverse is the case. The NSA leaks conveniently exemplify this tension. While the activities of the NSA were an infringement, if not a violation, of the privacy rights of individual US citizens and others, it is also the case that the Snowden leaks and subsequent publication in the media were an infringement, if not a violation, of the confidentiality rights of the NSA. Let us now turn to the notion of security.

Security

The notion of security is somewhat vague. Sometimes it is used to refer to a variety of forms of collective security, for example national security (in the face of external military aggression), community security (in the face of disruptions to law and order), and organisational security (in the face of fraud, breaches of confidentiality and other forms of misconduct and criminality). At other times it is used to refer to personal physical security. Physical security in this sense is security in the face of threats to one's life, freedom or personal property – the latter being goods to which one has a human right. Violations or breaches of physical security obviously include murder, rape, assault and torture.

Personal (physical) security is a more fundamental notion than collective security; indeed, collective security in its various forms is in large part derived from personal security. Thus terrorism, for example, is a threat to national security precisely because it threatens the lives of innocent citizens. However, collective security is not simply aggregate personal (physical) security. For example, terrorism might be a threat to the stability of a government and, as such, a national security threat – an example of which can be seen in the Islamic State's occupation of large parts of Iraq and Syria.

Aside from questions about the scope of security (for example the personal, organisational and national levels), security can be distinguished by type. Here a distinction between informational and non-informational security might be helpful. Informational security is self-explanatory and basically consists in ensuring that privacy rights are respected and confidentiality requirements are met.

Non-informational security pertains to physical or psychological harm to human beings, damage to physical objects, and certain forms of harm to institutional processes or purposes, for example by means of corruption. Non-informational security is both a constitutive human good and a constitutive institutional good. After all, a lack of non-informational security evidently implies harm to persons and/or institutions.

It is widely accepted that both privacy rights and confidentiality requirements can be overridden by the needs of non-informational security, since the latter may involve saving lives while the former might only involve some relatively unimportant disclosure of (private or confidential) information. It is perhaps less widely recognised that non-informational security can be overridden by privacy rights and confidentiality considerations. Examples here include intrusive surveillance of a suspected petty thief, or accessing the details of the locations of people under witness protection in order to interview them about a past minor crime.

Aside from the *scope* and *types* of security, there are also various *contexts* of security. These include domestic law enforcement, international organised crime, counter-terrorism, war, cyberwar, trade 'wars' and so on. These different contexts involve a variety of security concerns of differential moral weight; winning the Second World War was obviously of far greater importance than Australian farmers winning a commercial contract to supply live cattle to China. Intelligence gathering needs to be understood in these various different contexts and the stringency of privacy rights and confidentiality requirements relativised to them. In domestic law enforcement, for example, there is, as we saw above, a strong presumption in favour of the privacy rights of citizens, although these can be overridden in certain circumstances under judicial warrant. By contrast, in wartime military intelligence gathering is largely unfettered and the privacy rights of citizens curtailed under emergency powers. Moreover, the confidentiality rights of security agencies are increased under a 'cloak of secrecy' and the privacy and confidentiality rights of the enemy suspended until the cessation of hostilities. Counter-terrorist operations and so-called covert operations against hostile states with which one is not at war provide an additional problematic set of contexts. We return to some of these issues in the final section, below.

In the light of this discussion of security what are we to make of the NSA leaks? Speaking generally, these leaks were a breach of security in the sense that they infringed NSA confidentiality requirements and, indeed, US secrecy laws. However, the more important question is whether they undermined collective security in the stronger sense, for example by putting the lives of security personnel and, ultimately, citizens at risk. Moreover, as we have seen, these leaks involved two main categories of electronic data collection: wiretaps (involving the access of communicative content) such as phone taps and email interceptions; and metadata collection.[1] We shall now discuss these methods in light of our analyses of privacy and security, beginning with wiretaps.

Wiretaps: accessing communicative content

Wiretaps are interceptions of communications between one or more individuals, who are either residing in a country whose intelligence agency is doing the intercepting and/or are located overseas. In contrast with more recent methods of intelligence gathering, notably metadata collection, wiretaps have been used in the collection of national security and law enforcement intelligence for decades.

Importantly, most liberal democratic states have developed legislation in relation to the use of wiretaps in domestic criminal investigations which more or less mirrors underlying ethical principles. These principles may offer some direction to our investigation of wiretaps with respect to situations of interest here, for example the investigation of suspected terrorists domiciled in foreign liberal democratic states. The ethical principles in question include the following (Miller & Blackler 2005, pp. 111–40).

First, because the accessing and/or intercepting of such information is by definition an infringement of the right to privacy, the use of wiretaps ought to be avoided. But this presumption can be overridden by other very weighty moral considerations – in particular the need to protect other fundamental moral rights, such as the right to life – or by exceptional circumstances, such as might obtain in wartime.

Second, the benefits of such accessing and/or intercepting must offset the likely costs, including the erosion of public trust.

Third, the accessing and/or interception in question must be required in relation to serious crimes.

Fourth, there must be at least a reasonable suspicion, reasonable belief or probable cause that the person whose privacy is to be infringed has committed, or intends to commit, a serious crime and that the resulting information is likely to substantially further the investigation related to that crime. The more intrusive and sustained the infringement of the right to privacy, the more serious the crime in question needs to be (principle of proportionality), and the stronger the evidence that the person whose right to privacy is to be infringed is implicated in this crime ought to be.

Fifth, there must be no feasible alternative method of gathering the information that does not involve an infringement of privacy.[2]

Sixth, law enforcement officials must be subject to stringent accountability requirements, including the issuing of warrants in circumstances in which the justification provided is independently adjudicated.

Seventh, those whose privacy has been infringed must be informed that it has been infringed at the earliest possible point that does not compromise the investigation or connected investigations.

Accordingly, in so far as the Snowden leaks pertained to the interception of content by the NSA then, arguably, already existing legally enshrined moral principles can be used to determine whether these leaks were justified – on the grounds, for example, that the relevant NSA activities were a violation of these principles. Let us now turn to metadata.

Metadata

Metadata means 'data disassociated from the identities of its subjects or that can infer from gathered data any anomalous activity' (Sims & Gerber 2009, p. 7). It has generally referred to the bulk collection of telephone data (call numbers, time of call but not content of call) for domestic and international calls. The development of data mining and analytics techniques and technologies has resulted in faster and more efficient interception of telephone and other types of communications, as well as linking or associating various methods of electronic communication for the purpose of surveillance.[3] Intelligence agencies have widened their use of data mining and analytics technologies to include disparate data sources. At the same time, non-state actors such as terrorists have used various, more secure ways than telephone to communicate (Joye & Smith 2014, pp. 1, 11).

After 9/11, the US Foreign Intelligence Surveillance Court (FISC) authorised the collection of bulk telephone metadata, allowing the NSA access to all call records.[4] Both the government and the agency considered this to be the only effective way of continuously keeping track of all the activities, communications and plans of foreign terrorists who disguise and obscure their communications and identities (Clarke et al. 2013, pp. 95–6). Metadata intelligence-collection solutions such as those revealed in the Snowden leaks were also adopted because non-state actors (terrorists and transnational criminal syndicates) currently use technological developments (in data processing, open source information and commercially available encryption) to communicate, plan attacks or conduct their own surveillance on national security and law enforcement authorities. Hence intelligence agencies such as the NSA had to exploit similar communications technologies to track 'digital footprints' in multiple data feeds (metadata) – allowing them to respond more proactively to threat actor activities.

In addition to information about the telephone metadata program, Snowden's revelations also included material about NSA's PRISM program, which allows the agency to access a large amount of digital information – emails, Facebook posts and instant messages. The difference between telephone metadata and PRISM is that the latter also collects the contents of communications.

The collection of bulk metadata is morally problematic in that, as we saw above, there is a presumption against the gathering of citizen's personal information by government officials, including law enforcement and other security personnel. This problem is evident in the metadata collection of the Verizon and PRISM controversies. Verizon involved the collection by the NSA of the metadata from calls made within the US, and between the US and any foreign country, of millions of customers of Verizon and other telecommunication providers, whereas PRISM involved agreements between the NSA and various US-based internet companies (Google, Facebook, Skype and so on) to enable the NSA to monitor the online communications of non-US citizens based overseas. While privacy laws tend to focus on the content of phone calls, emails and the like, the Verizon episode draws our attention to so-called metadata, for example the unique phone number or email address of the caller/recipient, the time of calls and their duration and the location of the caller/recipient. It has been argued that since this data is not content, its collection is morally unproblematic. To this it can be replied, first, that such metadata is collected to facilitate the communication efforts of callers/recipients and their telecommunication providers, and its collection is consented to only for this purpose. Second, metadata enables the non-consensual construction of a detailed description of a person's activities, associates, movements and so on, especially when combined with financial and other data. The availability of such descriptions to security agencies is surely an infringement of privacy and therefore requires justification.

The Five Eyes and intelligence collection

As we saw above, Verizon and PRISM have raised legitimate privacy concerns, for both US citizens and foreigners, for example in relation to metadata collection and analysis. Regarding metadata collection and analysis in the context of domestic law enforcement, the solution, at least in general terms, is evidently at hand: extend the existing principles of probable cause (or, outside the US, reasonable suspicion), and the existing relevant accountability requirements, for example the system of judicial warrants.[5]

However, some of these privacy concerns pertain only to foreign citizens. Consider the FISA (Foreign Intelligence Surveillance Act) Amendments Act of 2008. It mandates the monitoring of, and data gathering from, foreigners who reside outside the US by the NSA. Moreover, data gathered but found not to be relevant for the purposes of, say, counter-terrorism is not allowed to be retained. Importantly, however, there is no probable cause (or reasonable suspicion) requirement unless the person in question is a US citizen.

This is problematic in so far as privacy is regarded as a *human* right and therefore a right of all persons, US citizens or otherwise. Moreover, these inconsistencies between the treatment of US citizens and foreigners are perhaps even more acute, or at least more obvious, when it comes to the infringement of the rights to privacy and, for that matter, confidentiality of non-US citizens in liberal democratic states allied with the US, for example EU citizens (see e.g. Kleinig et al. 2011).

Intelligence gathering, surveillance of citizens and suchlike by domestic law enforcement agencies is reasonably well defined and regulated, for example in accordance with probable cause or reasonable suspicion principles and requirements for warrants; hence the feasibility of simply extending the law-enforcement model to metadata collection within domestic jurisdictions.[6] However, this domestic law enforcement model is too restrictive, and not practicable in relation to intelligence gathering from, for example, hostile foreign states during peacetime – let alone during wartime.

The privacy rights of citizens during wartime are curtailed under emergency powers, and the privacy and confidentiality rights of enemy citizens are almost entirely suspended. Military intelligence gathering during wartime has few constraints and, given what is at stake in all-out wars, such as the Second World War, this may well be justified. However, these are extreme circumstances and the suspension of privacy rights lasts only until the cessation of hostilities. Accordingly, this military model of intelligence gathering is too permissive when it comes to covert intelligence gathering from, for example, fellow liberal democracies during peacetime.

The intelligence-gathering activities, notably cyber-espionage, of the NSA do not fit neatly into the law enforcement model or Just War theory. Questions arise about cyber-espionage in particular. On one hand, the US and its allies cannot be expected to defend their legitimate national interests with their hands tied behind their backs. So their recourse to cyber-espionage seems justified. On the other hand, there is evidently a need for moral guidance when it comes to cyber-espionage, or at least a review of the way it is currently conducted. In this context we make a couple of suggestions, which will be explained below: (i) the clustering together of nation-states; and (ii) a demarcation between government and security personnel on one hand and ordinary citizens on the other.

Under existing arrangements the US, UK, Canada, Australia and New Zealand – the so-called 'Five Eyes' – share information. These nation-states are, so to speak, allies in espionage, and cyber-espionage in particular; for example, they share intelligence. They are the members of the first cluster. There are, of course, other liberal democratic states outside the Five Eyes, such as various EU countries, which have 'shared core liberal democratic values' – with one another and with the Five Eyes – and, specifically, a commitment to privacy rights. This is a second cluster.

The members of these two clusters ought to make good on their claims to respect privacy rights by developing privacy-respecting protocols governing their intelligence-gathering activities in relation to one another. Of course, determining the precise content of such protocols is no easy matter given, for example, that there are often competing national interests in play, even between liberal democracies with shared values and many common political interests. But there does not appear to be any in-principle reason why such protocols could not be developed; and the fact that the task might be difficult is no objection to its attempt. Moreover, adherence to the protocols in question would consist, in so far as it is practicable, in ensuring compliance with some of the standard moral principles protecting privacy and confidentiality rights, such as probable cause and reasonable suspicion and use of judicial warrants. As such, these two clusters would essentially consist of an extension of the law enforcement model to cyber-espionage conducted within and between the included states.

Further, this process of clustering of liberal democratic states would be in accordance with a principle of reciprocity: each of the nation-states would need to agree to, and actually comply with, the privacy-respecting protocols in question.[7] What of authoritarian states known to be supporting international terrorism and/or engaging in hostile covert political operations, including cyber-espionage – for example China, Russia and North Korea?

With respect to authoritarian states of this kind, there are few, if any constraints on intelligence gathering and analysis, including cyber-espionage, if it is done in the service of a legitimate political interest such as national security.[8] Nevertheless, it is important to distinguish, within such an authoritarian state, between the government and its security agencies on one hand and private citizens on the other. Notwithstanding the applicability of the retrospective reciprocity principle, the need to respect the privacy rights of private citizens in authoritarian states remains intact; perhaps all the more so given that these rights (and, for that matter, human rights in general) are routinely violated by those citizens' own governments.

So a stringent principle of discrimination ought to govern cyber-espionage directed at authoritarian states. At the very least, the citizens of these states ought to be able to differentiate between morally justified infringements of the privacy and confidentiality rights of members of their government and its security agencies, on one hand, and violations of their own privacy and confidentiality rights, on the other, and be justified in believing that, while the former might be routine, the latter are few and far between.

Conclusion

In this chapter we have provided analyses of the key notions of privacy (and, relatedly, confidentiality) and security (bearing in mind the variety of security contexts, for example counter-terrorism versus ordinary law enforcement). Moreover, in doing so we have argued that privacy is a constitutive human good and confidentiality a constitutive institutional good, at least for security agencies. In relation to security we distinguished between informational and non-informational security, and argued that the latter is a constitutive good for both persons and institutions. We discussed wiretaps (interception of communicative content) and metadata collection, respectively, in the light of the right to privacy and the need for security, and argued that the question of whether privacy should override security or vice versa is a contextually dependent matter. So in wartime security rightly tends to override privacy, but this is not necessarily the case in law enforcement during peacetime. Counter-terrorist operations provide a somewhat different case. Finally, we considered the implications of our analyses for the intelligence-gathering activities of the so-called 'Five Eyes' (US, UK, Canada, Australia and New Zealand). We argued that cyber-espionage does not fit neatly into the law-enforcement model or the military model (as elaborated in accordance with Just War theory, for example). On one hand, recourse to cyber-espionage by the US and its allies is, in general terms, justified. On the other hand, there is evidently a need to review the moral guidance related to cyber-espionage as it is currently conducted, for example with respect to fellow liberal democracies and their citizens. In this context we suggested (i) clustering together certain nation-states, which could develop privacy-respecting protocols together with other liberal democratic states but not necessarily with authoritarian states; and (ii) a demarcation between government and security personnel on one hand and ordinary citizens on the other, the latter to be provided with a higher level of privacy protection.

Notes

1   The accessing, collection and analysis of data emanating from social media, such as Facebook and Twitter, by the NSA gives rise to the privacy concerns already discussed with respect to wiretaps and metadata collection. However, arguably these privacy concerns are much reduced given that the users of *social* media in many cases cannot reasonably

expect the same high levels of privacy accorded, for example, to those whose emails are intercepted or whose phone data is collected. At any rate, for reasons of space we do not discuss this issue here.

2 Recently this requirement has been weakened in some jurisdictions, e.g. to the requirement that the infringement be reasonable in the circumstances, including whether other methods would be as effective.

3 For a good discussion of the development of national security data-mining capabilities in the United States after 9/11 see Seifert (2008).

4 The FISC was established to provide judicial oversight of intelligence agencies (the NSA and FBI) seeking interception in the communications of suspects.

5 This is, of course, a simplification; however I do not have the space to go into details here. I have done so in my unpublished manuscript, Miller, S 'Cyber-security, privacy and confidentiality'.

6 This is not to say that this is likely to happen. For example, new legislation in Australia and the UK might allow intelligence agencies access to metadata without a warrant.

7 There are, of course, considerable difficulties here in relation to democracies outside the Five Eyes and NATO. For example, in part for historical reasons, some South American democracies do not necessarily trust, and have different and often competing political interests from, the US. Moreover, within the Five Eyes there are power imbalances, for example US in comparison to Australia, which might render the tit-for-tat procedure ineffectual. However, there is a possibility of smaller powers forming a collective and thereby reducing the power imbalance to an extent that could enable an effective tit-for-tat procedure.

8 Important questions arise here concerning what counts as a legitimate purpose, particularly in the context of the blurred distinction between political interests and economic interests, for example in China's cyber-theft operations. For reasons of space we cannot pursue these questions here.

References

Clarke, R, Morel, M, Stone, G, Sunstein, C & Swire, P 2013, *Liberty and security in a changing world*, Report and Recommendations, President's Review Group on Intelligence and Communications Technology, Washington, DC.

Harding, L 2014, *The Snowden files: the inside story of the world's most wanted man*, Guardian Books, London.

Henschke, A 2013, 'The morality of metadata: not just innocuous adornment', *The Conversation*, 13 December, http://theconversation.com/the-morality-of-metadata-not-just-innocuous-adornment-21160

Joye, C & Smith, P 2014, 'Most powerful spy says Snowden leaks will cost lives', *The Australian Financial Review*, 8 May.

Kleinig, J, Mameli, P, Miller, S, Salane, D & Schwartz, A 2011, *Security and privacy*, ANU Press, Canberra.

Lucas, E 2014, 'A press crops full of Snowdenistas', *The Wall Street Journal*, 29 January, http://online.wsj.com/news/articles/SB10001424052702303519404579350663554949356

Miller, S 2015, 'Cyber-attacks and "dirty hands": cyberwar, cyber-crimes or covert political action?' in F Allhoff, A Henschke & BJ Strawser (eds), *Binary bullets: the ethics of cyberwarfare*, Oxford University Press, Oxford.

Miller, S & Blackler, J 2005, *Ethical issues in policing*, Ashgate, Aldershot.

Seifert, JW 2008, *Data mining and homeland security*, CRS Report RL31798, Congressional Research Service, Washington, DC.

Sims, JE & Gerber, B 2009, *Vaults, mirrors, and masks: rediscovering U.S. counterintelligence*, Georgetown University Press, Washington, DC.

15

WIKILEAKS AND WHISTLEBLOWING

Privacy and consent in an age of digital surveillance

Jeremy Wisnewski

Surveillance has reached unprecedented levels in recent years. Our awareness of this fact is in no small part due to the actions of whistleblowers such as Chelsea Manning and Edward Snowden, acting in cooperation with organisations such as WikiLeaks (in the case of Manning) and with mainstream news organisations (in the case of Snowden and his confidant, Glen Greenwald). In what follows, I offer a partial defence of this kind of whistleblowing. I argue that knowledge of the possibility of invasions of privacy is required for our ability to consent to such invasions, and that consent is required if violations of privacy are to be justified. Whistleblowing on digital surveillance is thus justified at least to the extent that it preserves the conditions under which a democratic government maintains its legitimacy (namely, the consent of its citizens).

I begin by considering two related questions about privacy concerning digital surveillance: in what ways is the privacy of digital information important, and to what extent is such information actually private? I argue that digital information should be considered private, and that it is as private as anything *could* be for some persons. I then consider the conditions under which one could consent to this new form of privacy invasion. I conclude by arguing that the actions of Manning and Snowden were justified in so far as they made consent *possible*. Ironically, this may mean that these whistleblowers have contributed to the legitimation of the largest domestic spying program ever to exist.

Privacy and the digital panopticon

Foucault's image of the modern surveillance state as a panopticon has never been more apt. Contemporary panopticism is far more pervasive than even Foucault could have predicted: our electronic activities are now automatically collected and stored on a massive scale. This collection is carried out by both private companies and government agencies. Our data tells a story about who we are, what we think, and how we behave. The everyday collection of details about our electronic activity would thus seem to represent a fundamental challenge to our privacy.

The surveillance being carried out today is new in both its nature and scope: our digital communications and activities are now systematically collected and stored on a scale unthinkable even a decade ago. Almost none of this material *immediately* identifies anyone: the information is largely anonymised, though with a little investigation and correlation it is very easy to identify virtually anyone who has an active digital presence. And although someone *could* obtain very intimate details about a life by analysing this information, hardly any of the collected information will ever be seen *by anyone at all*. In the US programme of data collection, data sits in vast underground data storage centres for five years, and is then deleted.

It is a brave new world for espionage: everyone is being spied on, but no-one is really *doing* the spying. Government agencies like the NSA have access to information that would reveal many things we appropriately regard as private: our political views, our religious beliefs, what we like and desire, even the questions that interest us. For the most part, this information goes untouched and unseen. And yet the issue of privacy nevertheless looms large: why should anyone in government even *be able* to access such information about individual citizens?

Privacy has long been recognised as an important good. In many countries, a right to privacy has been enshrined in the law, which is meant to act as a bulwark against the overreaching arm of government. In many nations, a warrant is required to search a person's private possessions, or to enter a dwelling. We establish laws protecting particular kinds of information about persons, demanding confidentiality and swearing others to silence.

There is an intuitive link between privacy and the exercise of autonomy. The ability to maintain a degree of privacy over some areas of one's life facilitates the exercise of one's capacity to engage in legitimately autonomous action. This is so, in brief, because the awareness that one is being monitored can inhibit one's willingness to engage in actions that one might otherwise engage in. To the extent that one lacks privacy, in other words, one is less likely to engage in certain kinds of actions.

But our intuitions about this link are only partially accurate. There is some evidence that the mere presence of surveillance cameras actually has *no effect* on the way people behave (Welsh & Farrington 2004). Though the mere presence of cameras appears to have little effect, *active* surveillance *does* appear to have a significant impact (Oulasvirta et al. 2012). This stands to reason: if people know no-one is watching the camera feed, the presence of cameras will not deter them; if they believe they are actively being watched, they will adjust their behaviour accordingly.

This indicates something paradoxical: privacy seems to be connected with autonomy only as mediated through *belief*. One might be under constant surveillance and act in perfectly uninhibited ways *provided* one does not *know* that one is under surveillance. Likewise, one may be *completely* inhibited by the simple *belief* that one is under surveillance even if one is not. Thus one's beliefs about one's privacy are much more robustly connected to autonomy than is privacy itself. In this respect, surveillance only affects autonomy to the extent that we *know* about it.[1] The *manner* of surveillance also matters as to whether or not it has an effect on a person's action. If information about me is only passively collected, this will have little effect on my behaviour. If I believe an actual *person* is actively watching me, the effects on my action are significant.[2]

If, as Justice Anthony Kennedy argues, '[l]iberty presumes an autonomy of self that includes freedom of thought, belief, expression, and certain intimate conduct' (as cited in Rosen 2011, p. 72), then we had better be sure our intrusions into privacy leave some stones unturned. But the connection between privacy and autonomy is not a sufficient reason to reject *all* intrusions into privacy. In fact, some kinds of intrusions into the private lives of citizens may well *increase* our ability to exercise autonomy. Moreover, citizens routinely accept that some kinds of violations of privacy are necessary for the functioning of civil society. We accept the right of the police to question people, given just cause, about their private lives when investigating a crime (in standard police interrogation, for example). We likewise accept the right of the state to engage in searches, again given just cause, of homes, automobiles and even people. In various ways, these activities set aside the right to privacy for the sake of higher-order social goods (safety, security or justice).

Nevertheless, there is a presumption in modern democratic states that privacy is itself a condition of liberty. Glen Greenwald makes the following point:

> Only when we believe that nobody else is watching us do we feel free – safe – to truly experiment, to test boundaries, to explore new ways of thinking and being, to explore what it means to be ourselves. ... Mass surveillance by the state is therefore inherently repressive, even in the unlikely case that it is not abused by vindictive officials to do things like gain private information about political opponents. Regardless of how surveillance is used or abused, the limits it imposes on freedom are intrinsic to its existence.
>
> *(Greenwald 2014, p. 174)*

To accept surveillance, the argument goes, is necessarily to accept some basic hindrances to liberty. This is the very *design* of surveillance: the idea is precisely to limit the actions of those being observed: 'collective coercion is both the intent and effect of state surveillance' (Greenwald 2014, p. 178).[3]

In the end, though, whether or not digital surveillance is coercive is a *different question* from whether or not it constitutes an invasion of privacy. Even if we claimed that constant, active internet surveillance was not coercive in any way (a very implausible claim, to put it mildly), we would (probably) nevertheless regard such surveillance as an invasion of privacy. It is not a conceptual truth that autonomy requires privacy; it is an empirical one. Believing that we are being watched has a significant effect on our actions, at least in many circumstances. It is of course possible that things are different in the case of metadata. But even if digital surveillance isn't coercive, it might still violate a right to privacy. Indeed, the good of privacy need not be exhausted by its connection to liberty.

Adam Moore (2010, p. 142) argues that 'privacy, defined as a right to control access to and uses of bodies, locations, and information, is necessary for human well-being and flourishing. Simply put, there is compelling evidence that individuals who lack this sort of control suffer physically and mentally.' Assuming this view is correct, we should value privacy as a constitutive element of our wellbeing: the power to exert some control over not just our actions, but also *what people know about us*, shapes the kind of life we live.[4]

Of course, claiming 'some level of privacy' is required for both autonomy and wellbeing doesn't entail that the privacy in question must be *digital privacy*. Likewise, claiming that wellbeing requires 'some control' over the information others have about us doesn't entail that we must control our digital information. Although the general points both seem correct – privacy is both a condition for wellbeing and a condition for autonomy – it simply isn't obvious how these principles ought to apply to digital surveillance. One could maintain a high level of privacy if one simply stayed away from the internet, demonstrating that privacy *in some sense* is available whenever we want it, but not in any and every arena we choose. The digital realm, then, might be similar to other arenas in which we have elected to give up additional privacy in exchange for particular goods such as security (at airports, for example). Even if we need privacy for wellbeing, we might not need *digital* privacy in particular. An advocate of digital privacy would need to show how digital information in particular is crucial to autonomy, wellbeing, or both.

I think we should concede that the privacy of some citizens is *not* compromised by large-scale data collection. But this is small consolation if our aim is to protect privacy in general. Internet activities are closely related, in many cases, to core values and beliefs that are, in some ways, even more important than speech – my very interests and activities can be tracked by examining how I spend my time online. And while many people are not yet online, the internet has become the dominant mode of exploring and understanding the world for a huge number. It is the place they turn to get answers to questions, directions to stores, to do shopping and browsing, to interact with friends and to watch movies. Information about online activities provides a window into someone's life that can reveal any number of things that we regard as utterly personal. This suggests that digital privacy may be one of the most important forms of privacy, at least for some people.

There is an additional reason to think that digital privacy in particular is important for both autonomy and wellbeing – for at least *some* persons. In a programme of data collection as massive as that of the NSA, the possibility of abuse is incredibly high. This means that any benefits to be wrought from such a programme must also be of great and continuing value. It's hard to assess this publicly, given the national security interests at stake. Documents revealed by Snowden indicate that the programme of digital surveillance has not been particularly successful. Angwin (2014, p. 48) notes that the most *positive outcome of* digital surveillance that has been noted so far is that, in fifty-four instances, it 'contributed to our understanding' of cases 'at the margins'. This is hardly a glowing endorsement of an allegedly 'essential' weapon in the fight against terrorism.[5]

Privacy and consent

Is the right to privacy in fact violated by the collection of digital data? There are at least two arguments to the effect that it is not. First, one might argue that internet users have consented to having their data shared, and hence have voluntarily given up any right to privacy they once had. Indeed, the US Supreme Court has adopted a 'third-party doctrine': persons have no reasonable expectation of privacy regarding information they voluntarily disclose to third parties. When we click to give our consent in using various websites and applications, we also allow companies to collect and utilise the information we thereby provide.

A second argument one might make runs as follows: in general, the law does not recognise a 'right' to privacy in public places. The internet is not itself a 'private' place, so there can be no presumption of privacy in regard to one's digital activities. Thus, on this view, even if we *did not consent* to being observed, we have no particular right to privacy while in a public place such as the internet.

I will respond to the latter argument first. To monitor a person for a prolonged period of time, it might be argued, is itself a kind of search: it reveals things about a person that would otherwise remain hidden. Patterns emerge that would not be detectable in any single moment. Characterizing the opinion of Justice Douglas,[6] Jeffrey Rosen writes that:

> Prolonged surveillance is a search ... because no reasonable person expects that his movements will be continuously monitored from door to door; all of us have a reasonable expectation of privacy in the 'whole' of our movements in public.
>
> *(Rosen 2011, p. 71)*

The question is thus *not* whether or not internet activity is 'private' – let us concede that in some important senses it is not. The issue is whether massive surveillance *in a public domain* is itself a violation of one's right to privacy. Assuming Justice Douglas is correct, this would seem to be the case: prolonged surveillance reveals things about us that singular observations would not. Even if we have no right to privacy in relation to any particular actions carried out in public, we can reasonably expect privacy regarding the *totality* of our public actions, as the patterns these reveal can constitute some of the most intimate information about us – information that we have some legitimate right to keep private. The claim that the internet is a public domain, then, does not seem to justify massive surveillance of digital traffic (at least not by itself). Does the claim that all such surveillance involves consent fare any better?

Persons consent to terms of use for particular services, allowing companies to collect information about them in exchange for using the service in question. In this respect, it might well be argued that one *cannot* have a reasonable expectation of privacy in using such services. Indeed, one has consented to giving up one's data (which is usually anonymised) in exchange for free use of a service.

And yet the 'consent' in question does not seem to be informed, at least for the most part. People routinely click through the relevant terms without reading them, giving little thought to what they are consenting.[7] This may represent a genuine apathy about one's digital privacy. Such apathy may be the result of a failure to understand what kinds of sensitive information can be, and is, collected. It also may be that people simply do not care much about digital privacy of this sort.

But even if the consent we give is informed, it is consent to the actions of a company. It doesn't relate to large-scale *governmental* collection and use of the information collected by these companies. Consenting to a company's use of one's data is not the same as consenting to a government's use of this same data (even if the terms of service *include a statement that records are subject to government search*). My research interests, my hobbies, my location, my favourite political causes: all of these are easily accessed through a simple look at my internet search history, let alone an analysis of my internet activities over a longer period. Such an analysis would reveal the very content of my thoughts – *what I was thinking about* – as well as an intimate picture of those with whom I live and work.

At least in democratic states, there is a means by which we can give our consent to such uses of governmental power: we can re-elect those who create and perpetuate them. In principle at least, a democratic state *always* involves some level of consent on the part of those governed, bestowing the authority to make and enforce laws. The extent of this consent will depend on the exact laws already in place as well the exact authority invested in particular roles. Nevertheless, once laws allowing surveillance are created, an argument can be made that proper consent, through democratic election, has in fact been given. In this respect, it does not matter if one consents to governmental collection of digital information *directly*; one has *tentatively* consented to such collection through the democratic process itself.

Conditions of consent

In democratic societies, at least ideally, there are straightforward mechanisms in place for limiting intrusions into privacy, both in practice and as enshrined in law. The ability to elect leaders is the fundamental corrective mechanism in democratic societies today. This ability – again, in theory – acts as a safeguard against illegitimate intrusions into our private lives. Thus, if there is sufficient interest among citizens in changing the laws surrounding police interrogation, there is a mechanism by which this can be accomplished. This mechanism, one standard argument goes, provides intrusions of the state with their legitimacy: if a citizenry does not change the leadership that perpetrates or allows such intrusions, they have thereby consented to them. On a standard social contract view, then, intrusions into privacy (through things like surveillance) are justified provided that (i) there are mechanisms through which citizens may revoke their consent to said intrusions; and (ii) citizens do not use these mechanisms to revoke their consent.

In order for this argument to work, at least two conditions must be met. First, the citizens of a nation must be aware of the actions carried out by their government (at least in broad outline – this condition does not entail that every citizen should have full knowledge of covert operations). Without this awareness, it is impossible to revoke consent. If it is impossible to revoke consent, then the 'consent' in question is not worthy of the name. Second, the mechanisms that enable change in existing law must be plausibly regarded as functional. If these conditions are not met, the intrusions into privacy in question are illegitimate.

The first condition bears some comment. Certainly many actions undertaken by government agencies do not require the direct informed consent of citizens. Determining which roads to repair first, or what kind of landscaping would be most appropriate at City Hall, for example, are precisely the sorts of things we delegate to those in whom we invest authority. If informed consent were required for every action, this would ultimately impede *all* government action.

If informed consent requires abandoning surveillance all together, it may well be too high a price to pay. Perhaps current estimations of the optimal balance between privacy and security are askew; it seems right to insist nevertheless on some kind of balance. Calling for informed consent *tout court* would ultimately mean privacy *always* trumping security – a proposition too radical to entertain (it would mean the end of even standard police searches and standard forms of questioning in law enforcement).

George R. Lucas (2014, p. 31) argues that the NSA programme of large-scale surveillance should

> seek to inform, and to obtain voluntary consent from, the subjects of security surveillance, making it clear that there will be certain features of the program that subjects of a policy designed for their protection will knowingly and voluntarily consent to remain ignorant of for the sake of the effectiveness of that surveillance.
>
> *(Lucas 2014, p. 31)*

This seems to be the right level of consent required for programmes of massive surveillance: we need to know that our digital activities are being monitored, but we do not need to know precisely how, when or by whom. This allows the surveillance to be effective (we don't know enough about it to be able to stop it) but also voluntary (we do know that surveillance is going on).

The second condition states that the mechanisms that enable change in existing law must be plausibly regarded as functional. It is beyond the scope of the current chapter to determine the exact conditions for a mechanism of change to be called 'functional'. The mere existence of elections does not seem sufficient to guarantee that laws are in effect subject to the oversight of citizens. If elections are overrun with moneyed interests, or if large numbers of voters are so disenfranchised that they fail to vote, one *might* argue that the system in question does *not* have the functional mechanisms for change. Likewise, if the oversight that *does* exist is woefully inadequate, and if this oversight is enough to secure the acquiescence of the public, one might argue that the mechanisms for change have been stifled: people are prevented from acting by being made to believe there is no problem that needs to be addressed – adequate oversight is lacking precisely because people believe that it is already present.

In the US, the Foreign Intelligence Surveillance Act of 1978 is sometimes presented as the mechanism by which adequate oversight is achieved. This Act established a court to determine whether or not particular surveillance activity on the part of organisations like the NSA should be allowed. It is difficult to know with certainty what the review process of this court involves, since the rulings are automatically designated top secret. We *do* know, however, that:

> In its first twenty-four years, from 1978 to 2002, the court rejected a total of *zero* government applications while approving many thousands. In the subsequent decade, through 2012, the court has rejected just eleven government applications. In total, it has approved more than twenty-thousand requests.
>
> *(Greenwald 2014, p. 128)*

These figures *might* be consistent with perfectly adequate oversight: perhaps only sensible requests have been made. It is likewise possible that the oversight in question is much less significant than most people would imagine, and the surveillance much more extensive, and yet that those it affects (everyone!) simply do not care. For a governmental practice to be legitimate, it has to be something that citizens both know about and are able to change. Although I leave open the question of what mechanisms must be in place to judge the latter criterion met, surely open democratic elections are *one* such way, provided these elections are not undermined by corruption, fraud and so forth.

Let us say, for the sake of argument, that the US system has adequate means for changing laws and practices regarding which its citizens revoke their consent. If this is correct, it would seem that large-scale surveillance of metadata may turn out to be perfectly legitimate. Even if the collection of information far exceeds our suspicions, our apathy regarding such collection may ultimately justify it.

WikiLeaks and the corporate media

WikiLeaks provides a forum in which we can ensure that the first condition of consent is met. While it is implausible to claim that every page of the thousands released by the site is necessary for meeting this condition, nevertheless exposing government actions generally – and in particular the surveillance activity of the government – is essential for the legitimacy (or illegitimacy) of such surveillance. Whistleblowing makes consent (and revoking consent) possible.

The question of degree is important here. How much information should be released for public scrutiny? It is certainly possible that whistleblowers release more information than is required to insure the consent of the governed. Whistleblowing that endangers lives, for example, seems deeply morally problematic. Exactly *what* should be exposed is thus a serious issue: even if there is a moral justification for whistleblowing in general, it may nevertheless be difficult to determine what information should be made public and in how much detail.

The WikiLeaks approach to the question of degree – which seems to favour allowing the public to decide what's relevant and what is not – involves almost no oversight whatsoever, and no active collaboration with the government in order to protect sensitive information. The documents Julian Assange received from Chelsea Manning were initially released without any redactions whatsoever.[8] By contrast, Edward Snowden revealed information through the mainstream media, which in turn conferred with governmental officials about what should and should not be released. This allowed the US government to argue its case about what was important to national security and what was not. According to Glenn Greenwald (2014), these arguments were often weak, and were thus ignored in many cases. But the actions of Edward Snowden at least seem to make informed consent *possible*.

Snowden has been very articulate about his own motivations. As he describes it:

My sole motive is to inform the public as to that which is done in their name and that which is done against them. The U.S. government, in conspiracy with client states, chiefest among them the Five Eyes – the United Kingdom, Canada, Australia, and New Zealand – have inflicted upon the world a system of secret, pervasive surveillance from which there is no refuge.

(Greenwald 2014, p. 23)

Unlike Assange, who advocates total transparency, Snowden seems much more concerned with specific surveillance tactics than with the overall ethics of information. Snowden:

condones the violation of local or particular laws and statutes solely because of their incongruity with higher – and more fundamental – law.... Snowden's main claim, in short, is that *his* actions not only protect fundamental – but now systematically endangered – rights and laws, but that they also directly embody core legal virtues.

(Scheuerman 2014, pp. 4–5)

This leads Scheuerman (2014, p. 2) to argue plausibly that 'we should interpret Snowden's actions as meeting most of the demanding tests outlined in sophisticated political thinking about civil disobedience'. In this respect, I think it is a mistake to think of the acts of whistleblowing carried out by Manning and Snowden as treasonous.[9] Their actions have ensured that one of the necessary conditions of democratic legitimacy has been met: because of their actions, the public knows what kinds of data collection are currently being carried out, and on what scale.

But ironically and perversely, WikiLeaks, Snowden and Greenwald may turn out to be partially responsible for the future (and perhaps current?) *legitimacy* of widespread digital surveillance. In making the public aware of the large-scale collection of digital information, they also make it possible to claim the further consent of those affected. If citizens know that their digital information is being tracked but nevertheless continue to use the related digital technology, the argument might go, they are consenting to their data being collected – at least until they elect a government that would put an end to the practice. WikiLeaks and Snowden have thus made informed consent *possible*. But this is by no means a criticism. Even if it is lamentable that large-scale surveillance might be legitimated by our apathy, it is nevertheless *legitimated*. It will have passed the democratic test, even if it fails others.

Notes

1 It might be tempting for some, in light of this point, to claim that government surveillance was *made* harmful by its exposure rather than by its operation. I think there is something right about this claim, but it has to be understood correctly. Programmes of massive surveillance simply do not remain secret. While exposure of said surveillance may be the proximate cause of an interference with our liberty, the exposure itself is inevitable. It is thus *not* the case that somehow the whistleblowing itself *creates* the harm it exposes. There are obviously some complicated metaphysical issues lurking here that I will not address. I hope the reader will forgive me.
2 This matters a good deal if we are thinking about the relationship between passive digital surveillance and autonomy. If the data collection is done passively (no-one is examining all of what is collected), and if we further believe that it is extremely unlikely anyone will ever bother to look at this data in our own case, one could argue that there will be no significant effects on our autonomy in *this* case, though there could be in other forms of information collection.
3 There have been *many* studies on the way that surveillance affects actions. Some of this material is summarised in chapter 3 of Angwin (2014). Greenwald (2014) is talking specifically about *state* surveillance when he claims that surveillance is intrinsically coercive. The data available concerns surveillance generally understood.
4 It may be the case, of course, that wellbeing is connected to privacy *through* autonomy: privacy facilitates autonomous action, which in turn acts as a constitutive element of wellbeing. Alternatively, it may be that privacy is its own source of satisfaction, completely independent of autonomy. I have no allegiance to any particular view here.
5 Angwin (2014, p. 46) also lists six specific instances (all since 2001) where digital surveillance has *not* stopped a terrorist attack.
6 The opinion in question is *United States* v. *Maryland*, 615 F.3d 544 (D.C. Cir. 2010).
7 I suspect many readers will admit to having accepted Terms of Service in the past without having actually read them.
8 This is well documented.
9 It would be treasonous if we thought of government as a particular administration – namely, the one that decided to carry out a programme of surveillance that it did not want the public to know about. It is *not* treasonous to expose such a programme, however, if we think of the government as the set of democratic processes and procedures laid out in the US Constitution. Obviously, I think the latter way of understanding 'government' is much more sensible.

References

Angwin, J 2014, *Dragnet nation: a quest for privacy, security, and freedom in a world of surveillance*, Times Books, New York.

Greenwald, G 2014, *No place to hide: Edward Snowden, the NSA, and the US surveillance state*, Metropolitan Books, New York.

Lucas, G 2014, 'NSA management directive #424: secrecy and privacy in the aftermath of Edward Snowden', *Ethics and International Affairs*, vol. 28, no. 1, pp. 29–38.

Moore, AD 2010, 'Privacy, security, and government surveillance: WikiLeaks and the new accountability', *Public Affairs Quarterly*, vol. 25, no. 2, pp. 141–156.

Oulasvirta, A, Pihlajamaa, A, Perkio, J, Ray, D, Vahakangas, T, Hasu, T, Vainio, N & Myllymaki, P 2012, *Long-term effects of ubiquitous surveillance in the home*, Helsinki Institute for Information Technology, Helsinki.

Rosen, J 2011, 'The deciders: Facebook, Google, and the future of privacy and free speech', in J Rosen and B Wittes (eds), *Constitution 3.0: freedom and technological change*, Brookings Institution Press, Washington, DC.

Scheuerman, WE 2014, 'Whistleblowing as civil disobedience: the case of Edward Snowden', *Philosophy and Social Criticism*, vol. 40, no. 7, pp. 609–628.

Welsh, BC & Farrington, D 2004, 'Surveillance for crime prevention in public space: results and policy changes in Britain and America', *Criminology and Public Policy*, vol. 3, no. 3, pp. 497–526.

PART VI

Responsibility and governance

16

ETHICS FOR INTELLIGENCE OFFICERS

Michael Falgoust and Brian Roux

Instances of legislation that expand intelligence-collection powers raise serious concerns for privacy, autonomy, ethics and justice. Concerns about the erosion of civil liberties raised by philosopher Jeremy Waldron shortly after the passing of the PATRIOT Act (2003) have proven prescient – not least after Edward Snowden's revelation of mass surveillance and data-gathering programmes amongst global intelligence organisations such as the NSA (Greenwald & Snowden 2013). Justifications proposed by the organisations implementing these programmes are weakly supported by public evidence. Public scrutiny is avoided by pointing to the inherently secret nature of intelligence collection and national security concerns. Secrecy and lack of public oversight leave the ultimate judgment of the programme's effectiveness, weighed against the degree of privacy violations it entails, in the hands of officials with sufficient security clearance – which involves a conflict of interest. In addressing these concerns, we propose a code of ethics built around the framework of the Just War theory and democratic theories regarding privacy.

As an important component of liberty, the privacy of citizens must be respected. In liberal democracies judicial oversight is typically required for acts of law enforcement that would violate citizens' privacy. As much as these standards are jeopardised by the PATRIOT Act, citizens should still expect their privacy to be respected outside of circumstances sufficiently grave to warrant a violation. The Just War theory demands that military action be in proportion to the threat posed. We propose that a similar approach be taken with regard to intelligence operations. Given the potential to undermine trust between states, allied or not, intelligence operations must be carefully structured in terms of their objectives and methods, in order to avoid consequences more dire than those the operation might prevent. Where there is no specific threat to prevent, we argue that there is no clear justification for intelligence operations (or only justification for minimal, passive signals intelligence or 'SIGINT' operations). Only an extremely grave and imminent threat can justify wholesale domestic surveillance, and even then only until the immediate danger has passed.

In this chapter, we examine public information on existing mass intelligence-gathering programmes, and analyse these programmes with respect to the main elements of the Just War theory. In so doing, we try to determine whether each programme: (i) has a just cause, wherein the aim of the programme is compliant with international law and societal norms; (ii) is conducted by a competent authority established by and accountable to the sovereign government; (iii) maintains a right intention when executing its mandate in achieving the aims defined by its cause; (iv) is designed to strike a proportional balance between the harm it is intended to prevent and collateral damage to privacy interests; and (v) distinguishes between civilian and non-civilian targets, friendly and unfriendly governments, and other proper or improper targets. We present these questions as the basis for an ethical framework for evaluating future intelligence-collection programmes.

Just War theory and democracy

In proposing a code of ethics for intelligence officers, we encounter a collection of problems that have previously been outlined in scholarship on Just War theory, espionage, and cyber-conflict. A survey of existing literature will provide insights into the values in conflict. Here, key insights will be identified and incorporated into a general framework for just intelligence collection. This framework will show how the relevant values relate to one another in this context. From the skeletal structure, we develop a set of questions that can be asked of any intelligence-collection programme. Answers to these questions both provide an assessment of the programme in terms of just intelligence collection and offer normative guidance on how to constrain the programme to meet ethical requirements.

As intelligence collection primarily concerns defence of the state, Just War theory is the most generally applicable framework. Intelligence collection programmes operate in the context of standing international relations, foreign policy and military institutions. As Just War theory principles outline normative constraints in those domains, the same constraints should apply to intelligence collection as well.

The account of just intelligence collection offered here presumes that the respective sovereign state is a liberal democracy generally construed. As such, democratic theory and democratic accounts of justice underpin the sovereign authority assumed by Just War theory. Furthermore, insofar as intelligence-collection programmes may impact upon citizens in various ways, accounts of citizens' rights and duties must be available to ensure a complete ethical assessment. In particular, the kinds of harms citizens are most likely to suffer from intelligence collection involve privacy violations, so the importance and value of citizens' privacy in democratic theory must be brought into focus.

In liberal democracies, privacy defines the domain of liberty for individual citizens. John Stuart Mill refers to the private sphere as 'the sphere of self-regarding action'

(1859, p. 17). More recent scholars prefer to characterise privacy as a citizen's right to control flows of information (Nissenbaum 2009, p. 69). The shift in emphasis, from privacy as a negative liberty to informational privacy, is especially relevant to intelligence-collection programmes. Conceptions of privacy generally identify a connection between citizens' privacy and their autonomy. By defining a domain that is entirely subject to the individual, privacy rights foster a sense of autonomy (Reiman 1976, p. 39). Insofar as democratic legitimacy is grounded in the consent of the governed, without sufficient autonomy democratic governance is not possible. In a democratic state, legally recognised privacy rights ensure that the conditions for developing autonomy are distributed to all citizens. Privacy grounds individual freedom in liberal democracies; without a right to privacy in some form, citizens lack any specific guarantee of their freedom from government interference.

To examine the democratic value of privacy in terms of the principles of Just War theory, privacy violations should be understood as harming a person in some sense. This approach to privacy should follow naturally from the connection between privacy and autonomy. A violation of privacy compromises the integrity of a person, infringing the ability of an agent to take ownership of her personal domain (Moore 2003, p. 218). Luciano Floridi argues for a similar approach in framing privacy violations as attacks on the informational person (2005, p. 194). For our purposes, it is sufficient to understand privacy violations as attacks on the political person. If a democratic government violates its citizens' privacy in connection with intelligence collection, the freedom and self-rule that characterise a democracy are compromised. This issue is likewise well discussed in current scholarship regarding the difficulty (or incoherence) of trade-offs between privacy and security (Hildebrandt 2013, p. 374).

Beyond privacy, intelligence-collection programmes raise a number of moral questions that can readily be framed in the language of Just War theory. As intelligence collection is often associated with acts of war, preparation for war and defence, care must be taken to satisfy the *jus ad bellum* demands of Just War theory. At best, espionage can serve a functional role in alliances between nations. Mutual monitoring to ensure compliance with existing agreements can strengthen an alliance and encourage continued cooperation (Baker 2003, p. 1104). At worst, intelligence collection or covert operations compromise the sovereign state's control over its own information, constituting an attack on the state's sovereignty and placing diplomatic relations in jeopardy. Such actions should be taken with care, though potentially under less stringent constraints than the use of lethal force.

At the intersection of these two frameworks, democratic theory and Just War Theory, we see the most clearly identified problem with intelligence-collection programmes: the conflict between transparency and secrecy. Democratic institutions must operate in public view, otherwise they are not accountable to the citizenry from whose consent the institution's authority is derived (Rawls 1993). Nevertheless, intelligence collection necessarily operates in secret, well out of public view. Successful intelligence collection is in conflict with the transparency typically expected of public institutions. On any principled analysis, opaque government action cannot carry the legitimacy of democratic consent. Citizens simply lack knowledge of the operation and have no means to ensure that the action conforms to their interests or expectations. Abuses of the public mandate cannot be monitored, including encroachment on political rights. For example, there is no way for citizens to ensure that information gathered by an intelligence-collection programme will not be illicitly provided to law enforcement agencies, thus circumventing judicial oversight.

With this in mind, intelligence-collection programmes must be carried out with great care. In particular, the demand for just cause must be satisfied with reference to the interests of citizens, but the ethical approach to intelligence collection will also entail other specific commitments to the principles of Just War theory and democratic theory.

Legal backdrop

Fundamental to the ethical framework we propose is the concept of privacy and its importance to autonomy. In this context, a very important but often unspoken question concerns whose values should inform the extent to which such privacy must be protected. This is a normative question at its core, but one shaped by certain historical facts related to the continued development of technology generally, and the internet specifically. Since the internet originates from the United States, and due to the fact that the current locus of internet- and computer-oriented technological development is also located there, United States law has a predominating influence on this core normative question. The treatment of privacy in the context of the internet can no longer be confined to traditional US legal privacy norms, especially as US law begins to cognise technological objects differently from other tangible things. An ethical code for guiding intelligence officers through murky waters must account for these shifts and provide guidance that can keep pace with technology. It must do so in a way that embraces respect for privacy in a larger technical context, because forcing society to choose between privacy (and thus autonomy) and advanced technology is a false dilemma. However, in developing rules against the backdrop thus far presented, the current landscape of jurisprudence and how it developed must be understood.

The primary source of guidance on privacy in the US is the fourth amendment to the US Constitution. The courts' tendency to analogise in applying existing jurisprudence to novel fact patterns[1] involving technology has, until recently, created significant privacy concerns by treating electronic devices like any other tangible object, without acknowledging the uniqueness of such devices – especially given the current ubiquity of connectivity.

The Border Search Doctrine's application to technology is a good example of how this concept plays out.[2] Its jurisprudential basis is rooted in the right of a sovereign[3] to protect her territory at the physical border, which, conceptually, makes sense for tangible objects and containers. The laptop computer creates a problem for this doctrine because it represents a tangible object that the sovereign might rightly inspect for danger physically contained within it, but also intangible information that presents no danger to the physical territory of the sovereign. Three cases decided between 2005 and 2013 are informative.

In *Ickes*, a defendant convicted of transporting child pornography sought to overturn his conviction by arguing against evidence obtained from a border search of his van, in which images were found in a photo album and on his laptop computer.[4] As noted by the appellate court, the defendant argued that the sweeping nature of the ruling would make it possible to indiscriminately search any laptop crossing the border; but the court characterised his prediction as 'far-fetched'.[5] In its analysis, the court treated a laptop computer and its data just like any other 'cargo' or tangible thing.[6] *Ickes* was decided in 2005, two years prior to the first iPhone and three before the first Android-based phone.

In *Arnold*, a defendant faced similar circumstances, in that his laptop computer was searched and child pornography was found.[7] One divergence was that the search occurred at an airport as he landed from an international flight, and this was treated as a functional border for purposes of law.[8] A second divergence is that the district court originally found that information contained on computers at the border was protected by the Fourth Amendment.[9] In reversing the decision of the district court, the Ninth Circuit noted that the defendant 'failed to distinguish how the search of his laptop and its electronic contents is logically any different from the suspicionless border searches of travellers' luggage that the Supreme Court and we have allowed'.[10] The Ninth Circuit also discounted the argument that the storage capacity of a laptop should be considered in differentiating it from other mobile property.[11] *Arnold* was decided in 2008, contemporaneously with the introduction of the first iPhone and Android devices.

In *Cotterman*, a defendant's laptop was searched at a border and subsequently taken nearly 170 miles past the border to undergo forensic examination, which identified child pornography images therein.[12] *Cotterman* was decided *en banc* following an initial appellate decision that reasoned that the laptop was still in legal limbo, 'not yet admitted or released from the sovereign's control', and that the requirement of sophisticated equipment to conduct the search justified the removal as reasonable.[13] Viewing the situation through the lens of *Kyllo*, the Ninth Circuit confronted the privacy issues arising from the conflicting interests of the Border Search Doctrine and the Fourth Amendment.[14] Juxtaposing privacy interests against the needs of border protection, the Ninth Circuit drew a line after *Cotterman* and said that the removal of the computer for further searching was a step too far, and reasonable suspicion was required for this kind of forensic examination.[15]

The Border Search Doctrine cases, discussed *supra*, are instructive for the obvious reason that data, in the context of the internet, crosses borders through a network; how the law treats analogous crossings via sneakernet[16] is informative in predicting how the judiciary might treat this data in the future. Looking within the state, where Fourth Amendment protections are not minimised by the presence of a border, it is instructive to observe recent case law involving mobile phones, and smartphones in particular.

We have previously examined smart devices using external cognition as an intuition pump,[17] and have argued that, despite the then existing jurisprudence regarding border searches and vehicle searches incident to arrest,[18] smart devices represented a heightened privacy interest that should be protected due to the amount of information that can be stored, the personal nature of the devices, and the constant connectivity to cloud-data sources. Many points in our argument were timely, as shortly afterwards *Riley v. California* changed the landscape of jurisprudence to reverse the trend of treating such devices like any other tangible container.[19]

The *Riley* case begins by summarising the principles established in *Chimel, Robinson* and *Gant* that, generally, warrantless searches of the 'area within the arrestee's immediate control' are permitted during an arrest 'in the interests of officer safety and preventing evidence destruction'; that those interests are present even without a 'specific concern about the loss of evidence or the threat to officers in a particular case'; and that it is also permitted to search 'a car where the arrestee is unsecured and within reaching distance of the passenger compartment, or where it is reasonable to believe that evidence of the crime of arrest might be found in the vehicle'.[20]

In its analysis, the court changed how it treats electronic devices by acknowledging that physical analogy is not relevant when it comes to data stored on electronic devices.[21] More strikingly, and with the potential to impact future searches conducted at the border,[22] the court reasoned that 'data on the phone can endanger no one'.[23] Contrary to *Arnold*, where laptops were not distinguished from any other container and where storage capacity was discounted as a differentiation, *Riley* explicitly contemplates such differences.[24]

Extraterritorial searches expand the normative value of US Fourth Amendment jurisprudence into the international arena, and thus thrust US norms onto the world stage. Recent decisions in relation to warrants under the Stored Communications Act have created a problem whereby an entity existing within a US court's jurisdiction may have to produce the data it controls, even when the data physically resides in another country.[25] In essence, US law can ask the court to exercise jurisdiction by proxy. The reason that the cases identified, *supra*, are relevant to the present discussion of ethical frameworks for intelligence officers is that the public jurisprudential development embodied in case law shows a slow but steadily advancing understanding, on the part of US courts, of the unique privacy concerns presented by technologies such as the internet and connected mobile devices. What we cannot fully explore, however, is the type of jurisprudence that has developed in parallel under the jurisdiction of the FISA court,[26] which generally deals with the programmes in which intelligence officers are involved, and for which the proposed ethical code is pertinent. What goes on behind closed doors is fraught with potential for abuse.[27] For these reasons, we can be guided by the public jurisprudence's reaction to changing technical landscapes and rigorously apply the principles of the Just War theory to produce guidance applicable to an unknown, but theoretically consistent, hidden jurisprudence specific to intelligence officers. In the following section, we outline a series of questions designed to test key areas of concern and indicate constraints on intelligence-collection programmes. The questions presented have an analytical as well as a normative dimension, both of which will be explained in what follows.

Questions for just intelligence

In developing a code of ethics for intelligence officers, we also provide a tool for evaluating intelligence-collection programmes and activities. While any code of ethics must be grounded in principled arguments and abstract models of value hierarchy and conflict, an effective code should also offer tools for assessing situations and provide guidance for making decisions about complex controversies or in the absence of definitive resolutions. The challenge is to provide some means of structuring ethical issues, identify the relevant values in conflict and suggest acceptable courses of action. Relying on the ethical arguments surveyed above, the next step must be the creation of assessment criteria. When applied to a specific intelligence-collection programme, effective criteria should highlight ethical concerns, situate those concerns in relation to relevant moral values, and identify the normative constraints that are justified by the theoretical foundation.

In the interest of developing a more complete framework, the criteria developed here will be offered in the form of questions that can be asked of any intelligence-collection programme. Taken together, these questions suggest criteria for ethical assessment structured by a coherent chain of justification taken from Just War principles and democratic values. By building these criteria from evaluative questions, a general framework for ethical assessment is developed through structured application of the theory. This way of building the framework places focus on the desired outcome, guidance of the ethical design, and evaluation of intelligence-collection programmes. The questions begin with the issue of just cause and identify the concerns that follow by maintaining a strict commitment to just cause as it should be understood within a democratic state.

- Does the programme have just cause in compliance with international law and societal norms?
- Is the programme conducted by a competent authority, established by and accountable to a sovereign state?
- Does the programme maintain right intention when executing its mandate in achieving the aims defined by its cause?
- Does the programme design strike a proportional balance between the harms it is intended to prevent and collateral damage to privacy interests?
- Does the programme maintain a distinction between civilian and non-civilian targets, allied and non-allied states, and other proper or improper targets?

Each question highlights a specific principle of Just War theory related to an aspect of democratic theory. Before applying these questions to some controversial intelligence-collection operations, it will be necessary to explain the assessment framework that underlies them. In the following sections each question will be examine in order to identify its central concerns, the moral relevance of that concern, the normative constraints suggested and the implied justification for those constraints. By presenting the outlines of a code in this way, the insights of existing scholars directly translate to assessment criteria that can be applied by any agent or operative of an intelligence-collection programme. Perhaps more importantly, the normative constraints provide insight into both the extent of any ethical issue and the path that might uphold justice across both Just War theory and democratic theory.

Does the programme have just cause in compliance with international law and societal norms?

In the domain of Just War theory, just cause is a primary concern. If the motivation for employing force is morally compromised, any following action will be coloured by controversy. While this first question can be framed concisely, the answer must supply sufficiently robust justification in order to structure responses to the remaining questions.

As such, the first challenge is to provide some criterion of justice by which just cause can be evaluated. Just War theory traditionally leaves this domain largely untouched. Self-defence and protection of the innocent serve as easy justifications for war, but the context of intelligence collection makes even these motives difficult to assess. In general, just cause places more importance on prevention of harms than on retaliation, economic gain or other illicit motives. Reference to international law and internal social norms provides a more concrete way of assessing which motives should and should not count as illicit. A just cause must be consistent with both existing agreements with other states and the way in which intelligence collection may affect the state's relationship with the international community. Framing the just cause against societal norms reflects a limitation of the legitimacy of any decision. The action of a democratic state must have the support of its citizens, as evidenced through recognised legitimation procedures (Habermas 1996, p. 296). The clandestine nature of intelligence collection excludes the possibility of direct public consent. As such, there is a special burden on decision makers to consider how the public would perceive the anticipated harms and assess the risks attendant to taking action (or not). Where a cause cannot be justified according to widely held norms or explicitly recognised normative principles (e.g. political rights), state action would fail to uphold its mandate from the citizenry.

Three morally relevant concerns have now been identified: the risk/harm evaluation of possible actions; duties that accrue from established alliances; and the characteristic features of a democratic state. Where these concerns are all assuaged, the basis for just intelligence collection is established. And given these concerns, a just cause must be a very specific harm that should be prevented, or a clear vector of attack that must be monitored. Overly general or poorly defined causes make a reliable risk/harm evaluation difficult, as the scope of possible consequences becomes too broad. By contrast, a well defined aim offers clear criteria for success and failure, mitigating unforeseen consequences. The intelligence-collection programme should be constituted in such a way as to honour international law, and in the interest of upholding agreements and maintaining the confidence of allied states. These limitations in scope serve to mitigate the impact of unforeseen outcomes on foreign relations. Furthermore, the programme should respect the interests of citizens in order to maintain democratic legitimacy. In a democratic state, justice ultimately flows from the consent of the citizenry, such that no cause can be just without taking citizens' interests into account.

Is the programme conducted by a competent authority, established by and accountable to a sovereign state?

To meet the minimum conditions for just cause, the programme must be carried by an appropriate authority. Just War theory understands competent authority as a body with the recognised power to declare war (e.g. Congress in the United States). In the context of intelligence collection, where seeking a public mandate is impossible, responsibility for the programme must rest in some institution or office that is accountable to citizens. Locating responsibility in this kind of institution serves to isolate international political conflicts from the various interests of private firms and non-governmental organisations that may also have an interest in the outcomes or consequences of such a programme. Since just cause forbids the motives of economic gain or retaliation, only a publicly accountable body, responsible for acting in the interests of citizens in general, should bear responsibility for intelligence-collection programmes. Furthermore, responsibility should rest with an institution capable of overseeing the action itself and acting to mitigate harms or unforeseen consequences. Where the institution is a public body, democratic legitimacy is maintained in that the decisions of that body should be consistent with the principles of justice around which the state is constituted.

A simple normative constraint implied by this question is the cessation of non-government entities, commercial or otherwise, playing a role in intelligence collection. An entity that remains at a distance from public accountability risks polluting the just cause with various conflicts of interest. Lack of transparency, already a problem for intelligence programmes, is made more severe by the absence of any public accountability on the part of private firms. We recognise that this constraint would be difficult to enforce in the current landscape of intelligence collection, especially in the United States, where private contractors hold significant operational and support roles in government offices. Nevertheless, we hold that this impingement of the private into the public sector ultimately renders any intelligence-collection programme unjust. Placing private firms in such roles breaks a chain of accountability that should flow readily back to the citizenry, and creates significant confusion when it comes to assessing motives. A private firm must attend to a range of interests that are generally unlikely to coincide with those of citizens. For example, maintaining a satisfactory return on investment and generating revenue are orthogonal to preventing harms against citizens and strictly upholding agreements with political allies. Where a private firm must be involved in intelligence collection, there should be strict accountability to a public office empowered to both assign and withdraw responsibilities from contractors at its discretion, in the interest of maintaining strict accountability to the public.

Does the programme maintain right intention when executing its mandate in achieving the aims defined by its cause?

The central concern raised by this question is the transitivity of justification from the just cause to aims or objectives not directly entailed by the stated cause but made possible by the programme. As the just cause is the foundation of all further action in a just war (or, in this case, just intelligence collection), the cause must be understood as a constraint on the aims of the action. An intelligence-collection programme may cast a wide net in seeking the information required to fulfil the mission defined by the just cause. In such cases, maintaining focus on aims derived directly from the cause must be a primary concern. If a programme is intended to prevent a harm A identified by the just cause, but also enables outcomes B, C and D orthogonal to the just cause, then we must conclude that the programme is overly broad. A situation like this might require operational constraints in order to maintain focus on A or a total redesign to eliminate these additional outcomes. Just War theory does not allow for 'happy accidents' arising from warfare, so just intelligence should likewise avoid the happy accidents that might follow from intelligence collection.

The just cause should not be used to mask unjust intentions or aims. In addition, intelligence officers must guard against 'function creep' when there is pressure or interest in applying a successful programme to aims that extend beyond the just cause. While the lure of increased efficiency may be tempting, function creep undermines the legitimacy of an intelligence-collection programme. Even if the just cause enjoys citizen support (or is consistent with the requirements for democratic legitimacy described above), follow-on outcomes may not address the same configuration of interests as the cause. In a circumstance where transparency is impossible, function creep diminishes accountability to citizen interests. To avoid these circumstances, intelligence-collection programmes should have clear, specific aims that can be articulated to active officers so that they know when they are acting within the justification of the program. An absence of specific aims indicates disregard for democratic rule in allowing too much operational autonomy without transparency or accountability to the citizens. The aims should directly align with the motivating just cause, and they should serve as the primary objectives of the programme such that failure to achieve the aims constitutes total failure, even if unintended (orthogonal) outcomes are achieved. There can be no mitigated success if no aims directly related to the cause are achieved.

Does the programme design strike a proportional balance between the harms it is intended to prevent and collateral damage to privacy interests?

There should be no question that a principal concern in Just War theory is avoiding harm to those individuals who the use of force is intended to protect. To apply this concern to intelligence collection, invasions and violations of privacy must be framed as harms to the citizens of a democratic state. The connection between the privacy of citizens and the liberty of citizens is well travelled territory in democratic theory. Since intelligence collection can expose information lawfully held as private, a state must take care to avoid exposing its citizens in the interest of protecting them, in essence trading one kind of harm for another (Hildebrandt 2013, p. 376). As privacy is one of the foundations of liberal democracy, the erosion of privacy also harms the legitimacy of the state. Although foreign agents or governments are typical targets for espionage, the massive domestic surveillance programme of the NSA revealed in 2013 demonstrates an increased focus on monitoring for potential threats. When the lens of intelligence collection turns inward, the state treats its own citizens as outsiders or, at worst, enemies. Divisive behaviour on the part of a government towards its citizens is a hallmark of tyranny rather than democracy. Democratic states should avoid policies that set the people against the government.

If an intelligence-collection programme must place citizens' privacy at risk, minimising privacy violations must be a cardinal concern, of equal status to the aims defined by the just cause. Democratic states must rely on existing procedures for overseeing privacy violations, such as judicial approval for search and arrest warrants in US criminal law. Given the transparency issue already raised, employing judicial review in the form of closed courts, such as the US Foreign Intelligence Surveillance Court, is problematic regarding accountability to citizens. When domestic surveillance must be involved, the programme should have the smallest possible scope given well defined and specific aims. Special care must be taken to isolate the intelligence collection from other functions of government such as criminal law enforcement. While justifiable causes for domestic monitoring do exist, such as identifying foreign agents operating within the state, the collision between intelligence collection and law enforcement puts citizens' rights at risk, causing one harm in the interest of preventing another.

Does the programme maintain a distinction between civilian and non-civilian targets, allied and non-allied states, and other proper or improper targets?

The Just War principle of distinction is thought to be the most difficult challenge for conflicts taking place in cyberspace (Taddeo 2012, p. 117). Intelligence collection in the digital age raises the same concerns. Since the internet is an important channel for communication both within and between national borders, intelligence collection must utilise internet traffic as a potential source of valuable information.

As with the monitoring any other communication channel, care must be taken to see that monitoring is specifically targeted and avoids rampant violations of privacy. The scope of an intelligence-collection programme will define the scope of the programme's consequences. When defined by an overly broad scope, the information of citizens under no particular suspicion can be the subject of intelligence collection.

These concerns can be avoided in part by providing clearly defined targets in addition to clearly defined aims. Where distinction is made problematic by uncertain demarcation among hostile state actors, non-combatant civilians and civilians participating in a state-sponsored action such as a DDoS attack, intelligence collection must be handled carefully. If an intelligence-collection programme exposes allied states, civilians or other uninvolved individuals (i.e. individuals not associated with any harm that the just cause seeks to prevent), the programme has escaped the bounds of its justification. All too often, evaluating whether or not the programme fails to maintain distinction falls to the officers responsible for carrying out the programme, as only they will know the extent of the threat and associated targets that have been identified. If the programme contains no directives for excluding improper targets or avoiding violation of international agreements, distinction is unlikely to be maintained.

Insights and next steps

The questions offered above outline the concerns that intelligence officers should hold with regard to their work. Intelligence officers must recognise that they themselves should maintain the trust of the citizens to whom they are ultimately accountable. As both citizens and government personnel, there must be a sense of professional responsibility towards safeguarding the interests of citizens, including the sometimes conflicting interests of security and privacy. Given the necessity of secrecy with regard to maintaining oversight of intelligence collection, whistleblowing must be protected, accepted and encouraged. By extension of the above, those who undertake whistleblowing should endeavour to ensure that they do not endanger either other agents directly, or the security of citizens. Whistleblowers must provide the relevant information to the public, and should do so in a way that makes their moral grounding clear. To do so, the information released should be detailed enough to reveal the harm and clear enough to ensure censure of the commanders or decision makers who failed in their responsibilities to the citizenry.

In turn, commanding officers and other decision makers must recognise their ultimate responsibility to the citizenry at large, recognising the duty of their agents to exercise judgment in carrying out and maintaining the secrecy of operations. If it would be dangerous for a subordinate to expose an operation that is ethical as a whole but may appear problematic to someone with insufficient information, the commander must share the burden of knowledge with the subordinate. We recognise that intelligence operations are complex and may involve many degrees of subtlety, but the community of intelligence professionals must safeguard not only the security of the state but also the trust of the citizenry they are supposed to protect.

Notes

1 'Fact pattern' as used herein is a term of art which denotes the legally relevant facts in a given situation (real or hypothetical) against which the law can be applied to reach a result or answer.
2 'That searches made at the border, pursuant to the longstanding right of the sovereign to protect itself by stopping and examining persons and property crossing into this country, are reasonable simply by virtue of the fact that they occur at the border, should, by now, require no extended demonstration.' *United States v. Ramsey*, 431 US 606, 616 (1977).
3 The term 'sovereign' is somewhat archaic. In modern terms the term 'state' or 'state actor' would be more appropriate, conceptually speaking.
4 *United States v. Ickes*, 393 F.3d 501 (4th Cir. 2005).
5 Idem, pp. 506–7.
6 Idem, pp. 503–6.
7 *United States v. Arnold*, 523 F.3d 941 (9th Cir. 2008), *cert. denied*, 129 S. Ct. 1312 (2009).
8 Idem at 944 (explaining that searches of international passengers at a US airport are considered border searches).
9 *United States v. Arnold*, 454 F. Supp. 2d 999, 1000–01 (C.D. Cal. 2006) (requiring reasonable suspicion to search a laptop for data at the border).
10 *Arnold* 523 F.3d 941, 947 (9th Cir. 2008).
11 Idem (holding that storage capacity is not relevant to whether a search is particularly offensive).
12 *United States v. Cotterman*, 709 F.3d 952 (9th Cir. 2013) (*en banc*), *cert. denied*, 134 S. Ct. 899 (2014).
13 See *United States v. Cotterman*, 637 F.3d 1068, 1070 (9th Cir. 2011), *rev'd* 709 F.3d 952 (9th Cir. 2013), *cert. denied*, 134 S. Ct. 899 (2014).
14 See *Cotterman*, 709 F.3d 952, 956–57 (9th Cir. 2013) (quoting *Kyllo v. United States*, 533 US 27, 34 (2001)); see also *Kyllo* 533 US 27, 33–4 ('It would be foolish to contend that the degree of privacy secured to citizens by the Fourth Amendment has been entirely unaffected by the advance of technology.')
15 *Cotterman*, 709 F.3d 952, 957 (9th Cir. 2013) (finding, however, that the agents had reasonable suspicion in this case and reversing the district court's exclusion of the evidence).
16 The term 'sneakernet' is generally understood to mean the transport of data in a physical medium, such as a disk, as opposed to over a network. See RFP 1149, 'A Standard for the Transmission of IP Datagrams on Avian Carriers' (April 1, 1990) (laying out a humorous proposal for transmitting data by carrier pigeon). In this context, the physical conveyance of data on a laptop computer is conceptually the same as transmission by network.
17 Roux & Falgoust (2013).
18 See *Chimel v. California*, 395 US 752 (1969); see *United States v. Robinson*, 414 US 218 (1973); and see *Arizona v. Gant*, 556 US 332 (2009).
19 *Riley v. California*, 134 S. Ct. 2473, 2480 (2014) ('Held: The police generally may not, without a warrant, search digital information on a cell phone seized from an individual who has been arrested').
20 See *Riley*, 134 S.Ct. 2473, 2480 (2014).
21 See *Riley* at 2480 ('A conclusion that inspecting the contents of an arrestee's pockets works no substantial additional intrusion on privacy beyond the arrest itself may make sense as applied to physical items, but more substantial privacy interests are at stake when digital data is involved').
22 With the Border Search Doctrine, grounded in the sovereign's right to protect her territory, it would naturally follow that if data endangers no-one, then the doctrine cannot justify searching for it – for there is no protective interest in this case.
23 Idem.

24 *Riley* at 2489–90 ('But the possible intrusion on privacy is not physically limited in the same way when it comes to cell phones ... The sum of an individual's private life can be reconstructed through a thousand photographs labeled with dates, locations, and descriptions; the same cannot be said of a photograph or two of loved ones tucked into a wallet ... Finally, there is an element of pervasiveness that characterizes cell phones but not physical records. Prior to the digital age, people did not typically carry a cache of sensitive personal information with them as they went about their day.')

25 See in 'A warrant to search a certain e-mail account controlled & maintained by Microsoft Corp.' 2014 US Dist. LEXIS 59296, 42 Media L. Rep. 2275, 2014 WL 1661004 (S.D.N.Y. Apr. 25, 2014) (denying Microsoft's motion to quash a warrant issued under the Stored Communications Act, requiring it to produce data from a data centre in Ireland).

26 The United States Foreign Intelligence Surveillance Court, established by the Foreign Intelligence Surveillance Act of 1978.

27 See Electronic Frontier Foundation, 'Timeline of NSA Domestic Spying', viewed 12 November 2014, https://www.eff.org/nsa-spying/timeline.

References

Baker, CD 2003, 'Tolerance of international espionage: a functional approach,' *American University International Law Review*, vol. 19, no. 5, pp. 1091–1113.

Floridi, L 2005, 'The ontological interpretation of informational privacy,' *Ethics and Information Technology*, vol. 7, pp. 185–200.

Greenwald, G & Snowden, E 2013, 'The NSA files,' *The Guardian*, 1 November, www.theguardian.com/us-news/the-nsa-files

Habermas, J 1996, *Between facts and norms*, MIT Press, Cambridge, MA.

Hildebrandt, M 2013, 'Balance or tradeoff? Online security technologies and fundamental rights,' *Philosophy and Technology*, vol. 26, pp. 357–379.

Mill, JS 1859, *On liberty*, Project Gutenberg, www.gutenberg.org/files/34901/34901-h/34901-h.htm

Moore, AD 2003, 'Privacy: its meaning and value,' *American Philosophical Quarterly*, vol. 40, no. 3, pp. 215–227.

Nissenbaum, H 2009, *Privacy in context: technology, policy, and the integrity of social life*, Stanford University Press, Stanford, CA.

Rawls, J 1993, *Political liberalism*, Columbia University Press, New York.

Reiman, JH 1976, 'Privacy, intimacy, and personhood,' *Philosophy and Public Affairs*, vol. 6, no. 1, pp. 26–44.

Roux, B & Falgoust, M 2013, 'Information ethics in the context of smart devices,' *Ethics and Information Technology*, vol. 15, no. 3, pp. 183–194.

Taddeo, M 2012, 'Information warfare: a philosophical perspective,' *Philosophy & Technology*, vol. 25, no. 1, pp. 105–120.

Waldron, J 2003, 'Security and liberty: the image of balance★,' *Journal of Political Philosophy*, vol. 11, no. 2, pp. 191–210.

17

'DUE CARE' OR A 'DUTY TO CARE'? CODES OF ETHICS IN INTELLIGENCE GATHERING

Jill Hernandez

Michael Walzer's 'due care' criterion asserts that the public has an overriding right not to be put at risk, so that the government always has better reasons to pursue unhindered intelligence gathering than to ensure individual liberty (Walzer 1977 and 2006, p. 156). Civilians have, simply, a right to see that 'due care' is taken. Contemporary legal arguments use Walzer's due care doctrine to contend that there are no actual deontic constraints on the consequential interests of the state in using extraordinary measures to procure intelligence of high national security value (Horowitz 2008). In a post-9/11 shift away from deterrentist ideals towards jurisprudence that favours proactive, preventative measures (Dershowitz 2008), scholars have scrambled to provide a legal or moral check on unlimited governmental powers in the gathering of intelligence. Currently, intelligence work for US agencies is guided independently,[1] and there are no guidelines that govern intelligence gathering on the part of such agencies.[2] In the absence of a thoroughgoing code of ethics that can delineate professional, ethical behaviour in the intelligence community, most theoretical justification for these limits comes through appeals to a prisoner's right to privacy and/or individual freedom. The difficulty with appeals to privacy and individual freedom is epistemic: how can we know when (if ever) the intelligence community's obligation to protect its citizens oversteps the individual's rights to privacy and individual freedom?

This chapter takes a different tack. A jurisprudence of pre-emption and prevention is not inconsistent with certain deontic moral constraints, in particular deontic moral constraints that are rooted in a duty to ethically care. A due care criterion can be relevant in important national security cases, because the need to question those in custody can justify detaining enemy combatants during times of war, and the criterion can guide this questioning, especially when it aids the fighting of terrorist networks (Waxman 2008). Although in a detail-rich environment like that of intelligence gathering a single normative theory could well prove insufficient for guiding the decision-making procedures of intelligence professionals, this chapter will contend that an ethics of care could provide a guiding moral theory for agents in most cases – those in which there is not an immediate, pragmatic, utilitarian concern that trumps the duty to care.[3] By framing a code of ethics for the intelligence community as an ethics of care, the value of ethical caring functions as a morally necessary deontic check against the use of any-and-all means to gather intelligence. Since ethical caring functions as a built-in professional constraint in a code of ethics, its values must always be factored in when determining a course of action during intelligence gathering. The most significant moral reason for this is that the United States government creates, and is responsible for, a dependency relation with those it captures and detains. Dependency relations should be guided by an ethics of care. Indeed, on this basis, a code of ethics can consistently stipulate that there must be immediate, significant and epistemically determinable consequential *moral* benefits if the deontic base rooted in an ethics of care is ever to be overridden. Finally, the code of ethics used by intelligence professionals can stipulate the same thing: that there must be immediate, significant and epistemically determinable consequential benefits if the deontic moral base of the professional code is ever to be overridden.

The success of my argument depends upon several mitigating factors that weigh on the debate about the nature of potential codes of ethics in intelligence gathering. The first is whether there is epistemic indeterminacy about an inmate's status as an enemy combatant. When a suspect's citizenship and vested economic interest is unknown, or when there are justified reasons for intelligence agents to think that a detainee could be a US citizen, the government's duty to care cannot be immediately overridden by utilitarian reasoning. There have been, for example, many cases in which US citizens have not been afforded due process rights, typically constraining otherwise utilitarian pragmatic concerns in intelligence gathering.

The second factor is the assessment of potentially flawed information that links individuals to terrorism. One particular case, for example, is that of Maher Arar, a dual Canadian–Syrian national who was deported by the United States to Syria (where he was subsequently tortured) based on erroneous information linking him to terrorism (Austen 2006). If, as in Arar's case, faulty information can lead to violations of bodily autonomy that would ordinarily be preserved for citizens of allied states, deontic constraints on utilitarian thinking in intelligence gathering become relevant. Arar's case suggests that care and respect for bodily autonomy can guide the development of codes of ethics for use in intelligence gathering. If intelligence gathering requires violations of basic human rights and bodily autonomy, it must be guided by an ethics of care; and if these violations are permitted, they should never be so on the basis of anything except indubitable intelligence. Pragmatic, immediate utilitarian concerns can supervene only when there is no other option, and only when the action is guided by a code of ethics based on ethical caring.

Finally, as suggested by the Arar case, relationships with other countries can inform constraints on a governmental right to use utilitarian analyses. The case of Murat Kurnaz, a Turkish native and legal resident of Germany, is instructive.

Kurnaz was released from Guantanamo in August 2006 after being held for over four years (despite assessments by both German and American intelligence agencies that cast doubt upon his supposed links to terrorist cells or enemy fighters, Leonig 2007; Yost 2007). Kurnaz has written extensively of the abuse and torture he suffered at Guantanamo:

> I was in Pakistan, on a public bus on my way to the airport to return to Germany when the police stopped the bus I was riding in. I was the only non-Pakistani on the bus – some people joke that my reddish hair makes me look Irish – so the police asked me to step off to look at my papers and ask some questions ... The police detained me but promised they would soon let me go to the airport. After a few days, the Pakistanis turned me over to American officials. At this point, I was relieved to be in American hands; Americans, I thought, would treat me fairly. I was taken to Kandahar, in Afghanistan, where American interrogators asked me the same questions for several weeks: Where is Osama bin Laden? Was I with Al Qaeda? No, I told them, I was not with Al Qaeda. No, I had no idea where bin Laden was. I begged the interrogators to please call Germany and find out who I was. During their interrogations, they dunked my head under water and punched me in the stomach; they don't call this waterboarding but it amounts to the same thing. I was sure I would drown. At one point, I was chained to the ceiling of a building and hung by my hands for days ... I was transferred to Guantánamo. There were more beatings, endless solitary confinement, freezing temperatures and extreme heat, days of forced sleeplessness. The interrogations continued always with the same questions. I told my story over and over – my name, my family, why I was in Pakistan. Nothing I said satisfied them. I realized my interrogators were not interested in the truth.
>
> *(Kurnaz 2014)*

Examples like this demonstrate the value of integral allied trust in the use of extraordinary measures in intelligence gathering, even when related to the highest interests of national security. Not only was Kurnaz a European citizen, his detention was contested by Germany after the Germans confirmed American intelligence that Kurnaz was not a member of al-Queda and did not have links to terrorist groups within Germany (Seton Hall 2014).

There are two potential worries for my contention that an ethics of care could serve as a moral constraint on the US tendency towards utilitarian analysis in intelligence gathering. First is a formal dispute within an ethics of care. In its first twenty-five years as a robust moral theory, proponents of an ethics of care suggested that it was always opposed to an ethics of justice (justice concerns are paternalistic worries that are muted when using an ethics of care). Recently, scholars such as Virginia Held and Daniel Engster have argued (I think persuasively) that an ethics of care instead incorporates an ethics of justice, so that concerns about justice and rights just are concerns related to ethical caring. The second worry is substantive, and evidences itself in greater worries I will address below. A critic might contend that an ethics of care has no place in codes for intelligence gathering, and that the requisite environment for intelligence gathering requires anything but 'care' ('harshness', 'enhanced and coercive techniques' and 'dark side tactics' seem to preclude the warm-heartedness that is evoked by the term 'care'). But this criticism makes the mistake of equivocating 'care' and the emotions related to caring. Although an ethics of care demands respect for the reciprocity inherent in the lived experiences of others – between countries, between citizens, and even between inmates and information gatherers – it can ground a code of ethics that is rigorous, demanding and unwavering in its demand for truth. There may be, then, consequential moral reasons that can justify the government's use of extraordinary measures in intelligence gathering, especially during times of war. These reasons are not, however, absolute and they cannot in many cases – perhaps most cases – override. Rather than appealing to the epistemically problematic values of privacy and individual freedom to constrain government action, the extenuating factors of the status of the inmate, contextualisation of the information gathered and the relationship between different countries instead suggest a need for an ethics of care. An ethics of care can function as the foundation of a code of ethics for intelligence – an ethics of care can inform and serve as a proper jurisprudential moral check on an otherwise unlimited governmental interest in using extraordinary measures for intelligence gathering.

What does 'care' have to do with intelligence?

It should be noted that an ethics of care has not yet been implemented for intelligence professionals, although many care ethicists have observed how important it is to shift the application of care to global issues. Although Nel Noddings – the originator of care ethics – does not discuss global public policy issues, she does observe that:

> Extending care ethics to the level of international affairs is the second vital matter to introduce here. In the first couple decades of discussion on the subject, it was often assumed that care ethics could be usefully applied in families and small communities but that we must turn to a liberal theory of justice to address moral questions in institutional and international affairs. Now, there is good reason to argue that care ethics can be employed at every level of human activity.
>
> *(Noddings 2013, p. 206)*

Fiona Robinson has become a key figure in extending care ethics to global issues. She observes that 'relations and practices of care are central to the struggle for basic human security' (2011, p. 161). Her book demonstrates the ways in which peace-keeping, peacebuilding, the treatment of epic viruses and the transformation of what is considered 'women's work' can all be grounded on the principles of an ethics of care (she also develops a concept of what she calls *corporate social responsibility*: care-based guidelines for economic and political action for companies). David Geoffrey Smith argues that an ethics of care can constrain the global public policy shift towards 'the privileging of economistic interpretations of human life over political, cultural, and social ones' (2011, p. 247). Tove Petersen applies care ethics to issues of global poverty, and asserts that '[i]f we had adopted the ethics of care as our guide, we would see ourselves as caregivers, and those in poverty as the recipients of care. Whether or not we have a responsibility would not be the question' (2011, p. 187).

So, the call to apply care ethics in areas like intelligence has appropriately gone forth. But, prior to ascertaining what – if they exist – the deontic constraints on utilitarian moral reasoning in intelligence gathering might look like, it is important to understand the basic tenets of an ethics of care, specifically in response to the criticism that 'caring' has no place in the intelligence community. The potential criticism that an ethics of care could never ground a code of ethics for intelligence gathering because intelligence gathering by nature requires action that is uncaring is misplaced, but the criticism is based on a caricature of what an ethics of care really is. If critics take but a sample of ideas from care ethicists, they might find justification for this criticism. There are three main ideas in care ethics that lend themselves to such criticism: the relationality required by an ethics of care; the concept of a 'care relation'; and the notion of 'justice' employed by care ethicists. For example, it *is* true that an ethics of care is built around relationality, in the form of the belief that humans are relational creatures who depend upon care relations. Michael Friedman (2008, p. 540) explains that, '[a] moral theory that says or entails nothing about the nature, extent, and distribution of the responsibilities to care for … human beings is woefully incomplete'. The reason an ethics of care is framed by dependency relations is because, as Virginia Held argues, life itself is constituted relationally. The critic of care ethics who picks up on the idea of relationality may miss the empirical nature of Held's view. Held observes that, '[r]ather than assuming, as do the dominant moral theories, that moral relations are to be seen as entered into voluntarily by free and equal individuals, the ethics of care is developed for the realities, as well, of unequal power and unchosen relations; salient examples are relations between parents and children, but the ethics of care is not limited to such "private" contexts' (Held 2004, p. 143). Caring can include, but is not determined by, a positive feeling for someone. Noddings (2013, p. 207) confirms that, '[t]his does not imply that we must like, agree with, or work to advance the goals of this other. It means that, prepared to care, we will listen, enter dialogue. Second, by keeping open the avenues of communication, we may find a way to ameliorate the hate, distrust, or rage we've detected and, thus, be in a better position to protect others in the web of care.' An agent can care (in the sense of an ethics of care) for someone they do not *care* about (that is, someone for whom they do not have positive feelings). This is especially true in professions in which there are strong power and authority relations between the person acting and the person receiving the action. In the intelligence community, this gap exists between the intelligent agent and either the informant or the detainee, such that a dependency relation emerges. The dependency can be completely divorced from a positive feeling, and yet the consequences of the actions taken by the agent towards the dependent individual hinge on the care the agent takes. So, the critic who capitalises on the fact that care ethics requires relationality just misses that ethical and professional conduct emerges out of relations between persons; and in the intelligence community, these relations typically arise from some equivocal power dynamic.[4]

The concept of 'care relations' could also be cherry-picked as irrelevant or inapplicable to the intelligence community. In one regard, the critic would be correct: the 'care relation' is not myopic. It does not look solely at the goal and utility of one particular action, without reference to context and to the person impacted, nor does it look at 'good' in a vacuum, related to a single entity. Engster observes that care theories, instead, 'start with the individuals already existing in society and dependent upon one another for their survival, development, and social functioning, and highlights the unchosen obligations we all have toward others by virtue of our interdependency', and that this mutual dependency means that, 'all capable individuals have obligations to care for others in need regardless of our explicit or tacit consent' (Engster 2007, pp. 7–8). The scope of caring extends to those who will be impacted by injustices within communities – which means that intelligence gatherers must consider public safety, the corporate good and protecting our relationships with allies when they make decisions about ethical conduct. Since a 'care relation' includes a constellation of moral considerations, including a concern for the other person, sensitivity to the context of a situation, a concern for the needs and rights of distant persons and a desire to improve the world in – as far as possible – a nonviolent and democratic way (Friedman 2008, p. 542), the critic who suggests caring is irrelevant to the actions of the intelligence community fundamentally mistakes the object of ethical caring, as well as the manner in which care ethicists apply theory to action. The grounding value of the ethical relation is care itself: care is a universal moral value that is foundational for any social inter-action, and so is indispensable practically and morally, for both individuals and society (Mahowald 2006, p. 178). The goal of care is transformation, and the way in which care is applied in morally difficult situations is through caring. But 'caring' is not equivalent to a warm emotion, nor need it be detached (as I will argue below) from the goals of the intelligence community. 'Caring, by contrast, involves a subject confronting another subject and responding to his or her needs and abilities' (Engster 2005, p. 51).

Finally, critics could use the care ethicist's concept of 'justice' as fuel for the argument that an ethics of care cannot ground a code of ethics for intelligence gathering. They might start with the idea that 'justice' for the care ethicist is gendered, so that it is particularly attuned to, and thus suitable for, justice issues relating to women.[5] Once again, this observation is not without precedent in the literature. The ethics of care grew out of Nel Noddings' argument against biological essentialism in the 1970s. Men and women, though biologically different, are only *essentially* different if we understand essentialism as a facet of our social interactions. Gender is a social norm whose behaviours are socially bequeathed. These social norms have labelled some actions as 'feminine' or 'masculine', so that actions that are labelled 'feminine' and 'masculine' are simply social references. In practice, the differences within the same gender are so great and the differences between genders by comparison so small that it is not helpful to make gender-based, essentialist contrasts. Rather, Noddings thinks, what *is* helpful is to look at needs that transcend gender and social roles. The primary, universal need that transcends differences is the need for care (Noddings 2005), a need that has been referred to socially as 'feminine'. She writes (Noddings 2013, p. 206) that '[w]omen can and do give reasons for their acts, but the reasons often point to feelings, needs, impressions, and a sense of personal ideal rather than to universal principles and their application'. So, to the extent that we have linked the social behaviour of care to women, the critic might be onto something when they think of justice. But such a view is short-sighted. Justice is part of ethical behaviour, which for Noddings is a human affective response that arises naturally out of the simple sociological fact that we relate to one another. The caring relation forms the wider moral framework into which justice should be fitted (Friedman 2008, p. 540), and efforts at justice can miscarry if actions do not produce 'conditions under which caring-for actually occurs' (Noddings 2013, p. xxiv).

Justice is not, then, in this sense an expression of universal caring that results in rainbows and butterflies for the perpetrators of horrendous evils (on the contrary, universal caring is impossible to actualise because of its abstract nature, which should be welcomed by those who work in international relations, since its primary guiding normative principle – care – is neither ideal, abstract nor rooted entirely in reason (Noddings 2013, p. 208)). What a 'just' act connotes instead depends on the agents involved, the audience impacted and the social contexts in which the act occurs. When care and justice are 'meshed', care is the framework within which justice should fit (Held 1995). Justice, then, is always about the particular. A particular act is just only if it is rooted in receptivity (i.e. an understanding that one action perpetuates another), relatedness (i.e. on a macro level, our actions depend upon and impact others globally), and responsiveness (i.e. the agents respond to the specific characters in and context of a situation) (Smeyers 1999, p. 234–5). On a governmental level, morally just caring will take seriously the commitments (fiduciary, legally, morally and politically) that we have to other countries and to our own citizens. That a person is in custody and has lost her right to bodily autonomy, for example, is a morally relevant consideration that bears on the permissibility of an agent's using enhanced interrogation techniques to gather information. A necessary dependency relation is created by enforcing the law, but the dependency relation is marked by the vulnerability of the suspect and the utilitarian need of the government for information. The suspect is vulnerable because the agent 'is in a position to provide for [his needs]' and his physical integrity is wholly determined by outside factors (Morris 2001, p. 14).

So, the three main ideas of care ethics that could be erroneously critiqued have been detailed, and the criticisms answered. The intelligence profession is built around relationships – in particular power relations – that create dependencies, which can be justly adjudicated through care. Those relations are marked by the vulnerability of the suspect to the agent, rather than the positive feelings normally associated with a familial conception of 'care'. This vulnerability requires that the suspect's bodily autonomy be surrendered to the government, with the result that the government's actions can be guided in most cases by a code of ethics built upon an ethics of care. Now that the criticisms against an ethics of care have been addressed, we can see how it might help us in formulating a code of ethics for professional behaviour in intelligence gathering.

How an ethics of care can guide intelligence work

The application of care ethics to any act is usually a three-step process: a beginning in natural care, a distortion of social intervention, and a supplementing of natural care with ethical care (Noddings 2005). This process is helpful for intelligence gathering. The beginning of the interaction with a suspect can be characterised within the framework of 'natural care' – although typically from different cultures and backgrounds, and within the scope of an unequal power relationship, the suspect requires natural care – where the suspect provides information voluntarily. If the detainee refuses, the intelligence officer introduces a distortion to make the suspect change what he wants (as guided by an ethics of care, the distortion would occur by helping the suspect rationalise the reasons they might have to withhold information). But the intelligence agent then provides a supplement – a caring that comes alongside the rational component introduced by the agent through the distortion. Ethical care (which, again, need not be equivalent to a positive feeling) capitalises on a direct relationship between the agent and the suspect. This caring 'can be done well or badly; in a way that enriches or alienates, dignifies or humiliates either caregiver or the one cared for. Above all, caring is a practice that affects both the person receiving care and those providing it, the ethics of caregiving pertain to carer and care recipient alike' (Kittay, Jennings & Wasunna 2005, p. 444). If law enforcement and intelligence gatherers are caregivers – that is, if they are keepers of the autonomy and bodily integrity of another human being – then the ethics of care ought to guide a code of ethics for their behaviour.

Empirical evidence from FBI reports supports the care ethicist's view that the root of ethics is the universal experience of needing to be cared for and communicated with. Noddings suggests that these universal experiences can guide law enforcement:

> Care ethics advises us to maintain a caring relation – that is, to keep communication alive and remain prepared to care. In international relations, at the early signs of developing animosities, we should refuse to isolate the offending other. Instead of blaming, applying sanctions, and isolating these others, we should increase our interactions with them.

(Noddings 2013, pp. 207–8)

If care is inseparable from communication with the cared-for person, then one of the guiding tenets of a code of ethics for intelligence gathering would be communication (verbal, non-verbal, physical) that conveys care. The benefit of 'caring' communication is that intelligence gatherers will achieve better results by turning informants and getting actionable information by meeting the physical needs of suspects and rewarding their families.[6] But this benefit extends to the American public more generally. The positive values of justice and national security that justify rigorous interrogation techniques are actually effectuated when informed by an ethics of care. A democratic government has a responsibility to protect its citizens from risk, and if a detainee might have information that could impact upon national security, then the government has a duty to engage in enforcement activities that prevent those national security risks. The Department of Homeland Security's website (previous version) stated that it 'will direct every resource available toward prevention and preparedness, and empower Americans to live in a constant state of readiness, not a constant state of fear'.

A difficulty, however, in refocusing the moral justification for intelligence gathering is that doing so requires a review of the relations between management, agents and detainees. This difficulty is assuaged if an ethics of care can justify policy enforcement, since it grounds moral reasons in how people are related to others, and how they engage with one another. An ethics of care, if used as a guide for intelligence professionals for policy enforcement, sustains a broader moral framework into which justice fits, and actually provides more space for intelligence workers to prevent terrorist threats, since they work under the presumption that their actions are deontically constrained. Care as a normative base speaks at very least to the dissociations that can affect an employee's ability to work effectively.[7] Gilligan notes (1995, p. 125) that 'the vibrations and resonances which characterise and connect the living world' are 'numbed by the types of dissociations that present themselves when care is not present'. If the success of intelligence work relies in part on the normative model that frames its actions, then a model that provides an environment in which the agent can act without fear is preferable. All governmental employees are subordinate, but when they can work without fear, they are in a better position to contribute to their professions.[8] Rather than assuming, as do the dominant moral theories, that moral relations are entered into voluntarily by free and equal individuals, an ethics of care is developed for the realities of unequal power relations (Held 2004, p. 143), such as those that exist between agent and detainee, or between the government and its employees.

Another advantage of care ethics over utilitarianism in most cases of intelligence gathering is that it views the moral justification for actions as grounded in the claims of those with whom we engage. An ethics of care contends that we have a compelling moral interest in attending to and meeting the needs of others for whom we take responsibility (Held 2006, pp. 10–14). This makes the responsibility agents have over suspects action-guiding, which means it can found a code of ethics. Other moral rules (such as cost–benefit utilitarianism) are less compelling than the claims of others, because they are wholly independent from the agents the action will impact. But the claim of the other (more vulnerable) person can inform specific points within a code of ethics. The intelligence worker views the suspect in terms of the information she might possess, but also as a subject who carries with her a panoply of valued, subjective experiences that can motivate her in different ways. The agent who recognises this can prevent the suspect from being motivated by fear (anguish, and concerns about herself), and can respond instead to the care relation (Smeyers 1999, p. 236).

The result is not an abandonment of utilitarian principles for intelligence workers; which, as a purely pragmatic tool is extremely effective and which – in the face of an imminent terror threat – would be necessary to guide action. Neither does it mean that the government should not use any other reasoning besides the application of an ethics of care (rather, as stated from the outset, many thorny moral issues may require several normative standpoints). But, in terms of a code of ethics for non-imminent (i.e. emergency, ticking-bomb terror plots) intelligence gathering, the intelligence community's goals would be better served by utilising moral reasons that are informed and constrained by an ethics of care. If the consequences of actions within the interrogation room rely upon the dependency relation of suspect to agent, then the moral reasons deployed must be tied to that connection in order to be successfully justified.

One final criticism might be made. It could be argued that intelligence gathering is simply outside of the scope of morality, and instead falls within governmental policy. But such a view denies the human costs that influence the rationale behind intelligence gathering, and it obfuscates the dependency relation between our country and our allies. Allowing intelligence professionals to act within a code of ethics informed by care ethics – one that is sensitive to the political ties our country has to others – gives them a wider space within which to work, and minimises the error margin for epistemic indeterminacy when working with suspects. Care, then, can be the wider moral framework through which justice can be attained – one that provides not just for *due care* of citizens, but a due care that is ensured by a *duty to care*.

Notes

1 In 1989, President Bush signed an executive order that provided basic standards for professional conduct to guide the fourteen primary governmental agencies, which became a code of ethics for governmental workers more generally (see www.oge.gov/Laws-and-Regulations/Employee-Standards-of-Conduct/Employee-Standards-of-Conduct); a version for Department of Justice (DOJ) that does not include ethics of intelligence gathering (www.justice.gov/jmd/ethics-handbook); and a seven-sentence 'Core Values' CIA document (https://www.cia.gov/offices-of-cia/clandestine-service/code-of-ethics.html). The NSA has a 'Core Values Q&A' with its director online (https://cryptome.org/2013/08/nsa-core-values-inglis.htm), but no document that even approaches a code of ethics.

2 The Oversight and Review Committee of the Department of Justice Office of the Inspector General found that it was 'not aware of the existence of any MOU [Memoranda of Understanding] between the FBI or DOJ and the DOD or the CIA relating to standards for interrogation of detainees in DOD or CIA custody' (US Department of Justice, 2008, p. 19).

3 For our purposes here, I assume there might be an imaginable case in which the government has an imminent utilitarian need for information that could trump a deontic obligation. I do not take a position here on whether there are in fact such situations. But it is important to note that not everyone agrees that the government has even utilitarian interests in using harsh interrogation tactics for information gathering. 'Consequentialist harms of abusing some number of innocents will offset any gains obtained through harsh interrogations', concludes M. Wynia (2005, pp. 4–6). 'More importantly, there is no recorded instance of any systematic program of harsh interrogation that has been entirely confined to the guilty. For instance, military reports indicate that 70%–90% of the prisoners abused at Abu Ghraib were not terror suspects.'

4 For more on the dependency relation, see Held 2006, p. 144ff.

5 There *are* key differences between ethics of care theories and justice theories. Daniel Engster notes two of these: 'Justice theories have generally aimed to promote equality, autonomy, freedom, fraternity, the good life, and other such values, but rarely the decent care of all … Secondly, even in principled form, care theory remains far more concerned with process and relationship than most justice theories. Caring means more than just meeting needs, developing basic capabilities, and alleviating pain; it means doing so in a manner that is attentive, responsive, and respectful to the individuals in need of care. While caring can be formulated into a form of a justice theory, it is thus a unique sort of justice theory. It is a justice theory that designates caring for others in a caring manner as the most fundamental human value' (Engster 2005, p. 70).

6 Like all intelligence agencies, there is evidence the FBI participated after 9/11 in harsh interrogation techniques. But there is also significant anecdotal evidence that caring tactics produce better results. J. Wisnewski (2010, p. 157) writes that 'the FBI reported gaining intelligence concerning Al Qaeda operations by using standard forms of interrogation with Abu Zubaydah. In those initial weeks of healing, before the white room and the chair and the light, Zubaydah seems to have talked freely with his captors, and during this time, according to news reports, FBI agents began to question him using "standard interview techniques," ensuring that he was bathed and his bandages changed, urging improved medical care, and trying to "convince him they knew details of his activities." (They showed him, for example, a "box of blank audiotapes which they said contained recordings of his phone conversations, but were actually empty.") According to this account, Abu Zubaydah, in the initial days before the white room, "began to provide intelligence insights into Al Qaeda"'.

7 This point is also made by J. Hernandez (2011, pp. 157–74).

8 See, for example, Smeyers (1999, p. 236).

References

Austen, J 2006, 'Canadians fault U.S. for its role in torture case', *The New York Times*, 19 September, www.nytimes.com/2006/09/19/world/americas/19canada.html?pagewanted=print&_r=0

Dershowitz, A 2008, 'Visibility, accountability and discourse as essential to democracy', *Albany Law Review*, 71 Alb. L. Rev. 731.

Engster, D 2005, 'Rethinking care theory: the practice of caring and the obligation to care', *Hypatia*, vol. 20, no. 3, pp. 50–74.

Engster, D 2007, *Heart of justice*, Oxford University Press, Oxford.

Friedman, M 2008, 'Care ethics and moral theory', *Philosophy and Phenomenological Research*, vol. 77, no. 2, pp. 539–555.

Gilligan, G 1995, 'Hearing the difference: theorizing connection', *Hypatia*, vol. 10, pp. 120–127.

Held, V 1995, 'The meshing of care and justice', *Hypatia*, vol. 10, pp. 128–132.

Held, V 2004, 'Care and justice in the global context', *Ratio Juris*, vol. 17, no. 2, pp. 141–155.

Held, V 2006, *The ethics of care: personal, political, and global*, Oxford University Press, Oxford.

Hernandez, J 2011, 'The changing face of ethics in the workplace: care and the impact of immigration enforcement', in M Hamington & M Sander-Staudt (eds), *Applying care ethics to business*, Springer, Dordrecht.

Horowitz, RM 2008, 'Ethics in intelligence, security, and immigration', keynote address presented at the Pan American Collaboration for Ethics in the Professions Inaugural Conference, University of Texas-Pan American, 16 November.

Kittay, EF, Jennings, B & Wasunna, A 2005, 'Dependency, difference and the global ethic of longterm care', *Journal of Political Philosophy*, vol. 13, no. 4, pp. 443–469.

Kurnaz, M 2014, 'Notes from a Guantanamo survivor', *The New York Times*, 7 January, www.nytimes.com/2012/01/08/opinion/sunday/notes-from-a-guantanamo-survivor.html

Leonnig, C 2007, 'Evidence of innocence rejected at Guantanamo', *The Washington Post*, 5 December, www.washingtonpost.com/wp-dyn/content/article/2007/12/04/AR200712 0402307.html

Mahowald, M 2006, 'Review: ethics of care: personal, political, global', *International Journal of Feminist Approaches to Bioethics*, vol. 2, no. 1, p. 178.

Morris, J 2001, 'Impairment and disability: constructing an ethics of care that promotes human rights', *Hypatia*, vol. 16, no. 4, pp. 1–16.

Noddings, N 2005, 'An ethic of care', in M Timmons (ed.), *Conduct and character*, Oxford University Press, Oxford.

Noddings, N 2013, *Caring: a relational approach to ethics and moral education*, University of California Press, Berkeley, CA.

Petersen, T 2011, *Comprehending care*, Lexington Books, New York.

Robinson, F 2011, *The ethics of care: a feminist approach to human security*, Temple University Press, Philadelphia, PA.

Seton Hall 2014 'Murat Kurnaz: the story of Guantánamo detainee Murat Kurnaz', Seton Hall Law, Center for Social Justice Cases, http://law.shu.edu/ProgramsCenters/Pub licIntGovServ/CSJ/Murat-Kurnaz.cfm

Smeyers, P 1999, '"Care" and wider ethical issues', *Journal of Philosophy of Education*, vol. 33, no. 2, pp. 231–255.

Smith, DG 2011, 'Globalization and truth dwelling in the now', in JA Kentel (ed.), *Educating the Young*, Peter Lang, New York.

US Department of Justice 2008, *A review of the FBI's involvement in and observations of detainee interrogations in Guantanamo Bay, Afghanistan, and Iraq*, US Department of Justice, Office of the Inspector General, www.justice.gov/oig/special/s0805/final.pdf

US Department of Justice n.d., *Ethics handbook*, US Department of Justice, Justice Management Division, www.justice.gov/jmd/ethics-handbook

Walzer, M 1977 and 2006, *Just and unjust wars*, Basic Books, New York.

Waxman, M 2008, 'Detention as targeting: standards of certainty and detention of suspected terrorists', *Columbia Law Review*, vol. 108, no. 6, pp. 1365–1430.

Wisnewski, J 2010, *Understanding torture*, Edinburgh University Press, Edinburgh.

Wynia, M 2005, 'Consequentialism and harsh interrogations', *American Journal of Bioethics*, vol. 5, no. 1, pp. 4–6.

Yost, P 2007, 'German man held 4 years, but no link to al-Qaida found', *Seattle Times*, 6 December, http://seattletimes.com/html/nationworld/2004055664_gitmokurnaz06.html

18

CONCLUSION

A spy's perspective

Warren Reed

> Real democracy comes out of many subtle individual human battles that are fought
> over decades and finally over centuries ... [It] is a state of grace attained only by
> those countries that have a host of individuals not only ready to enjoy freedom, but
> to undergo the heavy labour to maintain it.[1]

These words, which capture the essence of democracy at work, were tooled by
one of the United States' best known novelists, Norman Mailer. But if a con-
templative person in a liberal democracy is asked to characterise the work of a spy
in the field, their thoughts usually point in the opposite direction, along the lines of
'an automaton trained by the state to break the laws of other countries and to
operate beyond the normal bounds of morality and propriety.' As understandable
as this common perception is, the truth with most spies is closer to the point raised
by Mailer on the role of the individual.

To explain this, and how it is manifested in an operational environment, spies as
individuals are best divided into three broad categories. First, there is a minority –
say, 5–10 per cent, who should never have been recruited into the profession and
who, once trained and placed in the field, act like cowboys. Among the intelligence services of the Western democracies, the Central Intelligence Agency (CIA)
has produced a regular (if minor) stream of such operatives. Some have had their
careers truncated early on, while others have been quietly nurtured and afforded
considerable resources on the basis that they can satisfy foreign policy requirements
of the day and 'get the job done', no matter how unpalatable the means employed.
No other Western service could match the Americans on this front, certainly not
in terms of the public profile that such rogue officers have sometimes gained. Of
course, regardless of how it is viewed, no other Western spy service operates on
such a broad global stage as the CIA.

Second, another 5–10 per cent are officers prone to succumb to the questionable ethics of their superiors when operations of a dubious moral nature are proposed. Little or no duress is needed for this breed to 'come on board', especially when the goal is cleverly cloaked in a national interest mantle. Enhanced promotional prospects are often a motivating factor for such people. Like operatives in the first category, those in the second are equally as likely to include as many crooks as cowboys, due to the large amounts of cash handled in their work overseas. These two groups are apt to treat lightly, or with disdain, the trust that is placed in them when serving overseas. Trust is, in various ways, crucial to all intelligence work and underpins the morality of each and every task that a spy undertakes. The gathering of human intelligence, or HUMINT in the jargon of the craft, is an intensely human affair.

Third, and most important of all, is the majority of intelligence officers who carry with them into the profession a keen sense of the standards and values with which a working democracy is imbued and who will generally stand firm against attempts by their service's management to diverge from those widely accepted norms of behaviour. Resistance can take various forms, ranging from direct confrontation to exquisite and imperceptible defiance. How an individual officer responds to such challenges when overseas will be rooted in his or her own sense of morality, before it is ever informed by the standards adhered to by their service as a whole. In this way, a spy in the field is to a significant degree – and sometimes totally – on their own in their moral decision making.

What sort of person makes up this majority? A typical assessment of an intelligence officer chosen for induction is: '[Smith] is an emotionally stable, mature, relaxed [man/woman] with good social skills. He is confident, self-assured and has a high level of assertive drive. The one characteristic that could well create some difficulties for him is his capacity for, and probably tendency towards, critical and analytical thinking. He has a high level of self-control and shows evidence of possessing the socially approved character responses of persistence, foresight and conscientiousness.' The craft that the majority is engaged in has been described by an American attorney and veteran CIA operative, Frederick Hitz. In his 2005 work, *The great game: the myths and reality of espionage*, he highlighted the uniqueness of the skills required for intelligence work:

> Spying and running spies have always been extraordinary occupations in the literal meaning of the word. Human qualities are called upon that either are not overly developed in many people, or, in the spy or spy runner, become outsized. Discretion, role-playing, and gregariousness are some of the characteristics that come to the fore.
>
> *(Hitz 2005, p. 142)*

Such people are not automatons. They work with a strong sense of purpose, knowing that 'a democratic state too gentlemanly to learn all it can about threats is a state that has betrayed its most fundamental responsibilities' (Frum 2014, p. 14).

At the operational level, spies customarily function from a pre-established intelligence base, often called a 'station', which is staffed by a number of colleagues who are usually proficient in the local language. An incoming spy will inherit from their immediate predecessor a stable of recruited agents, the most prized of which may have been 'on the books' and highly productive (and paid) for lengthy periods of time. The handover by a departing officer to their successor is one of the most delicate human relations tasks that confronts a spy. Its success depends upon the establishment of trust, which has to be mutual. By its very nature, it is unique in the way of human bonding. When an agent, who is by any measure a traitor to their country, is initially recruited and consents to the terms and conditions of their contract, a rare pact is entered into by the two parties involved. The foreign operative who engineers this intricate process, normally after a lengthy period of cultivation, is inveigling the agent into committing an act of treachery that is the antithesis of everything for which the spy stands. Perversely, for both sides, the recruitment deal is an act of supreme trust: if one party errs in the slightest way and their relationship is exposed, both lives can be lost and irreparable damage done in ways that far transcend the two individuals concerned. In all of this, there is a morality that is difficult to define.

At the point of recruitment, it is common for only two people to have ever met both the agent and the operative, and that is the agent and the operative themselves. Through inheriting an agent from a predecessor, three people will be involved and, in the case of long-standing agents, more, but not many. With each fresh recruitment, everything about the agent that is conveyed to the spy's headquarters is taken on trust, including the amount of money to be paid on a regular basis. It is in this area of cash payments that a spy, if susceptible to corruption, will first be tempted. A monitoring mechanism is built into the system where spies operate from a sizeable station run from inside an embassy. The station commander (in British parlance; station chief to the Americans) will generally be a senior officer in the service who is 'declared' to the government of the host country. That is, their intelligence status is known to the intelligence service of that country and an open though discreet liaison and exchange of secret material is carried out. The station commander is rarely able to run 'deep cover' agents like the other spies on the station whose true status is carefully disguised from the host country's agencies and government. The commander will, however, supervise and oversee the clandestine activities of the spies operating from that base. Nevertheless, with new recruitments, the spy will meet directly with the agent, and this provides space for potential corruption.

The station commander is generally the final arbiter in any disagreements or disputes that arise and will be afforded a high degree of respect in light of their seniority and track record. Corrupt commanders, however, are occasionally encountered. One, in a country of global significance, was bold enough to inflate the reputation and access of a local professor of international relations from a minor university to win for that person the highest status that the headquarters could assign to a fully fledged agent. This was done on the basis of a steady and timely flow of highly valued secret intelligence. In reality, the reports were concocted from articles in the local English-language newspapers and peppered with rephrased points, made in genuine secret reporting, that the station's deep-cover spies had procured from their agents. The station commander pocketed the so-called agent's salary. All of this was facilitated by well placed associates of the commander at headquarters. Needless to say, this was a demoralising experience for the station's deep-cover spies whose hard-earned reporting was regularly purloined without credit. The commander was aware that they knew.

Where is a moral line to be drawn in such cases? Who is obliged to act and when? With this example, the station commander's reputation and influence in that spy service, especially at the highest level of management, gave him an unchallengeable immunity. Any complaint lodged against him would not just be frowned upon and studiously swept under the carpet, but would blow back on those raising the issue. Careers were on the line.

In another case at a major station, a spy who had recruited its most prized agent was some months away from completing his posting. His successor was already in country undertaking a refresher language course, for which reason the outgoing spy had almost completed the process of introducing his successor to his stable of agents – always a delicate task.[2] For operational reasons, the first meeting between the agent and the incoming and outgoing intelligence officers had been left until last. Prior to that introductory meeting taking place, however, the declared station commander suddenly announced that he would take care of it himself; he had decided to take over the running of the agent. This broke one of the cardinal rules of the craft: an agent run by a deep-cover spy cannot be in contact with, let alone be handled by, a declared officer whose intelligence status is known to related agencies in the host country and elsewhere. The spy concerned refused to accept this decision and appealed to his headquarters to have it overturned. This was rejected. As the time of his departure from the post drew near, he remained adamant that he would not introduce the agent to his station commander. After threatening to take the matter beyond his service chief to the head of government in his home capital, the chief visited the post and resolved the matter resoundingly in the spy's favour. The agent was then duly handed over to the spy's successor. The station commander survived unscathed.

What that spy was upholding was a fundamental moral principle in agent-handling that went beyond the rash attempt by his commander to interfere in the case. At the point of recruitment, a spy makes a firm commitment to protect the agent, which covers not only their identity and the nature and extent of their betrayal, but also their life. If the agent in the above-mentioned scenario had been seen in company with the declared station commander by people aware of the latter's intelligence status, the odds were that the agent would have been discreetly apprehended, interrogated and had his throat cut. In turn, the agent's duty to his case officer is to guard his own actions so that neither is caught. It is a mutual obligation that provides security only if both strive to protect it. That is a highly professional requirement on the spy's part, which cannot be fulfilled merely by adherence to whatever moral standards apply in the spy's intelligence service. The foundation for an effective and safe relationship with an agent rests upon the personal moral standards of the spy himself or herself, before institutional values ever kick in.

Agent-handling entails much more than the mere tasking of an agent to utilise their access to obtain secret information much in demand. Without a broad understanding of the other dimensions of an agent's professional and personal life, their welfare and the security of the relationship cannot be guaranteed. For this reason, spies commonly become 'confessors' for their agents, often made privy to emotional and other vagaries in the life of the agent. A huge amount of a spy's time is necessarily devoted to servicing top agents in this way, usually in the late hours of the night. All of this is regularly documented for the spy's headquarters, though a deeper appreciation of how these various factors impact on an agent's stability and performance resides largely with the spy in the field. Only the agent-handler can ultimately decide at any given time whether the agent is up to having further demands placed upon them (in security or workload terms, or psychologically and emotionally). Nevertheless, it is common for a spy's headquarters to pile on pressure when certain international events are running hot and the government back home is demanding speedy access to vital secrets. Such secrets, if readily acquired, earn kudos from other closely allied intelligence services and their respective governments. The inordinate pressure that a headquarters places on a spy on such occasions to squeeze their stable of agents to the limit to produce secret material can oblige the spy to fabricate a scenario whereby it would appear dangerous to compel the agent to perform any better than is already the case. The moral tug and pull in all of this can be stressful for the spy, but has to be contained.

Morality is ever-present in a spy's reporting of secret intelligence. No matter how remote a spy's overseas operational bailiwick, one thing that distance does not erase is the awareness of the sort of secret material that is 'politically correct' and palatable back home. Without a firm moral anchor, some spies drift towards slanting reporting in a way that attracts positive attention in and beyond the headquarters. Promotion is a tantalising prospect for such operatives, but succumbing to this temptation can have dire consequences, especially when one's immediate superiors are caught up in the same self-centred process. A retired British Army officer, Colonel John Hughes-Wilson, an author and commentator on intelligence matters, articulates the dictum that should govern any spy's actions:

> Of course, there is another much older, cleverer and subtle advantage that good, accurate, timely intelligence can bestow to anyone wise enough to recognise the real truth. It is much less costly than any victory amid the blood, fire and horror of the battlefield, and it should be the ultimate goal of every professional soldier, diplomat and even politician. It is the ability, in the words of an ancient Chinese sage, 'to subdue your enemies and bend them to your will without having to resort to force'. Only intelligence can do that.
>
> (Hughes-Wilson 2004, p. 14)

Human intelligence gathering has long been supplemented by the product of electronic eavesdropping, commonly known in the spy world as SIGINT, or signals intelligence. In its modern form, this began with the introduction of the telegraph in the mid-1800s, followed by the telephone in the 1880s, radio in the early twentieth century, and ultimately today's world of satellite communications. For human spies, the tendency – let alone the professional purpose – is to focus the agent's attention on procuring secret intelligence on key requirements. Of course, there is always a temptation for some operatives to stray from that path and move into areas that appear attractive but are of only marginal relevance. Such diversions are fairly quickly picked up by a spy's headquarters at home, and they will generally be asked to explain their wavering focus and declining level of production.

With electronic eavesdroppers, however, the urge to digress and delve into the lives of individuals and organisations that should by any standard be off limits is more readily satisfied and often undetectable. Operatives with a voyeuristic bent can indulge themselves and intrude upon the lives of innocent parties without any noticable decline in their production of viable intelligence. In many cases, it is impossible to detect their professional immorality and the extent of their abuse of the trust placed in them. While electronic checks and balances built into the system sometimes warn of such activity, it is the wrongdoer's work colleagues who are usually the first to become aware of illicit behaviour. But if a group of co-workers share and enjoy the product of such intrusions, the damage incurred can be extensive before it is ever uncovered.

On this front, drones are the latest form of technology to throw up new challenges to the operatives involved. A wavering focus, laziness, carelessness, or just plain incompetence and immorality can have devastating consequences for the lives of innocent parties unaware of the fact that they have been targeted.

An endless tug and pull that those outside the secret world of intelligence rarely know about is the battle between those gathering and analysing HUMINT and those who put more store in SIGINT. In the American intelligence community in the latter decades of the twentieth century, the cost and effort put into human spies and their networks lost out to those who believed that SIGINT could provide all that was needed in the modern world. In more ways than one, the shocking failures in the system that led to the tragedy of 9/11 can be attributed to this skewered conviction. How to strike a balance between human spies on the ground and electronic eyes and ears all around us is, in many ways, an eternal battle. However, with realistic and professional management, it is generally possible to integrate both so that they supplement each other rather than compete for dominance.

A minefield of moral dilemmas was provided for British spies operating in the Middle East, and their colleagues back in London, in the lead-up to the 'shock and awe' invasion of Iraq in March 2003 by a massive, combined US and UK military force. Bold claims had been made, and so-called 'evidence' provided, of Saddam Hussein's possession of chemical and biological weapons of mass destruction (WMD) and his willingness to use them. Moreover, it was claimed that the Iraqi leader was keen to acquire nuclear weapons and that he had links to Al Qaeda through which he was implicated in the 9/11 terror attacks on New York and Washington in 2001. A briefing paper was drawn up for the British Prime Minister Tony Blair, purportedly based on secret intelligence which proved that Iraq had WMD and was ready to deploy them. Iraq, it was therefore claimed, posed a direct and imminent threat to the United Kingdom. This briefing paper, which later came to be known as the 'dodgy dossier', was used to justify Britain's involvement in the invasion. The Prime Minister's director of communications, who was a former journalist with no experience in the handling of secret intelligence, was directly implicated in the production of the dossier.

In 2009, the Chilcot Inquiry was established to look into the nagging question of what had and had not been known prior to the invasion. A former major-general and head of defence intelligence, Michael Laurie, wrote to Sir John Chilcot, the Inquiry's chairman, in 2011 stating that: 'We knew at the time that the purpose of the dossier was precisely to make a case for war, rather than setting out the available intelligence, and that to make the best out of sparse and inconclusive intelligence the wording was developed with care' (Norton-Taylor 2011, para. 2). Secret reporting provided by MI6 prior to the invasion was put under the microscope and was shown *not* to have been embellished or exaggerated in any way. The uproar over the dossier provided, especially for the democratic world, a worrying example of how easily the political process can commandeer the intelligence world for its own narrow purposes.

The effect of careless or deliberately distorted secret reporting, because of the cachet associated with any apparent intelligence 'scoop' by politicians and government advisers, is rarely considered by those officers who engage in the practice. Henry St John, Viscount Bolingbroke, a British statesman and political and philosophical writer, pointed to the consequences when he noted that, 'Truth lies within a little compass, but error is immense' (cited in Knowles 1999, p. 124). Accurate and timely intelligence is one thing; whether it is treated as such and acted upon is yet another. One usually follows the other, but not necessarily. Governments are sometimes dilatory for political reasons, or due to laziness or incompetence on the part of their aides and advisers. They are often deluged by secret reporting coming in on many fronts at the same time. The range of issues and emergencies with which governments deal, often in secret, are as varied as the human foibles of those working in the upper echelons of the system. Priorities are not always appropriately allocated. This was brought home in mid-2014 when the barbarity of the terrorist organisation ISIL in the Middle East burst into the public arena.[3] This led to clashes on both sides of the Atlantic between spies and politicians.

Harnden & Shipman (2014) report in *The Sunday Times* that the CIA and MI6 had blasted claims they were guilty of intelligence failures as the renegades swept into Iraq from Syria. 'Former CIA officers have accused the Obama administration of seeking to cover up its own policy failures by laying the blame at the door of America's spies after Iraqi soldiers fled from an attack by ISIS jihadists' (Harnden & Shipman 2014, para. 2). Similarly, sources close to the Secret Intelligence Service in London have blamed the Foreign Office and Downing Street for ignoring the growing menace of extremists in Syria.

When these sorts of situations arise, especially when the intelligence involved has been acquired at great risk to the spies concerned, they are as aware as any politician or government policymaker in their home capital that it has *not* been acted upon. If various appeals within the system for it to be considered go unheeded, where does the moral obligation to act further lie? Spies in the field often resolve this dilemma by privately briefing a foreign correspondent who is well acquainted with the situation on the ground. It will invariably be a journalist they already know and trust, and more often than not one who shares the same nationality. The resulting publicity generally warns unresponsive politicians and bureaucrats that unheeded warnings are unlikely to go away. Sometimes this works and sometimes it does not. When spies feel morally obliged to engage in such activity are they 'crossing a line' and acting like God, or are they simply doing their duty? But their duty to whom, and to what?

Because spies are at the beginning of the intelligence or informational process, blame is frequently sheeted home to them. This may be done by a government, directly or by insinuation, or by a bureaucracy, in addition to accusations of failure being made by the media and the community as a whole. If there was indeed a failure in the intelligence process, or if crucial intelligence had been obtained and appropriately distributed but not acted upon, is there a moral duty on the part of those spies who have first-hand knowledge of such matters to expose the truth? And, if so, how should they go about it?

To this spy's mind, the ultimate moral responsibility of every HUMINT spy is to work for the good of his or her country, to the best of one's ability – and never against it. Perhaps ironically, this is the antithesis of the spy's primary challenge, which is to inveigle and cajole other people in other countries, with prized access to secrets, to commit an act of betrayal and hand them over, clandestinely, in return for reward, usually monetary. That is the one solitary act that a loyal spy cannot imagine committing themselves. Yet some in the intelligence services of the world's liberal democracies do indeed betray their country's interests. There are many reasons for this, which, of course, need to be fully understood by a spy engaged in agent-handling. It goes to a fundamental precept of intelligence in any culture, anywhere, any time. That is, how do you appear through the eyes of others? The answer to this question is always instructive.

The leading agent-handler Victor Cherkashin, who ran two of America's most damaging traitors, Aldrich Ames and Robert Hanssen, commented in his 2005 memoirs that the US intelligence agencies were risk-averse (Cherkashin & Feifer 2005, p. 225). They concentrated on protecting their own and were in denial about the possibility of having traitors within their own ranks. Secrecy was aimed at avoiding scandal and maintaining careers. A similar disposition was in evidence in Britain's Secret Intelligence Service, commonly known as MI6. In the history of modern intelligence, there could be no more notorious gang of traitors than the Cambridge Five. A copious literature exists on these individuals and the harm they did, not only to their own country, but also to the Western world in its fight against communism and totalitarianism. Kim Philby, the best known of the five, was not only a longstanding Soviet spy, but someone in line to become chief of MI6. How somebody of that ilk could perpetuate their existence, undetected, within a sophisticated spy service leaves most people puzzled. To anyone who has worked, or does work, in secret intelligence – in that 'hothouse' environment – it is not necessarily an enigma.[4]

In summary, spies do indeed live in a moral world, though most people unacquainted with the realities of the craft generally assume that this is not the case. Another assumption is that, because spies are devoid of morality, they must be subjected to the closest scrutiny from outside. That is a healthy attitude to have with regard to any group of people in a democracy that operates in the shadows. But it should also be understood that, no matter how many checks and balances are put in place to stop spy services from abusing their powers and getting out of control, it is those *inside* the hothouse – that majority of men and women who diligently and honourably work for their country's good – who are a liberal democracy's first line of defence against wrongdoing. Whistleblowing inside a spy service is never a career-enhancing choice, as it rarely is for those who take cases outside their agency with legitimate cause.

Central in all of this is the concept of the national interest, which, in many ways today – especially in the fight against terror – extends into an 'international interest'. How the national interest is to be defined in the early decades of the twenty-first century, with liberal democracies increasingly among the world's most culturally and religiously diverse societies, is no easy task. Perversely, it is a country's spies who are closer to that dilemma than most other people.

In 2014, when the Australian government became aware of the danger posed by returning Australian citizens who had fought with ISIL jihadists in Iraq and Syria, legislation was put through Parliament to provide the country's intelligence agencies with additional powers seen as necessary to meet the threat. Understandably, a heated public debate ensued over these extra powers and the possibility that they might be abused. The media, and a fair slice of Parliament, focused exclusively on such lurking dangers and ignored the most obvious place to bolster corrective mechanisms already in place. A number of countries have an intelligence ombudsman. In Australia, this is the Inspector-General of Intelligence and Security (IGIS), which is a statutory office reporting at the end of each year to Parliament. It commenced operations in 1987 and oversees the activities of the country's six intelligence agencies. Claims were made in the 1990s, with some justification, that it was 'Canberra's Bermuda Triangle': cases taken to IGIS simply 'disappeared', with aggrieved intelligence officers pushed out into the public arena while those accused of wrongdoing retained their positions and went on to 'greater things'.

The overwhelming majority of men and women who work in intelligence agencies are representative of their society as a whole. They are our first line of defence against abuse. They will detect it before anyone outside the agencies does so, and if they report it internally and nothing is done, their next stop (as a professional obligation) is the ombudsman. What would have been useful, therefore, was a review of the effectiveness of IGIS since the office's inception. While there was no inference that IGIS was not currently fulfilling its responsibilities, men and women who had served, or were still serving, in the agencies, who had taken cases of abuse to IGIS, could have been invited by the Australian Parliament's Joint Committee on Intelligence and Security (a bipartisan body) to appear, *in camera* if necessary, to give evidence under parliamentary privilege on the effectiveness of the office. In such practical and realistic ways, liberal democratic systems can be readily cleansed through *existing* mechanisms.

In conclusion, and as Norman Mailer noted, 'Real democracy ... is a state of grace attained only by those countries that have a host of individuals not only ready to enjoy freedom, but to undergo the heavy labour to maintain it.' Most of those who work in our intelligence services and other protective agencies are doing just that.

Notes

1 Contained in an address given to the Commonwealth Club in San Francisco, February 20, 2003, when Norman Mailer was presented with the Club's Centennial Medallion in honour of the organisation's 100th anniversary.
2 Spies rarely have the luxury of months to devote to this handover process. It is generally a matter of a week or two at best, and sometimes only a matter of days. The range of introductions that need to be quickly and effectively facilitated may number between twenty and thirty.
3 ISIL is also referred to as ISIS as well as IS, the latter meaning Islamic State or Islamic Caliphate in the sense that the organisation aspires to create a state as a political entity.
4 An excellent work on how Philby pulled this off is Ben Macintyre's (2014) *A spy among friends*.

References

Cherkashin, V & Feifer, G 2005, *Spy handler: memoir of a KGB officer, the true story of the man who recruited Robert Hanssen and Aldrich Ames*, Basic Books, New York.

Frum, D 2014, 'We need more secrecy: why government transparency can be the enemy of liberty', *The Atlantic*, May, p. 14, www.theatlantic.com/magazine/archive/2014/05/we-need-more-secrecy/359820

Hamden, T & Shipman, T 2014, 'Obama ignored warnings over Iraq, say spies', *The Australian*, 30 June, www.theaustralian.com.au/news/world/spies-accuse-obama-of-ignoring-warnings-on-rise-of-isis/story-fnb64oi6-1226971111916

Hitz, F 2005, *The great game: the myths and reality of espionage*, Vintage Books, New York.

Hughes-Wilson, J 2004, *The puppet masters: spies, traitors and the real forces behind world events*, Weidenfeld & Nicolson, London.

Knowles, E 1999, *The Oxford dictionary of quotations*, Oxford University Press, Oxford.

Macintyre, B 2014. *A spy among friends: Kim Philby and the great betrayal*, Bloomsbury, London.

Norton-Taylor, R 2011, 'Iraq dossier drawn up to make case for war – intelligence officer', *The Guardian*, 13 May, www.theguardian.com/world/2011/may/12/iraq-dossier-case-for-war

References

Bendle, M 2006, 'History academic tells what's wrong with history academics', *The Australian*, 21 July.

Collins, L & Reed, W 2005, *Plunging point: intelligence failures, cover-ups and consequences*, HarperCollins, Sydney.

Friendly, A 1981, *The dreadful day: the battle of Manzikert, 1071*, Hutchinson, London.

Gibbon, E 1776, *The history of the decline and fall of the Roman Empire*, W. Strahan and T. Cadell, London.

Norwich, J 1995, *Byzantium – the apogee*, Alfred Knopf, New York.

Toynbee, A 1995, *A study of history*, Thames & Hudson, London.

INDEX

Note: page numbers followed by 'n' indicate endnotes.

Lightning Source UK Ltd.
Milton Keynes UK
UKHW020619160419
341091UK00005B/92/P